FAULT IN AMERICAN CONTRACT LAW

Representing an unprecedented joint effort from top scholars in the field, this volume collects original contributions to examine the fundamental role of "fault" in contract law. Is it immoral to breach a contract? Should a breaching party be punished more harshly for willful breach? Does it matter if the victim of breach engaged in contributory fault? Is there room for a calculus of fault within the "efficient breach" framework?

For generations, contract liability has been viewed as a no-fault regime, in sharp contrast to tort liability. Is this dichotomy real? Is it justified? How do the American and European traditions compare? In exploring these and related issues, the essays in this volume bring together a variety of outlooks, including economic, psychological, philosophical, and comparative approaches to law.

Omri Ben-Shahar is the Frank and Bernice Greenberg Professor of Law at the University of Chicago. He has written extensively in the areas of contract law, products liability, and law and economics. Ben-Shahar is the editor of the *Journal of Legal Studies* and, recently, the book *Boilerplate: Foundation of Market Contracts.*

Ariel Porat is Alain Poher Professor of Law in Tel-Aviv University's Faculty of Law and its former Dean, as well as Fischel-Neil Distinguished Visiting Professor of Law at the University of Chicago. Porat has written numerous articles in the areas of torts and contracts and is the author of the books *Contributory Fault in the Law of Contracts* and *Tort Liability under Uncertainty* (with Alex Stein).

FAULT IN AMERICAN CONTRACT LAW

Edited by

OMRI BEN-SHAHAR

University of Chicago Law School

ARIEL PORAT

Buchmann Faculty of Law, Tel-Aviv University

CAMBRIDGE
UNIVERSITY PRESS

CAMBRIDGE UNIVERSITY PRESS
Cambridge, New York, Melbourne, Madrid, Cape Town, Singapore,
São Paulo, Delhi, Dubai, Tokyo, Mexico City

Cambridge University Press
32 Avenue of the Americas, New York, NY 10013-2473, USA

www.cambridge.org
Information on this title: www.cambridge.org/9780521769853

First published 2010

Printed in the United States of America

A catalog record for this publication is available from the British Library.

Library of Congress Cataloging in Publication data
Fault in American contract law / Omri Ben-Shahar, Ariel Porat.
p. cm.
Includes index.
ISBN 978-0-521-76985-3 (hardback)
1. Breach of contract – United States. I. Ben-Shahar, Omri. II. Porat, Ariel. III. Title.
KF836.F38 2011 346.7302′2–dc22
2010023936

ISBN 978-0-521-76985-3 Hardback

To our parents,
Yael and Habash
– O.B.S
Adina and Haim
– A.P.

CONTENTS

IV. WILLFUL BREACH

V. COMPARATIVE FAULT

VI. THE MORALITY OF BREACH

CONTRIBUTORS

Barry E. Adler
Bernard Petrie Professor of Law
and Business,
New York University

Oren Bar-Gill
Professor of Law,
New York University School of Law

Omri Ben-Shahar
Frank and Bernice J. Greenberg
Professor of Law,
University of Chicago Law School

Fabrizio Cafaggi
Professor of Comparative Law,
EUI Florence

George M. Cohen
Brokaw Professor of Corporate Law,
Barron F. Black Research Professor,
University of Virginia School of Law

Richard Craswell
William F. Baxter Visa International
Professor of Law,
Stanford University

Melvin Aron Eisenberg
Koret Professor of Law,
University of California, Berkeley,
School of Law (Boalt Hall);
Stephen and Barbara Friedman
Visiting Professor of Law,
Columbia Law School

Richard A. Epstein
James Parker Hall Distinguished
Service Professor of Law,
University of Chicago School of Law;
Peter and Kirsten Bedford
Senior Fellow,
The Hoover Institution;
Visiting Professor of Law,
New York University
School of Law

Martha M. Ertman
Carole and Hanan Sibel
Research Professor,
University of Maryland Law School

Stefan Grundmann
Professor of Private
and Business Law,
German, European and International
Department,
Humboldt-Universität, Berlin

Dori Kimel
Fellow of New College and Reader in
Legal Philosophy,
University of Oxford

Roy Kreitner
Faculty of Law,
Tel Aviv University

Saul Levmore
William B. Graham Professor of Law,
University of Chicago Law School

Ariel Porat
Alain Poher Professor of Law,
Tel Aviv University;
Fischel-Neil Distinguished Visiting Professor of Law,
University of Chicago Law School

Eric A. Posner
Kirkland and Ellis Professor of Law,
University of Chicago Law School

Richard A. Posner
Judge, U.S. Court of Appeals for the Seventh Circuit;
Senior Lecturer,
University of Chicago Law School

Robert E. Scott
Alfred McCormack Professor of Law and Director,
Center for Contract and Economic Organization,
Columbia University

Steven Shavell
Samuel R. Rosenthal Professor of Law and Economics,
Harvard Law School

Peter Siegelman
Roger Sherman Professor of Law,
University of Connecticut School of Law

Steve Thel
I. Maurice Wormser Professor of Law,
Fordham Law School

Tess Wilkinson-Ryan
Assistant Professor of Law,
University of Pennsylvania Law School

PREFACE

Introduction

The basic rule of liability in tort law is fault. The basic rule of liability in contract law is no fault. This is perhaps one of the most striking divides within private law, the most important difference between the law of voluntary and the law of nonvoluntary obligations. It is this *fault* line (speaking equivocally) that this book explores. Is it a real divide – two opposite branches of liability within private law – or is it merely a rhetorical myth? How can it be justified?

For law-and-economics scholars, this fault/no-fault divide between contract and tort is all the more puzzling. In law and economics, legal rules are understood as incentives, evaluated within a framework in which parties take actions to prevent different types of loss. Tortfeasors can take measures to avoid accidents; contracting parties can take measures to avoid loss from breach. The context of the loss can diverge between contract and tort – accidents to strangers versus harm to a known breached-against party – but the underlying framework of incentives is similar, if not identical. Robert Cooter famously described this underlying framework as a unified "model of precaution,"[1] and Richard Craswell showed how to think of the breach-or-perform decision as a problem of precaution, mirroring the framework of tort law.[2] Thus, to those who take the idea of a unified model seriously, a significant puzzle looms large: If these two branches of law share the same underlying framework, why do they follow different liability regimes?

1 Robert Cooter, *Unity in Tort, Contract, and Property: The Model of Precaution*, 73 Cal. L. Rev. 1 (1985).

2 Richard Craswell, *Contract Remedies, Renegotiation, and the Theory of Efficient Breach*, 61 S. Cal. L. Rev. 629 (1988); Richard Craswell, *Precontractual Investigation as an Optimal Precaution Problem*, 17 J. Legal Stud. 401 (1988).

To be sure, the unified model takes a very general view of tort and contract. But the divergence puzzle is all the more challenging when we increase the resolution of our view and compare some of the main tort and contract doctrines, only to find again a clear divide. For example, tort law has a substantial causation requirement, but causation is seldom an issue in contract. Tort law recognizes claims for punitive damages; contract law by and large does not. Contract law limits the magnitude of recovery through doctrines such as foreseeability and certainty; tort law mainly employs proximate cause and duty of care, which exclude different sets of harms. And the list continues: economic harm (common in contract but not in tort), nonpecuniary losses (common in tort but much less so in contract), comparative fault (applied as a defense in tort but not in contract), and mitigation of damages (more common in contract than in tort).

Any explanation of the puzzling interface between contract and tort would have to begin with an account of the limited role that fault plays in contract law. This breaks down into separate lines of inquiry: (1) Should lack of fault be a defense against breach? Should the breaching party be able to escape liability if he can show that he worked hard to avoid breach? (2) Should a high degree of fault be an aggravating factor multiplying damages? Should the breaching party be liable for more than normal damages if breach was "malicious?" (3) Should contract law take the aggrieved party's fault into account? All of the contributions to this book deal with some aspects of these three fundamental questions.

I. A Positive Account

The first thing that an account of "fault in contract law" needs to do is to separate myth from reality and identify the extent to which fault does, or does not, play a role in contract liability. Almost every chapter in this book contributes some descriptive nuance to the fault picture. At one end of the spectrum, Melvin Eisenberg argues that contract law is substantially a fault regime, manifested in areas like unconscionability, unexpected circumstances, interpretation, mistake, and nonperformance.[3] In all these areas, fault plays an important role, and liability depends to a large extent on the parties' blameworthiness. Consistent with this descriptive line, Richard Epstein demonstrates that in many consensual relations, fault is built into the liability rule through a subtle definition of the content of the promise. Taking bailment

[3] Melvin Aron Eisenberg, *The Role of Fault in Contract Law: Unconscionability, Unexpected Circumstances, Interpretation, Mistake, and Nonperformance*, this volume.

as the prototype, he shows that the generic understanding of a promise is to take due care, not to guarantee a result.[4] George Cohen argues in this book that fault plays an important role in contract interpretation, in evaluating the promisee's behavior that contributed to the breach, and in shaping the doctrine of contractual damages. He explains that the emphasis commonly made on strict liability fails to recognize the role of fault in contract law.[5]

At the other end, other contributors highlight the strict liability side of contract law. Robert Scott, for example, argues that case law is largely consistent with the idea that the promisor's liability does not vary with his degree of fault. Willfulness of breach, he claims, is not an aggravating factor, despite some famous statements to the contrary in case law.[6] Richard Posner argues that the Holmesian notion of an option to breach and pay damages, embedded in a contractual promise, necessarily implies that liability is strict.[7] "It wouldn't make any sense," he argues, "to excuse you just because the cost of performance would exceed the benefits, for that would make the option nugatory."[8]

Between these poles, other contributors highlight additional contours of the fault doctrine and how it infiltrates contract law. In support of the no-fault-as-defense prong, Eric Posner identifies a broad set of cases in which promisors who are able to show that breach occurred with no fault of their own would escape liability.[9] Ariel Porat and Fabrizio Cafaggi, in separate contributions, explore the presence of a comparative fault defense – cases in which promisors, who are able to show that harm could have been avoided efficiently by promisees before or after breach took place, escape liability either in full or in part.[10] Saul Levmore suggests that the law actually allows parties to vary the scope of the comparative fault component embodied in the mitigation defense. He argues that parties who draft liquidated damage clauses do more than fix the magnitude of recovery – they opt out of the fault-based mitigation duties.[11]

A glimpse into continental European legal systems makes the "fault in contract law" puzzle even more mysterious. Stefan Grundmann provides a

[4] Richard A. Epstein, *The Many Faces of Fault in Contract Law: Or How to Do Economics Right, Without Really Trying*, this volume.

[5] George M. Cohen, *How Fault Shapes Contract Law*, this volume.

[6] Robert E. Scott, *In (Partial) Defense of Strict Liability in Contract*, this volume.

[7] Richard A. Posner, *Let Us Never Blame a Contract Breaker*, this volume.

[8] *Id.* at 1351.

[9] Eric A. Posner, *Fault in Contract Law*, this volume.

[10] Ariel Porat, *A Comparative Fault Defense in Contract Law*, this volume; Fabrizio Cafaggi, *Creditor's Fault: In Search of a Comparative Frame*, this volume.

[11] Saul Levmore, *Stipulated Damages, Superstrict Liability, and Mitigation in Contract Law*, this volume.

doctrinal journey through the ways continental European law merges both fault and strict liability. His discussion demonstrates that although fault plays a role in contractual liability, this role varies significantly between common law and the civil law prevalent in continental Europe: In fact, fault is often a condition to any imposition of contractual liability in European law. Fault has also varied over time in European law, with more recent reforms aimed at bolstering its role.[12]

II. Normative and Historical Accounts

The book provides a detailed depiction of the fault/no-fault divide and a distilled descriptive understanding of the role of fault in contract. But even after the many faces of fault in contract law are highlighted, it is all the more clear that the role of fault is limited. The primary ambition of this book, then, is to inquire into the reasons fault plays no more than a limited role and why it infiltrated some contract law doctrines, and perhaps to debate whether a bigger role for fault than it is currently accorded would be justified.

The first half of the book is organized along the normative positions toward fault in contract law. The first part – "The Case for Strict Liability" – includes three essays defending the traditional view that liability for breach of contract ought to be strict. Richard Posner and Robert Scott, in separate contributions, argue that fault should not be relevant to contractual liability, either as a no-fault defense or as a superfault damage booster. According to these writers, the Anglo-American contract law is efficient and should remain the way it is.[13] Richard Posner further argues against the interpretation of fault and "bad faith" doctrines in moral terms. Robert Scott offers two justifications for strict liability: reducing contracting costs, and supporting the parties' reliance on informal and relational modes of contracting.[14] A third essay by Stefan Grundmann explains the prominence of strict liability in the law of market contracts as a mechanism that improves the comparability of offers.[15]

The second part – "The Case for Fault" – responds by defending the roles of fault doctrines in contract liability. George Cohen explains that fault is necessary to interpret contract intent, to understand how damages are assessed, and to curb promisees' opportunism.[16] Eric Posner argues that negligence

[12] Stefan Grundmann, *The Fault Principle as the Chameleon of Contract Law: A Market Function Approach*, this volume.
[13] Posner, *supra* note 7; Scott, *supra* note 6.
[14] Scott, *supra* note 6.
[15] Grundmann, *supra* note 12.
[16] Cohen, *supra* note 5.

is superior to strict liability by eliminating the insurance element from the transaction. Under a strict liability rule, such insurance is forced on the victim, even though there is no reason for the victim to buy such insurance in the first place.[17] Melvin Eisenberg supports the role of strong moral norms in a contracting system that relies on legal remedies, reputation, and social norms for guidance of behavior.[18]

The third part – "Between Strict Liability and Fault" – provides various accounts of the division of labor between fault and strict liability in private law. The first two contributions here examine the more limited role of fault in contract, compared to its robust place in tort. They provide new insights into why English common law treated fault differently in tort and contract. Roy Kreitner argues that fault standards were historically considered to be socially imposed and thus inconsistent with the basic premise of contract law that the parties, not society, are the ones who create the content of the obligation. He also shows how the blurring of the contract/tort line in the area of products liability blurred the fault/no-fault distinction within each field.[19] Richard Epstein explores the origins of bailment law as a species of consensual obligation law and argues that the fault standard prevailed in it (and in other types of contractual arrangements) through the definition of the duty one party owed to another.[20] Taking a different perspective, but sharing Kreitner's view of fault standards as socially imposed, Martha Ertman explores the role of fault in contract law as a vehicle for ex post equitable concerns. General notions of fault can conflict with ex ante concerns of rational planning, certainty, and parties' autonomy, but particular recognition of the role of fault is necessary to fine-tune fair outcomes.[21]

III. Explaining Legal Doctrine

A. *Willful Breach*

Part IV collects four separate contributions – by Richard Craswell, Steve Thel and Peter Siegelman, Oren Bar-Gill and Omri Ben-Shahar, and Barry Adler – all addressing willful breach, which is one of the more puzzling fault-based pockets in contract law. The four contributions provide justifications

[17] Posner, *supra* note 9.
[18] Eisenberg, *supra* note 3.
[19] Roy Kreitner, *Fault at the Contract-Tort Interface*, this volume.
[20] Epstein, *supra* note 4.
[21] Martha M. Ertman, *The Productive Tension Between Official and Unofficial Stories of Fault in Contract Law*, this volume.

for the law's occasional harsher treatment of willful breach. They argue that what constitutes "willful" or "malicious" breach cannot be determined conceptually, but rather has to be the *conclusion* of the analysis that identifies situations in which normal damages are not high enough. There are occasions, these articles argue, in which normal damages do not suffice to create optimal deterrence and a damage booster is needed. These occasions have nothing to do with the mens rea of the promisor, the volition of his act, or its morality. They surely cannot be explained by reference to an infringement of the "sanctity of contract." Instead, the willful-breach cases have to do with incentives.

In the first of these four contributions, Craswell argues that the willful-breach add-on to damages can be explained in two ways. Higher damages are awarded when breach is clearly inefficient, or when normal damages are undercompensatory and do not provide enough incentive to perform.[22] Another willful-breach rationale is developed by Thel and Siegelman, who argue that higher damages are necessary when the social costs of avoiding breach are zero. They use the notorious example of breach in order to sell to a higher bidder as an example of a case in which there is no social cost to breach avoidance.[23]

A new theory of the role of willfulness is developed by Bar-Gill and Ben-Shahar. Unlike other theories, it offers an ex ante perspective. Willful breach, they argue, is often an indication of a systematic pattern of "nasty" but undetectable behavior, having to do with some failure by the promisor to make earlier investments in performance capacity. It is not the maliciousness of the observed infraction that is punished, but the revealed pattern of misconduct. The damage increase is needed to deter such propensities to shirk, and the subsequent mesh of subpar performance conduct that the underinvestment causes.[24]

Finally, Barry Adler argues that willfulness is not a device to increase damages for bad behavior, but rather a way to distinguish cases in which the true expectation remedy is higher.[25] These are cases in which the breached-against party's compensatory interest involves elements that are not measured by simple market-based damages. The added damages are paid in response not to the injurer's bad conduct but rather to the victim's true injury.

22 Richard Craswell, *When Is a Willful Breach "Willful"? The Link Between Definitions and Damages*, this volume.

23 Steve Thel & Peter Siegelman, *Willful Breach: An Efficient Screen for Efficient Breach*, this volume.

24 Oren Bar-Gill & Omri Ben-Shahar, *An Information Theory of Willful Breach*, this volume.

25 Barry E. Adler, *Contract Law and the Willfulness Diversion*, this volume.

Although these contributions are primarily normative, seeking justifications for the willful-breach rule, they also provide a more lucid picture of what types of conduct are considered willful under existing contract law. Collected here together, they provide the first attempt within law and economics to reconcile the perceived conflict between the notion of efficient breach and the doctrine of willful breach that has an eclectic appearance in case law.

B. *Comparative Fault*

Part V of the book explores the justifications for comparative fault rules in contract law. Ariel Porat advocates a broad recognition of a comparative fault defense in contract law.[26] He argues that in cases in which promisees failed to take low-cost cooperation measures or tended to overrely on the promisor's performance, such defense should be generally available. Saul Levmore studies a more specific application of the mitigation-of-damages rule.[27] He argues that a mitigation defense in not available, and for good reasons, when the parties stipulate liquidated damages. By stipulating a damage clause, parties want to avoid the ex post adjudication over issues relating to fault. Finally, Fabrizio Cafaggi explains the greater role of comparative fault rules in European law, with emphasis in Continental contract law on cooperation and corrective justice, in distinction from American contract law's emphasis on risk allocation.[28]

IV. The Morality of Breach

The final part tackles the fundamental question: Is it morally wrong to deliberately breach a contract? As opposed to those who argue that fault should not matter at all (like Richard Posner and Scott), and in contrast to the argument that no-fault breaches should (under certain conditions) be excused regardless of whether those breaches were deliberate or not (like Eric Posner), there is a position, recently made by Seana Shiffrin, that breach of a promise can be a moral wrong regardless of its efficiency. According to this position, parties who value performance as an end would not always permit willful breach, even if it were efficient.[29]

[26] Porat, *supra* note 10.
[27] Levmore, *supra* note 11.
[28] Cafaggi, *supra* note 10.
[29] Seana Shiffrin, *Could Breach of Contract Be Immoral?*, 107 Mich. L. Rev. 1551 (2009).

Continuing his previous dialogue with Shiffrin on the role of morality in contractual liability,[30] Steven Shavell argues that efficient breach merely mimics what a complete contract would have stipulated. When the contingency that eventuated and led to the breach of the contract was not explicitly addressed by the contract, the breach coupled with a payment of full-expectation damages is not a violation of a promise. In Shavell's view, the reason many individuals believe a breach is immoral is their mistaken perception that a contract is a simple set of promises, ignoring the fact that contracts are incomplete and it is the parties' intent that their contract be supplemented with a nuanced understanding of the obligations. The popular view that breach is immoral – so the argument goes – confuses the breach of a contract with the breaking of an explicit promise.[31]

In contrast to the argument made by some philosophers, that the law sanctions breach of contracts because the moral wrong is analogous to a breach of a promise, Dori Kimel offers a different view in this book. He argues that using state power to enforce contractual obligations is justified by the harm principle. According to that principle, the threshold for legitimate remedial responses to a breach of contract can only plausibly be harm. That explains why fault has a limited role in contract law: Because harm is the criterion for a remedial response, and because harm in contractual context is generally insensitive to fault, courts rightly tend to ignore fault.[32]

From a social-science experimental perspective, Tess Wilkinson-Ryan, in her contribution, explores people's moral sentiments toward breach. She surveys experimental research that documents people's opinion that promise breaking is wrong and that breach of contract is a form of promise breaking. Many people consider breach as a moral harm, even if it entailed no actual losses to the breached-against party. These sentiments affect people's decisions to breach, their willingness to settle after a breach takes place, and their predictions about legal rules of contract.[33]

Conclusion

With fault having a variety of roles in contract law, is there truly a tort/contract dichotomy based on a fault/no-fault line? With products liability sitting

[30] Steven Shavell, *Is Breach of Contract Immoral?*, 56 Emory L.J. 439 (2006); Seana Valentine Shiffrin, *The Divergence of Contract and Promise*, 120 Harv. L. Rev. 708 (2007).

[31] Steven Shavell, *Why Breach of Contract May Not Be Immoral Given the Incompleteness of Contracts*, this volume.

[32] Dori Kimel, *Fault and Harm in Breach of Contract*, this volume.

[33] Tess Wilkinson-Ryan, *Fault in Contracts: A Psychological Approach*, this volume.

on the interface between tort and sales law, is there any room for separate doctrinal grounds for liability? In the end, was Cooter right – can the two fields be regarded as unified, not only in economic theory, but also in the basis for liability? Against two traditions that provide clear answers – a doctrinal tradition of clear but rigid distinctions between tort and contract, and a law-and-economics tradition of ignoring the differences between the two fields – we hope that the contribution of this book is in *blurring* the answers while portraying a more interesting picture.

ACKNOWLEDGMENT

Many of the chapters in this book were previously published in full article length in a *Michigan Law Review* symposium issue, Vol. 107, No. 8 (June 2009), which was dedicated to the conference on "Fault in Contract Law" that took place at the University of Chicago Law School in September, 2008. The current volume provides a revised and abridged version of these articles, along with additional, new contributions.

PART I

THE CASE FOR STRICT LIABILITY

ONE

Let Us Never Blame a Contract Breaker

Richard A. Posner

Holmes famously proposed a "no-fault" theory of contract law: A contract is an option to perform or pay, and a "breach" is therefore not a wrongful act but merely triggers the duty to pay liquidated or other damages. This chapter elaborates the Holmesian theory, arguing that fault terminology in contract law, such as "good faith," should be given pragmatic economic interpretations, rather than be conceived of in moral terms. It further argues that contract doctrines should normally be alterable only on the basis of empirical investigations.

I.

My thesis is that concepts of fault or blame, at least when understood in moral terms rather than translated into economic or other practical terms, are not useful addenda to the doctrines of contract law. I have borrowed this thesis from Holmes, who in *The Common Law* (and later in *The Path of the Law*) drew a sharp distinction between tort and contract law, so far as issues of fault or blameworthiness are concerned.[1] In the case of an accident giving rise to a tort suit, he thought the loss should lie where it fell, that is, on the victim, unless the injurer was at fault, that is, negligent, and the victim faultless, that is, not contributorily negligent. He thus disapproved, in general, of strict tort liability. But a complication in his analysis arose from his belief in "objective" standards of liability; negligence was the failure of the average person to take proper care, even if the defendant was below average in his ability to do so.[2]

I thank Mark Sayson and Michael Thorpe for helpful research assistance.

[1] O.W. Holmes, Jr., The Common Law 107–10, 299–301 (Boston: Little, Brown, & Co. 1881) [hereinafter Holmes, The Common Law]; O.W. Holmes, Jr., *The Path of the Law*, 10 Harv. L. Rev. 457, 462 (1897) [hereinafter Holmes, *The Path of the Law*].

[2] Holmes, The Common Law, *supra* note 1, at 108–10.

That belief was not a fatal defect in Holmes's fault-based theory of tort law, however. As Bernard Williams has reminded us, consequences, and not just states of mind, influence our moral judgments. "[I]n the story of one's life there is an authority exercised by what one has done, and not merely by what one has intentionally done."[3] So inability to meet society's expectations concerning care to avoid inflicting injury can, when injury results, be considered a species of fault.

But Holmes was wrong to think that the pockets of strict liability in tort law were inconsistent with a fault-based theory of that law. Strict liability is based on recognition that care is too limited a notion of the duty to avoid doing harm. If you keep a lion in your backyard to ward off intruders and it escapes and mauls someone even though you took every precaution to minimize the risk of escape, there is still the question whether the expected costs of keeping a lion (the risk of injury discounted by the cost of the injury if the risk materializes) exceeded the benefits. To classify an activity as "abnormally dangerous," thus making the applicable tort standard strict liability, is to adjudge those costs to exceed the benefits.

Holmes's theory of contract law is as fault free as his theory of tort law is fault saturated. He thought of contracts as options – when you sign a contract in which you promise a specified performance (supplying a product or providing a service), you buy an option to perform or pay damages.[4] The option feature is particularly pronounced when the contract contains a liquidated damages clause. You are promising that you will either perform or pay the amount specified in the clause. As long as you pay the damages awarded by the court in the promisee's suit for breach of contract, whether they are specified in the clause or computed according to the principles of contract damages, no blame can attach to your failure to perform even if it was deliberate – even if, for example, you did not perform simply because someone offered you more money for the product or service that you had undertaken to supply in the contract and you did not have enough capacity to supply both the promisee and the new, more necessitous customer.[5] You have not *really* broken your promise, because what you promised (though that is not how the contract will have been worded) was either-or: not performance but *either* performance *or* compensation for the cost of nonperformance to the other party to the contract.

[3] Bernard Williams, Shame and Necessity 69 (1993); *see also* Bernard Williams, Moral Luck: Philosophical Papers 1973–1980 20, 28–30 (1981). This is the pre-Socratic Greek theory of blameworthiness.

[4] Holmes, *The Path of the Law*, *supra* note 1, at 462.

[5] *See* Restatement (Second) of Contracts ch. 16, introductory note (1981); *id.* § 309.

The fact that the victim of a breach of contract can sometimes obtain specific performance or some other form of injunctive relief might seem a great embarrassment to Holmes's option theory of contract. But it is not if we bear in mind that injunctive relief is possible only when the remedy at law – that is, damages – is unavailable. For in such a case the contractual undertaking loses its either-or character; instead of a promise of performance or damages, it is a promise of performance or nothing, and that is not a choice the promisee would have agreed to. In contrast, a *general* entitlement to specific performance would, indeed, make contract law fault based. A court would not be willing to command a nonperforming party to perform, on pain of civil and criminal contempt and potentially astronomical fines if he did not, without considering whether he was in some sense "at fault" in not performing – whether, in other words, the costs to him of performing would have exceeded the benefits to the other party. Moreover, a general entitlement to specific performance would thwart some efficient breaches.[6] If *A* breaks his contract with *B* to sell to *C* because *C* will pay more than the harm (which equals damages) to *B* from the breach, the breach increases the social product: *B* is no worse off, and *A* and *C* are both better off. But if *B* is entitled to specific performance, *A* cannot sell to *C* without paying *B* to agree to terminate *A*'s contract with him, creating a bilateral monopoly situation (of which more shortly).

The option theory of contract also implies that liability for the breach of a contract is strict, that is, that the victim of the breach need not prove fault by the contract breaker (another reason why specific performance can't be the standard remedy for breach). The promise is to perform or pay damages, and so if you choose not to perform – even if you are prevented from performing by circumstances beyond your control – you *must* pay damages. It wouldn't make any sense to excuse you just because the cost of performance would exceed the benefits, for that would make the option nugatory.

Another way to understand this point is to note that an option has an insurance component. If you promise me either performance or some compensation in lieu of performance you are insuring me against the consequences of your nonperformance. As Holmes explained with characteristic directness:

> The consequences of a binding promise at common law are not affected by the degree of power which the promisor possesses over the promised event.. .:. In the case of a binding promise that it shall rain to-morrow, the immediate legal effect of what the promisor does is, that he takes the risk of

[6] Ronald J. Scalise Jr., *Why No "Efficient Breach" in the Civil Law?: A Comparative Assessment of the Doctrine of Efficient Breach of Contract*, 55 Am. J. Comp. L. 721, 726–7, 763 (2007).

> the event, within certain defined limits, as between himself and the promisee. He does no more when he promises to deliver a bale of cotton.[7]

You will make such a promise – grant me such an option – if you are the cheaper insurer against the risk of nonperformance. Strict liability for nonperformance reduces transaction costs by optimizing risk bearing (the function performed in the tort setting by formal liability insurance).

The civil law approach to breach of contract is different from the common law approach. Liability is not strict; a party is in breach of his contract only if he "could reasonably have been expected to behave in a different way," that is, only if he was at fault in failing to perform.[8] And the victim's entitlement (to the extent actually honored) under civil law to specific performance discourages efficient breaches.[9] The duty of good faith – the common law version of which can, as we shall see, be explained in nonmoral terms – in civil law expands to include "[b]ad faith bargaining,"[10] which may not have a pragmatic, nonmoral, justification.

The common law and civil law conceptions of contract law may differ because the common law of contracts evolved from the law merchant and the civil law of contracts from canon law.[11] It is apparent which origin is more likely to produce efficient law. There is evidence that common law is, indeed, superior to civil law from the standpoint of promoting commercial activity.[12]

One might object to the common law rule of strict liability for breach of contract that a contracting party, at least if it is a corporation, either will be

[7] Holmes, The Common Law, *supra* note 1, at 299–300.

[8] Jürgen Basedow, *Towards a Universal Doctrine of Breach of Contract: The Impact of the CISG*, 25 Int'l Rev. L. Econ. 487, 496 (2005) ("[T]he fault principle is often considered to be an indispensable part of the law of obligations in civil law countries."); *see also* John Y. Gotanda, *Recovering Lost Profits in International Disputes*, 36 Geo. J. Int'l L. 61, 76 (2004). But the practical significance of the doctrinal differences between common law and civil law contract law has been questioned, as I note later.

[9] Scalise, *supra* note 6, at 726–7.

[10] William Tetley, *Good Faith in Contract: Particularly in the Contracts of Arbitration and Chartering*, 35 J. Mar. L. Com. 561, 568 (2004); *cf.* P.D.V. Marsh, Comparative Contract Law: England, France, Germany 65 (1994).

[11] Joseph M. Perillo, *Essay, UNIDROIT Principles of International Commercial Contracts: The Black Letter Text and a Review*, 63 Fordham L. Rev. 281, 308 n.190 (1994).

[12] *See, e.g.*, Edward L. Glaeser & Andrei Shleifer, *Legal Origins*, 117 Q. J. Econ. 1193, 1220–2 (2002); Paul G. Mahoney, *The Common Law and Economic Growth: Hayek Might Be Right*, 30 J. Legal Stud. 503 (2001); Salvatore Mancuso, *The New African Law: Beyond the Difference Between Common Law and Civil Law*, 14 Ann. Surv. Int'l & Comp. L. 39, 52 (2008); Simeon Djankov et al., *Debt Enforcement Around the World* 24–25 (Eur. Corporate Governance Inst., Finance Working Paper No. 147/2007, 2007), *available at* http://ssrn.com/abstract_id=953000. Yet by not distinguishing between liquidated damages clauses and penalty clauses, the civil law expands freedom of contract, although civil law judges do refuse to enforce "clearly unreasonable" damages clauses. Ugo Mattei, *The Comparative Law and Economics of Penalty Clauses*

risk averse (because its shareholders can eliminate firm-specific risk by holding a diversified portfolio of stocks) or can buy insurance from an insurance company, eliminating the need for an insurance component in its contracts. But even large corporations often buy a great deal of insurance; the reasons have to do with managerial risk aversion (a large part of a manager's wealth may be his firm-specific human capital), tax avoidance, and the deadweight costs of bankruptcy.[13] It is difficult, however, to buy market insurance against the risk of being the victim of a breach of contract, because the risk and its consequences cannot be calculated with the actuarial precision that insurance companies insist on[14]; there is too much heterogeneity among contracts – too much uncertainty about the likelihood and consequences of a breach. The difficulty of insuring against breach of contract has been demonstrated in the current financial crisis by the near collapse of American Insurance Group (saved only by a federal bailout), which through credit default swaps and other devices had offered default insurance on a large scale.

Probing deeper, we can see that strict liability for breach of contract, too, is a sensible default provision, which allows the parties to specify excuses for failure to perform, such as *force majeure*. There are also default excuse provisions, such as impossibility and frustration, but the justification is economic rather than moral; they allocate risk as the parties could be expected to have done had they negotiated over the issue.[15]

Then, too, determination of fault would necessarily be based on matters outside the contract itself, whereas it is highly desirable, in order to minimize the expense and uncertainty of litigation, that most breach-of-contract cases be decided by a simple comparison (made without a trial or even pretrial discovery) of the language of the contract with the fact of nonperformance.

Eric Posner pointed out in his contribution to this volume that negligence can be discussed in nonfault terms, such as the antiseptic terms of the Hand formula, and thus could be proposed as a rival to strict liability in contract law without entry into the morality thicket. But if I am right that contracts contain an important element of insurance, and that strict liability for nonperformance also facilitates contract negotiation and minimizes uncertainty, strict liability is a more efficient regime for contract cases than negligence would be.

in Contracts, 43 Am. J. Comp. L. 427, 442 (1995); *accord id.* at 441; Lucia Ostoni, translation, *Italian Rejection of Punitive Damages in a U.S. Judgment*, 24 J. L. & Com. 245, 261 (2005).

13 *See* Richard A. Posner, Economic Analysis of Law 471 (7th ed. 2007).

14 *Cf.* Alfred W. Cortese, Jr. & Kathleen L. Blaner, *The Anti-Competitive Impact of U.S. Product Liability Laws: Are Foreign Businesses Beating Us at Our Own Game?*, 9 J. L. & Com. 167, 182 (1989).

15 *See, e.g.*, Posner, *supra* note 13, at 96–7.

Strict liability for breach of contract is not logically inconsistent with treating *willful* breaches differently from involuntary ones, as by awarding punitive damages for the former but not the latter. But contract law does not do that, and for good reasons. For what exactly is a "willful" breach? In the usual case of breach of contract, the cost of performance to the defendant would exceed the benefit to the plaintiff. The cost might be or might include an opportunity cost, as in my example in which the defendant discovered that he could sell his product to a third party at a higher price than the contract price. An opportunity cost is a real cost. To deem a breach motivated by a desire to avoid such a cost "willful," and impose punitive damages or order-specific performance, would encourage inefficient conduct – providing a product or service to a party (the contract promisee) who valued it less than someone else did.

Of course, the three parties involved might bargain their way out of the situation. But the bargaining would be costly because of the bilateral monopoly setting. The promisor could get out of the contract only by negotiating with the promisee, and the promisee could extract concessions from the promisor only by negotiating with him. Each party would be pushing to maximize his share of the surplus value that the breach would enable, and such a negotiation is costly and may fail. If it fails, the surplus is lost, and that is a social and not merely a private cost.

There is an element of perversity, moreover, in arguing that efficient breaches, being deliberate rather than compelled, should be discouraged. Efficient breaches are efficient. Involuntary breaches are often inefficient: The promisor miscalculated his ability to comply with the contractual terms to which he had agreed. I am not suggesting that he should be "punished"; but if fault were taken seriously in contract law, he, like a negligent injurer sued in tort, would be thought at fault whereas a party that committed an efficient breach and thus increases the social product would not be.

The common law rule, consistent with the "no-fault" theory of contract that I am defending as a sound positive as well as normative theory, is that punitive damages are not recoverable in breach-of-contract cases.[16] The major judge-made exception[17] is for breaches by liability insurance companies of their contractual duty to defend.[18] Insureds, especially when they are individuals rather than firms (e.g., a driver who has injured someone in

[16] Restatement (Second) of Contracts § 355 (1981).

[17] Consumer protection statutes, such as the Fair Debt Collection Practices Act, frequently provide for the award of statutory damages, which are similar to punitive damages. *See, e.g.*, 15 U.S.C. § 1692k (2006).

[18] *See, e.g.*, 2 Allan D. Windt, Insurance Claims & Disputes: Representation of Companies And Insureds § 9:26 (5th ed., 2007).

an automobile accident), often lack the knowledge or resources required to obtain competent counsel. This may doom their defense to a tort suit and even result in a judgment that takes liability for the injury inflicted on the tort plaintiff out of the coverage of the insurance policy altogether. Yet proof of damages in a suit against the insurance company for breach of its duty to defend may be impossible, or at least very difficult, because it would require a comparison of the performance of the insured's lawyer with the hypothetical performance of the hypothetical lawyer whom the insurance company would have retained or paid for had it acknowledged its duty to defend. And it would require a determination whether, even if a good lawyer would still have lost the case, at least the court would not have made findings that vitiated the company's duty to indemnify.

The award of restitution in contract cases might be thought inconsistent with the no-fault theory of contract that I am advocating. Restitution is normally awarded when the law wants to deter the defendant's conduct rather than just make him internalize its costs. In a copyright case, for example, the infringer may be a more efficient exploiter of the copyrighted work than the copyright owner, but if so, limiting the latter to compensatory damages would create a regime of compulsory licensing. Anyone who thought himself the more efficient producer could infringe with impunity, treating the damages that he would owe the copyright owner as a licensing fee. Restitution of the infringer's profits, by making the infringement worthless to him, forces the would-be infringer to negotiate with the copyright owner, thus preserving the property rights regime of copyright law.

To award restitution in contract cases, however – other than in cases of rescission, where the object is to return the parties to their precontractual position, which may require one of the parties to give up a benefit it received from the other (perhaps because of a mistake, a common ground for rescission), or in extraordinary situations in which for one reason or another compensatory damages would not compensate the victim of the breach – would create a property right in the enforcement of a contract; and that would give rise to the bilateral monopoly problem discussed earlier. The promisor who had a superior opportunity to that enabled by the contract could not avail himself of it (more precisely, could obtain no profit from seizing the opportunity) without a negotiation with the promisee. The problem is less acute in copyright cases, where there are often multiple potential infringers, who if prevented from keeping profits from infringement will instead compete to obtain a license from the copyright owner.

Consistent with the economics of the situation, the traditional rule was that restitution was indeed not available simply to give the victim of a breach of contract a choice between his loss and the other party's gain. The traditional rule is under pressure, but it is too soon to determine whether it will give way; there is very little case law on the question.[19]

Professors Thel and Siegelman, in their contributions to this volume, discuss what is in substance, though not in name, restitution as a remedy for breach of contract: the award of windfall damages to middlemen.[20] Suppose *A*, a farmer, agrees to sell seeds to *B*, a seed wholesaler, for $100, and *B* agrees to resell the seeds to *C*, a nursery, for $150. Before delivery is due, the price of seeds doubles, and *A* breaks his contract with *B* and sells the seeds to *D* for the new market price of $200. If *B* is able to cover, and honor his contract with *C*, he will incur a loss that he can charge to *A*. But suppose *B*'s contract with *C* contains a clause that allows *B* to terminate the contract without liability. *B* does so, renegotiates the contract, and sells the seeds to *C* at a price that yields *B* the same profit as the original contract would have done. *B* has incurred no loss as a result of *A*'s breach, yet most courts would deem him entitled to obtain damages from *A* equal to the difference between the market price ($200) and the price in his contract with *A* ($100). In effect, he receives *A*'s profit from the breach.

But this result is sound, because the breach has not produced an efficiency gain; *A* is selling at the market price rather than to someone who values the seeds more than *B* does. And *B*'s inability to sell to his buyer, *C*, at the agreed-upon price may damage his business relationship with *C* (and perhaps with other customers as well).[21] Moreover, if the market price of seeds had fallen, *B* would have incurred an uncompensated loss by reason of having had to buy them from *A* at the higher contract price, which would limit *B*'s ability to resell at a profit. Thus, what seem "windfall" damages to *B* are really just the outcome of an agreed risk sharing. The expectation of a "windfall" compensates *B* for the possibility that he will have to confer a "windfall" on *A*, depending on which direction the market price moves in.[22]

Thel and Siegelman suggest another case in which restitution may be an efficient remedy for breach of contract.[23] A building contract specifies a particular brand of pipe; the builder deliberately substitutes another brand, which is just as good but cheaper, and so the builder saves money and yet the

[19] See the illuminating discussion in Andrew Kull, *Disgorgement for Breach, the "Restitution Interest," and the Restatement of Contracts*, 79 Tex. L. Rev. 2021 (2001).

[20] Steve Thel & Peter Siegelman, *Wilfulness vs. Expectation: A Promisor-Based Defense of Wilful Breach Doctrine*, this volume, at 164.5.

[21] *Id.*, citing Victor Goldberg, Framing Contract Law 225 (2006).

[22] *Cf.* Tongish v. Thomas, 840 P.2d 471, 476 (Kan. 1992).

[23] Thel & Siegelman, *supra* note 20, at 169. The case is a variant of *Jacob & Youngs, Inc. v. Kent*, 129 N.E. 889 (N.Y. 1921), but there the substitution was inadvertent, and the court said that all

buyer is no worse off. This looks like the efficient result, and one wonders therefore why the builder's conduct should be deemed a breach, let alone a willful one requiring a sanction even though the "victim" of the breach has incurred no loss. (Whether it should be deemed a breach with zero damages or not a breach at all is of little consequence.) But as Thel and Siegelman explain, the fact that the contract specified a particular brand may have been intended to curtail the builder's discretion out of concern that any deliberate substitution might well be inferior yet that this might be difficult to prove. Another possibility is that the buyer wanted that brand for some idiosyncratic reason, which a court could not value. In both situations, restitution of the builder's profit from the substitution might be justified.[24]

I say "might" rather than "would" be justified because it can be argued that building contracts are understood by the parties to give the builder leeway to make substitutions in response to changes in the price and availability of the various components[25] and that the buyer is compensated for the builder's freedom by the lower price that the builder will charge in exchange for obtaining such flexibility. The specifications in the contract still are legally enforceable, so that the buyer has a remedy against a substitution that whether or not approved by the architect (and there may not be an architect) reduces the value of the property. But if there is no reduction in value, no damages can be obtained.

My argument thus far may be criticized on the ground that compensatory damages for breach of contract are often inadequate to deter inefficient breaches. That is a common ground for wanting to carve out a class of "willful" breaches and punish them in some fashion, for example, by ordering restitution of the contract breaker's profits.[26] But if a supposedly compensatory remedy is not compensatory, then alter the remedy. Yet is that really necessary? The parties are free to specify in advance (within reasonable limits) the amount of damages to which the victim of a breach will be entitled.

I hope I will not be misunderstood to be arguing that there is never wrongful conduct in the negotiation or performance of contracts. I wrote an opinion recently that presented an interesting example of such conduct.[27] Here is a simplified version. *A* and *B* make a written contract. Later, *A* sues *B* claiming

the plaintiff would be entitled to was the reduction in the value of his property as a result of the substitution – which was probably zero.

[24] *See* Richard A. Posner, Law and Legal Theory in England and America 55–58 (1996).

[25] *See* Richard A. Posner, Cardozo: A Study in Reputation 106 (1990); Todd D. Rakoff, *Implied Terms: Of 'Default Rules' and 'Situation Sense,' in* Good Faith and Fault in Contract Law 191, 209 (Jack Beatson & Daniel Friedmann, eds., 1995).

[26] *See, e.g.*, George M. Cohen, *The Fault Lines in Contract Damages*, 80 Va. L. Rev. 1225 (1994).

[27] Extra Equipamentos e Exportação Ltda. v. Case Corp., 541 F.3d 719, 722–26 (7th Cir. 2008).

that during the negotiations *B* deliberately misrepresented the benefits that *A* would derive from the contract. But *A* does not sue for breach of contract. He can't; the parol evidence rule would bar a claim that promises made during the negotiations but not repeated in the contract should be deemed contractually binding. So *A* sues *B* in tort, charging fraud. The parol evidence rule is not a rule of tort law. But *B* has a defense: The written contract had included a clause stating that neither party was relying on any representations not embodied in the written contract. The "no-reliance" clause scotches *A*'s fraud suit because you cannot obtain damages for fraud unless you relied on the fraudulent representations, and *A* has disclaimed such reliance. So, although *B* is assumed to have acted wrongfully, *A* has no remedy in either contract or tort.

Is that a bad result? I think not. Provided (as was true in my case) that *A* is competently represented in the contract negotiations, so that he understands the meaning and significance of such a clause, he gave away his right to sue for fraud, with his eyes open, and presumably was compensated in other terms of the contract for making this concession. (Maybe *he* wanted the no-reliance clause, too, because he was worried that *B* might sue him for fraud.)

Neither am I suggesting that moral language never appears in contract cases. Obviously it does, as in the duty of "good faith" in the performance of a contract. But as Holmes explained in *The Path of the Law*, the fact that the law uses moral language doesn't mean that legal duties are moral duties. He famously wished to hold law and morality sharply separate.[28] The law uses moral language mainly because it supplies a familiar vocabulary in which to discuss duties and entitlements, and thus provides continuity between legal language and the language of everyday life. To take literally is a common source of mistakes in legal thinking. Here is an example: A class in an introductory course on contract law was asked why consideration is important in contract law. A student answered that it is because we want the parties to contracts to be considerate of each other's needs and objectives. Admittedly, it was a contract course in a business school rather than a law school. But law students and even sophisticated lawyers can stumble over the law's borrowings from moral language to describe legal obligations.

The idea of "good faith" is an example.[29] We generally want people to be honest and aboveboard in their dealings with others. But there is no general duty of good faith in contract law. If you offer a low price for some good to its owner, you are not obliged to tell him that you think the good is

[28] *See* Holmes, *The Path of the Law*, *supra* note 1, at 459.

[29] *See* Mkt. St. Assocs. Ltd. P'ship v. Frey, 941 F.2d 588 (7th Cir. 1991).

underpriced – that he does not realize its market value and you do.[30] You are not required to be an altruist, to be candid, to be a good guy. You are permitted to profit from asymmetry of information. If you could not do that, the incentive to discover information about true values would be blunted. It is an example of the traditional economic paradox that private vice can be public virtue.

And if through no fault of his own the other party to a contract with you cannot perform his duties under the contract, you are not obliged to forbear to enforce your contract rights, even if the result of your hardheartedness is to force him into bankruptcy. You may *want* to forbear, in your self-interest, because creditors don't usually do well in bankruptcy. But if forbearance were *required* by the law, interest rates would be higher because creditors' rights would be diminished.

There is a legally enforceable contract duty of "good faith," but it is just a duty to avoid exploiting the temporary monopoly position that a contracting party will sometimes obtain during the course of performance. More often than not, the parties to a contract do not perform their contractual duties simultaneously, and so one party may unavoidably deliver himself into the power of the other party for a time during the performance of the contract. *A* may agree to build a swimming pool for *B*, and *B* may agree to pay *A* upon completion. Suppose that when *A* has finished, *B* refuses to pay the agreed-upon price because he knows that *A* is desperately short of cash and will agree to a reduction in the contract price, having no possible source of cash other than *B*. *A*'s cash shortage, coupled with his having completed performance before *B* has begun and his having no alternative source of cash, gives *B* a monopoly position as *A*'s financier; monopoly is inefficient and so a modification of the contract to lower its price will not be enforced.

I am not using the word "monopoly" in the sense in which it is used in antitrust law. In my example, the breach is unlikely to have any effect on the market price of swimming pools. But it produces a social loss that can be rectified without an antitrust proceeding, just by refusing to enforce a modification of the contract. Think of the *Alaska Packers* case.[31] Seamen hired for the short Alaska salmon fishing season refused to work unless their pay was increased. The company reluctantly agreed. It had no alternative source of labor to which it could turn; its employees had effectively monopolized its labor supply. (A strike – which is what the case involved – is the exploitation of a temporary labor monopoly.) The court refused to enforce the contract modification,

[30] Laidlaw v. Organ, 15 U.S. (2 Wheat.) 178 (1817).
[31] Alaska Packers' Ass'n v. Domenico, 117 F. 99 (9th Cir. 1902).

reflecting as it did the seamen's temporary labor monopoly. Courts might describe the seller's conduct in such a case as coercive, extortionate, or in bad faith, but all they would mean by these highly charged words (more precisely all that, for the sake of clarity in law, they should be assumed to mean) would be that an implicit term of every contract (unless disclaimed) is that neither party shall take advantage of a temporary monopoly, conferred by the contract, of the supply of a key input into the output of the other party. One can, if one wants, denounce the temporary monopolist's conduct as wrongful, but the adjective adds nothing to the analysis.

Another example, this one involving the buyer's conduct rather than the seller's, is the rule that reads a "best-efforts" obligation on the part of a dealer into the dealership contract if his supplier has given him an exclusive right to sell the supplier's product. Exclusivity gives the dealer a monopoly during the life of the contract, and the best-efforts obligation prevents him from exploiting it. (The benefit of the monopoly to the supplier is that it gives the dealer an incentive to promote the supplier's product; the dealer doesn't have to worry about free riding by competing dealers in that product.) Nothing is gained by describing the dealer who, in the absence of a best-efforts duty, would exploit the monopoly conferred by the exclusive contract as "blameworthy."[32]

The duty of the victim of a breach of contract to mitigate his damages is also explicable in monopoly terms. A breach creates a bilateral monopoly: The parties would prefer to settle the victim's legal claim rather than litigate over it, but they can do so only by transacting with each other. The victim would like the damages that he has not yet incurred to mount up because that will increase the other party's maximum settlement offer. Suppose the contract entitles him to a million widgets, and the breach occurs after only a hundred thousand have been delivered and he could obtain the rest from another supplier cheaply but the cost to his original supplier of completing performance would be astronomical.[33] The duty to mitigate damages prevents the buyer from exploiting his temporary, contract-conferred monopoly in order to obtain a more generous settlement of his claim of breach of contract.

[32] *Frey*, 941 F.2d at 596 ("[T]o switch to another familiar example of the operation of the duty of good faith – parties to a requirements contract surely do not intend that if the price of the product covered by the contract rises, the buyer shall be free to increase his 'requirements' so that he can take advantage of the rise in the market price over the contract price to resell the product on the open market at a guaranteed profit. If they fail to insert an express condition to this effect, the court will read it in, confident that the parties would have inserted the condition if they had known what the future held." (citation omitted)).

[33] The example assumes that the original supplier could not obtain the needed quantity from the other supplier cheaply, and thus fulfill the contract at little or no increased cost.

In all these examples, the duty of "good faith" arises after the contract has been formed; that is why it is properly called the duty of good faith in performing a contract. If I may be permitted to quote again from my opinion in the *Frey* case (an opinion I had forgotten before I saw the reference to it in the chapter by Professors Bar-Gill and Ben-Shahar in this volume[34]),

> [b]efore the contract is signed, the parties confront each other with a natural wariness. Neither expects the other to be particularly forthcoming, and therefore there is no deception when one is not. Afterwards the situation is different. The parties are now in a cooperative relationship the costs of which will be considerably reduced by a measure of trust. So each lowers his guard a bit, and now silence is more apt to be deceptive.
>
> ... As performance unfolds, circumstances change, often unforeseeably; the explicit terms of the contract become progressively less apt to the governance of the parties' relationship; and the role of implied conditions – and with it the scope and bite of the good-faith doctrine – grows.[35]

There is, however, a limited duty of good faith at the contract-formation stage as well. It reflects the difference between *Laidlaw v. Organ*, where a knowledgeable buyer took advantage of an ignorant seller to obtain a valuable good at a below-market price, and a case of "unilateral mistake," in which the mistaken party is excused (for *Laidlaw v. Organ* really is a case of unilateral mistake, too), discussed by Professor Eisenberg in his chapter in this volume.[36] In the first case, allowing the knowledgeable person to take advantage of the ignorant one has a positive social product; in the second, as Eisenberg argues, it does not. Again I quote, as did Eisenberg, from my opinion in *Frey*:

> [I]t is one thing to say that you can exploit your superior knowledge of the market – for if you cannot, you will not be able to recoup the investment you made in obtaining that knowledge – or that you are not required to spend money bailing out a contract partner who has gotten into trouble. It is another thing to say that you can take deliberate advantage of an oversight by your contract partner concerning his rights under the contract. Such taking advantage is not the exploitation of superior knowledge or the avoidance of unbargained-for expense.... Like theft, it has no social product, and also like theft it induces costly defensive expenditures, in the form of overelaborate disclaimers or

[34] Oren Bar-Gill & Omri Ben-Shahar, *An Information Theory of Willful Breach*, this volume.

[35] *Frey*, 941 F.2d at 594–6.

[36] Melvin Aron Eisenberg, *The Role of Fault in Contract Law*, this volume.

investigations into the trustworthiness of a prospective contract partner, just as the prospect of theft induces expenditures on locks.[37]

The promisee's insistence on enforcing the contract with its mistake could be described as wrongful, but (here parting with Eisenberg) I do not see the utility of discussing it under the rubric of unconscionability or in any other morally charged language. I prefer to say that literal interpretation of contracts (specifically, a court's refusal to interpolate any implied terms – implied conditions, as they are rather confusingly described) creates opportunities for parties to extract surplus that the parties would not have agreed to had they foreseen and made provision against such behavior. It is clearer to speak in these terms than to invoke the moral sense.

The forgiving of unilateral mistakes illustrates that even the doctrine of unconscionability, which might seem to pose the sharpest challenge to the no-fault theory of contract law that I am expounding, may be explicable in nonmoral terms. A further illustration is the doctrine announced by Justice Traynor in *Monarco v. Lo Greco*:[38] If "either an unconscionable injury or unjust enrichment would result from refusal to enforce" an oral promise, a defense based on the statute of frauds will be denied.[39] I wrestled with this doctrine in a recent case,[40] and concluded that the doctrine is best understood as an effort to balance the value of protecting reasonable reliance against the policy that animates the statute of frauds of forestalling contract suits based on fraudulent or mistaken claims of an oral promise. It is not enough that the plaintiff relied on an oral promise; the statute of frauds would be too easily evaded if it did not apply to claims of promissory estoppel. Traynor's doctrine, I concluded from an examination of the cases, provides a substitute for the evidentiary function of a writing by requiring "a party that wants to get around the statute of frauds to prove an *enhanced* promissory estoppel, and the enhancement consists of a kind or amount of reliance unlikely to have been incurred had the plaintiff not had a good-faith belief that he had been promised remuneration."[41] The words "unconscionable" and "unjust" conceal the actual character of the doctrine.

[37] *Frey*, 941 F.2d at 594.

[38] 220 F.2d 737 (Cal. 1950).

[39] *Id.* at 741.

[40] Classic Cheesecake Co. v. JPMorgan Chase Bank, N.A., 546 F.3d 839 (7th Cir. 2008).

[41] *Id.* at 845. In *Monarco*, for example, "When the plaintiff reached 18 and wanted to leave home and make his own way in the world, his mother and stepfather promised him that if he stayed and worked on the family farm they would leave almost all their property (which was in joint tenancy) to him. He stayed, and worked hard, receiving in exchange only room and board and spending money. The farm prospered. But when the stepfather died 20 years later, he left his half interest in the farm to his own grandson." *Classic Cheesecake*, 546 F.3d at 843.

II.

The analysis that I have presented for preserving our "no-fault" regime of contract law is, of course, not conclusive, but even if it were less persuasive than an analysis that reached the opposite conclusion, I would be disinclined to favor changing the law. This is a general point, having nothing in particular to do with the fault issue. It applies to any default rule of contract law. Such a rule is by definition one that the parties can contract around. If they do not do so, or at least do not do so frequently, there is an inference (except in the case of contracts with consumers for inexpensive items) that the rule is optimal. The reason is that the costs of contracting around, in any but the smallest contracts (which is why I am excepting small consumer contracts), are – or so one might think (this qualification will be explained shortly) – small relative to the other transaction costs.

Observation of contracting-around behavior can thus provide an empirical test of the efficiency of a contractual default provision.[42] Given the availability of this empirical test, it would be imprudent to change the law on the basis of purely theoretical arguments unless the arguments were compelling and hence unrebutted by responsible students of contract law. And that is not the case with regard to the arguments for injecting fault (or more fault) into U.S. contract law.

Granted, studies have found that rules are often not contracted around even if they are inefficient.[43] Some of these studies attribute this result to a psychological bias in favor of the status quo. But such a bias is rational in the contracting process because very few contract disputes result in litigation, so that the transaction costs of negotiating a change in a standard provision will therefore often exceed the benefits.[44] Whatever the reason for the persistence of inefficient default rules, the phenomenon weakens the empirical approach

[42] *See* Jeffrey L. Dunoff & Joel P. Trachtman, *Economic Analysis of International Law*, 24 Yale J. Int'l L. 1 (1999); William H. Widen, *Corporate Form and Substantive Consolidation*, 75 Geo. Wash. L. Rev. 237, 263–4 (2007).

[43] *See, e.g.*, Omri Ben-Shahar & John A.E. Pottow, *On the Stickiness of Default Rules*, 33 Fla. St. U. L. Rev. 651 (2006); Lisa Bernstein, Comment, *Social Norms and Default Rules Analysis*, 3 S. Cal. Interdisc. L. J. 59, 71–2 (1993); Russell Korobkin, *The Status Quo Bias and Contract Default Rules*, 83 Cornell L. Rev. 608 (1998). *Cf.* Robert E. Scott & Mitu Gulati, Sticky Contracts (or Why Don't Law Firms Have R&D Departments?) (Nov. 8, 2008) (unpublished manuscript, on file with author).

[44] This is a possible explanation for contract lawyers' tendency, noted by Scott & Gulati, *supra* note 43, to swallow their objections to conventional contract terms that may not fit the circumstances of the particular contract in negotiation. In addition, just raising a question about a familiar term may alarm the other party or be taken as a signal that the party raising the question is not committed to the deal or seeks an unwarranted advantage.

that I am suggesting, but it also exposes an additional reason to go slow in pushing for changes ("reforms") in contract law. Lawyers and their clients place substantial reliance on the rules of contract law. Even when contracts are individually negotiated, a form contract (which may simply be a form in a lawyer's office rather than something published in a book of form contracts) is very often the basis for the negotiation, and the form reflects existing law. In addition, contract negotiations and choice of terms (including price) are heavily influenced by the lawyers' and clients' understanding of the legal framework. Changing a common law rule creates a period of uncertainty, as courts explore the boundaries of the rule in case-by-case adjudication.

Another reason for proceeding cautiously along the path of contract law "reform" is the high degree of uniformity in contract law, not only across the fifty American states but also across different legal systems altogether. Although specific performance is said to be the default regime in European contract law and fault does, as I have said, play a larger role in that law than in Anglo-American contract law, the differences in outcome appear to be small and are narrowing.[45] Civil law judges exercise discretion to award damages rather than order-specific performance, and often the same outcomes are reached in common law and civil law systems under different doctrinal rubrics. Thus, in answer to a question by Douglas Baird at the conference, Stefan Grundmann explained that civil law courts reach results similar to *Hadley v. Baxendale* under the rubric of a precontractual duty to mitigate damages by requiring the buyer to warn the seller of any unusual damages that a breach would cause.

Global consensus (to exaggerate a bit) is further evidence – of course, not conclusive – for the optimality of our existing law. It also suggests the importance, under modern conditions of commerce, of having a degree of global uniformity of contract law. Because there is no international convention on contract law that would make it possible to change the whole world's contract law at a stroke, a change in that law would have to be implemented piecemeal, jurisdiction by jurisdiction; the process of attaining global uniformity would be protracted, and that is another reason to go slowly in changing domestic contract law.

[45] *See* Wayne R. Barnes, *Contemplating a Civil Law Paradigm for a Future International Commercial Code*, 65 La. L. Rev. 677, 751–2 (2005); Gotanda, *supra* note 8, at 63–4; Julian Hermida, *Convergence of Civil Law and Common Law in the Criminal Theory Realm*, 13 U. Miami Int'l & Comp. L. Rev. 163, 167–70 (2005); Barry Nicholas, *Fault and Breach of Contract*, *in* Good Faith and Fault in Contract Law, *supra* note 25, at 337; Patricia Pattison & Daniel Herron, The Mountains are High and the Emperor is Far Away: Sanctity of Contract in China, 40 Am. Bus. L. J. 459, 475 (2003); *cf.* Werner F. Ebke & Bettina M. Steinhauer, *The Doctrine of Good Faith in German Contract Law*, *in* Good Faith and Fault in Contract Law, *supra* note 25, at 171, 190.

Against all this it may be argued, in the spirit of Professor Shiffrin's recent article,[46] that it is often immoral to break a contract deliberately and that the law should be shaped accordingly, and thus, for example, punitive damages should be allowed in many cases of willful breach. The other side of this coin, presumably, is that a nonperformer should be held in breach of contract only if the breach was willful, opportunistic, or perhaps negligent, but in any event in some way wrongful. I have no wish to debate the morality of contract breaking, but I don't understand the "accordingly." The law does not enforce every violation of the moral code, let alone enforce it to the hilt (as by awarding punitive damages for, or affixing criminal sanctions to, every violation), and I doubt that Shiffrin would want it to. Nor does the law excuse all injuries that are not the result of a breach of the moral code. (Does she want to abolish strict liability in tort?) She needs to give reasons why recasting contract law in moral terms would be a *sensible* step to take and not merely the logical implication of a philosophical theory.

[46] Seana Shiffrin, *Why Breach of Contract May Be Immoral*, 107 Mich. L. Rev. 1551 (2009).

TWO

In (Partial) Defense of Strict Liability in Contract

Robert E. Scott

Many scholars believe that notions of fault should and do pervade contract doctrine. This chapter argues that contract liability is strict liability at its core. This core regime is based on two key prongs: (1) the promisor is liable to the promisee for breach, and that liability is unaffected by the promisor's exercise of due care or failure to take efficient precautions; and (2) the promisor's liability is unaffected by the fact that the promisee, prior to the breach, has failed to take cost-effective precautions to reduce the consequences of nonperformance. The chapter offers two complementary normative justifications for contract law's stubborn resistance to considering fault in either of these instances. First, it argues that there are unappreciated ways in which courts' adherence to strict liability doctrine at the core of contract reduces contracting costs. In addition, it argues that a strict liability core best supports parties' efforts to access informal or relational modes of contracting, especially where key information is unverifiable.

Introduction

The Restatement's oft-quoted assertion about the nature of contract liability is one of the most imprecise generalizations ever made about the common law of contract. Numerous scholars have pointed out that, in fact, many notions of fault infuse contract law, ranging from prescriptions against intentional "bad behavior" to assessments of the reasonableness of an actor's behavior in assessing both liability and damages. But while there are, indeed, many "fault lines" in contract, speaking at that level of generality has little analytic purchase. In short, from a distance the fault lines in contract appear broken and indistinct.

In this chapter, I propose to defend the notion of strict liability that lies at the core of the Restatement's claim. By its terms, the Restatement does not rule out fault-based considerations for claims based on promissory estoppel, fraud, bad faith, mistake, excuse, or a host of other issues. But the availability of these principles only in select circumstances justifies a core no-fault regime. This core regime is based on two key prongs: (1) the promisor is liable to the promisee for breach, and that liability is unaffected by the promisor's exercise of due care or failure to take efficient precautions; and (2) the promisor's liability is unaffected by the fact that the promisee, prior to the breach, has failed to take cost-effective precautions to reduce the consequences of nonperformance. In terms of the Restatement conception, then, contract law is strict liability without a contributory negligence defense.

Notwithstanding the many illustrations of fault lines in contract, the Restatement's assertion, as limited above, is descriptively accurate. The core of contract law *as applied in the courts* is a no-fault regime. This is so even though theorists mount powerful arguments on efficiency grounds for a cost-benefit analysis of promisor and promisee behavior in particular cases, and even though contract doctrine appears to invite just such an analysis. For example, if the promisor carelessly fails to take efficient precautions ex ante, which result in breach ex post, the "willful breach doctrine" invites courts to increase damages to deter such inefficient behavior. Similarly, if the promisee fails to take efficient precautions prior to the breach that would reduce or eliminate losses, the mitigation principle invites courts to apply a "contributory negligence" bar to recovery. However, a large sample of cases shows that courts decline to employ the willful breach doctrine to deter an inefficient breach. And despite evidence that the promisee has failed to take precautions prior to breach that would have reduced losses, courts adhere strictly to the rule that the promisee's mitigation responsibility is not triggered until the promisor breaches.

The courts' reluctance to adopt a comparative fault standard in assessing the core question of liability for breach is all the more surprising given that comparative fault principles are found elsewhere in contract law, most notably in the doctrines of unjust enrichment and unilateral mistake. Viewed in this light, the question is not why contract law fails to acknowledge explicitly the many fault principles it embraces implicitly. Rather, the puzzle is why courts adhere to a no-fault regime at the core of contract liability even though contract doctrine invites them to consider fault in other instances.

In Part I of this chapter, I set out the case that courts are committed to a strict liability regime at what I call the "core" of contract law. This part focuses on the evidence of strict liability as demonstrated by (a) courts' reluctance to use the willful breach doctrine to deter inefficient breach by promisors; and (b) courts' reluctance to use the mitigation principle to deter inefficient overreliance by promisees. In Part II, I offer two complementary normative justifications for contract law's stubborn resistance to fault principles at its core. I argue that there are unappreciated ways in which courts' adherence to strict liability doctrine reduces contracting costs. In addition, I argue that a strict liability core best supports parties' efforts to access informal or relational modes of contracting, especially where key information is unverifiable. Part III briefly summarizes.

I. The Strict Liability Core of Contract Law

A. *The Promisor's Behavior: The Willful Breach Doctrine*

Among the many debates about fault in contract law, one principle remains unchallenged: A promisor is strictly liable for defective performance or nonperformance despite her exercise of due care. Even the most fervent adherents of fault in contract law concede that the law always applies this rule strictly. Thus, the promisee does not have to prove that the promisor failed to take cost-effective precautions against breach. Nor, for that matter, can the promisor escape liability by showing that the breach was caused by exogenous factors beyond her control.

But there *is* a doctrine in contract law that invites courts to adjust liability or damages if the promisor's breach was "willful." Courts have attached this doctrine primarily to the choice of damage measures in cases involving breach of a contract for services. In such cases, promisees commonly sue for the "cost of completion" – the price of purchasing a substitute performance in the market. However, the cost of completion sometimes exceeds the gain that the seller's performance would have produced. This problem usually occurs in construction contexts. In *Jacob & Youngs v. Kent*, for example, the contractor deviated from the agreed-upon performance in an apparently minor way, but the costs of remedying that defect were much greater than the reduction in property value that the deviation had caused.[1] Similarly, in *Peevyhouse v. Garland Coal & Mining Co.*, a lessee agreed to restore the lessor's property after the lessee had used it, but the costs of restoration turned out to be much higher than the resultant increase in property value.[2] In cases like these, where repair involves unreasonable destruction of the contractor's work or the cost of completion is grossly disproportionate to the benefit obtained, the owner can recover only the diminished market value on the ground that the standard remedy would produce "economic waste."

[1] 129 N.E. 889 (N.Y. 1921).
[2] 382 P.2d 109 (Okla. 1962).

There is substantial uncertainty, however, as to the appropriate circumstances for applying the "economic waste" doctrine. A key doctrinal prerequisite is the finding that the contractor has substantially performed the contract in good faith and that the breach was not "willful."[3] In both of the celebrated cases noted above, the court declined to find fault with the promisor's breach. In *Jacob & Youngs*, Justice Cardozo invoked the economic waste doctrine to limit the owners' damage award to the diminution in value caused by the breach. He found (at least implicitly) that the contractor's breach was accidental and not willful. In *Peevyhouse*, the majority did not address the willful breach doctrine directly, but Justice Irwin dissented on the ground that the breach "was wilful and not in good faith." Thus, the majority at least implicitly rejected application of the willful breach doctrine to the facts in the record.

To be sure, the precise behavior intended to be captured by the willful breach doctrine is unclear. However, the concept should be sufficiently capacious to embrace "inefficient behavior" of the promisor. By this standard, a breach is willful when the promisor fails to take cost-effective precautions in performing a contract that is ex ante efficient and then breaches the contract to avoid incurring substantial losses. In using this standard to evaluate the actions of promisors in cases such as *Jacob & Youngs* and *Peevyhouse*, it is important to recognize that the promisees in such cases will have *prepaid* for the service in a master contract. The fact of prepayment is often ignored by courts and commentators because, in such a contract, the services are bundled together and are not separately priced. For example, the royalty on the mineral lease in a case such as *Peevyhouse* is smaller if the mining company agrees to restore the land at the end of the lease term, but rarely if ever is there an explicit "subprice" for the agreement to restore. Likewise, the cost of constructing a building is seldom disaggregated into separate prices for the promise to install the plumbing and the promise to correct defective work. Yet, no one would claim that the mining lessee agreed to restore for nothing or that the building contractor did not charge for having to replace nonconforming plumbing.[4]

[3] As Cardozo famously stated, "the willful transgressor must accept the penalty of his transgression." *Jacob & Youngs*, 129 N.E. at 891.

[4] Alan Schwartz & Robert E. Scott, *Market Damages, Efficient Contracting, and the Economic Waste Fallacy*, 108 Colum. L. Rev. 1610 (2008). The standard construction contract contains a separate promise by the contractor to correct any defective construction. This promise remains binding even after substantial performance of the contract. *See e.g.*, American Institute of Architects, AIA Document A201–1997: General Conditions of the Contract for Construction (1997).

The fact of prepayment reduces the incentives for the promisor to take precautions ex ante that would reduce the ex post cost of completion. Promisors such as the contractor in *Jacob & Youngs* and the mining company in *Peevyhouse* can sometimes reduce the cost of performance below the promisee's value by taking precautions between the time of contract and the time of completion. But a prepaid promisor's incentive to invest efficiently in cost reduction is materially reduced if her damage exposure for failing to invest is capped by the diminished value measure.

A finding of fault based on "inefficient behavior" in these situations is appropriate if four key conditions are satisfied. First, the promisor is able to take a precaution during the course of performance that reduces the expected cost of the contractually required service below its expected value to the promisee. Second, the promisee is an imperfect monitor and is unlikely to detect the promisor's lack of precaution. Third, the promisee may never (or only later) discover the promisor's failure to take precautions. And fourth, the promisor is able to perform the contractually required service ex post, albeit at a much more expensive price. Where these conditions are satisfied, the economic waste rule should not be applied: Restricting promisees' awards to diminished market value creates an incentive for sellers not to take the efficient precaution. Rather, courts should invoke the "willful breach" doctrine: an award of cost of completion damages that creates a positive incentive for sellers to take efficient precautions. Cost of completion damages in such a case is an efficient deterrent against this moral hazard.

The question, then, is whether the contractor's behavior in *Jacob & Youngs* sufficiently satisfied the "inefficient behavior" test to justify invoking the willful breach doctrine and considering fault in the assessment of damages. Virtually all the ensuing commentary has accepted Cardozo's characterization of the contractor's behavior in *Jacob & Youngs* as accidental and has justified the nonwillful characterization of the breach. Unfortunately, however, that characterization appears to be false. The extraordinary costs of completion in *Jacob & Youngs* resulted from the contractor's failure to inspect the pipe to ensure that it complied with the contract specifications. In dissent, Justice McLaughlin recited the key facts from the record and concluded that the failure to inspect was "due to gross neglect." The record in *Jacob & Youngs*, thus, shows that each of the four conditions supporting a finding of inefficient behavior was satisfied:[5]

[5] Note that we must assume, per Cardozo, that the failure to install the contract-specified pipe was, in fact, a breach. This assumption is supported in the case by the architect's refusal to give his certificate.

> There was (1) an apparently efficient precaution – checking the pipe as it was delivered to insure that it met contract specifications; (2) evidence that the owner, through his architect, was an imperfect monitor (he was able conveniently to check only the first installment of pipe but not the remainder); (3) difficulty in discovering the unsatisfactory performance because most of the pipe was embedded in the walls of the house; and (4) performance that was inefficient ex post: The high cost of removal caused the ex post market price of performance to exceed the [diminished market value] by so much as likely to exceed the buyer's value from performance.[6]

An analysis of the facts in *Peevyhouse* supports the same conclusion: The breach was a result of the mining company's failure to take ex ante precautions, and a fault-based analysis should have invoked the willful breach doctrine. As Judith Maute has shown, the mining company in *Peevyhouse* could have stripped the land with restoration costs in mind.[7] Also, the plaintiff, Garland, admitted at trial that (1) the owners had insisted that the regrading provisions be included in the contract; (2) they would not agree to the coal mining lease unless the promise to regrade was included; (3) heavy rains caused the plaintiff to postpone the promised remedial work; and (4) in the interim, plaintiff relocated the grading equipment to another profitable site and decided not to return to complete the remedial work.

In short, declining to apply the willful breach doctrine and restricting the promisee to the diminished value measure in the contexts these cases exemplify is inefficient. This inference is supported by a more systematic examination of the case law. In order to evaluate how contemporary American courts treat economic waste claims, I recently analyzed a sample of 110 cases, most of which were litigated in the past two decades.[8] In twenty-nine cases, the courts were faced with the question of the appropriate measure of damages when the evidence showed that the cost to complete would greatly exceed the value of performance to the plaintiff. Nineteen cases had facts that were sufficiently clear to permit an inference that the seller could have taken cost-effective precautions to reduce the cost of performance. In these cases, where the sellers' actions likely would have reduced costs, the buyers' capacity to monitor was also likely imperfect: they were mostly amateurs, and they could not constantly be on site. As discussed above, in cases such as these it is efficient for courts to award cost of completion damages, even where the ex post cost of performance significantly exceeds the buyer's ex post valuation. Such

[6] Schwartz & Scott, *Market Damages, supra* at 1654 n. 108.

[7] *See* Judith L. Maute, Peevyhouse v. Garland Coal & Mining Co. *Revisited: The Ballad of Willie and Lucille*, 89 Nw. U. L. Rev. 1341, 1429 (1995).

[8] Schwartz & Scott, *supra* at 1624–34.

an award is efficient as it induces the seller to take the precaution that would forestall the excess costs. Yet, in only one of the thirty cases did a court apply the willful breach doctrine and award the larger damages measure.

The evidence from *Jacob & Youngs*, *Peevyhouse*, and their progeny points in a single direction. Courts continue to follow the strict liability principle that the promisor's behavior is irrelevant to the issues of liability and damages. In particular, courts decline the open invitation of the willful breach doctrine to apply fault-based principles in cases where strong arguments suggest that the breach was inefficient and should have been deterred. Before trying to justify this surprising conclusion, I next examine the second prong of the core strict liability idea: that the promisee's behavior prior to the breach is irrelevant to questions of liability or damages.

B. *The Promisee's Behavior: The Mitigation Principle*

Common law courts have consistently held that a promisee need not take steps to avoid losses so long as the promisor has not clearly and definitively repudiated the contract. This rule limits the ability of courts to encourage both parties to take cost-effective precautions that will reduce the expected losses from a contract breach. Moreover, it is well established that, absent a legal restraint on the promisee's reliance actions, the promisee will overrely when there is an expectation damages default rule. These inefficiencies can be moderated, however, by careful application of the rules governing anticipatory repudiation. If promisors repudiate as soon as they are aware of events that will ultimately lead to nonperformance, they can, at least in theory, induce the promisee to mitigate sooner rather than later.

A comparative fault analysis, therefore, should focus on the rules governing anticipatory repudiation: The more likely that the promisee's behavior is contributing to the losses from breach, the more likely a court should be (1) to find that the actions of the promisor constitute a repudiation of the contract; and (2) to invoke *at that time* the doctrine of avoidable consequences and the promisee's mitigation responsibility. By interpreting anticipatory repudiation rules in this way, courts could motivate parties to avoid or reduce the breach costs that would otherwise result if the promisee were allowed to delay mitigation until the time of performance.

To see this, consider an example in which Adam agrees on July 1 to deliver an air conditioning unit to Christy on December 1 at a cost of $500,000.[9]

[9] The discussion that follows draws on Robert E. Scott & Jody S. Kraus, Contract Law and Theory 815–18 (4th ed. 2007).

Assume that an explosion in Adam's plant on September 1 causes a two-month delay in delivery that will cost Christy $100,000. Suppose, however, that if Adam informs Christy on September 1 of his inability to meet the contract deadline, Christy can redesign the building under construction to accommodate an air conditioning unit that is equivalent in quality but differently designed. Christy's total losses due to Adam's breach would then be only $40,000 – that is, the $20,000 additional price of the substitute air conditioner plus the $20,000 additional cost to redesign the building. Adam would obviously prefer limiting his maximum loss to $40,000 by having Christy redesign her building. By repudiating on September 1, at the time of the plant explosion, Adam would hope to induce Christy immediately to mitigate her damages by making the necessary adjustments.

The doctrine of anticipatory repudiation thus can be used to extend the duty of mitigation to a period before the time for performance has expired. Because it potentially enables the parties to avoid wasteful actions taken in reliance on performance, applying the doctrine in this way brings actual contracts closer to the ideally efficient contract, one that would require parties to make all cost-effective adjustments to events occurring after the contract was formed.

But courts have been reluctant to require mitigation at the time of repudiation. The common law rule remains well established: The promisee can either seek damages at the time of repudiation or wait until the time of performance and recover market damages at that later date. As a result, promisees operating under the common law rule are free to exacerbate their damages by waiting until the time of performance to mitigate. And when promisees exercise this option, they undermine the possibility of mutually beneficial postcontract adjustments. The common law rule thus seems inconsistent with the fault-based, cost-benefit analysis embodied in the doctrine of avoidable consequences. Returning to our earlier example, giving Christy the option of waiting beyond the time of repudiation is inefficient because she will not internalize the cost of delay to Adam. Moreover, she will be motivated to wait as long as she can, since she retains any benefits from a declining market, while Adam must bear all the costs.

C. *Summary*

As the preceding discussion has shown, in cases where courts are directly asked to consider the relevance of promisor and promisee behavior in assessing the core questions of liability and damages, the strict liability regime announced in the Restatement is alive and well. To be sure, the fact that these core questions remain grounded in a system of strict liability does not undermine familiar claims that elsewhere contract embraces fault-based notions. But it does deepen the puzzle as to why those fault lines have failed to penetrate the two core questions: Will the promisor's liability be increased if it appears that breach was caused by her inefficient behavior, and will the promisee's recovery be diminished by evidence that his inefficient behavior contributed significantly to the quantum of loss? In both cases, the answer at common law and in contemporary litigation is a clear "no." In the next part, I ask whether this rejection of a fault-based system at the core of contract can be justified.

II. The Normative Case for Strict Liability

The normative case for strict liability rests on two complementary arguments. Both are based on the claim that commercially sophisticated parties prefer strict liability rules over fault-based rules, especially at the core of contract. These arguments center on the revealed preference of commercial parties for precise or bright-line rules over broad standards and on a revealed preference for party autonomy in selecting precisely when and where standards are preferable to rules. In the first case, the preference for autonomy in selecting between rules and standards permits parties to optimize contracting costs by shifting them between the front end and the back end of the contractual process. In the second case, the preservation of formal rules offers parties the choice of improving contractual incentives by relying on informal or relational contracting as a complement to the formal contract. In this part, I first consider the theoretical arguments that support the claim that commercial parties prefer formal rules in general and strict liability at the core of contract in particular. Thereafter, I evaluate the evidence that supports the theoretical claims.

A. *Contract Design and the Choice Between Rules and Standards*[10]

Why might commercial parties prefer strict liability to a fault-based regime? One answer lies in the trade-off between contracting costs and the goal of improving contractual incentives. Commercial parties will weigh front- or back-end contracting costs against the incentive *gains* that they produce – what George Triantis and I have referred to elsewhere as the incentive "bang"

[10] This discussion draws on Robert E. Scott & George G. Triantis, *Anticipating Litigation in Contract Design*, 115 Yale L.J. 814 (2006).

for their contracting-cost "buck." And they will prefer improved incentives of the sort we examined earlier only if those incentives do not generate even greater contracting costs. To understand parties' apparent preference for formal rules like strict liability, one must consider the contract design challenges that they face in writing incomplete contracts.

Incomplete contracts are challenging because the parties must attempt to balance two seemingly inconsistent goals. One goal is to encourage "relation-specific investments" that enhance the expected surplus from the transaction. But the commitment that is necessary to motivate surplus-maximizing specific investments will typically conflict with the goal of preserving flexibility – which is necessary to halt those transactions that prove to have insufficient net value when uncertainty is resolved.

One way to encourage initial investments is for the parties to write a contract with precise, unchanging terms or "rules", that is, determinate outcomes that apply across the board regardless of the eventual state of the world. But because the rules are inflexible, they may not respond to what actually happens and may be inefficient ex post. Alternatively, if the future is very uncertain, the parties may instead emphasize the value of flexibility by drafting a contract with vague standards, that is, "soft" terms such as those that require subsequent adjustment in good faith to new facts as they arise. But a promisor with the discretion to adjust performance is likely to choose the best alternative for *him* even though the self-interested choice is unlikely to be the best way to maximize the parties' joint welfare.

In short, neither precise rules nor vague standards can, standing alone, solve the problem of incomplete contracts. Parties therefore predictably seek to optimize total contracting costs by trading off the respective benefits and costs of commitment and flexibility. They can do this by shifting their costs between the front and back end of the contracting process. For example, when the parties agree to bright-line rules, such as the buyer's obligation to purchase a precisely specified, customized machine at a fixed price, they encourage the seller to undertake the required investment by limiting the court's authority to determine their particular performance obligations. But this strategy requires the parties to rely on mere estimates of the likelihood of future events. Alternatively, when the parties agree to a vague standard, such as to adjust the price of the machine in good faith as conditions subsequently require, they effectively delegate the specification of performance requirements to a court at the back end of the contracting process. This provides flexibility and allows them potentially to benefit from the court's hindsight advantage, but at a cost of undermining the buyer's commitment to pay and the seller's willingness to invest. The parties thus choose between these front- and back-end specification mechanisms by comparing the benefits of ex ante commitment against the flexibility offered by the court's hindsight advantage.

This model of contract design suggests that courts should refrain from filling contractual gaps with broad standards in cases where the parties are silent. A court may be tempted (with the encouragement of one of the parties) to see gaps and to use fault-based doctrines such as mistake, excuse, or frustration as devices for implying standards into the parties' agreement. But this is generally an error. Commercial parties can include standards in their contract at relatively low cost. They also have superior knowledge regarding the context of their contractual relationship, which provides the basis for determining the optimal mix of precise and vague terms. As a rule of thumb, therefore, courts are wise to assume that the absence of vague standards in commercial contracts is an instruction from the parties to focus interpretation on the precise terms of the contract.

This preference for party autonomy in selecting what standards to use and when to use them supports the claim that commercial parties will prefer strict liability rules to broad, fault-based standards. In addition to the trade-off between front- and back-end contracting costs, bright-line rules offer commercial parties the opportunity to resolve their disputes without a full-blown trial. It is plausible that the more complex the factual issues in litigation, the easier it will be for one party to create disputes regarding the appropriateness of the other's behavior. Thus, litigation is likely to be more costly in a fault-based regime because the parties more frequently will have full trials. When parties weigh their contract design choices, they will not only consider the costs and gains from creating the deal initially; they will also consider the likelihood and costs of later disputes. The fact that fault regimes increase the likelihood and cost of disputes explains why parties may prefer contracts that only crudely encourage efficient behavior but significantly reduce the contracting costs of enforcement.

B. *Rules v. Standards and the Choice Between Formal and Informal Enforcement*[11]

As suggested in the earlier discussion, contract design is not merely a matter of calculating the costs and benefits of negotiating particular terms in a contract. In addition to handling the front-end cost of negotiating a contract,

[11] This discussion draws on Robert E. Scott, *A Theory of Self-Enforcing Indefinite Agreements*, 103 Colum. L. Rev. 1641 (2003).

parties must attend to the back-end problems of verifying and enforcing their respective obligations in court. Focusing on the costs of verifying contractual obligations motivates parties to consider the choice between formal and informal means of enforcement.

In many instances, an agreement between two commercial parties will be self-enforcing because both parties want to earn and preserve a good reputation so as to enhance their self-esteem and future business prospects. Moreover, agreements will also be self-enforcing to the extent that the parties anticipate that the expected profits from future dealings are greater than the gains from breaching the existing contract.

Even where loss of reputation and the threat of retaliation are insufficient to induce performance, powerful norms of reciprocity appear to enhance and extend the reach of informal enforcement. A substantial body of experimental evidence shows that a preference for reciprocity – that is, the willingness to reward cooperation and to punish selfishness – can motivate cooperation even in arms-length interactions between complete strangers. This evidence suggests that contracting parties frequently can (and do) turn to informal means of enforcement based on trust and reciprocity in addition to the desire to maintain a good reputation or the prospect of profitable future dealings. And if parties are able to rely on these informal methods of enforcement, they may be able to create contractual commitments that are at once sufficiently credible to motivate efficient investments ex ante and sufficiently flexible to ensure efficient adjustment ex post.

So, what role does (and should) legal enforcement play in a world where informal enforcement is pervasive and robust? First, note that informal enforcement generally is cheaper than formal enforcement because a party needs to expend costs only to observe the other's behavior, while formal enforcement requires additional resources to verify that behavior to a court. Moreover, informal enforcement is often better than formal enforcement: Parties can make credible promises regarding observable but nonverifiable measures of performance, thus achieving contractual objectives that may not be possible with formal enforcement. To be sure, there is still an important role for formal contract enforcement. Common sense tells us that relationships relying on informal enforcement can break down, and when they do, the parties will resort to costly litigation. When reciprocity breaks down in complex transactions, the courts can serve a valuable function by making factual determinations to unravel complex behaviors.

Thus, a central question remains: How do the various means of enforcement interact with each other? The available evidence suggests that legal enforcement is often imperialistic; that an effort to superimpose legal enforcement on a regime of self-enforcement can displace or "crowd out" informal mechanisms.[12] The experimental evidence of crowding out undermines the argument that courts should adopt a broad, fault-based approach to enforcing contracts. The understandable instinct to deter inefficient behavior may well prove counterproductive in the long run. As the evidence suggests, extending legal enforcement to the difficult-to-verify questions of willful breach and overreliance may well impair the efficacy of informal means of enforcement that rely instead on reciprocity norms.

As we have seen, common law contract doctrine has resisted the invitation to imply broad fault standards of behavior at the core of contract. Thus, if a promise falls within the core of legal enforcement, contract law fills only a few gaps, using simple, verifiable strict liability rules when it does so. The evidence that there are informal means of enforcing commitments that courts cannot readily verify supports this approach. The more general lesson for courts, therefore, is that an effort to judicialize notions of comparative fault and reciprocal behavior may well destroy the very informality that makes these mechanisms so effective in the *absence* of judicial enforcement.

C. *The Evidence*

While there are good theoretical reasons to believe that commercial parties prefer a strict liability regime to one based on fault, critics may argue that theoretical inferences about parties' intentions are fraught with peril. If commercial parties prefer a formal, strict liability regime, it may be argued, then why don't they say so?

The short answer is that they do. Following is a common provision found in many alliance agreements:

> The Parties' legal obligations under this Alliance Agreement are to be determined from the precise and literal language of this Alliance Agreement and not from the imposition of state laws attempting to impose additional duties of good faith, fair dealing or fiduciary obligations that were not the express basis of the bargain at the time this Agreement was made.
>
> The Parties are sophisticated business entities with legal counsel that have been retained to review the terms of this Alliance Agreement and the Parties represent that they have fully read this Alliance Agreement, and understand and accept its terms.[13]

[12] For discussion see Scott, *supra* note 11, at 1688–92.

[13] Alliance Agreement between E. I. du Pont de Nemours & Co. and EarthShell Corp. (Jul. 25, 2002), *available at* http://contracts.onecle.com/earthshell/dupont.collab.2002.07.25.shtml.

In addition to such anecdotal evidence from individual contracts, the available data support the strict liability theory. First, Lisa Bernstein's pioneering work shows that parties who are members of trade associations – and thus who rely both on informal or relational enforcement and on third-party enforcement – carefully preserve formal, strict liability rules and reject broad standards in assessing performance, breach and liability.[14] Bernstein argues that this regime can best be understood as a mechanism for preserving the space for both formal and informal norms to operate.

Second, recent work by Eisenberg and Miller studying choice of law and choice of forum clauses in a data set of 2,865 contracts provides empirical support for the claim that commercial parties prefer the binary strict liability regime of the traditional common law.[15] Specifically, their study showed that parties choose New York law in 46 percent of the contracts and New York as the forum state in 41 percent of the contracts. California, on the other hand was chosen for its contract law in less than 8 percent of the contracts even though its commercial activity, as measured by the place of business of the contracting parties, was second only to that of New York.

The significance of this striking differential in party preference is illuminated in a recent paper by Geoff Miller that analyzes the differences between contract law in New York and California.[16] Miller's analysis confirms the conventional wisdom: New York strictly enforces bargains and displays little tolerance of efforts to balance interests ex post. California, by contrast, is far more willing to adopt fault-based considerations and to revise contracts on the grounds of fairness, equity, or public policy. As Miller concludes, "[t]he revealed preferences of sophisticated parties support arguments by Schwartz, Scott and others that formalistic rules offer superior value for the interpretation and enforcement of commercial contracts."

The theory and evidence that support the normative case for strict liability in contract are partial in two respects. First, they are partial because the theory and evidence largely apply to commercially sophisticated parties. Thus, the normative claims for strict liability have less force, if any, when applied to other areas of contract law, and particularly those that concern contracts

[14] Lisa Bernstein, *Merchant Law in a Merchant Court: Rethinking the Code's Search for Immanent Business Norms*, 144 U. Pa. L. Rev. 1765 (1996); Lisa Bernstein, *Private Commercial Law in the Cotton Industry: Creating Cooperation Through Rules, Norms and Institutions*, 99 Mich. L. Rev. 1724 (2001).

[15] Theodore Eisenberg & Geoffrey P. Miller, *The Flight to New York: An Empirical Study of Choice of Law and Choice of Forum Clauses in Publicly-Held Companies' Contracts* (N.Y.U. Ctr. For Law & Econ., Working Paper No. 124, 2008), *available at* http://lsr.nellco.org/nyu/lewp/papers/124.

[16] Geoffrey P. Miller, *Bargaining on the Red-eye: New Light on Contract Theory* (N.Y.U. Ctr. For Law & Econ., Working Paper No. 131, 2008), *available at* http://lsr.nellco.org/nyu/lewp/papers/131.

made by relatively unsophisticated parties. The case is partial in a second respect as well: Strict liability in contract exists largely in a narrow domain – the primary behavior of the promisor and promisee, respectively, in the performance of the contract and in reliance on that performance. Nevertheless, the theory and evidence supporting strict liability rules within those two domains is largely unchallenged.

Conclusion

The claim that strict liability in contract is a myth faces two formidable obstacles. First, the claim is descriptively inaccurate. At the core of contractual obligations, strict liability is alive and well. If one focuses on what courts actually do, there is substantial evidence that they decline opportunities to use the willful breach doctrine to deter inefficient promisor breaches, and, in addition, they decline opportunities to deploy the mitigation principle to deter inefficient overreliance by promisees. Second, the claim is normatively problematic. Notions of autonomy and efficiency both support the claim that, in assessing performance and the response to nonperformance, commercial parties will prefer strict liability rules to fault-based rules. While the evidence is incomplete, it is nevertheless significant that the available theory and evidence point in one direction – significant enough to shift the intellectual burden of proof.

THREE

The Fault Principle as the Chameleon of Contract Law: A Market Function Approach

Stefan Grundmann

This chapter begins with a comparative law survey showing that not all legal systems opt exclusively for fault liability or strict liability in contract law, but often adopt a more nuanced approach. This approach includes intermediate solutions such as reversing the burden of proof, using a market ("objective") standard of care, distinguishing between different types of contracts, and providing a "second chance" for breaching parties. Taking this starting point seriously and arguing that it is highly unlikely that all legal systems err, this chapter argues that the core question is how and when each liability regime should prevail or how and when the regimes should be combined. When asking how best to combine the regimes, the simple answer is that market expectation, and specifically the ability to compare offers, should be the core criterion.

Introduction

When Ernst Rabel came to the United States, some seventy-five years ago, he brought with him his conception of comparative law as a discovery device for all countries,[1] and sought to develop this international discussion into more concrete results, namely, into a unification of sales law as the core of contract law.[2] Moreover, when Rabel later wrote his treatise on (comparative) sales law[3] – which became highly influential for the Hague Uniform Sales Law of

For more extensive footnote documentation, see 107 Michigan Law Review 1583 (2009).

[1] *See* Ernst Rabel, *Aufgabe und Notwendigkeit der Rechtsvergleichung*, 13 Rheinische Zeitschrift für Zivil-und Prozessrecht 279, 283 (1924), *reprinted in* 3 Ernst Rabel, Gesammelte Aufsätze 1, 5 (1967).

[2] Rabel initiated his work on sales law unification in 1929 with his so-called "Blue Report." 3 Ernst Rabel, *Rapport sur le droit comparé en matière de vente, in* Gesammelte Aufsätze, *supra* note 1, at 381. He is considered to be the "mastermind behind the draft uniform international sales law." Bernhard Grossfeld & Peter Winship, *The Law Professor Refugee*, 18 Syracuse J. Int'l. L. & Com. 3, 11 (1992).

[3] Ernst Rabel, Das Recht des Warenkaufs (1958).

1964[4] and subsequently the Vienna Convention on the International Sale of Goods of 1980 (CISG)[5] – one of the central questions where his new surroundings heavily influenced him was fault. In fact, he strongly advocated a strict liability regime, a trademark of Anglo-American contract law, which was ultimately introduced into Article 79 of the CISG. And because of the eminence of the CISG, this regime has remained on the international agenda; it is evident in more general sets of contract law principles developed over the last decades at the Unidroit level[6] and in Europe.[7] The Principles of European Contract Law opt for a strict liability regime in which the only permissible excuse is *force majeure*,[8] and the breaching party bears the burden of proof.[9] The Unidroit Principles share, in essence, this singular focus on force majeure,[10] but they do so in a more refined manner: Article 5.1.4 distinguishes "obligations de resultat" (promises of result) from "obligations de moyen" (promises of best efforts). Such a distinction could, of course, be bargained for in a contract under any regime.[11]

The importance of another development for which Rabel strongly advocated, the introduction of the so-called German *Nachfrist* into the CISG regime, is less obvious. But in fact, this was no less influential on the current European regime than the incorporation of the strict liability approach. In principle, Nachfrist limits the most onerous sanctions for breach of contract to those cases where the party not only breached but also did not cure when given a "second chance" (after an additional period of time), both in the CISG and in the current European system.[12]

4 Ronald H. Graveson et al., The Uniform Laws on International Sales Act 1967 (1968); Berndt Godenhielm, *Some Views on the System of Remedies in the Uniform Law on International Sales*, 10 Scandinavian Stud. L. 9 (1966).

5 United Nations Convention on Contracts for the International Sale of Goods, Apr. 11, 1980, 1489 U.N.T.S. 3 [hereinafter CISG].

6 For the influence of the CISG, see Int'l Inst. for the Unification of Private Law [UNIDROIT], *Principles of International Commercial Contracts, passim* (2004), *available at* http://www.jus.uio.no/lm//unidroit.international.commercial.contracts.principles.2004/portrait.pdf [hereinafter Unidroit Principles].

7 For the influence of the CISG, see Principles of European Contract Law, Part I (Ole Lando & Hugh Beale, eds., 1995); Part II (Ole Lando et al., eds., 1999); Part III (Ole Lando et al., eds., 2003). While the Unidroit and the so-called Lando principles are not official and are not law, the role of the UN Convention as a model for future EC legislation is also accepted officially. Commission of the European Communities, *Communication from the Commission to the Council and the European Parliament on European Contract Law*, paras. 18–20, COM (2001) 398 final (July 11, 2001), *available at* ec.europa.eu/consumers/policy/developments/contract_law/cont_law_02_en.pdf.

8 Principles of European Contract Law, Part II, *supra* note 7, art. 8:101.

9 Principles of European Contract Law, Part I, *supra* note 7, art. 1:108.

10 Unidroit Principles, *supra* note 6, art. 7.1.7.

11 Some scholars interpret the Principles of European Contract Law to mirror this approach. *See* Ole Lando, *Non-Performance (Breach) of Contracts*, *in* Towards a European Civil Code 505, 509 (Arthur Hartkamp et al., eds., 3d ed. 2004).

12 CISG, *supra* note 5, art. 64(1)(b); Parliament and Council Directive 1999/44/EC, art. 3(5), 1999 O.J. (L 171) 12, 15 [hereinafter EU Sales Directive]. For an explanation of the "second chance" and

Several questions arise from this cross-Atlantic trip into history. The first is whether the example of Rabel and the contract law developments he spawned speak in favor of the superiority of a strict liability regime in contract law (explicitly leaving aside torts). The second question is whether the core argument advanced by Rabel, that only strict liability can mirror the promise initially given, is one that works particularly well in sales law (and in an industrial society), but less well in services (and in a service society). A third question is whether, instead of following Rabel's regime, all legal systems really follow a nuanced approach with a mixture of strict liability and fault liability elements, and use other governance devices such as the "second chance" principle. Finally, a fourth question is what guidelines can be given for satisfactorily combining the two liability regimes. This chapter suggests the answer to this final question is that market expectations should be the core criterion for combining strict and fault liability and that legal scholarship and legal regimes should therefore take a market function approach.

I. Nuance as the Common Denominator in a Comparative Law Perspective

The traditional view among contract scholars is that civil law systems opt for fault liability in contract law while common law systems opt for strict liability. Yet this impression is the result of too much abstraction on both sides. In fact, all systems opt for a nuanced combination of the two – for which only a few examples, and now systematic survey, can be given. Contract law development in Europe now often occurs at the European Community ("EC") level. EC contract law is an amalgam of the civil law and common law systems of its member states, and thus provides a valuable additional perspective.

A. *The Most Important Nuances in Civil Law Systems*

The nuanced approach is evident in several civil law systems. The core breach-of-contract rule in the German Civil Code (section 276), after the fundamental reform in 2002, reads as follows[13]:

> (1) The obligor is responsible for intention and negligence, if a higher or lower degree of liability is neither laid down nor to be inferred from the

its economic rationale, *see* Fernando Gomez, *Introduction*, *in* EU Sales Directive: Commentary 13, para. 108 (Massimo C. Bianca & Stefan Grundmann, eds., 2002); Stefan Grundmann, *Regulating Breach of Contract – The Right to Reject Performance by the Party in Breach*, 3 Eur. Rev. Cont. L. 121, 129–37 (2007).

[13] The German law (and more) can be found in English. *E.g.*, Cases, Materials and Text on Contract Law 659–63, 667–9 (Hugh Beale et al., eds., 2002); Basil S. Markesinis et al., The German Law

> other subject matter of the obligation, including but not limited to the giving of a guarantee or the assumption of a procurement risk.... (2) A person acts negligently if he fails to exercise reasonable care.[14]

The practical impact of this rule is heavily influenced by the second phrase of section 280(1), which says that, in contracts, the burden of proof for negligence is the reverse of the burden in tort law. Therefore, absent a provision to the contrary, the breaching party is responsible for any nonconformity with the contract unless he can prove that no negligence can be imputed to him.

The German law is interesting here in three respects. First, it is a law that has been reformed very recently and therefore reflects current policy, not outdated views. For instance, C.W. Canaris, the scholar who was most influential in the legislative process, has very strong feelings about the ethical superiority of the fault principle over strict liability.[15] Second, notwithstanding Canaris's apparent preference for fault liability, section 276 is very clear in that liability is neither based entirely on fault nor entirely on strict liability, but on a nuanced combination of both approaches. As section 276(1) states, German law tolerates both regimes more favorable to the breaching party – such as assigning responsibility only where there is gross negligence or even willful conduct, or alternatively simple negligence with the burden of proof on the nonbreaching party – and a regime more favorable to the nonbreaching party – namely strict liability, the so-called liability by warranty, or "*Garantiehaftung*." Rules that are more favorable to the breaching party are not commonly part of the German legal scheme (the Code itself), but rather appear in the terms of individual contracts. Conversely, rules favoring the nonbreaching party, namely, those introducing strict liability, can be found both in the Code – namely, in case law interpreting the Code – and, most important in the context of our discussion here, either implicitly or explicitly in an agreement between the parties.

Third, German law is in fact rather close to a strict liability regime even where it formally provides exclusively for fault liability. The reversal of the burden of proof, mentioned above, is one factor in this regard. A second

of Contract 444–51 (2d ed. 2006). *See also* Stefan Grundmann, *Commentary*, *in* 2 Münchener Kommentar zum Bürgerlichen Gesetzbuch (Wolfgang Krüger, ed., 5th ed. 2008) (providing a more extensive commentary on section 276).

14 Bürgerliches Gestzbuch [BGB] [Civil Code] § 276, 2002 Bundesgesetzblatt I 42, *translated at* Bundesministerium der Justiz: BGB – translation, http://www.gesetze-im-internet.de/englisch_bgb/german_civil_code.pdf (official translation of the German Ministry of Justice).

15 *See* the recent article on the article quoted by Claus-Wilhelm Canaris, *Die Einstandspflicht des Gattungsschuldners und die Übernahme eines Beschaffungsrisikos nach § 276 BGB*, *in* Norm und Wirkung: Festschrift für Wolfgang Wiegand 179 (Eugen Bucher et al., eds., 2005). For discussion of the argument of ethical superiority, *see infra* Part II.

factor is that, in fault liability, the standard of care applied is a market, or "objective," standard. Therefore, behavior is negligent if it does not meet the standards that the market would expect of good contract partners – and if the partners are professionals, of good professional partners in a particular business sector.[16] A third factor is that fault is irrelevant for the duty to perform in the first place as well as for the availability of rescission as a remedy.[17] This has repercussions for damages, because restitution awards that accompany rescission are often equivalent to damages for breach and because any noncompliance outside cases of force majeure gives rise to damages, at least when the breaching party is given a second chance after performance has fallen short of the terms of the contract and if the contract is about the supply of goods in mass transactions.[18]

Nonetheless, in one, perhaps two, highly important respects, the fault principle is still paramount in German law. The first concerns sales of prefabricated products in mass transactions. Under German law, as well as Italian law, the seller is not responsible for the fault of a third-party producer – although there is vicarious liability in principle.[19] Instead, the seller becomes responsible and owes damages only if – after having been informed by the third-party producer and given an opportunity to make alternative arrangements – he does not act. Moreover, this implies that the seller owes the purchaser damages only to the extent that the damages are due to the seller's negligence after breach by the third party. A second aspect is not strictly about fault but has a similar effect. Article 3, paragraph 5 of the EU Sales Directive,[20] which is pan-European, states that the nonbreaching party can rescind a contract only after having given the breaching party a second chance. Therefore, it is possible that the breaching party faces rescission only under conditions that are often even more protective than those associated with fault liability. This

[16] Karl Riesenhuber, *Damages for Non-Performance and the Fault Principle*, 4 Eur. Rev. Cont. L. 119, 130 (2008). There is abundant case law on the degree of education and specialization necessary for doctors and lawyers. *See* Grundmann, *supra* note 13, paras. 110–13, 125–37.

[17] BGB §323.

[18] In these cases, a guarantee to supply a good of the standard owed – at least on the second try – is implied in section 276. *See* BTDrucks 14/6040 at 132; Grundmann, *supra* note 13, paras. 177–80; Hansjörg Otto, *Die Grundstrukturen des neuen Leistungsstörungsrechts*, 24 Juristische Ausbildung [JURA] 1, 1–11 (2002); *supra* note 14. Reference can be made to a fourth, less well-known factor, a rule contained in §311a(2) German Civil Code, which brings German law close to a common law strict liability regime more generally: *see* Stefan Grundmann, *Der Schadensersatzanspruch aus Vertrag*, 204 Archiv für die civilistische Praxis 569, 580–2 (2004).

[19] *Helmut Heinrichs*, in Palandt, Bürgerliches Gesetzbuch, § 278(1) (Peter Bassenge et al., eds., 66th ed. 2007); Grundmann, *supra* note 20, at 580 (sharply criticizing this result). The rule is already different under French Law. *See* Cases, Materials and Text on Contract Law, *supra* note 13, at 663–5.

[20] *See supra* note 11.

regime also applies to damages that stem from the rejection of performance by the breaching party, for instance, the return of the good delivered. In fact, remedies that result from the rejection of performance in kind by the breaching party typically require willful omission on the side of the breaching party. Thus, considering fault or strict liability without the mechanism of a second chance may be questionable.

French civil law is very similar to German law (although perhaps less explicit) in the most important respects named above – namely, liability for fault serves as the underlying principle, but the breaching party is presumed to be negligent if the contracted-for result is not reached.[21] In French law, the market standard approach is less explicit than in German law, but as a practical matter, the situation is similar to that in Germany; therefore, the French objective standard also comes very close to a strict liability regime.[22]

French law is interesting – and even outstanding – in a different respect. In France, there is a longstanding tradition, developed by René Demogue early in the twentieth century, of distinguishing between "obligations de moyens" (promises of best efforts) and "obligations de résultat" (promises of result). The difference between article 1137 and article 1147 of the French Civil Code served as the basis for Demogue's distinction.[23] In the obligations de résultat, a specified result must be reached – for instance, construction must be finished – and there is an excuse only in case of force majeure, while in obligations de moyens, only best efforts are required – for instance, in cases where medical treatment is offered.

B. *Some Striking Nuances in Common Law Systems*

A wide swath of literature explains fault and strict liability in common law systems – although perhaps fewer devoted solely to British law – and this chapter will not attempt duplicate this effort at great length. Nonetheless, a few aspects of the common law norms – elements of fault within traditional strict liability systems – are important here.

First, in stark contrast to the civil law convention wherein liability is not accorded for the acts of third parties, the common law makes breaching parties

[21] The law (and more) can be found in English. *See* Cases, Materials and Text on Contract Law, *supra* note 13, at 663–5, 667–9; Anthony Ogus & Denis Tallon, *Remedies*, *in* Contract Law Today: Anglo-French Comparisons (Donald Harris & Denis Tallon, eds., 1989).

[22] *See* Philippe Malaurie et al., Les Obligations para. 945 (2d ed. 2005) (citing the exceptions in section 1927 Code Civil, which serve as basis for an e contrario argument in the other cases).

[23] *See, e.g.*, Muriel Fabre-Magnan, Les obligations 418, 439–48 (2004) (specifying that the burden of proving fault is on the nonbreaching party unless the case falls into an intermediate category called "obligation de moyens renforcée," in which case the burden of proof is reversed).

strictly liable for their own defects *and* for those caused by third parties.[24] The core argument for this regime is that without it, the splitting of performance between all contributing parties (e.g., producer and retailer) would lead to a situation without liability because the purchaser typically does not have a contractual relationship with the producer.[25]

The second point worth highlighting in this context is that some common law countries have a particular regime for particular service contracts that, in many cases, subjects particular service providers to liability only in cases of negligence or fault.[26] In these countries, the traditional strict liability regime of common law is superseded by statutory law for particular situations, namely, for service contracts such as those for medical treatment. This is similar to the already-mentioned and longstanding practice in France of distinguishing between obligations de moyens and obligations de résultat because, as with obligations de résultat, success is not guaranteed when particular service contracts are breached. French law is, however, still more to the point in that it names the core criterion directly: From a policy perspective, it is by no means correct to assume that we should allow for a fault exception for all supply-of-services contracts. To the contrary, it is necessary to ask separately for each type of (service) contract whether success has been promised, albeit implicitly, or not.

A third point worth highlighting is that the common law limits damages to those consequences that were foreseeable or, as English law puts it, were not too remote.[27] This is also the rule in the CISG.[28] One point on the melding of fault and strict liability is striking, although not often highlighted in English or American literature: Foreseeability (of a certain danger) is a classic criterion for fault in civil law, albeit in another context, in establishing whether precautions were necessary.[29] Thus, a fault element slips in; that is, the strict liability regime is not "pure" even in its core scope of application. The reasons for this will be taken up after strict liability is discussed from a policy point of view.

[24] Daniels v. White & Sons, Ltd., (1938) 4 All E.R. 258 (K.B.); *see also* Raineri v. Miles, [1981] A.C. 1050, 1086 (H.L.) ("[F]or damages for breach of contract, it is, in general, immaterial why the defendant failed to fulfil his obligation, and certainly no defence to plead that he had done his best.").

[25] *See, e.g.*, Guenter Treitel, The Law of Contract 839 (11th ed. 2003).

[26] *See* Supply of Goods and Services Act, 1982, c. 29, § 13 (Eng.); Wilson v. Best Travel Ltd., (1993) 1 All E.R. 353. More generally on fault in common law, *see* Barry Nicholas, *Fault and Breach of Contract, in* Good Faith and Fault in Contract Law 337 (Jack Beatson & Daniel Friedmann, eds., 1995); Guenter H. Treitel, *Fault in the Common Law of Contract, in* Liber Amicorum for The Rt. Hon. Lord Wilberforce 185 (Maarten Bos & Ian Brownlie, eds., 1987).

[27] *See., e.g.*, Hadley v. Baxendale (1854) 9 Exch. 341; Hugh Collins, The Law of Contract 410–13 (4th ed. 2003).

[28] CISG, *supra* note 5, art. 74(2) and standard commentaries cited there.

[29] For a collection of the extensive case law, *see* Grundmann, *supra* note 13, paras. 52, 70, 142, 148.

C. *Particular Refinement in European Investment Services Law*

The European Parliament's second (2004) directive on investment services law provides another approach to the combination of fault and strict liability.[30] Since the rules are so detailed on the European level, a fairly uniform standard remains even after transposition into different national laws.[31] One core issue motivating this directive was determining how investment service providers should best execute their clients' orders. Investment service providers typically have many alternative markets where they can execute a client's order; they can also bundle orders or execute them individually, and best execution is typically different for bonds, shares, and other securities. The EC legislature did not feel capable of prescribing specific guidelines as a result of the wide variety of cases. On the other hand, the legislature in the new regime did not want to use a general clause – like "best efforts" – either. Instead, the legislature opted for the following scheme: Each service provider has the discretion to shape its own procedure for handling clients' orders. This procedure, however, has to be made public, and the provider has to periodically assess its performance under the chosen procedure compared with other procedures and publish the results. There is no liability as long as the provider observed the procedure and it had no obvious flaws (which would be an extraordinary case, as one would not expect many clients to choose providers with highly flawed procedures). The EC legislature's approach to investment services is interesting in that it tries to tackle the problem of service contracts. In many service contracts, the result reached through performance of the contract does not indicate with sufficient certainty the quality of the provider's efforts toward execution. The EC directive nevertheless aims to make the quality of providers' efforts measurable. On the other hand, there is less need for liability as long as clients can diversify and the incentive for good performance of providers is particularly high. High incentives exist here: Providers' performance will become highly visible, and the future success of their business will therefore depend on these figures.

[30] Parliament and Council Directive 2004/39/EC, 2004 O.J. (L 145) 1.

[31] *See* Clifford Chance LLP, *EU Legal and Regulatory Developments: Safeguarding of client assets: CESR's technical advice in relation to Directive 2004/39/EC on Markets in Financial Instruments (MIFID)*, 11 Derivatives Use, Trading & Reg. 67 (2005); Guido Ferrarini, *Contract Standards and the Markets in Financial Instruments Directive (MiFID): An Assessment of the Lamfalussy Regulatory Architecture*, 1 Eur. Rev. Cont. L. 19 (2005); Angela Knight, *The Investment Services Directive – Routemap or obstacle course?*, 11 J. Fin. Reg. & Compliance 219, 221 (2003).

II. A Market Function Approach

A. *Ethics or Economics – The Wrong Question*

The majority of civil law scholars endorse the idea that the fault principle is ethically well founded, and some scholars clearly see it as ethically superior to strict liability.[32] The core argument is the following: A system that grounds damages in fault gives the breaching party more freedom, since he does not have to answer for developments that he could not control. In a Kantian tradition, it is seen as an act of freedom to choose between breach or conformity with a contract. Others, however, argue that a regime of strict liability may also foster some level of freedom by furthering the principle of *pacta sunt servanda*, that agreements must be kept[33] – a principle of equal importance with freedom of will. Therefore, balancing both principles seems necessary. In fact, this reasoning is used to explain why most systems include both fault and strict liability elements.[34]

While it is true that most systems follow a nuanced approach, the above explanation is misguided. First, freedom and pacta sunt servanda are not of equal importance, at least not in the context discussed here. There is actually a clear hierarchy between them, and pacta sunt servanda is clearly more important for the following reason. Those who advocate the ethical superiority of the fault principle because it gives the breaching party the freedom to answer only for those acts and events for which he is responsible forget one rather simple fact: There is an earlier type of freedom that allows each party to decide what offers he makes and to which standards he wants to bind himself, that is, the freedom of contract. In fact, fundamental concepts such as normative individualism or Böhm's concept of a private law society[35] are significant because they clarify one thing: The most vital tenet

[32] Karl Larenz, Lehrbuch des Schuldrechts: Erster Band, Allgemeiner Teil 286 (14th ed. 1987), at 276–9; Canaris, *supra* note 15, at 251; Erwin Deutsch, *Die Fahrlässigkeit im neuen Schuldrecht*, 202 Archiv für die civilistische Praxis 889, 892 (2002); Stephan Lorenz, *Schuldrechtsmodernisierung – Erfahrungen seit dem 1. Januar 2002*, *in* Karlsruher Forum 2005: Schuldrechtsmodernisierung – Erfahrungen seit dem 1. Januar 2002 59 (Egon Lorenz, ed., 2006).

[33] Riesenhuber, *supra* note 16, at 145.

[34] *See id.* at 148.

[35] Franz Böhm, Freiheit und Ordnung in der Marktwirtschaft 105–68 (1980); *see also* David J. Gerber, *Constitutionalizing the Economy: German Neo-liberalism, Competition Law and the "New" Europe*, 42 Am. J. Comp. L. 25 (1994) (describing and commenting on this concept in English); Stefan Grundmann, *The Concept of the Private Law Society: After 50 Years of European and European Business Law*, 16 Eur. Rev. Private L. 553 (2008); Manfred E. Streit & Werner Mussler, *The Economic Constitution of the European Community: From "Rome" to "Maastricht"*, 1 Eur. L. J. 5 (1995) (on the influence of Böhm's ordo-liberalism).

of freedom in modern times (and Böhm sees this time as starting with the French Revolution and the "private law society" it installed) is the right of each person to decide, to the greatest extent possible, which obligations to assume. This freedom – which comes first – is disregarded if the question of whether fault or strict liability should govern is decided, not on the basis of the parties' expressed or implicit intentions, but rather on the basis of an "ethical credo" about the superiority of fault or of strict liability. If the freedom of the parties is taken seriously, the question is how to interpret their intentions, not to impose on them a regime judged by scholars, legislatures, or any other third party to foster their freedom and therefore be ethically superior. Replacing the choice made by the parties – even if justified as fostering freedom – is paternalistic. Normative individualism, on which the economic analysis of contract law rests, has mainly ethical foundations, too, including the assumption that each individual is given the freedom of choice as far and as early as possible.

The core question is therefore which regime best fosters the intentions the parties had in mind when entering the contract. Does strict liability better mirror their expectations or does fault liability? Is the answer the same for all contracts? Does a requirement of foreseeability mirror parties' expectations? The next section uses party and market expectation as a guideline for answering these questions.

B. *Party and Market Expectation as Guidelines*

Liability in contract law is not really an issue when it comes to the recipient of goods or services. Payment is generally owed under a strict liability rule (some exceptions are discussed in the following section). Liability of the provider of goods or services, therefore, is the real issue. It is helpful to keep in mind that liability results in compensation. Damages account for what the recipient has bargained for but has not fully received. Thus, liability in all its forms helps to make the recipient whole if the performance he receives is not in conformity with the contract.

If liability requires more than mere nonconformity, however, the recipient's expectation of receiving the benefit of the contract for which he bargained is not fulfilled in those cases where the additional requirement – for instance, fault – is not satisfied. Therefore, liability based exclusively on nonconformity with the contract – that is, strict liability – has the advantage of making different offers easier to compare. All costs resulting from a certain behavior, for instance, the production of the good sold in conformity with the contract – and the production of the good sold in nonconformity – are calculated into the prices if liability is strict.[36] This is so because the buyer either receives the benefit of the contract for which he bargained or he receives full compensation without any additional requirement. The benefit bargained for will be received irrespective of whether performance is in conformity with the contract (or at least something close to the benefit when potential litigation costs are factored in).

It would seem to be a cornerstone in a model of competitive markets that clients be put in a situation where comparability is best guaranteed. But any requirement of fault reduces comparability: A party that bargains for a specific benefit receives the full benefit only where the other party fulfills his contractual obligations, but a fault regime obligates him to fulfill an additional requirement before receiving the full benefit where the other party breaches. Under strict liability (if one ignores litigation costs), nonconformity does not matter. The buyer who receives performance in conformity with the contract is just as well off as the one who does not receive performance in conformity with the contract. Thus, strict liability reduces the influence of nonconformity on whether the full benefit of the bargain is received, and it increases comparability because developments in the future that the buyer cannot foresee (namely, breach) become irrelevant for the (value of the) benefit he derives from the contract.

An additional advantage of strict liability is related to governance. In strict liability, the person who can best influence and assess the quality of the performance, that is, the provider of goods or services, carries all costs of conformity. Therefore, no external person – for instance, a judge applying the Hand formula – has to make this assessment.[37]

C. *Promise of Results or Promise of Best Efforts – The Core Criteria*

If strict liability better fosters freedom of contract, or freedom to bind oneself to a standard that the other party expects, and it also fosters comparability of offers, the core question is how to justify exceptions to strict liability. As a starting point, the distinction between contracts for results or best efforts, which is so fundamental in French law, would seem to be highly sensible. There are promises where no result has been promised or no such promise

[36] *See* Robert Cooter & Thomas Ulen, Law & Economics 208–12 (5th ed. 2008); Steven Shavell, *Strict Liability versus Negligence*, 9 J. Legal Stud. 1, 4–8 (1980).

[37] *See* Shavell, *supra* note 36. The same line of reasoning can be applied to the question whether there should be a *force majeure* excuse or not. *Compare* Fabre-Magnan, *supra* note 23, at 573–4 (civil law) on the one hand, *with* Treitel, *supra* note 25 (common law), at 838 on the other.

can be inferred from the parties' typical interests because in some cases too many other factors can obstruct a certain result. In other words, where an obligation is such that the result can be promised because it is within the party's control, strict liability is acceptable (and indeed fosters comparability and thus market and party expectations). But where this is not the case, strict liability is just not appropriate because parties would not expect a guarantee of result.

The first category, where strict liability is appropriate, includes virtually all sales of goods and some sales of services. For example, strict liability should typically apply to mass-production contracts. The German rule, which would hold that the seller is not accountable for the defects caused by the third-party producer, is clearly suboptimal in this context. This rule is not suboptimal (only) because of the shortcomings of the fault principle. In fact, it goes beyond fault and excludes liability if there clearly was fault on the side of the third-party producer. One way around this result would be to design vicarious liability differently, that is, to make the seller responsible at least for the fault of other members of the distribution chain (including the producer). But strict liability provides a much easier solution: The seller's liability would be beyond doubt (vicarious liability would not matter) and, as a result, the producer's recourse from the seller would also be known. The effect is that ultimately the person who caused the nonconformity is subject to liability and not exempt for reasons such as privity of contract. Uniform international law and its development confirm the correctness of applying strict liability to these contracts: Article 79 of the CISG, which covers sales, is the most prominent rule in which strict liability is carried through consistently.[38]

The second category – where strict liability is inappropriate – is composed of some, but by no means all, services. This is the really difficult category. The distinctive feature should not be the type of contract, but rather the question of whether reaching a certain result is within the party's control or, more precisely, within a typical party's control. In cases where the answer is negative, no promise of result can be inferred from the parties' typical interests. In these cases, a guarantee is the exception, rather than the default, and must be proved by the nonbreaching party. The parties could agree to a guarantee, but the law should not infer it from the typical interests of the parties in such a case. If, however, the result is within a typical party's control, a promise of result can be inferred from the parties' typical interests, because such a promise is reasonable and it fosters comparability and thus market and party

[38] On the strict liability concept and the exact shape of the exceptions in this case, *see, e.g.*, Hans Stoll & Georg Gruber, *Exemptions, in* Commentary on the CISG, *supra* note 5, art. 79, paras. 10–13, 30–2.

expectations. In a contract for services, therefore, one has to ask whether the result intended is within the control of the seller (or within the control of the network he gathers around him). This explains why, for instance, in the case of credit transfers strict liability should indeed be applied. Credit transfers constitute one of the few classes of cases on liability – fault or strict – that the EC has decided, and indeed the legislature decided in favor of strict liability.[39] The payment chain has control over whether the credit arrives at the beneficiary's account – within a fixed period of time and without getting lost in the chain. Because of all this, a guarantee can easily be given; and the EC directive interprets the parties' understanding as implying such a guarantee. It is worth noting that this is not even a very exceptional case in the area of services. Contracts that specifically provide for success or a particular result (so-called works' contracts in European terminology)[40] – and this is a large number of cases – fall into this category.

Deciding whether strict liability should apply based on whether the contract is within the party's control would seem to be convincing on the side of the recipient as well. The recipient typically just owes payment. While this duty is a strict one and the recipient cannot simply claim he was not at fault for a lack of money, many legal systems nevertheless accept excuses for late payment, such as illness.[41] This result is justified by the fact that comparability is not an issue. As recipients do not make offers on the market, there are few factors that suppliers of goods or services use to compare potential recipients. While solvency is certainly one, temporary illness is not. And while a suitable contingency for coping with such "unexpected" obstacles is a factor for which a "guarantee" is expected on the side of the supplier, it is probably not on the side of the purchaser (client). This is because illness is not seen as being within the purchaser's control, while the capacity to cope with illness *is* seen to be within the control of a supplier enterprise; that is, the supplier enterprise can more easily organize his affairs to deal with illness.

Similar criteria can be applied to long-term contracts in which a party can control whether he applies certain procedures, and otherwise refrains from acting in a grossly negligent way, but cannot control the outcome.[42]

[39] Parliament and Council Directive 2007/64/EC, 2007 O.J. (L 319) 1, 8. *See, e.g.*, Despina Mavromati, The Law of Payment Services in the EU (2008); Johannes Priesemann, *Proposal for a Directive on Payment Services in the Internal Market: Overview and initial comments*, 1 Euredia 15 (2006).

[40] In the German context, *see* BGB § 631 and standard commentaries on this section. In the French context, *see, e.g.*, Fabre-Magnan, *supra* note 23, at 418.

[41] For German Law, *see* Heinrichs, *supra* note 19, § 276, para. 28.

[42] At least if it is a long-term relational contract that takes up most or all of the breaching party's working power for a considerable time.

The business-judgment rule in corporate law[43] – which certainly is as well grounded in the policy aspect that risk taking by managers should be encouraged – may also be explained by this idea. In contracts, this idea has been developed only in the context of labor law, where it is obvious that employers should diversify or insure the risk of breach because employees cannot do so as easily in most cases. But it could readily be developed in other areas, and a market expectations approach would be helpful in a discussion of exactly how the duties should be shaped in these areas.

In summary, strict liability best fosters comparability as the core criterion for party expectations by determining the parties' will at the moment the contract is formed. Exceptions to the strict liability regime have to be justified by the fact that a contract involves a type of performance wherein the result is not within the (typical) party's control. If the contract is a long-term one, an additional allowance, embodied by a negligence standard, for instance, could be made for the likelihood that breach will occur at some point.

D. *Fault, Foreseeability, and Other "Softeners" of Strict Liability*

Fault is one alternative to strict liability. As discussed in the previous section, a fault regime can be justified when a result is not within the control of the breaching party (or his partners in the chain). This control-oriented divide works quite well where the intention of the parties is the criterion that decides the case. In some cases, however, we look beyond the intention of the parties and consider public policy motives. One such case is antidiscrimination rules.[44] There, public policy concerns justify a strict liability regime even where the party in violation cannot be seen as being in control of the result.

Another way to deviate from strict liability is with foreseeability. The rationale for a foreseeability requirement is that the purchaser (client) is in the best position to anticipate exceptional circumstances that may give rise to

[43] For a definition, *see* 1 Am. Law Inst., Principles of Corporate Governance § 4.01(c) (1994). The lead case in Delaware is *Aronson v. Lewis*, 473 A.2d 805 (Del. 1984). For a comparative and economic perspective, *see* Holger Fleischer, *Die "Business Judgment Rule" im Spiegel von Rechtsvergleichung und Rechtsökonomie*, *in* Festschrift für Herbert Wiedemann 827 (Rolf Wank et al., eds., 2002).

[44] The European Court of Justice also decided that the duty not to discriminate on the basis of gender was subject to strict liability. *E.g.*, Case C-177/88, *Dekker v. Stichting Vormingscentrum voor Jong Volwassenen (VJV-Centrum) Plus*, 1990 E.C.R. I-3941, 3975. It is not just cases involving willful and particularly offensive discrimination that are subjected to liability. Given that "indirect" discrimination can be quite tricky, the result reached by the ECJ is not easily explained by an argument that it is "in the hands" of the employer not to discriminate.

a loss.[45] Therefore, he should carry the risk of not being compensated when he does not disclose this risk during contract formation. Why this reasoning – itself a pocket of fault – should be restricted to strict liability regimes only, and not apply to fault regimes, is not evident at all. Thus, the German regime would need correction not only with respect to the principle (strict liability), but also with respect to the excuse. The question of foreseeability is, however, more complex than that. Because it is not always easy to prove damages, compensation for breach is typically suboptimal as a general rule. Therefore, it may well be that the risk of incurring liability that is not foreseeable to the breaching party reduces his inclination to breach the contract where performance avoids the problem of proof of damages. When assessing the well-foundedness of a foreseeability rule, the following alternative must therefore be kept in mind: The criterion may well place the onus of disclosing on the party who has better information, but it may also reduce the already suboptimal deterrence value of damage remedies.

Yet another way to deviate from strict liability is with the "second chance" principle. If a breaching party faces certain remedies only after having a chance to cure its nonconformity, then remedies are not immediately available in all cases of breach. Under European and German law, the second-chance principle applies not only to the nonbreaching party's restitutionary remedies, but also to his damages, insofar as the damages consist of the return of the defective performance and a claim for money to buy a substitute. The requirement of a "second chance" may deviate from strict liability even more than a mere fault requirement, because breaching parties may have a right to a second try even if they acted in a grossly negligent – not just a negligent – way. From a policy perspective, this deviation from strict liability can be justified by the fact that the second chance postpones more invasive remedies only if the chance is used promptly and without considerable hassle.[46] Thus, this justification for deviation does not reduce the amount of compensation, but affects only the form of compensation.

Conclusion

Fault *or* strict liability? This is too simplistic a question. Strict liability and some fault liability is more or less the reality in all countries – with larger exceptions in the area of services. Furthermore, if the aim of the fault requirement is to not excessively restrict the freedom of the breaching party, there

[45] *Cooter & Ulen*, *supra* note 36, at 274.

[46] For an extensive discussion, *see* Stefan Grundmann, *Regulating Breach of Contract – The Right to Reject Performance by the Party in Breach*, 3 Eur. Rev. Cont. L. 121, 129–37 (2007).

are other – probably more appropriate – governance devices in contract law to be taken into account. These include the "second chance" and the foreseeability principles. Thus, this chapter highlights two trends with respect to the fault principle. First is that both general approaches have nuances. Second is the use of functionally related instruments, which traditionally have not been seen in conjunction with the fault principle but have a similar effect.

PART II

THE CASE FOR FAULT

FOUR

How Fault Shapes Contract Law

George M. Cohen

This chapter describes three defects in the traditional strict liability paradigm of contract law to demonstrate how fault significantly shapes contract law. First, justifications for strict liability focus on implementing contractual intent when contract law's main focus is interpreting contractual intent. Fault helps interpret contractual intent. Second, the strict liability paradigm excessively emphasizes a single fault variable – the ability of the promisor to control his own performance – and downplays other relevant fault variables. In particular, the strict liability paradigm ignores the potential for opportunistic behavior by the promisee, which creates a "negligence-opportunism trade-off." A broader conception of fault emphasizes the potential for fault by both parties and the need to make relative fault assessments. Third, the strict liability paradigm overlooks doctrinal avenues in contact law that incorporate fault. One important example is the law of contract damages. Fault helps explain contract damages doctrine.

Law is an inherently normative enterprise, and so it is inevitably concerned with fault. Contract law is no exception. Yet the application of fault to contract law remains controversial. Theories and doctrines of contract law teach that contract law is and should be a regime of strict liability, rather than a fault-based regime. In my view, however, the theoretical and doctrinal justifications for strict liability in contract law are flawed, incomplete, and misleading. They unduly obscure the role of fault in contract law and hinder its effective use.

In this chapter, I describe three defects in the strict liability paradigm, and use these to demonstrate how fault significantly shapes our contract law.

This chapter draws heavily on George M. Cohen, *The Fault That Lies Within Our Contract Law*, 107 Mich. L. Rev. 1445 (2009), but incorporates my earlier work more than that essay.

First, the justifications for strict liability frame the issue as one of implementing contractual intent when the main problem of contract law is interpreting contractual intent. Fault helps us interpret contractual intent.[1] Second, the strict liability paradigm focuses too much on a single fault variable – the superior ability of the promisor (which I use as a shorthand for the breaching or nonperforming party) to control his own performance – and downplays other relevant fault variables. In particular, the strict liability paradigm ignores the potential for opportunistic behavior by the promisee, which creates what I call the "negligence-opportunism trade-off" in contract law.[2] A broader conception of fault recognizes and emphasizes the potential for fault by both parties as well as the need to make relative fault assessments. Third, the strict liability paradigm overlooks doctrinal avenues in contract law that incorporate or accommodate fault. I will discuss one important set of such doctrines: the law of contract damages. Fault helps explain contract damages doctrine and fill doctrinal gaps.[3]

I. Fault and Uncertain Contractual Intent

The essence of the strict liability conception of contract law is that the reason a contracting party fails to perform does not matter. According to traditional contract doctrine, when one party promises to perform some service for another party or supply some good to another party in exchange for a price, and subsequently fails to perform, that party has breached the contract. The promisor's fault or the lack of it is irrelevant.[4] The only fault that matters is the promisor's failure to perform. The primary justification for strict liability is that it best implements what many perceive to be the main goal of contract law, which is to facilitate voluntary transactions with minimal state interference. (For purposes of this chapter, I take this goal as given and leave third-party effects and interests for another day, though they are, in my view, more important than is usually supposed.) If one is committed to "freedom of contract" and sees "fault" as a social judgment independent of the parties'

[1] George M. Cohen, *Implied Terms and Interpretation in Contract Law*, in 3 Encyclopedia of Law and Economics 78 (Boudewijn Bouckaert & Gerrit De Geest, eds., 2000) [hereinafter Cohen, Interpretation].

[2] George M. Cohen, *The Negligence-Opportunism Tradeoff in Contract Law*, 20 Hofstra L. Rev. 941 (1992) [hereinafter Cohen, *Negligence-Opportunism Tradeoff*].

[3] George M. Cohen, *The Fault Lines in Contract Damages*, 80 Va. L. Rev. 1225 (1994) [hereinafter Cohen, Fault Lines]; George M. Cohen, *Finding Fault with Wonnell's "Two Contractual Wrongs,"* 38 San Diego L. Rev. 137 (2001) [hereinafter Cohen, Finding Fault].

[4] Restatement (Second) of Contracts § 235 cmt. b ("[A]nything short of full performance is a breach, even if the party who does not fully perform was not at fault. ...") (1981).

intentions, then naturally one sees fault as inconsistent with contract law. In this view, fault is a means to "regulate" contracting parties rather than to facilitate their transactions.

The problem with this justification is that it depends crucially on two assumptions: that the mutual intentions of contracting parties are known or easily determined, and that these mutual intentions do not themselves incorporate fault standards of performance. In many cases, however, these assumptions are contestable, if not false. Parties' expressions of intent, whether written, oral, or conduct-based, are often unclear, contradictory, and incomplete. Questions of interpretation inevitably arise. Contractual intent is particularly likely to be uncertain in situations in which the parties cannot resolve contractual disputes amicably but resort to the courts; in fact, uncertain intent is often the cause of such disputes. In litigated contract disputes, out of which the bulk of contract law comes, parties typically offer competing meanings of contractual intent. Contract law aims to guide courts in resolving these disputed interpretations; thus, the very existence of contract law belies the assumption of easily determined contractual intent. One might usefully view contract law as a set of presumptions for resolving contested contractual intent.

The determination of contractual intent is so contested that courts and contracting parties often try to constrain the interpretive methodology courts use in ascertaining intent. Notable examples of this technique are the parol evidence rule and its contractual counterpart, the merger clause, both of which try to limit the source of contractual meaning to a writing. The debate over textualist versus contextualist methods of interpretation also falls into this category. Constraining interpretive methodology is an example of a common technique in law: Resolve (sidestep) difficult substantive questions via procedure. The technique is never fully successful, however, and again contract law is no exception. Interpretive methodologies themselves raise further interpretive questions. Instead of focusing on what the parties want to have happen under the contract (substantive or primary intent), the question shifts to how the court should go about determining what that intent is (procedural or secondary intent). Moreover, the potential exists for conflict between primary and secondary intent, adding new interpretive complexity.[5]

If contractual intent is often contested and the need for interpretation is common, the case for strict liability weakens. Strict liability no longer follows naturally or logically as a consequence of honoring the parties' known intent.

[5] For example, the parties may prefer a textualist interpretive methodology, but may prefer more that the court get the substantive term right even if that goes against the textualist methodology. *See* Cohen, Interpretation, at 96–7.

Rather, proponents of strict liability must defend it as the best proxy for interpreting uncertain intent. It may well be that contracting parties in many cases intend that the reason for nonperformance does not matter. The parties may intend that the promisor provide a kind of insurance or warranty of performance. On the other hand, in many cases, the parties may also intend that a court take fault into account in the event of an unsettled dispute. They may intend, for example, that "best efforts" or "reasonable care" suffice. If the parties intend fault standards to apply, then fault implements contractual intent. If the parties' contractual intent is uncertain, fault can help interpret contractual intent. So long as fault represents a reasonable presumption of contractual intent, there is no inconsistency between the two.

II. An Expanded Law and Economics Approach to Fault

Law and economics theories of contract law try to answer the question of how to interpret uncertain contractual intent by hypothesizing "efficient" contract terms or rules, which potentially make both contracting parties better off (at least prospectively) by increasing the size of the contracting "pie." From a law and economics perspective, then, strict liability makes sense in the face of uncertain contractual intent to the extent that the promisor is most often in a better position than the promisee to take cost-effective measures to ensure or enhance the promisor's performance. If the promisor is generally the "superior risk bearer," most contracting parties would agree to strict liability, and so courts should deem them to have intended strict liability even if they do not expressly say so (which they often do not do). Strict liability thus incorporates a fault-based presumption: The promisor's nonperformance is presumptively his fault; therefore, it makes sense to impose liability on him.

The superior risk-bearer approach to contract law views contractual nonperformance as analogous to a tort accident.[6] Although the analogy may seem odd at first blush, since contractual nonperformance is usually an intentional act, the analogy makes sense if one moves back one step to the event that motivates nonperformance. After the parties enter into the contract, some "regret contingency" may occur (or some previously existing and unknown risk may surface), which raises the cost of performance to the performing party or reduces the benefit of performance to the paying party to the extent that the adversely affected party would prefer not to perform.[7] Viewing

[6] *See, e.g.*, Robert Cooter, *Unity in Tort, Contract, and Property: The Model of Precaution*, 73 Cal. L. Rev. 1 (1985).

[7] *See* Charles J. Goetz & Robert E. Scott, *The Mitigation Principle: Toward a General Theory of Contractual Obligation*, 69 Va. L. Rev. 967 (1983).

contractual nonperformance as resulting from an accident, the superior risk-bearer analysis naturally focuses on precaution taking, though it can encompass insurance and mitigation as well. Possible precautions include quality control, backup supplies, insurance, and the avoidance of promising in the first place.

The problem with the superior risk-bearer justification for strict liability is that it pushes the analogy between contract breaches and tort accidents too far, leading to an unduly cramped view of fault. Theorists agree that contract breaches differ from tort accidents (at least those involving strangers) because contract law must take account of the parties' mutual intent – the contract. Law and economics theorists typically do this by arguing that most contract law rules are default rules, which apply only in the absence of an agreement by the parties that displaces the rule. Although the original Coasian analysis concludes that the default specification of legal rules is irrelevant when contracting around legal rules is costless, if "transaction costs" impede such contracting around, the theory holds that courts should set defaults so as to minimize transaction costs. One way to minimize transaction costs is to pick default rules that a majority of contracting parties would want.[8] In this view, a contract is just another form of precaution. Since a promisor can often write a contract that protects him from liability in the event that various contingencies occur, using a force majeure clause, for example, the difference between contract and tort does not seem to affect the strict liability argument.

This view fails, however, to capture the key differences between contract breaches and tort accidents, differences that suggest a much larger role for promisee fault. First, promisees often have a greater ability to take cost-effective steps to mitigate losses caused by regret contingencies (both after and before their occurrence) than tort victims have to mitigate physical harm caused by accidents. Moreover, compared to promisors, promisees may be superior mitigators. Similarly, effective contractual performance often requires mutual cooperation rather than simply unilateral conduct; for example, investments by the promisee may affect the ability of the promisor to take precautions. Promisees may fail to engage in this cooperative conduct. The more that promisee fault matters, the weaker the case for strict liability becomes.

Second, the risk of opportunistic behavior looms much larger in contract breaches.[9] Opportunistic behavior occurs when one party in a contractual relationship takes, or fails to take, some action contrary to the other party's

[8] *See, e.g.*, Robert Cooter & Thomas Ulen, Law and Economics 200–02 (3d ed. 2000).

[9] *See, e.g.*, Richard A. Posner, Economic Analysis of Law 93–4 (7th ed. 2007); Timothy J. Muris, *Opportunistic Behavior and the Law of Contracts*, 65 Minn. L. Rev. 521 (1981).

reasonable expectations based on the parties' agreement, contractual norms, or conventional morality in a way that creates the possibility of loss to the other party.[10] In many cases, opportunistic behavior involves one party deliberately withholding information from or providing false information to the other party or the court. Contracts often depend on full and truthful disclosure of information, not simply an exchange of goods or services for money, and there is no general reason to presume that promisors have a greater ability or motivation than promisees to lie, distort, or obfuscate. Promisee dissembling, whether during negotiations or in contract performance, can adversely affect the promisor's ability to take precautions or perform. It can exaggerate or exacerbate a promisee's losses from nonperformance or minimize the risk or effect of a regret contingency. Moreover, a promisee who has in fact agreed to bear a certain risk may find it convenient to deny that agreement when the risk materializes, and may seek to shift responsibility for that risk to the promisor by pointing to some failure of performance or precaution taking by the promisor.

Law and economics theories of contract recognize the importance of opportunistic behavior in contracts but tend to minimize the importance of opportunistic behavior in contract doctrine. One way the theories do this is by limiting the concept of opportunistic behavior to cases in which one contracting party makes a relationship-specific investment, allowing the other party to threaten to deprive the investing party of his investment. For example, if one party contracts to build a house for the other, and construction precedes payment, then the buyer can force the builder to renegotiate the contract by threatening to withhold payment even though no other circumstances change. A party's vulnerability created by specific investments is certainly an important condition that facilitates opportunistic behavior, but opportunism can occur even in the absence of specific investments.

All that opportunism requires is some change in position ("reliance") growing out of the contractual relationship that exposes one party to loss that the other party can intentionally impose. This vulnerability can arise in a number of ways. If performance is sequential, one party may provide a benefit to the other party who then tries to keep that benefit without performing his reciprocal obligations. Or one party may forgo other contracting opportunities, which then become unavailable when market conditions change. Or one party may provide information to the other party, who then uses the information to the first party's disadvantage. Or one party may act negligently and the other party knowingly tries to exploit rather than correct the problem.

[10] Cohen, Negligence-Opportunism Tradeoff, at 960–1.

Finally, contract terms and contract law doctrines often create the potential for opportunistic exploitation by a party seeking to apply those rules to unintended situations.

Another way law and economics theories minimize the importance of opportunistic behavior in contract doctrine is to assert that the parties can handle most opportunistic behavior without court intervention, by choosing contractual partners wisely or drafting contract well. Unfortunately, contracting parties cannot solve all problems of opportunism on their own; thus, legal rules matter. Not only do contracting parties regularly fail to foresee opportunistic behavior, even when they foresee it, they simply cannot write "self-enforcing" contracts that protect against all forms of opportunistic behavior. Reputation can be a powerful deterrent to opportunism but it is often ineffective; for example, it is often difficult to know whether a potential contracting party has behaved opportunistically in the past.

Like mitigation, opportunistic behavior is crucial to the strict liability versus fault debate because the promisee may be the more likely opportunist. In general, the fact that promisees are just as likely to behave opportunistically as promisors significantly undercuts the law and economics argument for strict liability.

What if both the promisor and promisee are at fault? In particular, if one party is better able to take precautions against regret contingencies, but the other party is the more likely opportunist, who should prevail? I call this problem the "negligence-opportunism trade-off," because the court in this situation must choose between placing priority on deterring negligence or on deterring opportunism.[11] In my view, deterring opportunistic behavior must take presumptive priority over deterring negligent behavior in contract law, as it does elsewhere in law. Opportunistic behavior entails higher social costs than negligent behavior, and the social costs of avoiding it are lower. Opportunism often entails investments that are socially wasteful, whereas negligent behavior is often an unintended byproduct of useful conduct. Furthermore, opportunistic behavior imposes higher third-party costs by impairing the level of social trust necessary for efficient contracting to occur.

The main objection to giving priority in contract doctrine to deterring opportunism is that it is too difficult for courts to detect opportunism. There are a number of responses to this objection. First, the difficulty of detecting opportunism is just a variation of the idea that contractual intent is uncertain. There is no reason for courts to presume that the parties intend courts to

[11] See Cohen, *Negligence-Opportunism Tradeoff*, at 983–90, for a more detailed discussion.

resolve uncertain intent by considering only the evidence of that intent that is easiest to determine. Second, identifying the superior risk bearer may also be difficult in certain cases. So long as courts are at least equally confident in the "most likely opportunist" judgment as they are in the superior risk-bearer judgment, deterring opportunism should take priority. Third, in many cases, courts can just as easily gather information relevant to determining opportunism – such as the parties' purposes in contracting, the commercial context of the deal, and the reasons for nonperformance – as they can collect information relevant to the superior risk-bearer determination – such as precaution costs, expected losses, and insurance capabilities. Courts can also develop rebuttable presumptions of opportunistic behavior by identifying situations in which opportunistic behavior is more likely to occur. These situations include those in which one or more of the following is present: The market price has moved against a contracting party who now seeks to escape the contract based on some contractual formality; one party has incurred significant sunk investments and the other appears to be trying to rewrite the deal; reputational effects are likely to be weak; the market for substitutes is "thin" rather than "thick"; or self-help protection is costly.

Perhaps the best example of the negligence-opportunism trade-off in contract law is the much-discussed case of *Jacob & Youngs v. Kent*.[12] An owner who contracted to have a residence built withheld the final payment upon discovering that the builder had not used the Reading brand of pipe required by the contract but instead had used other wrought-iron pipe made by other manufacturers. The owner demanded that the non-Reading pipe be replaced even though much of the pipe was already encased within the walls of the house. Judge Cardozo and the New York Court of Appeals held that the owner had to make the final payment. Cardozo's reasoning, albeit using different terminology, was essentially that the builder's breach was merely negligent ("the result of oversight and inattention of the [builder's] subcontractor"[13]), whereas the homeowner was likely acting opportunistically in insisting on the strict letter of the contract.

Cardozo devotes most of the opinion to identifying facts that would support a presumption of owner opportunism. The installed pipe was "the same in quality, in appearance, in market value, and in cost as the brand stated in the contract."[14] There was no evidence of any idiosyncratic preference for Reading pipe and most people would view pipe as serving functional rather

[12] 129 N.E. 889 (N.Y. 1921). I discuss my view of the case in more detail in Cohen, *Negligence-Opportunism Tradeoff*, at 990–1000.

[13] 129 N.E. at 890.

[14] *Id.*

than esthetic purposes. The contractor was in a vulnerable position, having incurred substantial sunk costs. Even though the contractor had protected itself to some degree against owner opportunism by insisting on progress payments, the amount owing was still a significant sum. The costs of "mitigating" the breach and replacing the pipe were high because the defective pipe was encased rather than "in shape to be returned." One could add to Cardozo's list the fact that owner was a one-shot contractor who might not be concerned about any reputation for opportunistic behavior among other builders, and so might be insufficiently deterred from "holding up" the builder for more money in the absence of court action.

My point is that contract disputes often present questions not only about which party is the best precaution taker, but also about which party is the best mitigator and the most likely opportunist. The case for strict liability is strongest when the promisor is all three. In my view, however, the likelihood that the promisee is more at fault on one or more of these criteria is high enough in litigated cases that courts should not presume that strict liability generally best represents contractual intent.

III. A Fault-Based Approach to Contract Damages

Having addressed the main arguments for strict liability in contract law, based on mutual intent and economic theory, I turn finally to the question of the role of fault in contract doctrine. In my view, the language and architecture of contract doctrine strongly reflect the pervasive influence of fault, though not always in obvious ways. In this final section, I focus on a particular area of contract doctrine – contract damages – to show how a seemingly strict liability doctrine in fact leaves ample room for fault considerations.

The law of contract damages purports to follow the strict liability paradigm because it claims to focus on the goal of "compensation" for the promisee's loss. If compensation is the goal, then the reason for the breach must be irrelevant. Contract law then claims expectation damages as the primary compensatory damage measure. The problem is that the apparent dominance of expectation damages as "the" unifying compensatory damages measure is an illusion. Contract law recognizes other compensatory interests, namely, reliance and restitution. Moreover, contract law recognizes a number of "limitations" on expectation damages, including mitigation, foreseeability, and certainty. Courts even have two different ways of measuring expectation damages: cost of completion and diminution in value. What explains the dizzying array of contract damage measures?

In my view, the law of contract damages as courts actually apply it is best understood as a fault-based system.[15] Courts apply different damage measures depending on the reason the contract fails and the relative fault of the parties. By adjusting the level of damages awarded, courts try to give optimal incentives to both parties. In general, higher damage measures, such as expectation damages and the disgorgement version of restitution, reflect a greater concern with promisor fault. Lower damages measures, such as reliance damages and the reimbursement version of restitution, reflect a greater concern with promisee fault. Contract damages are often undercompensatory relative to the expectation interest because they are as much about deterrence and incentives as about compensation.

More specifically, courts tend to use expectation damages when they believe that the promisor has acted opportunistically, the promisor is the superior mitigator, or the contract otherwise should be performed because it remains jointly profitable. The primary purpose of expectation damages is to deter opportunistic breaches. Expectation damages generally deter opportunistic breaches by depriving the promisor of gain that he has illegitimately expropriated in violation of the parties' intentions or some broader social norm. This justification for expectation damages is broader than the traditional economic justification for expectation damages, based on the theory of efficient breach, which holds that expectation damages optimally deter inefficient breaches. Inefficient breaches are generally considered breaches involving situations in which circumstances unexpectedly change after the formation of the contract, making the contract sufficiently more costly or less desirable to the promisor that it is no longer profitable for him, although the contract remains jointly profitable. Opportunistic breaches, by contrast, include cases in which no such change occurs. The stated primacy of the expectation damage remedy, of course, makes these extreme cases of opportunism relatively rare; if reliance damages were the predominant contract damage remedy, however, these cases would be more common.

To make this point more concrete, consider four paradigmatic cases of pure opportunistic breach.[16] In the first case, the half-completed exchange, one party provides a service to another for an agreed price, but the other party then simply refuses to pay. If the service provider (the promisee) were limited to reliance damages, and these damages are less than the contract

[15] For a more detailed discussion of the points in the next two paragraphs, *see* Cohen, *Negligence-Opportunism Tradeoff*, at 1245–316.

[16] I discuss these cases in more detail in Cohen, *Finding Fault*, at 140–54. The examples themselves come from Christopher T. Wonnell, *Expectation, Reliance, and the Two Contractual Wrongs*, 38 San Diego L. Rev. 53 (2001).

price, the paying party (promisor) would always have an incentive to breach because he would, in effect, get the service for less than the contract price. In the second case, one party makes a relationship-specific investment and the other tries to exploit that vulnerability to extort a modification of contract terms. If the extortionist promisor expects that some percentage of vulnerable promisees will agree to the modification and not have the resources to sue later, the promisor will not be deterred from repeatedly attempting extortion if the promisees who do sue are limited to recovering reliance damages. Expectation damages are more likely to deter the repeated extortion attempts. In the third case, an insurer refuses to pay out on insurance after the insured contingency occurs. Reliance damages in this case, if they are defined as simply a refund of the premium, could lead to the collapse of the insurance market, because no insurers would have an incentive to pay out. They would simply keep the premiums of all who suffered no loss and refund the premiums for promisees who suffered losses. The same argument would apply to other contracts with a risk allocation component, such as those with warranty provisions. In the final case, a party with valuable private information contracts with another party. When the less-informed party discovers the information, that party may breach the contract but try to exploit the information in other transactions. Again, if the better-informed promisee is limited to recovering reliance damages, the promisor will not be deterred from the opportunistic expropriation. By contrast, to the extent it captures the value of the promisee's information to the promisee, the expectation damage measure will deter such opportunistic breaches.

The idea that the main purpose of expectation damages is to deprive a promisor of illegitimate gain will strike some as more like the restitutionary goal of avoiding unjust enrichment than the goal of compensation. That depends on how restitution is defined. Sometimes, the restitution remedy is conceived of as a kind of reimbursement. In a half-completed exchange involving goods, rather than services, this version of restitution would simply involve returning the goods, or the money paid. The reimbursement restitution remedy is not sufficient to deter opportunistic breaches. In other cases, however, restitution is conceived of as a disgorgement remedy. That is analogous to the function I see expectation damages as playing. In fact, in some cases, courts will use the disgorgement version of restitution instead of expectation damages where they believe that expectation will not sufficiently deter opportunistic breach.

Courts tend to use reliance damages when breach is nonopportunistic; that is, the promisor breaches not to expropriate some illegitimate gain, but to avoid an unanticipated loss. There are two main examples of nonopportunistic breach, which differ mainly in whether the contract was a bad deal from the outset or became a bad deal only after it was made.[17] In the first case, the contract itself is an "accident" or a "mistake," a contract that should not have been made because it never was jointly profitable, or simply would not have been made if both parties had known all the relevant facts existing at the time. Accidental contracts are distinguishable from contracts in which one party fraudulently induces the other party to enter into the contract by withholding information or providing false information; those contracts that should not have been made are opportunistic breach cases. In the second case, an unanticipated contingency (as opposed to an opportunistically manipulated or exaggerated one) renders the contract not jointly profitable and therefore one that should not be performed. In the absence of promisor opportunism, the failed contract in both cases becomes more like a tort accident; reliance damages are then appropriate, because they aim not at encouraging performance, but rather at encouraging efficient precaution taking to avoid reliance losses. Expectation damages applied in cases of nonopportunistic breach would overdeter promisors; promisors would take too many precautions, including not promising. The real difficulty in these cases is deciding whether opportunism is truly absent, that is, whether the contract really was an unintentional mistake or the regret contingency really was unanticipated. This problem is just another variation of uncertain contractual intent.

Finally, courts use various doctrines that limit damage recoveries, such as foreseeability, mitigation, and certainty, to give promisees incentives to take precautions and mitigate and to deter promisee opportunism. Reliance damages generally have the same effect. In fact, the limitations on expectation damages often leave the promisee with reliance damages or something close to it. To the extent that the reliance damage measure may itself lead promisees to make excessive reliance investments, take insufficient precautions, or engage in opportunism, courts can apply the damage limitations to a reliance damage recovery, or alternatively use the lower reimbursement version of restitution, to restrict the promisee's recovery.

A fault-based theory of contract damages explains the variety of damage doctrines courts actually use in a unified way that does not depend on ad hoc principles or a resort to measurement difficulties. The theory also explains the predominance of the expectation damage measure. Many litigated cases involve opportunistic behavior by promisors or situations in which the contract remains jointly profitable and the promisor is the superior mitigator. Yet courts and scholars continue to resist the "intrusion" of fault in contract

[17] *See* Cohen, *Finding Fault*, at 154–63.

damages. In the remainder of this section, I consider three important ways that economically oriented scholars have manifested this resistance to a fault-based theory of damages, which is comfortably grounded in economic theory. These paths of resistance are the theory of efficient breach, the critique of the penalty clause doctrine, and the importance of market damages.

Economic theorists have used the theory of efficient breach to justify and explain the privileged position of expectation damages. The theory says that only expectation damages optimally deter inefficient breaches and encourage efficient breaches. To the extent these are important goals of contract law, expectation damages should thus be the dominant damage measure. The problem I have always had with the efficient breach theory is that it takes a reasonable economic concept – efficient nonperformance – and combines it with a controversial commitment to limited court involvement in contract damage determination, that is, strict liability. The theoretical attraction of the efficient breach theory is that a uniformly applied expectation damage measure avoids costly court determinations of the reason for a particular breach – that is, fault. All a court has to do in a contract dispute is decide whether a contract has been made, whether a breach has occurred, and what the expectation damages are.

In reality, however, the net benefits of this "pricing mechanism" are, at best, far from clear and, at worst, illusory.[18] The theory assumes that it is generally easier for courts to measure the expectation interest accurately than it is to determine accurately whether a particular breach is efficient. That may not be the case. Some argue that courts can save on the costs of gathering information about fault under a strict liability regime. But contract law has many doctrines that allow introduction of evidence that would be useful for making a fault determination: excuse, promissory estoppel, and good faith, as well as the damage rules already discussed, to name a few. If one of these doctrines is potentially applicable in a particular case, contract law does very little to cut off information relevant to distinguishing among breach types when the parties think it is worth the effort to produce such information. Moreover, a strictly applied expectation damage rule would insufficiently deter some promisor and promisee opportunism as well as insufficiently encourage promisee precaution taking and mitigation. Unsurprisingly, then, contract law has never implemented anything close to the regime the efficient breach theory contemplates. If anything, the law of contract damages is closer to the idea that courts tend to award expectation damages for inefficient breaches and reliance damages for efficient breaches.

[18] *See* Cohen, *Finding Fault*, at 159–63.

Although the efficient breach theory of expectation damages does not describe the contract damage regime we have, it at least has a patina of plausibility to the extent that expectation damages are the predominant remedy. The continuing objection of law and economics scholars to the rule against enforcing penalty clauses[19] more directly challenges existing law. The critique, however, is similarly grounded in the strict liability paradigm and the argument that strict liability best comports with contractual intent. In many contracts, parties do not express their views on damages or other remedies. A seldom acknowledged corollary to this observation is that no court, to my knowledge, has ever held a contract unenforceable on the grounds of uncertainty for lack of a remedy term. In these cases, the contracting parties must expect courts to set reasonable damage default rules, and as I have already discussed, there is reason to think parties expect courts to use fault concepts to determine the appropriate measure of damages, as well as to interpret contracts generally.

But if the parties contract for a liquidated damage clause, then why does the law not always enforce these clauses? One concern is that parties may not have intended the clause to act as a penalty at all; the fact that it has become a penalty may be an "accident." In addition, the parties may not have intended that a promisee be able to use a penalty clause opportunistically by looking for ways to assert breach, no matter how trivial.[20] (A similar concern helps explain contract law's avoidance of punitive damages, as well as the concern that such damages would too greatly deter promise making.) To critics of the penalty doctrine, however, the doctrine appears anomalous because it seems to single out a particular kind of contract term for special scrutiny and possible nonenforcement. From the perspective of a fault theory of contract, by contrast, strict enforcement of liquidated damage clauses would be the anomaly. Strict enforcement of liquidated damage clauses is a form of strict liability. If strict liability does not make sense generally in contract law, why should we impose it on this one term? Put another way, by not strictly enforcing liquidated damage clauses when they act as penalties, courts treat those clauses the same way that they treat other contract clauses, which are also not strictly enforced regardless of the circumstances and the fault of the parties.

The one pocket of contract damage doctrine where strict liability makes sense is market damages, which are based on the difference between the contract price and the market price of a substitute performance at the time of

[19] *See, e.g.*, Posner, Economic Analysis of Law, at 127–30.

[20] *See* Kenneth W. Clarkson, Roger LeRoy Miller, & Timothy J. Muris, *Liquidated Damages v. Penalties: Sense or Nonsense?*, 1978 Wis. L. Rev. 351, 368–72.

breach.[21] It is therefore no surprise that one of the most famous statements of the strict liability view that the reason for breach of contract does not matter in determining damages, by Justice Holmes in *Globe Refining Co. v. Landa Cotton Oil Co.*,[22] comes in a case involving market damages. The market damage measure incorporates two fault-based presumptions. The first is that when a promisor breaches after the market price changes to his disadvantage (a price increase for a seller, a price decrease for a buyer), that breach is presumed to be for the opportunistic purpose of taking advantage of the new market price. In response to that presumption, the market damage rule disgorges any profit that the promisor would earn from making a new contract with a different party at the new market price. In this sense, the market damage rule is a restitution rule, and serves to deter opportunistic breach. At the same time, the market damage rule presumes promisees can easily mitigate, by procuring a substitute contract, and encourages them to do so when such mitigation is efficient.

If these presumptions hold, then the market damages rule obviates the need for a court to make any fault determinations. It need not inquire into the promisor's motives for breach or the reasonableness of the promisee's mitigation efforts or lack thereof. The problem is that the presumptions may not hold. Promisees may not be able to mitigate, or promisors may be able to do so more easily. Moreover, if other economic variables change simultaneously with a change in the market price, such as an increase in the seller's costs or a decrease in the buyer's valuation, the breach may not be opportunistic, and the market damage measure may not create optimal incentives. In these cases, a role for fault resurfaces and courts, at least implicitly recognizing this fact, tend to create exceptions to the market damages rule. Thus, the market damages rule does not justify a strict liability approach to contract damages. Rather, it is part of the menu of contract damage rules from which courts choose depending on the circumstances, and including fault considerations.

Conclusion

I do not deny that strict liability captures an important part of contract law. Strict liability reflects contract law's commitment to deterring promisor fault, and promisor opportunism in particular. Presuming promisor fault makes sense in a number of contexts, especially those in which promisors can easily

[21] *See* Cohen, *Fault Lines*, at 1316–48.

[22] 190 U.S. 540, 544 ("If a contract is broken the measure of damages generally is the same, whatever the cause of the breach."), 547 ("The motive for the breach commonly is immaterial in an action on the contract.") (1903).

procure substitute performance, such as sales of goods. But contracts and contract law encompass a much broader range of economic activity in which the presumption of promisor fault is less defensible or outweighed by other concerns, including promisee opportunism. In these cases, especially cases in which contractual intent is uncertain, economic theory supports a significant role for fault. Courts, whether guided by such theory or by a more intuitive sense of justice, on the whole share (or act as if they share) this view, which has, as a result, become embedded in contract doctrines like those concerning damages. Rather than continue to reach for some theoretically pure, yet impractical, unattainable, inefficient, and undesirable paradigm of strict liability, we should learn to live with, and improve, the contract law we have, with all its fault.

FIVE

Fault in Contract Law

Eric A. Posner

A promisor is strictly liable for breaching a contract, according to the standard account. However, a negligence-based system of contract law can be given an economic interpretation. This chapter shows that such a system is, in some respects, more attractive than the strict liability system. This may explain why negligence ideas continue to play a role in contract decisions, as a brief discussion of cases shows.

Introduction

Anglo-American contract law is said to be a strict liability system, but it could just as well be a fault-based system. Indeed, one can make a plausible case that a fault-based contract law would be superior to the strict liability system. A fault-based system would result in courts enforcing optimal contracts more systematically than they do currently – if courts could implement the system with sufficient accuracy. The disadvantage of such a system is that courts would need to make difficult inquiries and could make more errors. How the advantages and disadvantages balance out is hard to determine.

As many authors have noticed, although Anglo-American contract law is usually called a strict liability system, it does contain pockets of fault. Faultlike notions, such as good faith and best efforts, recur in the cases; and terms are often implied in order to ensure that obligations are reasonable rather than absolute. These doctrines reflect some of the advantages of the fault-based system, and strengthen the theoretical basis for the claim that fault ought to play a role in contract law.[1]

Thanks to Oren Bar-Gill, Omri Ben-Shahar, Richard Craswell, Daryl Levinson, Ariel Porat, Giesela Ruhl, Eyal Zamir, participants in a seminar at the European University Institute, and participants at the Conference on Fault in Contract Law, for their helpful comments.

[1] Cohen's article is the most comprehensive discussion; however, he focuses on damages rules, which I will for the most part ignore. George M. Cohen, *The Fault Lines in Contract Damages*, 80 Va. L. Rev. 1225, 1237–9 (1994).

This chapter is divided into two parts. Part I lays out the case for a fault-based contract law. Part II shows ways in which this idea is reflected in doctrine – not in all doctrine, but in some cases and rules. In both parts, I limit my discussion to fault in the performance or breach decision: The question is whether the promisor's breach may be excused because the breach was not his fault, or was not negligent. For the most part, I ignore negligent representation and other doctrines related to the decision to enter a contract in the first place.[2] I also use a very simple model; a more complex model could well lead to different results.

I conclude that the case for strict liability for breach of contract is not particularly strong, and so we should not be surprised that so many pockets of fault-based liability exist in contract law.

I. Theory

A. *A Model*

Consider a contract where Buyer values a good at V, Seller's cost in producing the good is c_H, with probability q ("bad state of the world"), and c_L, with probability $(1 - q)$ ("good state of the world"), where $c_H > V > c_L$. Buyer pays in advance a price, p, such that p just covers Seller's expected costs. Prior to performance, Seller can incur some cost x; if Seller incurs this cost, q drops to 0; in other words, Seller can ensure that performance will be at the low cost. The contract is made at time 0; Buyer pays at time 1; Seller invests x or not at time 2; Seller's cost of performance (c) is determined at time 3; and Seller performs or breaches at time 4. Damages (d), if any, are paid at time 5. Renegotiation is assumed to be impossible.

The conventional analysis of this setup in the literature is as follows.[3] Performance is desirable if and only if the cost is low (the good state of the world), because $V > c_L$ and $V < c_H$. The investment x is desirable if and only if x is less than the cost savings from reducing the probability of c_H from q to 0.

[2] On this, *see id.* at 1245–56.

[3] I use a simplified version of the model that has been developed in the literature. *See* Lucian Arye Bebchuk & I.P.L. Png, *Damage Measures for Inadvertent Breach of Contract*, 19 Int'l Rev. L. & Econ. 319 (1999); Robert Cooter, *Unity in Tort, Contract, and Property: The Model of Precaution*, 73 Cal. L. Rev. 1 (1985); Richard Craswell, *Performance, Reliance, and One-sided Information*, 18 J. Legal Stud. 365 (1989); Richard Craswell, *Precontractual Investigation as an Optimal Precaution Problem*, 17 J. Legal Stud. 401 (1988); Lewis A. Kornhauser, *Reliance, Reputation and Breach of Contract*, 26 J.L. & Econ. 691 (1983). These articles focus on the extent to which different damage measures provide the promisor with proper incentives to take precautions. With a few exceptions to be noted, they do not discuss whether a fault-based liability rule should be used.

Those cost savings equal the social benefit of the transaction being consummated (generating $V - c_L$), where otherwise it would not go through (with probability q). Thus, efficient investment requires that $x < q(V - c_L)$.

Optimal incentives can be easily provided in this setup. To ensure efficient performance or breach, let Seller pay damages if she does not perform, and set those damages equal to V ($d = V$). This remedy also ensures efficient investment. Because Seller pays Buyer's lost valuation if Seller does not perform, Seller fully internalizes the cost of breach. Here, Seller will invest x as long as $x < q(V - c_L)$, as this reduces expected costs from $qV + (1 - q)c_L$ to c_L. And if Seller does not invest x because x is high, Seller will perform in the good state of the world and not perform (instead paying damages) in the bad state of the world.

B. *Fault*

As has frequently been noted, this analysis does not depend on any notion of fault. Seller is strictly liable for breach of contract.

However, we can imagine a fault-based approach that yields the same behavior. Suppose that Seller is liable for breach of contract only if her breach was the result of fault or willful action. Let us use the following definitions:

Seller's breach is *willful* if the cost of performance is less than Buyer's valuation ($c = c_L$); efficient breach is not willful.

Seller's breach is *negligent* if the cost of performance is higher than Buyer's valuation (i.e., $c = c_H$), and Seller could have taken a cost-justified action to prevent this from happening (i.e., $x < q(V - c_L)$) but did not. In other words, breach, whether or not efficient, after failure to engage in efficient investment is negligent.

Seller's breach is *inadvertent* (not her fault, and not giving rise to liability), if the cost of performance is higher than Buyer's valuation (i.e., $c = c_H$), and Seller could not have taken a cost-justified action to prevent this from happening (i.e., $x > q(V - c_L)$). Efficient breach after efficient investment is not negligent.

Seller pays damages only if the breach was willful or negligent. In either case, let damages equal d.

It can be shown that this fault system produces efficient performance at time 4 and efficient investment at time 2. Efficiency requires that performance occur if and only if $V > c$, that is, where $c = c_L$. Suppose that Seller engaged in efficient investment at time 2. Her cost is then c_L, and at time 4 she will perform if $d > c_L$.

Now consider whether Seller will engage in efficient investment at time 2. If Seller does, she incurs cost x; and she will perform if $d > c_L$ (see above), resulting in cost, c_L. Thus, the cost of investment is $x + c_L$. If Seller does not engage in investment, she does not incur cost x. In the good state of the world ($c = c_L$), she will perform, at cost c_L, because $c_L < d$. In the bad state of the world ($c = c_H$), she will breach and pay d. Thus, her cost of not investing is $qd + (1 - q)c_L$. She will invest only if it is cheaper than not investing, that is, where $x + c_L < qd + (1 - q)c_L$, or $x < q(d - c_L)$, which is also the condition for efficient investment if $d \geq v$.[4]

C. A Comparison: Strict Liability Versus Negligence

Although the strict liability system and the fault system lead to the same outcome – efficient breach and efficient performance – they have several important differences.

First, the fault system requires the court to make the negligence determination, which might be difficult. The strict liability system does not. In particular, the negligence approach, but not the strict liability approach, requires the court to determine whether both $V > c$ and $x < q(V - c_L)$ – so it must determine V, c, x, and q. The strict liability system requires that the court make an accurate damages determination – so it must determine V and c only. Thus, along the dimension of administrative and error cost, strict liability is superior to negligence.[5]

Second, the negligence system reduces the expected costs of transacting relative to the strict liability system. In the negligence system, the potential breacher knows that he does not have to pay damages in the bad state of the world if he could not have prevented it from happening at reasonable cost. In the strict liability system, he does have to pay.

To see this difference more clearly, return to our example. Recall that Seller charges a price that just covers her cost. Suppose also that x is arbitrarily close to zero, so that Seller will always incur x in order to eliminate the risk of $c = c_H$. Under the strict liability system $p = x + c_L$. In the negligence system, we have the same result: $p = x + c_L$.

Now imagine that x is arbitrarily high. In the strict liability system, $p = qV + (1 - q)c_L$. The price must cover damages in the bad state (where $d = V$) and the cost of performance in the good state. In the negligence system, $p = (1 - q)c_L$. In the negligence system, Seller does not have to pay $d = V$ in the bad state of the world, as long as the bad state could not have been avoided in

[4] In a more realistic model, cost would be a continuous function of the investment, x. The optimal x would minimize $q(V - c_L)$, and d would need to be greater than this level of investment, rather than V, as in the text.

[5] *See, e.g.*, Cooter, *supra* note 3, at 31.

cost-justified fashion. So for a range of x's, the price difference is somewhere between 0 and qV.

Thus, for any contract where x is not arbitrarily close to zero, the price will be higher under the strict liability system than under the negligence system. In return for the higher price, Buyer gets de facto insurance against the bad state of the world – a damages payment equal to V.

From an ex ante perspective, the parties would almost certainly prefer the negligence regime along this dimension. Buyer has no reason to purchase from Seller insurance against the bad state of the world. Although it is possible that in some cases, Buyer is more risk averse than Seller, and therefore would be willing to purchase insurance from Seller, in the vast majority of cases either both parties will be risk neutral, Buyer will be less risk averse than Seller, or Buyer can more cheaply purchase insurance from a third-party insurance company. The default rule should therefore not supply insurance (which is the same thing as saying that there should be a negligence regime), allowing the parties to opt out and agree to insurance in those rare cases when doing so is in their mutual interest. The strict liability system, in effect, forces Seller to sell an insurance policy to Buyer, unless the parties incur drafting costs or renegotiation costs to avoid this outcome.[6] If, as I have argued, the parties will rarely want to engage in a collateral insurance transaction, then the negligence regime is superior.

A comparison to tort law is instructive. In a simple setup, where only one party can cause the accident and take care, strict liability provides optimal incentives for that party both to take care and to choose the level of activity. In particular, the party chooses the efficient activity level precisely because it pays damages if it causes an accident, even if it is not at fault. Strict liability forces the party to internalize all the third-party costs of his behavior.

But this activity-level logic does not carry through to contract law.[7] The promisor does not impose an externality on the promisee by entering a contract with him. Thus, the only effect of strict liability in contract law is to force the promisor to pay money to the promisee in the bad state of the world, and

[6] *See* Charles J. Goetz & Robert E. Scott, *Liquidated Damages, Penalties and the Just Compensation Principle: Some Notes on an Enforcement Model and a Theory of Efficient Breach*, 77 Colum. L. Rev. 554 (1977). This point has also been made about supracompensatory damage measures, such as punitive damages. *See, e.g.*, Richard Craswell, *Contract Remedies, Renegotiation, and the Theory of Efficient Breach*, 61 S. Cal. L. Rev. 629, 643–4 (1988); Richard Craswell, *Deterrence and Damages: The Multiplier Principle and Its Alternatives*, 97 Mich. L. Rev. 2185, 2229 (1999).

[7] Except in the context of products liability, where the normal justification for strict liability is that buyers are unlikely to discover information about the riskiness of the product except (implicitly) through the price system. *See* Steven Shavell, *Strict Liability versus Negligence*, 9 J. Legal Stud. 1, 20–2 (1980).

demand a higher price ex ante (or a lower price if the relevant promisor is the buyer) – or incur extra transaction costs in order to bargain around the rule. As noted, the promisee will not usually gain from insurance, and so strict liability makes the parties worse off than a negligence regime would – either because it creates an unnecessary insurance contract or because it raises transaction costs.

II. Doctrine

Contract law is conventionally understood to be unconcerned with fault. In the influential words of the Restatement:

> Contract liability is strict liability. It is an accepted maxim that *pacta sunt servanda*, contracts are to be kept. The obligor is therefore liable in damages for breach of contract even if he is without fault and even if circumstances have made the contract more burdensome or less desirable than he had anticipated.[8]

If the analysis demonstrating the potential benefits of a negligence standard in Part I is correct, however, it would be surprising if negligence ideas played no role in contract law. In fact, as many scholars have noticed, they do.[9] Here, I will briefly describe some of this doctrine, and then explain how it fits or does not fit the theoretical analysis.

Throughout, the focus is on doctrines that excuse the promisor from liability, or dramatically reduce damages when the promisor could not avoid breach by taking cost-justified precautions. I do not try to prove that all or most or even many cases actually reflect negligence-style thinking. I argue instead that, in some cases, negligence-style thinking provides a natural interpretation of what the court did.

I should be clear that I am not claiming that negligence plays the same role in contract law as it does in tort law. In tort law, the plaintiff must, in most cases, prove that the defendant acted negligently, and a court will evaluate the defendant's behavior against some substantive standard of fault in the course of determining liability. Clearly, courts do not routinely and clearly engage in [illegible]lar process in breach of contract cases. What I do argue, however, [illegible]nder doctrinal cover, courts sometimes apply an implicit fault stan[illegible]n the sense of releasing defendants from liability if the alleged breach was "inadvertent" rather than the result of negligent or willful behavior.

[8] Restatement (Second) of Contracts ch. 11, introductory note (1981).

[9] *See* Cohen, *supra* note 1; *see also* G.H. Treitel, *Fault in the Common Law of Contract, in* Liber Amicorum for The Rt. Hon. Lord Wilberforce 185 (Maarten Bos & Ian Brownlie, eds., 1987).

A. *Impossibility/Impracticability*

The impossibility and impracticability doctrines (henceforth, I will mention only the latter) provide that a promisor is excused from performance when performance is "impracticable." The standard interpretation of this doctrine is that performance is excused only when it is extremely costly, not when it is merely not cost-justified to perform in the sense meant in this chapter. Thus, one might be led to believe that the impracticability doctrine applies only when performance is rendered excessively costly on account of risks that could not have been prevented, and when the promisee is the cheaper risk-bearer.[10] On reflection, however, this argument turns out to be unconvincing. The problem is that most contracting parties who end up in litigation – businesses, chiefly – are probably risk neutral or close to it, because they are big or can purchase insurance from a third party.[11]

The impracticability doctrine has another possible meaning. Suppose that a carrier promises to deliver goods to a destination by a certain time, but then is unable to keep the promise because of an event outside its control – a war that shuts a canal, for example.[12] In cases such as this, courts do not automatically find against the carrier (as strict liability would imply), nor do they evaluate the relative risk aversion of the parties. Instead, they examine whether the promisor could have kept its promise by taking reasonable precautions. For example, suppose the carrier could have stopped the ship at a distance from the canal, waited a reasonable time for further developments, and then taken a less onerous alternate route if the canal turned out to be closed. A court is more likely to release the carrier from liability if it takes this precaution (but ultimately continues on the same route and is blocked) than if it

[10] Posner and Rosenfield state as follows:

> The foregoing discussion indicates the factors that courts and legislatures might consider in devising efficient rules for the discharge of contracts. An easy case for discharge would be one where (1) the promisor asking to be discharged could not reasonably have prevented the event rendering his performance uneconomical, and (2) the promisee could have insured against the occurrence of the event at lower cost than the promisor because the promisee (a) was in a better position to estimate both (i) the probability of the event's occurrence and (ii) the magnitude of the loss if it did occur, and (b) could have self-insured, whereas the promisor would have had to buy more costly market insurance.

Richard A. Posner & Andrew M. Rosenfield, *Impossibility and Related Doctrines in Contract Law: An Economic Analysis*, 6 J. Legal Stud. 83, 92 (1977).

As will become clear, my argument is that (1) should be sufficient for discharge and (2) is irrelevant.

[11] Victor P. Goldberg, *Impossibility and Related Excuses*, 144 J. Institutional & Theoretical Econ. 100 (1988); Alan O. Sykes, T*he Doctrine of Commercial Impracticability in a Second-best World*, 19 J. Legal Stud. 43, 66–7 (1990).

[12] *See, e.g.*, Am. Trading & Prod. Corp. v. Shell Int'l Marine Ltd., 453 F.2d 939 (2d Cir. 1972).

does not. Here, again, the court is influenced by notions of fault. It examines whether the cost of the relevant precaution would have been low enough, and the benefit great enough.

Section 261 of the Restatement recognizes the role of fault in the impracticability doctrine:

> Where, after a contract is made, a party's performance is made impracticable *without his fault* by the occurrence of an event the non-occurrence of which was a basic assumption on which the contract was made, his duty to render that performance is discharged, unless the language or the circumstances indicate the contrary.[13]

If taken literally, this rule would seem to recognize that a negligence regime already exists – almost. Recall that under the negligence regime, the promisor is liable if (1) he fails to perform when performance is cost justified; or (2) he fails to perform and performance is not cost justified only because the promisor failed to take cost-justified precautions. If "impracticable" means "not cost justified," and if "fault" means "failure to take cost-justified precaution," then Section 261 has the same meaning as the negligence rule: The promisor is excused if performance is not cost justified and if it would not have been cost justified if the promisor had taken a cost-justified precaution.

The phrase "basic assumption" would need to be interpreted as any event that rendered performance not cost justified. This interpretation might seem implausible, but, on the other hand, no one has supplied a satisfactory definition of "basic assumption." Some judges and scholars fall back on the notion of foreseeability, arguing that the impracticability doctrine applies only when the supervening event is unforeseeable. But this argument makes little sense. The relevant question for the parties is not whether a particular event occurs or can be foreseen but whether the parties' costs rise, and everyone can foresee that costs may rise. That is, for example, all sellers know that their input costs might rise even if they cannot always foresee the particular events that *cause* those costs to rise. It does no violence to the sweeping language of Section 261 to interpret it as consistent with a negligence standard.

B. *Reasonable or Substantial Performance*

Courts distinguish between material and technical breaches, and between substantial and full performance; these distinctions often turn on the question of fault. In Louisiana, courts can decline to dissolve a lease at the request

[13] Restatement (Second) of Contracts § 261 (emphasis added).

of the lessor "where it finds that the breach of the lease is not major or where the breach was not the fault of the [lessee] or where the [lessee] was in good faith."[14] The Restatement similarly provides that, in determining whether a material breach occurred, a court should take account of "the extent to which the behavior of the party failing to perform or to offer to perform comports with standards of good faith and fair dealing."[15] In one of the Louisiana cases, the lessor had the right to cancel the lease if the lessee violated a municipal ordinance and failed to correct the violation within ten days. The court found that because the violations were "technical," did not threaten immediate harm, and were difficult to correct because of the complexity of municipal law, the breach was not the result of the lessee's fault, and thus could not justify termination.[16]

This line of cases provides important evidence that fault matters in contract law. However, the cases do not unambiguously conform to the model described in Part I. To see why, observe that victims of breach retain the right to obtain damages even for "technical" breaches; what they do *not* have is the right to *terminate* the contract on account of such breaches. Thus, the victim of a technical breach has the right to damages; the victim of a material breach has the option to terminate (and sue for damages) or to sue for damages alone. Clearly, the victim of the material breach has a more valuable remedy, inasmuch as his remedy encompasses the remedy of the victim of the technical breach; and he can, in effect, obtain supracompensatory damages whenever the breacher is willing to pay him some amount not to terminate. By contrast, in the model, the negligent breacher pays compensatory (rather than supracompensatory) damages and the non-negligent breacher pays zero (rather than compensatory) damages.

The usual explanation for the right to terminate for material breach is not to punish the breacher, but to ensure that the victim of breach can protect himself in a world in which breachers are often judgment-proof. In other words, the right to sue for damages is often worth nothing, while the right to terminate is worth a great deal. If this is the case, then we can redescribe the cases in a manner that brings them roughly in line with the model. When the breacher is negligent (or willful), courts ensure that the victim has a remedy; when he is not, courts do not ensure that the victim has a remedy.

[14] *Karno v. Bourbon Burlesque Club, Inc.*, 05–0241, p. 5 (La. App. 4 Cir. 5/10/06); 931 So. 2d 1111, 1115 (quoting *Karno v. Joseph Fein Caterer, Inc.*, 02–1269, pp. 9–10 (La.App. 4 Cir. 4/16/03); 846 So. 2d 105, 110) (emphasis omitted).

[15] Restatement (Second) of Contracts § 241(e).

[16] *Bourbon Burlesque Club*, 05–0241, at 9–10; 931 So. 3d at 1117.

C. *Good Faith and Best Efforts*

In *Feld v. Henry S. Levy & Sons, Inc.*,[17] the contract required the defendant, a bread-baking business, to sell to the plaintiff all of its breadcrumbs output for a certain period. Later, the defendant decided to stop production of breadcrumbs in order to create space for a computer room. Because the contract required defendant only to sell its output, and its output ceased when it dismantled the equipment for making breadcrumbs, the defendant argued that it had not breached the contract. The plaintiff argued that the defendant had breached the contract by failing to act in good faith. The court agreed.

The court acknowledged that the defendant could have reduced its output without violating the contract, and could even have ceased production if its losses were "more than trivial." But it held against the defendant because the defendant asserted in a "conclusory" fashion (i.e., without evidence) that the breadcrumb operation had become "uneconomical."[18] The court also mentioned that the six-month cancellation clause allowed the defendant to protect itself to some extent, that the defendant offered to resume breadcrumb production if plaintiff paid a slightly higher price than that stipulated in the contract, and that the defendant did not take steps to obtain "more economical equipment."[19]

The court appeared to believe that the defendant's breach was willful. The defendant had simply discovered that the price it obtained was less than its costs, including its opportunity costs, tried to hold out for a higher price, and then shut down operations when the plaintiff refused the offer. What is relevant to the argument here is the reference in the opinion to the conditions under which defendant's behavior might have been excused. The language implies that defendant could have avoided liability by showing that it could not have taken reasonable steps to reduce its costs to a tolerable level.[20] Because the defendant did not make such a showing, we do not know whether the court would have excused liability based on the absence of fault (on the cost-benefit interpretation or any other), but the language does suggest such an outcome.[21]

[17] 335 N.E.2d 320 (N.Y. 1975).

[18] *Id.* at 322–3.

[19] *Id.* at 321.

[20] However, the court expressed doubt about whether such a test would be feasible. *Id.* at 323 ("In any event, 'economic feasibility', an expression subject to many interpretations, would not be a precise or reliable test.")

[21] *Cf.* Charles J. Goetz & Robert E. Scott, *Principles of Relational Contracts*, 67 Va. L. Rev. 1089 (1981). Goetz and Scott similarly argue that in such "relational contracts," courts cite the doctrines of good faith and best effort when they are really just trying to determine whether continued performance would be value maximizing.

D. *Interpretation/Implied Terms*

One might respond by arguing that the court in *Feld* was not so much relying on notions of fault as interpreting the contract. The case was a strict liability case; it is just that the court (in effect) interpreted the contract to implicitly provide that the baking company could cease output when cost-justified steps could not ensure efficient performance and not otherwise. Having construed the contract in that way, the defendant was strictly liable for failing to engage in cost-justified behavior.

But this is just an argument by definition. We could say that courts import fault principles when they interpret contracts in order to preserve strict liability in making the liability determination; or we could say that courts interpret contracts literally and use a negligence rule in the liability determination. The two statements amount to the same thing. The larger point is that courts, one way or the other, try – at least sometimes – to eliminate or limit damages when the promisor could not have avoided breach through cost-justified actions – that is, was not negligent.

Consider the following illustration from the Second Restatement of Contracts. A mining company hires an engineer to help reopen a mine for "$10,000 to be payable as soon as the mine is in successful operation."[22] The engineer performs but the mine cannot be reopened. The Restatement says that the engineer should nonetheless be paid.[23]

The point seems to be that the mining company most likely hired the engineer to provide a service, and not to provide insurance in case that the service does not result in successful opening of the mine. The only possible interpretation of this argument is that the engineer should supply cost-justified efforts and no more. Again, the negligence idea reappears. It is idle to argue about whether the doctrinal reason for this result is that the contract "really" provides for only cost-justified performance or that the contract requires performance but the engineer will be excused from liability as long as the performance that he actually provides is cost justified. In both cases, contract law operates as a negligence-based system rather than as a strict liability system.[24]

[22] Restatement (Second) of Contracts, § 227 cmt. B, illus. 2 (1981).

[23] *Id.*

[24] To be sure, if the contract explicitly provides for a negligence standard of liability – that is, it says that the promisor must take cost-justified actions – then "strict" enforcement of such a contract would produce the same outcome as fault-based enforcement.

E. *Conditions*

Many contracts contain express conditions, and the promisor is obligated to perform only if those conditions are met. Even when contracts do not contain express conditions, courts frequently imply conditions. There are no hard and fast rules governing when conditions are implied, but there are patterns. For example, courts frequently make payment conditional on performance even when the contract does not say so.

Courts also imply conditions in much the same way that they imply other sorts of terms, based on a judgment about what the parties would have agreed to. This kind of judgment will reflect principles of fault when courts believe that parties would have wanted such principles in their contract. For example, in *Jacobs & Youngs, Inc. v. Kent*, a contractor breached a contract by failing to install the type of pipes that the contract specified.[25] The promisee refused to pay, invoking the traditional rule that payment is conditional on performance.[26]

The court appeared to believe that the cost of performance, tearing down the building and installing the correct pipes, exceeded the value of performance, installation of the correct pipes, which apparently were not functionally different from the pipes that were installed;[27] the question is whether it also believed that the failure to notice the mistake before installation occurred was inadvertent rather than negligent. In pointing out that an architect inspected but failed to notice the error, the court implied that the error was inadvertent.[28] In the face of explicit contractual language to the contrary, the court eliminated liability (or greatly reduced it) because the breach was not negligent or willful.[29]

For another example, consider *Royal-Globe Insurance Co. v. Craven*.[30] An insurance contract conditioned payout on notice of the claim within twenty-four hours of the accident. Theresa Craven, the insured, was unconscious during that period and so could not provide notice, but failed to give notice until three months after she was released from the hospital. The court excused her from the promise to give notice within twenty-four hours but held that she failed to comply with an implicit obligation to give notice within a reasonable time after she had recovered, and thus was not entitled to payment.[31] Alternatively, one could describe the result in terms of a negligence system. Craven's breach of her promise to give notice within twenty-four hours was

[25] 129 N.E. 889 (N.Y. 1921).

[26] *Id.* at 890.

[27] *Id.*

[28] *Id.* at 890. The brand was printed on the outside of the pipe in intervals but the pipe was otherwise indistinguishable from other pipes.

[29] *Id.*

[30] 585 N.E.2d 315 (Mass. 1992).

[31] *Id.* at 316–18.

not willful or negligent – she was unconscious. Further, there was nothing she could have done prior to the date of performance to ensure that she could have given notice when her duty to do so arose. By contrast, the failure to inform promptly after she returned to health was clearly negligent (or even willful). It would have cost Craven very little, while notice gives the insurance company a chance to verify the claim before the evidence becomes stale.

F. *Damages*

George Cohen argues that the damage measures reflect fault principles. He points out that courts sometimes award restitution damages when breach is willful, and sometimes award reduced damages – reliance damages, for example – when the breach is inadvertent or negligent.[32] Similarly, the draft Third Restatement of Restitution and Unjust Enrichment provides that the remedy for "opportunistic breach" may be disgorgement of the breacher's gains.[33] When the breacher's gains are significant, the victim's remedy may be supracompensatory.

In fact, in a fault-based system, courts should award zero damages rather than reliance damages when breach is inadvertent, and should award at least full damages (V minus any unpaid portion of the price) when breach is negligent. Thus, a negligence regime would operate by excusing conduct through liability rules rather than adjusting damages. Nonetheless, Cohen may well be right that the range of damage remedies reflects different attitudes toward willful, negligent, and inadvertent breach. In a strict liability system of contract liability, a supracompensatory remedy for breach makes no sense. Putting aside special cases,[34] a supracompensatory remedy just deters efficient breach under strict liability.[35] In a negligence regime, by contrast, a supracompensatory remedy for opportunistic breach does not deter efficient breach, as long as opportunistic breach means that $V > C$ – that is, as long as breach would be, in fact, inefficient. The promisor should always perform when performance is efficient. There is no reason to award greater damages when breach is willful than when breach is negligent, but no harm comes from this practice, either.[36]

32 Cohen, *supra* note 1.

33 Restatement (Third) of Restitution and Unjust Enrichment § 39 (Tentative Draft No. 4, 2005). For similar principles, *see* Restatement (Second) of Contracts § 357 (1981).

34 Special cases include the use of damage multipliers when breach is difficult to detect. *See* Craswell, *supra* note 6, at 2230.

35 *See* Alan Schwartz, *The Myth that Promisees Prefer Supracompensatory Remedies: An Analysis of Contracting for Damage Measures*, 100 Yale L.J. 369 (1990).

36 Again, a similar result can be found in the literature on tort law. *See, e.g.*, Shavell, *supra* note 7.

SIX

The Role of Fault in Contract Law: Unconscionability, Unexpected Circumstances, Interpretation, Mistake, and Nonperformance

Melvin Aron Eisenberg

It is often asserted that contract law is based on strict liability, not fault. This assertion is incorrect. As this chapter demonstrates, fault is a basic building block of contract law, and pervades the field. Contract law discriminates between two types of fault: the violation of strong moral norms, such as the prohibition of deception, and the violation of somewhat weaker norms, such as the requirement of due care. Where both types of fault are relevant, one party's violation of a strong moral norm will normally override the other party's violation of a weaker moral norm. Fault is pervasive in contract law because it should be. If moral obligation and fault were removed from contract law, the contracting system would be much less efficient. The efficiency of the contracting system rests on a tripod whose legs are legal remedies, reputational effects, and the internalization of social norms – in particular, the moral norm of promise keeping. All three legs are necessary to ensure the reliability, and therefore the efficiency, of the contracting system.

Introduction

The Second Restatement of Contracts states that "[c]ontract liability is strict liability. It is an accepted maxim that *pacta sunt servanda*, contracts are to be kept. The obligor is therefore liable in damages for breach of contract even if he is without fault."[1] Similarly, Farnsworth's treatise states that "contract law is, in its essential design, a law of strict liability, and the accompanying system of remedies operates without regard to fault."[2] These statements, and many others like them, are incorrect.

As a normative matter, fault *should* be a building block of contract law. One part of the human condition is that we hold many moral values concerning

[1] Restatement (Second) of Contracts ch. 11, introductory note (1981).

[2] E. Allan Farnsworth, Farnsworth on Contracts § 12.8, at 195–6 (3d ed. 2004).

right and wrong. Contract law cannot escape this condition. Accordingly, the basic principle that tells us how to make the best possible rules of contract law must accommodate not only policy and empirical propositions, but also moral values, including values concerning various types of fault. This basic principle is as follows:

> *First.* If, but only if, appropriate conditions are satisfied, and subject to appropriate constraints, the law should effectuate the objectives of parties to promissory transactions.
>
> *Second.* The rules that determine the conditions to, and the constraints on, the legal effectuation of the objectives of parties to promissory transactions, and the way in which those objectives are to be ascertained, should consist of those rules that best take into account all relevant moral, policy, and empirical propositions.

Based on this principle, it should not be surprising that fault is a pervasive element in contract law. In this chapter I discuss some important areas of contract law in which fault should and does figure very heavily. The point is not to exhaust the areas in which fault should and does play an important role, but to illustrate how contract law is fault-based to a significant extent, and to examine the different ways in which fault figures in contract law.

Fault comes in different flavors and degrees. For contract-law purposes, fault can be divided into the violation of strong moral norms, such as the norm against lying, and the violation of somewhat weaker moral norms – in particular, the norm that an actor should give due regard to the legitimate interests of others. The major type of contract-law fault in the latter category is negligence, or lack of due care. In this chapter I discuss the role of different kinds of fault in five important areas of contract law: unconscionability, unexpected circumstances, interpretation, mistake, and liability for nonperformance.

I. Unconscionability

One of the most important developments in modern contract law is the emergence of the principle that an unconscionable contract or term is unenforceable.[3] Traces of that principle can be found in some older cases, and equity courts have long reviewed contracts for fairness when equitable relief was sought, but unconscionability was not a recognized principle under classical contract law. The position of contract law changed radically beginning in the 1960s, following the lead of Section 2–302 of the Uniform Commercial Code,

[3] For convenience, hereinafter I will use the term "contract" to include contract terms.

which provides that if any contract or contract clause is unconscionable, a court may refuse to enforce the contract or clause or limit the application of the clause to avoid an unconscionable result. Section 2–302 was adopted by almost every state, and the principle it embodies has been embraced in other uniform acts, the Second Restatement of Contracts, the Second Restatement of Property, and the case law. However, the meaning and reach of the unconscionability principle is still not fully established.

Early on, an effort was made to reconcile the unconscionability principle with the bargain principle – the principle of classical contract law that bargains are enforceable according to their terms, without regard to fairness.[4] A major step in this direction was a distinction, drawn by Arthur Leff and later adopted by many courts and commentators, between procedural and substantive unconscionability.[5] Essentially, Leff defined procedural unconscionability as fault or unfairness in the bargaining *process*, and substantive unconscionability as fault or unfairness in the bargaining *outcome* even if unaccompanied by unfairness of process.

Procedural unconscionability is easy to reconcile with the bargain principle. That principle rests in significant part on the predicate that private actors are the best judges of their own utility. This predicate, however, only justifies the application of the bargain principle where both parties act voluntarily and are fully informed, and the bargaining process is fair. Therefore, where the bargaining process is unconscionable – unfair – a major predicate of the bargain principle is not satisfied, and that principle cannot properly be applied to enforce the contract.

In contrast, it may seem difficult to reconcile the bargain principle with a regime that allows judicial review of contracts for pure substantive unconscionability, because under such a regime a contract could be found unconscionable even if the bargaining process was fair. Accordingly, the effect, if not the purpose, of the distinction between procedural and substantive unconscionability was to suggest that pure substantive unconscionability should not be sufficient to render a contract unconscionable.

The distinction between procedural and substantive unconscionability is useful, but it takes us only so far and in some ways clouds the relevant issues. Often the distinction is artificial, because unfairness in the bargaining process will be significant only if the resulting bargain is unfair. Conversely, under some circumstances extracting an unfair contract is unfair in itself.

[4] *See* Melvin Aron Eisenberg, *The Bargain Principle and Its Limits*, 95 Harv. L. Rev. 741 (1982).

[5] Arthur Allen Leff, *Unconscionability and the Code – Emperor's New Clause*, 115 U. Pa. L. Rev. 485, 487 (1967).

Finally, the distinction does not address the crucial question, how should it be determined whether a contract *is* unconscionable?

The answer is that two elements – a predicate and a principle – should figure in a determination of unconscionability. The *predicate* is the nature of the market on which the contract was made. Contracts made on competitive markets will rarely be unconscionable. However, when contracts are made off-market or on markets that are not competitive, the stage is set for unconscionability. The *principle* is that unconscionability normally turns on whether the contract involved moral fault on the part of the promisee. Regardless of the nature of the market on which a contract is made, a contract will not be unconscionable without the element of moral fault.

A. *Markets*

In this chapter, I use the term "competitive market" to mean a market that is either perfectly or reasonably competitive. A *perfectly* competitive market has four characteristics: a homogeneous commodity; perfect, cost-free, and readily available information; productive resources that are sufficiently mobile that pricing decisions readily influence their allocation; and participants whose market share is so small that no participant can affect the terms on which the commodity is sold, so that each participant takes those terms as given. A *reasonably* competitive market is a market whose characteristics approximate those of a perfectly competitive market. There are relatively few perfectly competitive markets, but many reasonably competitive markets.

Now assume a perfectly competitive market, and let the parties to a bargain be S, a plaintiff-seller, and B, a defendant-buyer. Given the elements of a perfect market, the contract price will be the market price. This price will rarely if ever be unconscionable, because in our society a perfectly competitive market is generally regarded as a fair mechanism to set prices. (1) By normal measures of value, the contract price will be equal to the benefit S has agreed to confer upon B. (2) S would not voluntarily have agreed to transfer the commodity to B at any lower price, because if B had not agreed to pay the market price, S could have sold it to another buyer at that price. (3) Since cost-free information is readily available on such markets, the parties to the transaction will almost always be fully informed. (4) The contract price will normally equal the seller's marginal cost plus a normal profit.

The price in a perfectly competitive market will also normally be efficient. Given that pricing decisions on such a market readily influence the allocation of productive resources, any prospect of above-normal profits will provide an incentive to increase supply, leading to an increase in capacity and a new and lower equilibrium price that yields only normal profits.

These effects are scaled down where a market is only reasonably competitive. For example, because commodities sold on a reasonably competitive market normally will not be homogeneous, and information is not cost free, exploitation is a possibility. In general, however, transactions on reasonably competitive markets are unlikely to be unconscionable, for many of the same reasons that transactions on a perfectly competitive market are rarely if ever unconscionable.

In this connection, however, it is important to distinguish between commodities and the markets on which they trade. In the case of commodities that are sold on competitive markets, contracts are normally made on physical or virtual markets in which the public can readily participate. However, a commodity that is normally sold on a public market may occasionally be sold privately – that is, away from any public market that is readily accessible to both parties. Where that occurs, the contract should be treated as having been made off-market, even where the commodity is also traded on a competitive market. Unconscionability is most likely to be found where a transaction occurs either off-market or on a public market that is not competitive.

B. *Moral Fault*

In short, contracts made on perfectly competitive markets are rarely, if ever, unconscionable, and contracts made on reasonably competitive markets are not often unconscionable. However, the converse is not true: A contract that is made off-market or on a noncompetitive market is not unconscionable for that reason alone. Instead, such a contract will be unconscionable only if it involves moral fault on the part of the promisee. Moral fault, for contract-law purposes, should normally refer to social morality – moral standards that are rooted in aspirations for the community as a whole and that, on the basis of an appropriate methodology, can fairly be said to have substantial support in the community, can be derived from norms that have such support, or appear as if they would have such support.

The importance of moral fault in this connection is made explicit in many civil-code and civil-code-based rules that operate like the unconscionability principle. For example, the German Civil Code provides:

> [A] legal transaction is void by which a person, by *exploiting* the predicament, inexperience, lack of sound judgment or considerable weakness of will of another, causes himself or a third party, in exchange for an act

of performance, to be promised or granted pecuniary advantages which are clearly disproportionate to the performance.[6]

Although the essential role of moral fault is not as explicit under American law as it is under some civil-code and civil-code-based rules, it is implicit in the concept of unconscionability: What kind of conduct is not conscionable must depend on what kind of conduct involves moral fault.

II. Unexpected Circumstances

I now turn to the area of unexpected circumstances, in which the most salient type of fault is lack of due care. A basic rule in this area is that relief will not be granted where the adversely affected party is at fault for having caused the relevant event.[7] Under this rule, fault operates in a binary fashion, like an on/off switch, to bar the adversely affected party from employing an unexpected-circumstances excuse that she would otherwise be entitled to invoke. However, there is another way to view this problem; fault might instead operate on a continuum, like a dimmer switch. A promisor's fault in causing the unexpected circumstance may be slight or severe. At one extreme, the promisor's fault may consist of reckless conduct or gross negligence. At the other extreme, the promisor's fault may consist only of minor negligence. The location of the promisor's conduct on the fault continuum should affect the promisee's remedy. Where a promisor would be excused by reason of unexpected circumstances but for her fault, and her fault is minor, a reasonable accommodation is to require the promisor to pay reliance damages – the costs that the promisee incurred in reliance on the promise – but not expectation damages. The promisor should be required to pay reliance damages, because she is at fault and her fault has caused the promisee to be worse off than he was before the promise was made. However, the promisor should be excused from paying expectation damages, because but for her fault she would be excused from liability; the fault is minor; and the promisee will have no loss in the usual sense of that term – that is, no diminution in his precontract wealth – after he is compensated for his costs by reliance damages. Accordingly, Restatement Second Section 272(2) provides that: "[i]n any case governed by the rules stated in this chapter [on impracticability and frustration], if those rules … will not avoid injustice, the court may grant relief on such terms as justice requires including protection of the parties' reliance interests."[8]

[6] Bürgerliches Gesetzbuch [BGB] [Civil Code] Aug. 18, 1896, as amended, § 138(2) (F.R.G.) (emphasis added). *See also* Principles of European Contract Law art. 4:109(1) (1998) (emphasis added); UNIDROIT Principles of Int'l Commercial Contracts art. 3.10(1) (2004).

[7] *See, e.g.*, Restatement (Second) of Contracts §§ 261, 266(1), § 265.

[8] *Id.* § 272(2).

A series of decisions by the Massachusetts Supreme Court exemplifies this remedial approach. The decisions all arose out of a contract between John Bowen Company, a general contractor, and the Massachusetts Department of Health. The contract provided for the construction of the Lemuel Shattuck Hospital in Boston. The series began with *Gifford v. Commissioner of Public Health*,[9] which concerned the validity of that contract. This case did not involve unexpected circumstances, but it set the stage for the other decisions. Under a Massachusetts statute, contracts like the one at issue had to be put out to bid and awarded to the lowest qualified bidder. The contract was awarded to Bowen, but another bidder, Slotnik, challenged the award. The Massachusetts Supreme Court held that in setting out the components of its bid, Bowen had failed to fully comply with the statute, and that if Bowen had fully complied, Slotnik would have been the lowest qualified bidder. Accordingly, the court canceled the award of the contract to Bowen. The remaining decisions in the series involved suits against Bowen by subcontractors who had entered into contracts with Bowen before Bowen's contract with the Department of Health was canceled in *Gifford*.

M. Ahern Co. v. John Bowen Co.[10] was an action by a plumbing subcontractor, Ahern, for unpaid labor and materials furnished on the hospital project before Bowen's contract was canceled. The court held that Bowen was not liable for Ahern's expectation damages by reason of the cancellation of Bowen's contract with the Department of Health, but recovery could be granted for the benefits conferred on Bowen before the cancellation, based on "what the court holds to be *fair and just* in the unanticipated circumstances." In *Ahern* itself, the court concluded that what was fair and just turned at least in part on the role Bowen's fault had played in making the contract with Ahern impossible to perform:

> This is not a case where the defendant stands fully apart, as the plaintiff does, from the circumstances which caused the unexpected destruction of the subject matter of the contract. The defendant did those things with respect to the subbids discussed in Gifford v. Commissioner of Public Health which caused its bid to appear the lowest, although in fact it was not. The Gifford decision has held that what the defendant did was not properly done. Even though we assume, as the defendant urges here, that it acted in good faith, and in respects as to which the prescribed course was not clear, the fact is that its actions, in a field where it had a choice, had a significant part in bringing about the subsequent critical events – the awarding to it of an apparent contract which turned out to

[9] 105 N.E.2d 476 (Mass. 1952).
[10] 133 N.E.2d 484 (Mass. 1956).

> be void and the ensuing decision of this court. In the circumstances it is plain that this is not a case of fully excusable impossibility.[11]

In *Albre Marble & Tile Co. v. John Bowen Co.*,[12] Albre, another subcontractor, had contracts with Bowen for the installation of marble and tile for the hospital. Bowen refused to perform its contracts with Albre on the ground that performance had been made impossible by the Health Department's cancellation of its contract with Bowen, and Albre sued Bowen in four counts. The first and second counts sought expectation damages for Bowen's breach of Albre's contracts. Bowen pleaded impossibility, and the court dismissed these two counts on summary judgment. Albre's third and fourth counts sought to recover the value of its work and labor under its contracts, which consisted of the " 'preparation of samples, shop drawings, tests and affidavits' " rather than labor or materials furnished in the construction of the hospital. To put this differently, Albre sought reliance damages in its third and fourth counts. Accordingly, a major issue in the case was whether a promisee could recover reliance damages against a promisor who was excused from paying expectation damages by reason of unexpected circumstances. The court concluded that even though Bowen was not sufficiently at fault to be liable for expectation damages, it was sufficiently at fault to be liable for reliance damages:

> [T]his is not a case of mere impossibility by reason of a supervening act.... Although the defendant's conduct was not so culpable as to render it liable for breach of contract, nevertheless, it was a contributing factor to a loss sustained by the plaintiff which as between the plaintiff and the defendant the latter ought to bear to the extent herein permitted.

In short, the principle, supported by Section 272(2) of the Second Restatement, and exemplified by the Lemuel Shattuck Hospital series, is that where the occurrence of an unexpected circumstance would warrant judicial relief except that the promisor is proven to have been at fault, and the fault was minor, the promisor normally should be relieved from liability for expectation damages, but not reliance damages. Of course, if the promisor's fault is more extreme, she will not be able to set up an unexpected-circumstances defense, and therefore normally will be liable for expectation damages.

III. Interpretation

In the area of unconscionability, the most salient kind of fault is moral fault. In the area of unexpected circumstances, the most salient kind of fault is lack

[11] *Id.*

[12] 155 N.E.2d 437 (Mass. 1959).

of due care. In some other areas of contract law, both kinds of fault play a role. The play of different kinds and degrees of fault in a single area is well illustrated by four central principles of interpretation.

> *Principle I.* If contracting parties subjectively attached different meanings to an expression, and the two meanings were not equally reasonable, the more reasonable meaning prevails.[13]

Principle I is based in large part on fault. If A and B engage in the formation of a contract, A is negligent if she uses an expression that she should realize would lead a reasonable person in B's position to understand that A attaches a given meaning, *x*, to the expression, when in fact A attaches meaning *y*. If B attaches meaning *x*, and as a result suffers wasted reliance or the defeat of a legitimate expectation when A insists on meaning *y*, A should be liable to B.

> *Principle II.* If contracting parties subjectively attached different meanings to an expression, and the two meanings were equally reasonable, neither meaning prevails.

Principle II is associated with *Raffles v. Wichelhaus* (the *Peerless* case).[14] In *Peerless*, the seller agreed to sell the buyer 125 bales of Surat cotton to arrive at Liverpool "ex [ship] 'Peerless' from Bombay." There were, however, two ships named Peerless that sailed from Bombay: One sailed in October, and one in December. The seller meant the December Peerless and accordingly shipped Surat cotton to the buyer on that ship. The buyer meant the October Peerless and refused to accept the cotton shipped on the December Peerless. The seller sued for breach of contract. The court held for the buyer on the ground that there was no "consensus ad idem [meeting of the minds]," so that no contract was formed.

Principle II applies only if both parties are either fault-free or equally at fault. In *Peerless* itself, it is likely that both parties were equally at fault. A.W. Brian Simpson found that at the time of the case, ships commonly shared names, and there were reports of at least eleven ships called Peerless that were sailing the seas.[15] Ships bearing the same name could be differentiated by using their unique registration numbers or, much more commonly, by the names of their captains. On these facts, the buyer and the seller in *Peerless* were equally careless in assuming that the term *Peerless* was unambiguous.

[13] These four principles are embodied in Restatement (Second) §§ 20, 201.

[14] *See* 2 H & C 906, 159 Eng. Rep. 375 (Ex. 1864).

[15] A.W. Brian Simpson, *Contracts for Cotton to Arrive: The Case of the Two Ships* Peerless, 11 Cardozo L. Rev. 287, 295 (1989).

> *Principle III.* If contracting parties subjectively attached the same meaning to an expression, that meaning prevails even though it is unreasonable.

Where both parties negligently attached the same (unreasonable) meaning to an expression, both parties are at fault, but the fault has caused no injury. Rather, a party would be morally at fault to later claim a meaning that she herself did not attach to the expression.

> *Principle IV.* If contracting parties, A and B, attached different meanings, *m* and *n*, to an expression, and A knew that B attached meaning *n*, while B did not know that A attached meaning *m*, meaning *n* prevails even if it is less reasonable than meaning *m*.

Although Principle IV allows a negligently adopted meaning to prevail, it is supported by a fault analysis. B may have been negligent in attaching meaning *n* to the expression, but A was at greater fault in allowing B to proceed on the basis of an interpretation that A knew B held. A's greater fault outweighs B's negligence.

In sum, when parties assign different meanings to contractual expressions, blameworthiness – in the form of either morally wrongful behavior or negligence (itself a special kind of moral fault) – plays a key role in determining which meaning prevails.

IV. Mistake

Mistake, like interpretation, is an area of contract law in which both negligence and strong moral fault are salient. Traditionally, contract law has recognized several categories of mistake, one of which is known as unilateral mistake. In this chapter, I will focus on that type of mistake.

The term "unilateral mistake" normally refers to transient mechanical errors in the actor's mental machinery. For example, an actor may write "65" when she intends to write "56," or may make an error in addition. Characterizing these kinds of blunders as mistakes assumes that for the actor in question the blunder is transient. If an actor wrote all his numbers backward, we would not characterize his acts as mistakes. Instead, we would say that the actor had some type of disability. I will call mistakes of this kind – that is, blunders that result from transient errors in the actor's mental machinery – mechanical errors. Among the most common types of mechanical errors are mistaken computations, mistaken payments, misidentifications of property that is to be bought and sold, auditory or visual misperceptions, and misunderstandings of specifications, formulas, or plans.

Mechanical errors resemble the kind of mistakes sometimes made in the transcription of DNA. Almost invariably, that transcription is correct, but every once in a while it goes awry.

A. *The Paradigm Case: The Nonmistaken Party Is Aware of the Mistaken Party's Mechanical Error*

I begin with the paradigm case, in which the nonmistaken party, B, is aware of the mechanical error that was made by the mistaken party, A. In that case, the mistaken party should have no contractual liability. It is true that in the event of a mechanical error, normally the mistaken party, A, is at fault because she did not exercise due care. In the paradigm case, however, B would be more strongly at fault if he tried to take advantage of this kind of error. Of course, B might have formed an expectation that by concluding a contract he could benefit from A's mistake. As a matter of morality, however, if that were B's intention he would be viewed as improperly taking advantage of A. Accordingly, B's expectation would be unjustified, like the expectation of a person who finds lost property and knows who the owner is, but thinks that he is entitled to benefit from the owner's carelessness – "finders keepers."

B. *The Nonmistaken Party Had Reason to Know of the Mistaken Party's Mechanical Error*

Suppose that the nonmistaken party is not proven to have been aware of a mechanical error, but had reason to know of the error. Here the fault analysis is not as clear as it is in the paradigm case. In the paradigm case, B knowingly attempts to take advantage of A's mechanical error; in the reason-to-know case, he does not. Nevertheless, although A is at fault for making the mistake, B is at fault for his negligence in failing to realize that a mistake was made when a reasonable person would have done so. Furthermore, administrability considerations strongly favor relief in the reason-to-know case. Only the nonmistaken party knows with certainty whether he was actually aware of a mechanical error. Proving actual (subjective) awareness by the nonmistaken party therefore will usually be too difficult a burden for the mistaken party to shoulder. Where the nonmistaken party had reason to know of a mechanical error, he probably did know. Accordingly, the reason-to-know case should be treated like the paradigm case to protect the integrity of the rule that governs that case.

C. *Cases in Which the Nonmistaken Party Neither Knew nor Had Reason to Know of the Mechanical Error*

Suppose the nonmistaken party, B, did not know or have reason to know of the mechanical error made by the mistaken party, A. This kind of case presents two issues. First, should A be liable for B's reliance damages? Second, should A be liable for B's expectation damages?

In the paradigm case, where B is aware of A's mechanical error, B's reliance should make no difference. If B is aware that A made a mechanical error, B's reliance is unjustified. However, if B relies when he is neither aware nor has reason to be aware that A made a mechanical error, then B's reliance is justified; A's fault has caused a loss to B; and at a minimum, A should compensate B for that loss by paying reliance damages.

Whether the mistaken party should be liable for expectation damages in such a case is a more difficult issue. Older contract law took the position that a mechanical error (or, in the traditional nomenclature, a unilateral mistake) was not a defense against expectation damages unless the nonmistaken party either knew or had reason to know of the mistake. In contrast, modern contract law takes the position that a mechanical error is a defense to expectation damages, at least where the result of enforcing the contract through expectation damages would be unconscionable.[16]

It is true that where B neither was aware nor should have been aware of the mistake, A is at fault, and B has formed a justified expectation as a result of A's fault. That, however, is not dispositive. For example, if A negligently makes a mistaken payment to B, and B neither knows nor has reason to know that the payment is mistaken, then as a result of A's fault B may form a justified expectation that the payment is his to keep. However, that expectation is not protected by the law.[17] Similarly, where A has negligently lost personal property, and B, who finds the property, reasonably believes that the property was abandoned, B forms a justified expectation that the property is now his. Again, however, that expectation is not protected.

As in those cases, the fact that the nonmistaken party in a mechanical-error case formed a justified expectation does not mean that he acts fairly in insisting on full enforcement of the contract after he understands that

[16] *See, e.g.*, Restatement (Second) of Contracts § 153(a) (1981).

[17] *See, e.g.*, Glover v. Metro. Life Ins. Co., 664 F.2d 1101, 1105 (8th Cir. 1981) ("In all the circumstances, it would be unjust, in our view, for [an unknowing mistaken payee] to keep the money. This result disappoints an expectation on her part that she had every reason to believe, at one time, to be legitimate, but to decide otherwise would be intolerably unfair to [the mistaken payor].").

his counterparty had made such an error. On the contrary, just as a payee is morally obliged to return a mistaken payment once he learns the payment was mistaken, and a finder is morally obliged to return lost property once he knows that it was lost rather than abandoned, so too would a party to a contract that is based on a mechanical error be morally overreaching if he insisted on full enforcement after he learned of the error. This principle is embodied in Section 153 of the Second Restatement and the modern cases.[18]

Normally, the principle of unconscionability is applied ex ante, at the time a bargain is made, to determine whether the bargaining process, the bargain, or both conformed to moral standards. In the context of mechanical errors, however, the concept of unconscionability refers to cases where it is morally improper to seek full enforcement of a promise that was based on such an error.[19] In these cases, the nonmistaken party will be restored to his precontract wealth by an award of reliance damages. A fair-minded person who is made whole in this way would not try to take advantage of a mechanical error by inflicting a further loss on the mistaken party so as to make a gain that is not earned by knowledge, skill, or diligence. As in other areas of contract law, therefore, fault should and does play a significant role in the outcomes in this category of mistake cases.

V. Nonperformance

The subjects discussed in Parts I through IV do not exhaust the areas of contract law in which fault plays a significant role. Other such areas – to name just a few – are fraud, duress, undue influence, and the duty to perform in good faith. Of course, some rules of contract law turn exclusively on policy and empirical considerations. Examples are the mailbox rule, the parol evidence rule, and the statute of frauds. In still other areas, such as disclosure, fault considerations are largely although not entirely trumped by policy considerations. However, that some contract-law rules are not driven by fault does not mean that contract law is not fault based, any more than the existence of some strict-liability rules in tort law means that tort law is not fault based.

Why, then, do various authorities conclude that contract law is based on strict liability, not fault? Perhaps these authorities have in mind not contract law but rather one area of contract law: liability for nonperformance of a bargain promise. The idea that liability in this area is strict, not fault based, has

[18] *See* Donovan v. RRL Corp., 27 P.3d 702 (Cal. 2001).

[19] McMaster Univ. v. Wilchar Constr. Ltd., [1971] 3 O.R. 801, 811 (Can.); *see also* Stepps Invs. Ltd. v. Sec. Capital Corp., [1976] 14 O.R.2d 259, 271 (Can.).

a superficial appeal. In torts, the plaintiff normally prevails only if the defendant acted wrongfully by intentionally inflicting an injury or failing to exercise due care. In contracts, the plaintiff normally prevails if a contract was formed and the defendant did not perform her part of the contract. It is therefore tempting to reach the conclusion that liability in contract for nonperformance is strict, and is based on policy reasons rather than moral reasons.

However, this is an oversimplified view of the morality of promising and the basis of liability for nonperformance. In the area of nonperformance, law and morality, although not identical, tend to converge rather than diverge. Morally, a promise is a commitment to take a certain action, such as the achievement of a given result, even if at the time the action is to be taken the promisor would prefer not to fulfill her promise, all things considered. The mere fact that a promisor has not failed to perform intentionally or negligently is not a moral excuse for nonperformance, because the moral commitment of a promisor extends further. Neither is it a moral excuse for nonperformance that when the time comes to perform the promise, it would hurt to do so. To believe that any of these reasons are moral excuses for not performing a promise would be to misunderstand the nature of promising.

On the other hand, nonperformance of a promise *is* morally permissible if there is a moral excuse for not performing. One such excuse is that performance would not only hurt, but hurt very badly. As Thomas Scanlon says,

> Saying "I promise to ..." normally binds one to do the thing promised, but it does not bind unconditionally or absolutely.... It does not bind absolutely because, while a promise binds one against reconsidering one's intention simply on grounds of one's own convenience, it does not bind one to do the thing promised whatever the cost to oneself and others.[20]

Similarly, the fact that performance of a promise hurts very badly may be a legal excuse under the doctrine of impracticability, which rests in significant part on whether a promised performance has become much more costly than was contemplated at the time of contract formation.

More generally, it is inaccurate to say that liability for nonperformance is established by showing contract formation and nonperformance. To these elements must be added the lack of an excuse for nonperformance. The legal structure of liability for nonperformance builds on the moral structure of promising, and neither the moral nor the legal obligation is an example of strict liability. If I promise you that I will meet you for lunch and I don't show

[20] Thomas M. Scanlon, *Promises and Practices*, 19 Phil. & Pub. Aff. 199, 214 (1990).

up, I am at fault, and "strict liability" doesn't enter the picture. The same is true if I promise to sell you one hundred widgets and don't deliver. Of course, in the lunch hypothetical, if I have a good excuse for not showing up – for example, if I suddenly fell ill – I wouldn't be at fault. Similarly, if I have a good excuse for not delivering the widgets, such as a blockade or a fire, I won't be liable. It's true that what constitutes a good excuse in the widgets hypothetical may be different from what constitutes a good excuse in the lunch hypothetical, but that is largely because of the different context and subject matter, not because one nonperformance is judged under a fault standard and the other is judged under a strict liability standard.

The fault basis of liability for contractual nonperformance is well summarized by Barry Nicholas:

> Fault is ... absent from the conventional common law conception of liability for breach of contract only because it is in substance incorporated in the meaning of "contract." So in a formulation such as that in Restatement 2d Contracts, § 235(2): "When performance of a duty under a contract is due any non-performance is a breach," the part played by fault is incorporated in the duty.[21]

Conclusion

It is not surprising that fault plays a significant role in contract law. On the contrary, it would be surprising if it did not. For one thing, moral norms are basic building blocks in all fields of law. For another, the efficiency of the contracting system would be materially impaired if fault did not play a significant role. The efficiency of that system rests on a tripod whose legs are legal remedies, reputational effects, and the internalization of social norms – in particular, the moral norm of promise keeping. These three legs are mutually supportive. Legal rules rest in significant part on social norms, reputational effects rest in significant part on social norms, and social norms are reinforced by legal rules and reputational effects.

All three of these legs are necessary to ensure the reliability, and therefore the efficiency, of the contracting system. Legal rules alone are not sufficient, because dispute settlement under law is expensive and chancy. The moral norm of promise keeping alone is not sufficient, because not all actors fully internalize moral norms. And reputational effects alone are not sufficient,

[21] Barry Nicholas, *Fault and Breach of Contract*, *in* Good Faith and Fault in Contract Law 337, 345 (Jack Beatson & Daniel Friedmann, eds., 1995).

because reliable information concerning a promisor's history of breach is often hard to come by and often disregarded even when known.

Because all three legs are necessary to support the efficiency of the contracting system, anything that weakens one leg seriously threatens the efficiency of that system. Giving effect to a theory that fault does not play an important role in contract law would remove the moral force of promising in a bargain context and would thereby decrease the efficiency of the contracting system in three ways. First, it would lead contracting parties to make greater use of costly noncontractual measures, such as security deposits, to ensure performance. Second, it would diminish the force of reputational constraints, because such constraints rest in significant part on moral norms. Finally, and most important, it would increase the need to resort to litigation, which is very expensive, as opposed to achieving performance of contracts through the internalization of the moral norm of promise keeping, which is very inexpensive.

PART III

BETWEEN STRICT LIABILITY AND FAULT

SEVEN

Fault at the Contract-Tort Interface

Roy Kreitner

The formative period in the history of contract and tort may be characterized by the cleavage of contract and tort around the concept of fault: tort modernized by moving from strict liability to a regime of "no liability without fault," while contract moved toward strict liability. Nineteenth-century scholars of private law offered explanations for the opposition, reasoning that alternative ideas about fault account for the different character of state involvement in enforcing private law rights: Tort law governs liabilities imposed by law on nonconsenting members of society (and thus, it should limit itself to fault-based conduct), while contract law governs bargained-for duties and liabilities of parties who exercise freedom of contract (and thus, liability voluntarily undertaken need not consider fault). It is argued in this chapter, that these theories are problematic, especially because they cannot offer a complete account of contract or tort. Tort retains too much strict liability to be thought of as a regime of no liability without fault, and contract has too many fault-based rules to be conceived of through strict liability. While these justifications for the distinction between contract and tort were questioned in ensuing generations, they still structure much of the debate over the current boundary between contract and tort.

Introduction

Despite a number of notable exceptions, the concept of fault has not been central to contemporary contracts scholarship.[1] I would like to suggest that this

For discussions and comments on previous drafts, I am grateful to Yishai Blank, Sharon Hannes, Talia Fisher, and Ariel Porat. Thanks to Abigail Faust for excellent research assistance. This research was supported by The Israel Science Foundation (grant No. 014014371).

[1] For some of those notable exceptions, *see* Good Faith and Fault in Contract Law (Jack Beatson & Daniel Friedmann, eds., 1995); George M. Cohen, *The Fault Lines in Contract Damages*, 80

is no simple oversight. Indeed, fault may be a good prism through which to understand the modernization of contract and tort – or, in other words, the making of modern private law. Moreover, an enhanced role for the analysis of fault in contract might go some way in clarifying persistent puzzles that revolve around the relationship between contract and tort.

In short, my thesis is as follows: The second half of the nineteenth century was a formative period for contract and tort, during which the understanding of these categories modernized by shifting and, in a sense, switching positions regarding fault. Tort modernized by moving from causality-based liability to a regime of "no liability without fault," while contract modernized by abandoning the relevance of fault and adopting, at least rhetorically, a theory of strict liability. While this shift vis-à-vis fault was never complete and never represented a truly adequate account of the working rules of contract or tort, it was important for the conceptualization of the different aspects of private law. That conceptualization was powerful and long lasting, but in important ways misleading, particularly because it implied a strict separation between public regulation and private ordering. Further, it is precisely that misconception that haunts our current attempts at making sense of the contract-tort boundary, particularly with respect to the range of problems that reach courts under the guise of warranty products liability.

I. Modernizing Tort and Contract Around Fault

The familiar part of the story of modernization and fault deals with the development of tort law. While the level of historical nuance may be increased nearly indefinitely, the dominant narrative holds that prior to modernization, the common law was concerned chiefly with the causation of damage and not with the fault of the actor. James Barr Ames's articulation of the shift remains cogent a century after he wrote:

> The early law asked simply, "Did the defendant do the physical act which damaged the plaintiff?" The law of today, except in certain cases based upon public policy, asks the further question, "Was the act blameworthy?" The ethical standard of reasonable conduct has replaced the unmoral standard of acting at one's peril.[2]

Va. L. Rev. 1225 (1994) [hereinafter Cohen, *Fault Lines*]; George M. Cohen, *The Negligence-Opportunism Tradeoff in Contract Law*, 20 Hofstra L. Rev. 941 (1992) [hereinafter Cohen, *Negligence-Opportunism*]; and Ariel Porat, *The Contributory Negligence Defence and the Ability to Rely on the Contract*, 111 Law Q. Rev. 228 (1995).

[2] James Barr Ames, *Law and Morals*, 22 Harv. L. Rev. 97, 99 (1908).

Tort scholars from the late nineteenth century until today have squabbled about the details,[3] but most would agree in summing up that, "It is most likely that theories of strict liability were dominant during the formative years of the common law. But during the nineteenth century ... there was a decided and express shift towards the theories of negligence."[4]

Two points bear emphasis in this account of the modernization of tort law. First, it is only a generalized historical hindsight that can locate the shift in the basic background assumptions that organized the field, or that created "classical legal thought." The accounts of such a shift are persuasive, but only when one acknowledges that the shift took place over the course of decades (rather than, say, through one key judgment of an individual court) and that it solidified quite late in the nineteenth century. The evidence lies not only in the new framework for thinking about torts, visible in treatises and scholarly articles, but also in the development and refinement of particular doctrines, most notably contributory negligence, assumption of risk, and *damnum absque injuria*. Second, the importance of the shift in background assumptions about liability could hardly have been imagined early in the nineteenth century, when the number of serious injuries from industrial activity was miniscule in comparison to what would emerge in the last third of the century. By the last two decades of the nineteenth century, the question of the extent to which injuries from industrial accidents could go uncompensated had become a major economic battleground in ways that would have been difficult to appreciate early in the century.[5]

So much for the familiar story in tort. The distinctly less familiar aspect of the story deals with the modernization of contract. Everyone is familiar with the idea that contract rests on a species of strict liability, namely, the claim that, in general, "duties imposed by contract are absolute."[6] While a few scholars have challenged this view on both descriptive and normative

[3] For a representative sampling of some of the early haggling, *see* Oliver Wendell Holmes, Jr., The Common Law (Mark DeWolfe Howe, ed., 1963; 1881); Nathan Isaacs, *Fault and Liability*, 31 Harv. L. Rev. 954 (1918); Jeremiah Smith, *Tort and Absolute Liability – Suggested Changes in Classification* (pts. 1–3), 30 Harv. L. Rev. 241, 319, 409 (1917); Ezra Ripley Thayer, *Liability without Fault*, 29 Harv. L. Rev. 801 (1916); and John H. Wigmore, *Responsibility for Tortious Acts: Its History* (pts. 1–3), 7 Harv. L. Rev. 315, 383, 441 (1894). For modern articulations with greater historical complexity, *see* Morton J. Horwitz, The Transformation of American Law, 1780–1860, at 85–99 (1977); Duncan Kennedy, The Rise and Fall of Classical Legal Thought 228–34 (2006; 1975); John Fabian Witt, The Accidental Republic: Crippled Workingmen, Destitute Widows, and the Remaking of American Law 43–54 (2004); and Gary T. Schwartz, *The Character of Early American Tort Law*, 36 UCLA L. Rev. 641 (1989).

[4] Richard A. Epstein, *A Theory of Strict Liability*, 2 J. Legal Stud. 151, 152 (1973).

[5] *See* Witt, *supra* note 3, at 51–2, 67–70.

[6] E. Allan Farnsworth, Contracts 617 (3d ed. 1999); *see also* Restatement (Second) of Contracts, ch. 11, introductory note, 309 (1981).

grounds, it remains an ingrained aspect of mainstream understandings of contract. What generally escapes appreciation is that the understanding of contract as a strict liability regime is anything but an age-old phenomenon. In fact, such a regime emerged in the United States only at about the same time as the solidification of the no-liability-without-fault regime in tort, during the final decades of the nineteenth century.

During the first half of the nineteenth century, although this view receded slowly in the decades following, contract was understood as a fault-based regime. The most important reason for this is that contract as a *category* was understood in direct reference to the typical contractual relationships that constituted it. This world of contract was inhabited by people in relational pairs: bailor and bailee, principal and agent, master and servant, principal and factor, landlord and tenant, vendor and purchaser, husband and wife. Within those relational pairs, actors had standardized duties, whose contours were shaped by the relation itself.[7] Individual agreement tailored these duties only on the margins. And while some of the relations included duties we could characterize as absolute, it was far more typical for duties to be framed in terms of reasonable skill, reasonable diligence, or reasonable care. It was a failure to meet the standard of care, often phrased directly in terms of negligence, that triggered *contractual* liability.[8] Thus, the basic standard of liability was one of fault, even if fault of an objective variety.[9]

Only late in the nineteenth century did the strict, or almost absolute, version of contractual liability come into its own, and then only through a thorough reworking of the framework for thinking about contract.[10] The transformation in the concept of contract entailed a reevaluation of the source of contractual obligation as well as its basic purpose. In terms of the source of obligation, the parties were conceived as making private law for themselves, rather than

[7] For one of many accounts, *see* William M. Wiecek, The Lost World of Classical Legal Thought: Law and Ideology in America, 1886–1937, at 102 (1998). For a detailed statement of the relational idea in the common law as opposed to the idea of will in Roman law, see Roscoe Pound, *The End of Law as Developed in Juristic Thought* (pt. 2), 30 Harv. L. Rev. 201, 211–17 (1917).

[8] This point is intuitive regarding a category like bailment, in which various standards of duty aligned with the different types of bailment, and where slight, ordinary, or gross negligence could trigger liability, or their absence shield from it. But the same idea is actually applicable to a host of other contractual relations that made up the early nineteenth-century scheme of contract law.

[9] Of course, fault in late nineteenth century under a regime of no liability without fault is also objective fault, and not a simple version of moral blameworthiness. For the early articulation, see Holmes, *supra* note 3, at 161–3.

[10] *See* Grant Gilmore, The Death of Contract 46–8 (1974); James Gordley, *Contract, Property, and the Will – The Civil Law and Common Law Tradition, in* The State and Freedom of Contract 66, 79 (Harry N. Scheiber, ed., 1998).

entering into preexisting standardized relations; in terms of contract's basic purpose, the view of parties entering into a type of cooperative endeavor declined and the vision of parties allocating particularized and accountable risks rose.[11] A simple comparison should render this claim intuitive. Early nineteenth-century lawyers saw bailment as a paradigmatic contractual relationship, and they understood the content of the duties as part of the relationship itself. The level of care required by the bailee was a function of the type of bailment. The bailee was responsible for his behavior and liable only for failing to exercise the proper level of diligence in caring for the bailed property. Compare this with a transaction that late nineteenth-century – or for that matter, early twenty-first-century – observers of contract might think of as paradigmatic[12]: mutual promises for the future delivery of an agricultural commodity. Even if we assume that the parties contemplate actual delivery,[13] the observer of their contract does not need to imagine anything but minimal cooperative activity; in fact, the parties are allocating risks regarding the future price of the commodity and nothing more. They act, in a sense, as mutual insurers, and thus considering anything but absolute liability would be an anomaly.

As noted, the no-liability-without-fault regime in tort required, in addition to a new organizational scheme, the development of new doctrines or innovative revision of old ones. The same was true for contract. Thus, the late nineteenth century saw the expansion and refinement of the rules on formation; a thorough reworking of the rules of consideration; and a heightened emphasis on intention in the rules on interpretation, even while contract theory was becoming more and more adamant about its objective basis. In all, then, contract and tort formed the central pillars of classical legal thought, and their modernization entailed switching their respective positions on the question of fault.

II. Explaining the Fault Swap

There is abundant evidence explaining why nineteenth-century American jurists made "no liability without fault" a rallying cry in their attempt to reformulate tort law. The evidence regarding the purging of fault from contract is

[11] *See* James Gordley, The Philosophical Origins of Modern Contract Doctrine 158–60, 201–13 (1991); John V. Orth, *Contract and the Common Law, in* The State and Freedom of Contract, *supra* note 10, at 44, 45–9.

[12] For the rise of mutual promises (or executory contracts) as the paradigm of modern contract thought, *see* P.S. Atiyah, Essays on Contract 10–31 (1986) and P.S. Atiyah, The Rise and Fall of Freedom of Contract 420–40 (1979).

[13] Of course, this is a counterfactual assumption if the transaction is conducted on an organized commodity exchange, rather than between actual farmers or merchants whose specific trade is in this type of commodity.

role through their promises made consented-to, freely undertaken obligations central, and imposed duties marginal and anomalous.[18] Contract was thus established as the very center of the private realm, in part by purging its fault-based standards. Indeed, it is the image of strict liability that heightens the sense of party control and autonomy, since it is always assumed that the parties could, if they wished, contract for any other standard of liability within their contract.[19]

It has often been remarked that classical legal thought imposed a firm boundary between contract and tort.[20] The reason this was important, as already alluded to, is that distinguishing between tort and contract was part of a wider project of distinguishing between the public or regulatory realm, on the one hand, and the private realm, on the other. This may seem odd to some, since tort and contract are both typically considered part of private law. But late nineteenth-century legal thinking certainly viewed them as private in different ways. Contract was essentially private, a creation of rights and obligations initiated entirely by free, consenting parties. The idea that their obligations would be absolute was not only an absence of intervention, but also a testament to their own power to generate obligations independently of the state; tempering the parties' self-imposed obligations was conceived to be a threat to their autonomy. Tort, on the other hand, was private law in the sense that the law was protecting the legal entitlements of private individuals. But at the same time, that protection required the state to impose standards of behavior, or limitations on freedom of action, to which the parties never consented. In this sense, the public involvement in tort was considered to be different in kind from the involvement in contract. Tort was, indeed, private law, and classical legal thinkers found it important to emphasize that as private law it should not be used as a redistributive mechanism, but rather only as a mode for vindicating rights. But it was contract that served as the true core of private law, with tort always retaining an air of public regulation. This conceptualization was a significant departure from eighteenth- and early nineteenth-century legal thought, where negligence, contract, and tort (none of them fully formed) mixed promiscuously. Teasing contract and tort apart was one aspect of erecting a firm divide between the public and the private, and one of the key doctrinal tools in doing so was exchanging their positions on fault.[21]

18 *See* K.N. Llewellyn, Forward, *On the Complexity of Consideration*, 41 Colum. L. Rev. 777 (1941); Ian R. MacNeil, *The Many Futures of Contracts*, 47 S. Cal. L. Rev. 691, 696 (1974).

19 *See, e.g.*, Leavitt v. Dover, 32 A. 156 (N.H. 1892).

20 W. David Slawson, Binding Promises 3 (1996); Wiecek, *supra* note 7, at 103.

21 *See* Horwitz, *supra* note 15, at 85–94; Kennedy, *supra* note 3, at 240–1.

For most legal scholars today, the explanation for the shape of private law offered by classical legal thought is unconvincing. It simply no longer makes sense to believe, as many late nineteenth-century legal minds apparently did, that the particular doctrinal structure expounded by the classics is the instantiation of the idea of freedom. Some of the reasons for this are based on internal critiques of the system. Since the realist critique of the early twentieth century, we are more accustomed to see a doctrine like damnum absque injuria as a question-begging statement of liability (or no liability), rather than a justification for the conclusion.[22] It is little more than an unsupported conclusion of a judge that in the particular case before him, no liability should attach. By imposing externally determined levels of care, objective standards of behavior to define negligence blurred the boundary between negligence and strict liability. Many areas of tort law, such as that applying to common carriers, still carry strict liability by common law or by legislation. Objectivism in contract blurs the boundary between liability based on actual consent and liability based on law-imposed standards of behavior, or, in other words, it blurs the boundary between contract and tort. The protection (even sporadic) of reliance where no contract has been concluded again brings contract and tort perilously close together. And the presence of restitution for cases of quasi-contract seems less suspect and less marginal than the classics claimed – yet again raising the specter that private law is infused, through and through, with public decision making and a limited role for actual consent.[23] Finally, on top of all this, waves of legislation in fields like workers' compensation, workplace safety, and eventually consumer protection made the regulatory environment in which contract and tort were embedded a feature that could not be ignored in viewing the system as a whole. Overall, the realist attack made the explanatory basis of the classical structure an easy target for critique.[24]

But the story does not end here. One of the fascinating aspects of late nineteenth-century legal thought is its structural staying power, well beyond the explanatory or justificatory force of its central tenets. The structural features

[22] *See* Witt, *supra* note 3, at 47–50.

[23] For a leading view of contract as public law, see Morris R. Cohen, *The Basis of Contract*, 46 Harv. L. Rev. 553 (1933). For analyses, see Horwitz, *supra* note 15, at 35–63, and Witt, *supra* note 3, at 51–70.

[24] For a sample of some of the more self-conscious examples of this assault, see John R. Commons, Legal Foundations of Capitalism (1924); Richard T. Ely, Property and Contract in Their Relations to the Distribution of Wealth (1914); Robert L. Hale, *Coercion and Distribution in a Supposedly Non-Coercive State*, 38 Pol. Sci. Q. 470 (1923); K.N. Llewellyn, *The Effect of Legal Institutions upon Economics*, 15 Am. Econ. Rev. 665 (1925); and Roscoe Pound, *Liberty of Contract*, 18 Yale L.J. 454 (1909).

of the system – such as the ideas that contract is centered on party sovereignty; that liability beyond consent is marginal and anomalous; that contract is more private than tort, which is more regulatory; or that strict liability is more interventionist than negligence – all survive, unmoored from the idea of justifying the mass of existing rules as instantiating freedom.[25] For classical legal thought, the "animating idea [was] the effort to make patent the hidden legal content of a free political and economic order."[26] This pretension has given way to visions of law that recognize that regulation and redistribution can be legitimate aspects of government, not simply consistent with the idea of freedom, but at times necessary requirements for the effective enjoyment of rights. And yet, the structure within which the interpretation of existing legal rules or the discussion of even wide-scale reforms is conducted is still closely tied to the basic strategies of organization of late nineteenth-century law. The puzzles engendered by this remainder or aftertaste of classical thought, as they arise at the boundary between contract and tort, are the focus of the remainder of this chapter.

III. Products Liability and Fault at the Border Between Contract and Tort

The border between contract and tort is a long one. It stretches from questions of how to deal with misrepresentations during contract negotiations,[27] to questions of interpretation of actions (or words) during formation,[28] to questions of liability for deceitful or fraudulent behavior during contract performance,[29] and, of course, to questions of remedy.[30] Indeed, after legal realism and its revival of the idea that tort principles are *internal* to the concept of contract, there is scarcely a contracts issue that may not in some way be

[25] *See* Roberto Mangabeira Unger, What Should Legal Analysis Become? 41–52 (1996).

[26] *Id.* at 41.

[27] In contract (via a doctrine like *culpa in contrahendo*) or in tort (through negligent misrepresentation)? Friedrich Kessler & Edith Fine, Culpa in Contrahendo, *Bargaining in Good Faith, and Freedom of Contract: A Comparative Study*, 77 Harv. L. Rev. 401 (1964). Or perhaps using something (somewhat) different, in the shape of promissory fraud? Ian Ayres & Gregory Klass, Insincere Promises 59–82 (2005).

[28] Clarke B. Whittier, *The Restatement of Contracts and Mutual Assent*, 17 Cal. L. Rev. 441 (1929).

[29] Gregory Klass, *Contracting for Cooperation in Recovery*, 117 Yale L.J. 2 (2007).

[30] The literature on reliance damages is voluminous; for my purposes here, it is sufficient to note that some commentators are adamant that the reliance interest is simply not contractual and that reliance damages, when awarded, are therefore best understood through tort. Peter Benson, *The Unity of Contract Law*, *in* The Theory of Contract Law 118, 174–7 (Peter Benson, ed., 2001); Daniel Friedmann, *The Performance Interest in Contract Damages*, 111 Law Q. Rev. 628, 632 (1995).

informed by tort thinking.[31] But in products liability, the meeting of responsibility based in tort and that based in contract is particularly salient.

The meeting of contract and tort in products cases is at once obvious and mysterious: obvious because both historically and today, claims for redress from product injuries may be phrased in contract or tort language; mysterious because it is unclear whether one set of principles or another should govern, or even whether such a choice would determine much about outcomes. To make this concrete, I present a cumulative rundown of some of the places where the boundary is touched, and where sketching a boundary might have impact. This account shows how the issue of products liability proceeds to change the form of contact between the categories of contract and tort. After laying out these points of contact, I return to the question of how understanding the development of contract and tort in their relations to fault may help in grappling with these problems.

Products, whether mass produced or custom made, complex or simple, built for the consumer or for industry use, may cause damage to users or their property or to bystanders. An injured party may sue for damages under a number of headings that, at least at first glance, seem to have distinctive doctrinal features.

Warranty is the contractual home for the suit. From the plaintiff's perspective, warranty's attractiveness depends on who he is. On the one hand, warranty does not require proof of fault but only that the product did not do what such products are supposed to do (i.e., fulfill its role without injuring the user); on the other hand, warranty, at least early in the day, requires privity just as any other claim on the contract would require privity. So, if the injured party is not the buyer of the product (or the seller is not the manufacturer, etc.), privity may be a serious obstacle to recovery. The creation of a regime that would come to be known as products liability is, on one level, located entirely here: Most of the cases that scholars would eventually liken to an "assault upon the citadel" were cases that sounded in warranty and eroded the obstacle of privity of contract.[32]

But, of course, the injured party may also sue in tort. There, the major obstacle would be proving fault – that is, negligence – but a lack of contractual privity would not normally arise as an obstacle.

[31] For a clear expression of this recurring idea in realist work on contract, *see* George K. Gardner, *An Inquiry into the Principles of the Law of Contracts*, 46 Harv. L. Rev. 1 (1932).

[32] George L. Priest, *The Invention of Enterprise Liability: A Critical History of the Intellectual Foundations of Modern Tort Law*, 14 J. Legal Stud. 461, 505–11 (1985). For earlier explanations of the development, *see* Friedrich Kessler, *Products Liability*, 76 Yale L.J. 887 (1967); William L. Prosser, *The Assault upon the Citadel (Strict Liability to the Consumer)*, 69 Yale L.J. 1099 (1960).

Cases such as *Henningsen*, *Escola*, and *Greenman*, famous as the groundwork of products liability, combined the contract and tort issues into a single policy discussion.[33] That discussion took on a somewhat canonical formulation in section 402A of the Second Restatement of Torts, setting out strict liability in tort for manufacturing defects. This was conceived of as a tort problem, whose solution was abandonment of the general requirement of fault in response to what was understood as a public policy–inspired vision of legal responsibility. This vision of responsibility and the policy behind it will remain hot topics of debate (on which more will be said momentarily), but structurally this is the basic contract-tort combination that animates products liability.

Note, then, that the foundation of products liability works on both contract and tort axes and that in each a basic tenet of the modernizing moment is jettisoned. When seen through the contract perspective, the parties to the contract are no longer the authors of all obligations, since some contractual obligations will even run to nonparties.[34] From the tort perspective, we see an adoption of liability without fault, or responsibility "although … the seller has exercised all possible care in the preparation and sale of his product."[35]

Once a products liability regime is in place, a number of practical issues arise in drawing and maintaining the boundary between contract and tort, three of which I will briefly mention. The first is a question of the degree of overlap between a products liability action sounding in tort and one in contract. Is there any difference, in terms of liability, if the basis for the suit is the implied warranty of merchantability found in UCC 2–314, or a tort rule akin to Restatement 402A? Or, in other words, could a product be defective under one rule and not defective under the other? In *Denny v. Ford Motor Co.*, the New York Court of Appeals dealt precisely with this problem and found that regarding design defects, each claim will rely on a different test for liability.[36] The case brings to the fore the question of whether there is a complete overlap between contract and tort in this situation, with the court resting its

[33] Greenman v. Yuba Power Prods., Inc., 377 P.2d 897 (Ca. 1963); Escola v. Coca Cola Bottling Co., 150 P.2d 436, 440–4 (Ca. 1944); Henningsen v. Bloomfield Motors, Inc., 161 A.2d 69, 77–8, 80–4 (N.J. 1960).

[34] UCC § 2–318 (2005).

[35] Restatement (Second) of Torts § 402A.

[36] 662 N.E.2d 730 (N.Y. 1995). The court found that a plaintiff relying on the warranty of merchantability could succeed in a design defect claim by showing that the design did not meet consumer expectations, while a tort plaintiff would have to show that the design did not meet a risk-utility test. *Id.* at 737–9. In this case, the Ford Bronco at issue could pass the risk-utility test when all its possible uses (on road and off road) were taken into account, but might fail the consumer expectation test, because consumers would be expecting on-road safety (i.e., a car that would not roll over during on-road driving). *Id.* at 738–9. *See* Jay M. Feinman, *Implied*

conclusion of distinct causes of action on the idea that a "negligence-like risk/utility approach is foreign to the realm of contract law."[37]

The second boundary issue deals with the scope of protection and takes legal form in the economic loss rule. While some commentators see the economic loss rule as an arbitrary obstacle to recovery in tort,[38] others, including the Supreme Court, have analyzed the doctrine in terms of "the need to keep products liability and contract law in separate spheres."[39] The Court engaged in an extended analysis of the types of damage appropriate to contract and tort, distinguishing broadly between the economic realm and the realm of safety.[40] The interesting common feature in *Denny* and *East River Steamship Corp.* is the argument that contract and tort have distinctive characteristics, making them applicable to different spheres or realms, and that the overlap in fact situations should not cloud that difference.

The third boundary issue is the question of whether producers or sellers will be allowed to use contractual provisions to disclaim liability for damage caused by their products. Historically, courts held relatively fast to the rule that parties could not contract out of liability for their own negligence.[41] On the other hand, parties are traditionally thought to have wide latitude in fashioning remedies, including limiting the remedies for breach of warranty (when the warranty is not disclaimed). As will become clear in a moment, much of the discussion over how to think about products liability today centers on using contractual disclaimers, or what might be termed "freedom of tort." Again, a crucial theme here is that tort and contract seem to have functional differences that make the categories distinctive, despite the existence of factual overlap.

The question of whether producers would be able to contract out of liability was the chief animating feature of the backlash against the expansion of products liability that held the field from the early 1960s to the early 1980s. Beginning with the economic analysis of law and quickly spreading to tort theory from the doctrinalist tradition as well as more philosophical attitudes, the 1980s and early 1990s saw an onslaught of scholarship assailing

Warranty, Products Liability, and the Boundary Between Contract and Tort, 75 Wash. U. L.Q. 469 (1997).

37 Denny, 662 N.E.2d at 738.

38 *See, e.g.*, Linda J. Rusch, *Products Liability Trapped by History: Our Choice of Rules Rules Our Choices*, 76 Temp. L. Rev. 739 (2003).

39 East River Steamship Corp. v. Transamerica Delaval, Inc., 476 U.S. 858, 870–1 (1986).

40 *Id.* at 869–74.

41 N.Y. Cent. R.R. Co. v. Lockwood, 84 U.S. (17 Wall.) 357 (1873); Witt, *supra* note 3, at 51; Charles W. McCurdy, *The "Liberty of Contract" Regime in American Law, in* The State and Freedom of Contract, *supra* note 3, at 161.

the expansion of products liability.[42] Of interest to our present inquiry is that much of this scholarship was framed directly in terms of a preference for contract over tort. Richard Epstein's retrospective statement sums up the spirit of much of the critique:

> The rules of product liability law are like poorly designed all-purpose screwdrivers – ill-suited and far too complex and convoluted for the many tasks that they must perform. And the source of this complexity is the familiar one – the inveterate tendency to use complex collective, or tort, solutions in preference to contractual ones.[43]

Before jumping into the discussion of whether the contractual solutions for products liability are attractive, it pays to take note of the shifting valence of contract: At the early stages of the development of products liability, contract contained within it both expansion (since it was no-fault liability) and limitation (since it was based on privity) of liability. Doctrinal details of possible overlap similarly contain potential expansion or contraction. For example, the economic loss doctrine sees contract as a possible source of expanded liability, but almost always in the context of disclaimed responsibility. Finally, the neocontract approach to products liability is all about limitation of liability.[44]

One of the strange things that happened in the course of products liability development is that a rhetoric of strict separation of spheres eventually reemerged in the field that opened as a hybridization of contract and tort. If legal scholars in the early 1960s saw products liability as a regulatory field where contracts and torts mixed, by the late 1980s the voices calling for the separation of spheres had grown ascendant. And those calls for separation of spheres seemed to rely on precisely that element of classical legal thought that had once seemed discredited, that is, the idea that tort was regulatory while contract was private. The idea that contract is wholly private and not regulatory is more of a rhetorical motif than an argument in the neocontract literature on products liability (which is based primarily on arguments about efficiency), but it recurs with enough force and frequency to warrant notice.

42 Some of the leading pieces of scholarship included Richard A. Epstein, *Products Liability as an Insurance Market*, 14 J. Legal Stud. 645 (1985); Richard A. Epstein, *The Unintended Revolution in Product Liability Law*, 10 Cardozo L. Rev. 2193 (1989); George L. Priest, *The Current Insurance Crisis and Modern Tort Law*, 96 Yale L.J. 1521 (1987); Priest, *supra* note 32; Alan Schwartz, *Proposals for Products Liability Reform: A Theoretical Synthesis*, 97 Yale L.J. 353 (1988).

43 Richard A. Epstein, Simple Rules for a Complex World 213 (1995); *see also* Mark Geistfeld, *The Political Economy of Neocontractual Proposals for Products Liability Reform*, 72 Tex. L. Rev. 803, 803 (1994); Schwartz, *supra* note 42, at 413.

44 *See generally*, Peter W. Huber, Liability: The Legal Revolution and Its Consequences (1988); Geistfeld, *supra* note 43, at 803–04.

This is not the place for a full-blown evaluation of neocontractual positions on products liability.[45] My intention is to focus only on those aspects of the argument that may be illuminated by rethinking them through the prism of fault and its related framework of public regulation and private ordering. Recall that the modernizing maneuver of classical legal thought positioned tort as a field that ought to be governed by fault so as to limit regulatory encroachment to behavior that infringed on the rights of others. Recall also that it positioned contract as strict liability in order to highlight that the source of the obligations was the parties' agreement, and not any societally imposed standard of behavior. As we will see, elements of the neocontract or contractualist position on products liability replicate this maneuver.

The basis of the contractualist position on products liability is that purchasers and sellers will negotiate contracts that yield efficient levels of investment in safety and efficient levels of compensation for injuries caused by products. This much is considered nearly beyond argument if parties are perfectly informed,[46] and thus most of the discussion centers on the question of the extent of imperfect information and its effects.

However, even under assumptions of perfect information, certain limitations to the contractualist position should be apparent. The problem with the contractualist position in general is that the scope of interests considered when imagining a system through individual exchanges is too narrow to capture fully the social stakes of the system.

A concrete example is the issue of damages for pain and suffering – or more generally, nonpecuniary damages. As noted above, contractualists have usefully distinguished between two elements that informed buyers and sellers would contract for: investments in safety (in design and manufacture) on the one hand, and compensation for injury (or insurance) on the other.[47] Buyers would want optimal (not maximal) investments in safety, and they would want insurance (compensation by the seller) as long as sellers were better placed to insure than the buyer. As far as pecuniary damages are concerned, there is a happy coincidence, in that one element can act as a guarantee for the other: So long as sellers are responsible for damage caused by their products, they will invest optimally in safety (anything more or less would cost more than it would save), and buyers would be willing to pay sellers for insurance for pecuniary losses, just as they would be willing to insure these losses elsewhere. However, the happy coincidence ceases when nonpecuniary losses are

[45] For such an evaluation, *see* Steven P. Croley & Jon D. Hanson, *Rescuing the Revolution: The Revived Case for Enterprise Liability*, 91 Mich. L. Rev. 683 (1993).

[46] Geistfeld, *supra* note 43, at 811–12.

[47] *See id.* at 809–14; Schwartz, *supra* note 42, at 362–8.

taken into account. As contractualists have been quick to point out, most perfectly informed buyers would not be willing to insure against nonpecuniary loss, and thus would forgo insuring such loss by paying a premium to sellers.[48] However, this does not mean that buyers view nonpecuniary losses as unreal, or as nondamage. Thus, they actually would want sellers to take such losses into account when investing in safety precautions. But in the absence of liability for such losses, sellers have no incentive to do so (since hypothetically, it is the liability structure through which sellers optimize their investments in safety). Therefore, there is a flaw in the contract setting: The informed rational buyer will not want to buy insurance for pain-and-suffering damages but will want the seller to consider such damage when investing in safety. Unless the parties can rely on some obligation outside their bargaining, there is a built-in tension preventing the optimal arrangement between them.[49]

I began with the concrete example of nonpecuniary damages because it is an area that contractualists themselves have noted as a potential stumbling block to their view of products liability.[50] But the point is open to generalization. Direct and compensable injuries to buyers are actually only a subset of the damages that ensue from unsafe products. Family members, employers, friends, and others who count on daily interactions with people who are injured by products typically suffer losses as well. Collateral damages, although almost always losses that are well beyond the imagination of any compensation structure, are nonetheless part of the social cost of unsafe products.

Even more obviously than with regard to nonpecuniary losses to the injured party, these are losses no rational buyer would contract to insure. Yet they are no less real in terms of social cost, and thus they should ideally fit into the calculus of investment in safety. In fact, one way to make sure that sellers do not ignore these costs is to impose a safety calculus that is not based on what particular rational buyers would contract for, but rather on a much wider basis of the social costs of accidents.

Acknowledging this means admitting that the proper baseline for manufacturer–seller duties is socially imposed and does not have its source in a narrow vision of the parties' agreement. In other words, it implies a vision of contract where some of the duties are determined externally to the parties' interests, narrowly construed. Or, to put it in slightly different terms,

[48] *See* Schwartz, *supra* note 42, at 408–11.

[49] The parties will be able to bargain to a second-best solution, some compromise that takes into account the desire for more safety than the insurance component warrants, but there is no happy coincidence aligning their bargaining interests with a socially ideal level of investment in safety.

[50] *See* Schwartz, *supra* note 42, at 410.

it acknowledges that part of what parties to a contract are involved in is the generation of a public good – in this case the public good of safe products.[51] This idea should not sound farfetched. It is intuitive that contracting parties generate a public good in the shape of trust in the market, or the idea of safe contracting. Consider, for example, the difference between analyses of nondisclosure and misrepresentation: When dealing with silence regarding features of the transaction, we are willing to consider information as a possible entitlement whose allocation should be sensitive to efficiency concerns.[52] But the analysis of misrepresentation is fundamentally different, quintessentially fault based, and obviously reliant on sources outside the parties' own agreement – and yet, no less contractual for that. Nondisclosure can theoretically be overcome simply by asking the right question. Misrepresentation, however, threatens to unravel the basic background trust without which market transactions would be far more difficult.

Conclusion

The point of this analysis has obviously not been to suggest the optimal scheme for governing problems of products liability. Rather, the much more modest goal has been to show that whichever side of the tort-contract boundary is relevant for solving the problem, the parties cannot be conceived of as sole originators of the solution. To paraphrase Leon Green, the polity is a party to every contract.[53] Contract, like tort, is a mode of social regulation whose rules ought to serve social goals. The idea that the parties' own interests, narrowly construed and bargained over, could exhaust the relevant social goals was a pipe dream of late nineteenth-century legal science. Today, at times, it appears that contracts enthusiasts tap into the rhetoric of that dream – and its resurrection does more to confuse than illuminate current thinking. Recalling the roots of contract as a fault-based regime and the reasons that drove nineteenth-century theorists to characterize it as based on strict liability reminds us of the socially imposed duties that function as building blocks of contract. One may hope the reminder will serve as a mild corrective for some of the confusion.

[51] For an analogous argument in the context of medical malpractice, *see* Jennifer Arlen, *Contracting over Malpractice Liability* (Law & Economics Research Paper Series, Working Paper No. 08-12, 2008), *available at* http://ssrn.com/abstract=1105368.

[52] *See* Anthony T. Kronman, *Mistake, Disclosure, Information, and the Law of Contracts*, 7 J. Legal Stud. 1, 22–7 (1978).

[53] Leon Green, *Tort Law Public Law in Disguise* (pts. 1 & 2), 38 Tex. L. Rev. 1, 257 (1959–60). For the contract version of the claim, see Cohen, *supra* note 23.

EIGHT

The Many Faces of Fault in Contract Law: Or How to Do Economics Right, Without Really Trying

Richard A. Epstein

Modern law often assumes that a uniform cost-benefit formula is the proper way to determine fault in ordinary contract disputes. This chapter disputes that vision by defending the view that different standards of fault are appropriate in different contexts, in line with Roman law classifications adopted in *Coggs v. Bernard* in 1703. Typically, parties in gratuitous transactions should be held only to the standard of care that they bring to their own affairs. The higher objective standard of ordinary care governs in commercial transactions. That bifurcation leads to efficient searches. Persons who hold themselves out as merchants or experts warrant their ability to achieve uniform standards, while individuals who seek favors from their friends are incentivized to choose them carefully. The basic principle has surprising durability in dealing with agency, medical malpractice, occupier liability, guest statute, and frustration cases. Often the efficient analysis of fault is given only to those who do economics without really trying.

Introduction: From Fault to Negligence – and Back

The concept of fault plays a dominant role not only in contract but also in tort. Often "fault" is the equivalent of the term "negligence." Commonly, its definition is said to track the Hand formula, which compares the burden of precaution (B) with the expected losses, equal to the probability of loss (P) multiplied by the expected severity of the loss (L).[1] Hand's earlier discussion of custom in *The T.J. Hooper*[2] is often ignored.[3]

My thanks to Omri Ben-Shahar and Ariel Porat for their insightful comments on an earlier draft of this paper, to the members of the UCLA Law and Economics Workshop, and to Jack O. Snyder, University of Chicago Law School, Class of 2010 for his excellent research assistance.

1 *See* United States v. Carroll Towing, 159 F.2d 169, 173 (2d Cir. 1947).

2 60 F.2d 737 (2d Cir. 1932).

3 *See* Richard A. Posner, *A Theory of Negligence*, 1 J. Legal Stud. 29 (1972). For my rejection of the Hand formula, *see* Richard A. Epstein, *A Theory of Strict Liability*, 2 J. Legal Stud. 151, 155–60 (1973).

In this chapter, I reject on both normative and positive grounds the claim that the Hand formula exhausts the idea of fault in contract law. Sometimes the two definitions overlap. But in the thesaurus,[4] "fault" and "negligence" fall into separate domains without overlap. The list of synonyms for fault includes "error," "weakness," "responsibility," "liability," and "burden." "Negligence" for its part connotes "fault," in ways that imply some want of care: "carelessness," "inattention," "laxity," "slackness," and "disregard."

These ordinary usages of fault carry over into the law of contract. The key question is in what sense and why. The task is difficult because the huge class of enforceable agreements is highly heterogeneous. The standard of care for the nondelivery of goods need not track the standard of care for complex partnership transactions. Second, the level of variation increases if certain tort-like cases are governed by contract, most notably those involving the destruction or loss of property arising out of a consensual transaction. Reserve the tort law for harms that occur between strangers, and the variation in the use of fault in contract law will increase.

In order to work out the arrangements between these various crosscurrents, I proceed as follows. I argue that as a first principle, this tort-contract line should be placed between (1) physical injuries that arise between neighbors and strangers; and (2) physical injuries that arise between parties who are bound together by a prior consensual arrangement that could, in principle, allocate the risk of loss between the parties. Part I sketches out the reasons, based on the comparison of sporting events with sharp boundary lines, why negligence should tend to be the odd man out, with strict liability and intentional harms doing the bulk of the work in both stranger and consensual arrangement cases. Part II argues that physical harms that arise in the course of consensual arrangements should be treated under a contract law framework. It also explains why we rightly expect a greater variation in the use of fault in the consensual cases than we do in the neighbor and stranger cases. Part III then turns to the Achilles' heel of the common law: the proper treatment of gratuitous transactions, first for bailments and agency relationships, and then, briefly, in medical malpractice, occupier liability, and guest statute contexts. Throughout this section, I focus a great deal on Roman law conceptions of fault, identifying how modern courts have made use of them, and suggesting that even greater use would have been beneficial, resulting in a lot less confusion over what should be the proper standard of fault. Finally, Part IV examines the influence of the seminal case of *Coggs v. Bernard*[5] in traditional frustration cases and compares

[4] Namely, the thesaurus feature on Microsoft Word.

[5] (1703) 2 Ld. Raym. 909, 92 Eng. Rep. 107 (Q.B.).

the approach that allows for multiple standards of fault with the modern tendency to collapse all questions on the standard of care into a cost-benefit formula, concluding that the earlier approach is superior to the modern one – even on economic grounds.

I. Tort Law

Historically, tort law deals chiefly with trespass and nuisance, fire, animals (including cattle trespass),[6] and liability under the rule of *Rylands v. Fletcher*.[7] In these cases, I have long defended the view that a strict liability system is simpler and more effective than a negligence rule, and will not repeat that defense here, except to say that it is easier to judge the outcome after the fact than it is to determine care levels before the fact.[8]

Historically, however, the bifurcation between stranger and consensual cases was cast aside in *Vaughan v. Menlove*,[9] which is generally credited with introducing the objective standard of care in negligence cases. Most suggestively, the defendant in *Vaughan* drew on the law of bailments[10] – cases where one party delivers a chattel with a promise for its return at some future date – for inspiration, even though the unavoidable division of control in bailment cases makes them a poor analogy for disputes between neighbors.

In *Vaughan*, the defendant built a hayrick near the plaintiff's land. Although often warned that internal fermentation could lead it to burst into flames, he did nothing to correct the situation, noting that since he had insurance, "he would chance it."[11] The decision speaks at times of the defendant's "neglect," "gross negligence," and want of "ordinary prudence."[12] The court declined, however, to let liability turn on whether the defendant "had acted honestly and bona fide to the best of his own judgment," which to all appearances he had not, by insisting on an objective standard.[13]

[6] *See generally* Restatement (Second) of Torts §§ 157–64 (1965) (trespass to land); *id.* §§ 504–05 (livestock); *id.* §§ 506–18 (animals other than livestock); *id.* § 520 ("Abnormally Dangerous Activities"); *id.* §§ 821A–840E (nuisance). For a defense of the negligence approach in animal cases, *see* Glanville L. Williams, Liability for Animals (1939).

[7] (1868) 3 L.R.E. & I. App. 330 (H.L.), *aff'g* Fletcher v. Rylands, (1866) 1 L.R. Exch. 265.

[8] *See* Epstein, *supra* note 3.

[9] (1837) 3 Bing. (N.C.) 468, 132 Eng. Rep. 490 (C.P.).

[10] *Id.* at 493.

[11] *Id.* at 491.

[12] *Id.* at 493.

[13] *Id.* The accurate (and economic) definition of good faith requires a defendant to treat the potential loss of the plaintiff as having equal weight to his own. For its application in relation to the duty to settle insurance claims within policy limits, *see* Merritt v. Reserve Insurance Co., 110 Cal. Rptr. 511 (Ct. App. 1973).

Under the Roman law of bailments, the standard of care for loss of or damage to goods varies from strict liability to good faith.[14] In *Vaughan*, ironically, any conscientious application of the law of bailments would have imposed onerous duties on the defendant precisely because he gained all of the benefit (such as it was) from storing hay in so precarious a position.[15] The question is what more can we learn from the law of bailments?

II. Moving the Tort-Contract Boundary: In Praise of Heterogeneity

Our point of departure is this simple proposition: Any restriction of the domain of tort necessarily expands the domain of contract. In the Anglo-American system, the doctrine of consideration has hampered the growth of contract law. That shortfall, moreover, is corrected only in part by the principle of detrimental reliance in Section 90 of the Second Restatement of Contracts.[16] Most gratuitous transactions thus revert by default into tort law. This netherworld covers gratuitous bailments, gratuitous licenses to enter the property of another, gratuitous principal-agent relationships, and the gratuitous provision of medical services.

When the modern law switches these problem areas from contract to tort, it upsets the overall structure of both areas, and thus increases the difficulty in applying the elusive fault principle. Intuitively, gratuitous transactions are not fertile ground for the strict liability rules that dominate stranger cases. Far from seeking to make the plaintiff bear the cost of an activity from which the defendant obtains all the gain, now the plaintiff seeks to hold liable a defendant who has provided her with a service at no charge. Pulling these cases out of tort law makes it easier to adopt a uniform tort theory, be it strict liability or objective negligence. In all cases, the concern is with having a defendant "keep off" the plaintiff.

Keeping parties separate is usually not the object of cooperative ventures. No longer must the law neutralize a defendant's efforts to internalize gain and externalize losses. Instead, the dominant inquiry asks what ex ante rule maximizes the joint welfare of the parties to the transaction. So stating the question, it becomes instantly clear that the huge variety of contractual transactions resists the adoption of any uniform standard of liability or damages. One-size-fits-all is never the correct approach in a world of heterogeneous

[14] *See* discussion *infra* Section III.A.

[15] *See* Vaughan v. Menlove, (1837) 3 Bing. (N.C.) 468, 475, 132 Eng. Rep. 490, 493 (C.P.) (Tindal, C.J.).

[16] Restatement (Second) of Contracts § 90 (1981).

transactions. How, then, does the case law deal with the tort-contract interface?

III. Gratuitous Transactions: Bailment and Agency

A. Coggs v. Bernard

Historically, the most important treatment of gratuitous transactions is *Coggs v. Bernard*, which lies at the crossroads of Roman and English law.[17] *Coggs* arose out of the following prosaic circumstances. The plaintiff owned a number of casks of brandy, which the defendant had moved from one place to another. During the move, the casks split open, and much of the brandy was lost. The plaintiff sued to recover for his losses, in what could be easily seen as a tort action for harm caused by the defendant. The defendant defended on the grounds that the plaintiff had not alleged either that the defendant was a common porter or that he had received any reward or consideration from the plaintiff for his work.

Both elements of the defense have their purpose. Common porters always hold themselves out by making the implicit representation that they will conduct themselves in accordance with industry standards. To use the old but accurate Roman expression, their standard of care was *culpa levis in abstracto*, where the "abstracto" signaled an objective standard of care that allowed for no variation among defendants within the designated class.[18] There is a good information-cost explanation for this rule. The usual business cases involve persons who handle a large volume of traffic from customers with whom they have no prior contact. Employing a subjective standard would force individual customers to figure out the level of care of which this particular defendant is capable, a tricky task in the absence of any past relationship. In contrast, the use of an abstract, or objective, standard encourages a potential merchant to withdraw from the field if he cannot meet that objective standard. Minimizing search costs enhances the security of transactions.

In contrast, *culpalevis in concreto* refers to the particular or "concrete" circumstances of each case, and thus invites use of a subjective standard. The Roman definition here speaks of *"talem igitur diligentiam praestare debet, qualem in suis rebus adhibere solet,"* or "the defendant ought furnish only that

[17] (1703) 2 Ld. Raym. 909, 92 Eng. Rep. 107 (Q.B.). *Coggs* explicitly overrules Southcot v. Bennet, (1601) Cro. Eliz. 815, 78 Eng. Rep. 1041 (Q.B.), which held the gratuitous bailee to a high objective standard of care.

[18] Literally "slight negligence by an objective standard," which means that slight negligence is sufficient to create liability.

standard of care that he brings to his own affairs."[19] That subjective standard rightly applied under Roman law, as Chief Justice Holt observed,[20] where a property owner has asked a favor of a friend. The friend is not normally in business, and this is known to the owner. Both reasons for the objective standard drop out of the picture. Asking the defendant to use the same level of care that he does in his own affairs imposes a standard that is always attainable. In these informal transactions, the owner of the brandy, faced with this sliding standard of care, protects himself by selecting the right friends to do the work.[21]

Chief Justice Holt, moreover, did not stop there. Rather, he borrowed wholesale the Roman approach to bailments. He finessed the defendant's objection based on consideration as follows: "[T]he owner's trusting him with the goods is a sufficient consideration to oblige him to a careful management. Indeed if the agreement had been executory, to carry these brandies from the one place to the other such a day, the defendant had not been bound to carry them."[22] His formulation closely tracks Roman law. To be sure, these arrangements involve a gift of services, not a gift of goods. But the two situations follow the same general rule, which refuses any executory enforcement of a gift promise, while recognizing that the gift is complete on delivery.

Denying executory enforcement does not, however, fill out all the incidents of this arrangement. What is the proper standard of care if the goods are damaged, destroyed, or stolen while in the hands of the bailee? That problem never arises with the outright gift of goods or services, where the risk of loss passes to the new owner under the maxim *res perit domino*, literally, the thing perishes for the owner, who thus bears the risk of loss. The Romans applied that solution to the gratuitous contract of *mutuum* – a transfer of fungible goods for consumption, where the obligation is the return of goods of like *kind* sometime in the future.[23] But bailed goods must be returned, so that the loss cannot be easily assigned to one party or the other.

In *Coggs*, Chief Justice Holt held the standard of ordinary care applied, deviating from the Roman principles he had incorporated into English law. To see Holt's error requires understanding the six different kinds of bailments developed in Roman law.[24] The first of these is *depositum*, the gratuitous

[19] *See* Dig. 10.2.25.16 (Paulus, Ad Edictum 23).

[20] *See Coggs*, 92 Eng. Rep. at 110–11.

[21] *Id.*

[22] *Id.* at 113.

[23] On *mutuum* generally, *see* Barry Nicholas, An Introduction to Roman Law 167 n. 4, 169–70 (1962).

[24] For a general discussion of the rules of bailment, *see* W.W. Buckland, A Text-Book of Roman Law: From Augustus to Justinian (Peter Stein, ed., 3d ed. 1963) 459–62 (discussing *mutuum*),

bailment for safekeeping – a transaction done for the benefit of the bailor. The standard of care reflects the bailee's favor, by making bad faith or gross neglect the standard of liability. The bailor thus takes the risk that the chosen bailee will not meet some objective standard of care – yet another deviation from the Hand formula, $B = PL$. Nor is the bad-faith/gross-negligence test difficult to administer for stored goods, because the rule does not typically turn on a psychological examination of the defendant's capabilities, but is governed by a general nondiscrimination principle: Does the defendant bring the same level of care to the plaintiff's goods as he brings to his own? If the plaintiff's goods are stored together with the defendant's possessions, the risk of loss falls on the plaintiff. If not, and less care is taken, the risk falls on the bailee. If the parties want a different standard, they can stipulate expressly.

Now suppose the defendant agreed to manage, not just to store, the bailed goods gratuitously. Holt referred to the Roman contract of limited agency, called *mandatum*, which follows the risk-allocation rule for gratuitous bailments. The principal cannot demand executory enforcement of the contract, which allows the promisor to back out of the job, at least so long as he gives the owner an opportunity to set up alternative arrangements, including some that could require payment for the same services. But once the agent begins to manage goods, the work done is governed by the same good-faith standards in *Coggs*. In this context, the simple negligence standard to which both Chief Justice Holt and Justice Gould gravitate does not fit the Roman pattern, which predicates liability on gross neglect. Yet Holt appears to set the standard far higher than simple negligence, noting that for the bailee to escape he would have to show the wrongful act of a third party, as if, say, a stranger punctured a hole in the casks.[25]

Coggs is at the opposite pole from the converse situation of *commodatum*, or loan for use, where goods are lent for the benefit of the bailee. Commodatum typically requires a higher level of care, even if the bailor knows of the defendant's personal foibles and shortfalls. Accept goods for your own advantage, and you are usually duty bound to return them unharmed. But here, too, fault in contract law does not collapse into the Hand formula. Rather, as in the fire cases, strict liability applies except when the destruction of the goods is attributable to acts of God – huge storms and the like – or to violent actions by third persons, to which Holt alluded.[26]

464–7 (discussing *depositum*), 467–70 (discussing *commodatum*), 470–8 (discussing *pignus*, or pledge), 494–504 (discussing *locatio*, or lease), and 512–18 (discussing *mandatum*).

[25] Coggs v. Bernard, (1703) 2 Ld. Raym. 909, 919, 92 Eng. Rep. 107, 113 (Q.B.).

[26] *Id.* ("As if a drunken man had come by in the streets, and had pierced the cask of brandy.")

The rule can be further refined to reimpose liability on the bailee who has some antecedent awareness of the risk, which would allow him to move the bailed goods to a safer location. But the plaintiff's loss is not compensable if the same natural or human events would have destroyed the goods if they had remained in the hands of its original owner. Incremental, not total, risk determines liability.

Last are the commercial cases undertaken for the mutual benefit of both parties. The term "benefit" covers all forms of tangible gain, but excludes the warm glow that animates most gratuitous transactions. These transactions include the simple pawn (*vadium*), where the goods stand as security for an unpaid loan; the contract of hire; or bailments where the bailee is paid a fee to manage or operate the thing bailed. These paid variations of the simple deposit or mandate call for a standard of ordinary care given the prospect of mutual gain. But even this deviates from a strict cost-benefit approach of the Hand formula. Now, ordinary care has a closer affinity to the customary standard of care normally observed in a given trade or business.

To be sure, this ordinary-care standard and the Hand formula both seek to identify efficient levels of precaution by the parties. But the Hand formula applies on a case-by-case basis. Its use of costly and unreliable expert evidence has two negative consequences. First, it gives no information about the appropriate standard in advance. Second, it increases the cost of litigation after the fact because of the wide variation in estimates that rival experts can easily gin up. The ordinary-care standard is hardly perfect, but it supplies better information at both stages. The key point, therefore, is that this standard does not allow a plaintiff to show, as in *The T.J. Hooper*,[27] some supposed gap between an established industry custom and the efficient standard of care. No court could, in the older view, reject custom because of its own independent cost-benefit analysis. That custom yields only to a legislative override, which takes place solely because statutes outrank custom in the legal hierarchy.[28] The endless number of misguided lawsuits that rest on frontal assaults on custom is testimony to the wisdom of the earlier position.[29]

[27] 60 F.2d 737 (2d Cir. 1932), *aff'g* 53 F.2d 107 (S.D.N.Y. 1931). For a showing of how Hand mangled the evidence on custom, *see* Richard A. Epstein, *The Path to* The T.J. Hooper: *The Theory and History of Custom in the Law of Tort*, 21 J. Legal Stud. 1 (1992).

[28] For the most influential statement, *see* Ezra Ripley Thayer, *Public Wrong and Private Action*, 27 Harv. L. Rev. 317, 321–3 (1914).

[29] *See, e.g.*, Barker v. Lull Engineering Co., 573 P.2d 443 (Cal. 1978) (announcing a two-part test of product defect that exposed the manufacturer of its High-Life Loader to the misconduct of both its purchaser and driver).

B. Thorne v. Deas

The errors in the Anglo-American law governing gratuitous transactions have also led to other errors. In *Thorne v. Deas*,[30] the plaintiff and defendant were co-owners of a ship of which the plaintiff was the captain. The defendant had promised the plaintiff before he set sail that he, the defendant, would insure the ship, which he failed to do. The plaintiff then sued him for his share of the loss when the ship was wrecked at sea. Chancellor Kent held that *Coggs* did not govern because no specific goods had been bailed.[31] The transaction was, under the Roman classification, mandatum: a simple mandate. Accordingly, in the absence of consideration, the defendant could not be sued for gross neglect in the absence of misfeasance, of which there was none since he had just forgotten to take out the insurance.

Unfortunately, Chancellor Kent misapplies the misfeasance-nonfeasance distinction. The two parties in *Thorne* were not strangers, to whom the no-duty-to-rescue rule applied. They were co-owners.[32] In terms of their ordinary business expectations, the total failure to act is a greater breach than a good-faith effort to fill out forms that goes awry (for which a defense might actually be available). Calling the latter conduct a misfeasance cannot paper over the difference between entering the wrong information on an insurance form and the use of force, the setting of traps, or the accumulation of dangerous substances, to the detriment of a stranger. So long as notice must be given to back out of gratuitous transactions, the defendant should be liable for his unexcused neglect, in the absence of any act of God or third party.

C. Siegel v. Spear *and* Comfort v. McGorkle

Thorne, in turn, led to further wrong turns in the road. In *Siegel v. Spear & Co.*,[33] the plaintiff purchased furniture from the defendant subject to a mortgage to secure the price. The plaintiff made a collateral promise not to remove the furniture from his apartment until the mortgage had been paid off. Subsequently, he approached the defendant's credit officer for help while he was away during the summer months. A deal was struck that the furniture would be moved into the defendant's warehouse. Since it was not insured, the defendant's credit officer offered free of charge to insure the goods while in

[30] 4 Johns 84 (N.Y. Sup. Ct. 1809).
[31] *Id.* at 99.
[32] *Id.* at 84.
[33] 138 N.E. 414 (N.Y. 1923).

storage, billing the plaintiff for the fees. He failed to do so, and an action was allowed when the goods were destroyed.

The court distinguished *Thorne v. Deas* on the ground that in *Siegel* the promise to insure was incident to the bailment, whereas in *Thorne* it was a "naked" promise not tethered to any property transaction.[34] The court extended *Coggs* to cover a collateral promise that went beyond the care of the thing – a cross between bailment and mandate. But it nonetheless rejected the Roman view of gratuitous agency, or mandate, unrelated to the delivery of the property. A decade later, in *Comfort v. McCorkle*,[35] the court duly distinguished *Siegel* by denying recovery where the defendant had simply promised to process the plaintiff's proof of loss in a timely manner with the insurance carrier, wholly unrelated to any bailment. The Roman solution is simpler, more elegant, and more coherent.

D. *Medical Malpractice, Occupier's Liability, and Guest Statutes*

Coggs v. Bernard and the Roman categories of fault remain influential outside the context of bailment and agency. Three areas deserve some brief mention: medical malpractice, liability of owners and occupiers to persons lawfully on their premises, and liability of automobile drivers to their guests.

In medical malpractice cases, the patient who receives charitable care has received a gift of expensive services. No payment covers a premium for liability insurance, so the standard of ordinary negligence is out. Some cases against hospitals and physicians could turn on gross neglect, but liability would be infrequent. Stranger cases were still judged by a strict liability rule.[36]

The traditional law of owner and occupier liability sets different standards of care for licensors – really, owners of residential premises – and invitors – owners of commercial premises.[37] The ordinary houseguest does expect safer conditions than the owner or occupier creates for himself and his family, so liability arises when an owner exposes a guest to latent dangerous conditions of which they have knowledge and the guest does not. As with bailments, the guest's best defense lies in the selection of those persons to visit. Businesses take all comers and thus are subject to the same objective standards used for

[34] *Id.* at 415.

[35] 268 N.Y.S. 192 (N.Y. Sup. Ct. 1933).

[36] Just this distinction is taken in Powers v. Massachusetts Homeopathic Hospital, 109 F. 294, 304–05 (1st Cir. 1901).

[37] For an articulation of the old distinction, *see* Robert Addie & Sons (Collieries), Ltd. v. Dumbreck, [1929] A.C. 358 (H.L.) (appeal taken from Scot.) (U.K.). For the American reception, *see* Restatement (Second) of Torts § 342 (1965).

warehousemen in bailment cases. These categories have tended to give way, by both statute and common law decision, to a uniform reasonable care standard. But that false generalization hardly counts as an overall improvement. *Rowland v. Christian*[38] is known for Justice Peters's assault on the traditional classification. Yet at the end of the day, the facts of *Rowland* strikingly confirm the older rule: The plaintiff recovered for harm caused by a latent defect in a bathroom fixture known to the defendant but not the plaintiff. So long as an owner risks injury from any latent defect, the entrant is still protected by a nondiscrimination principle.[39] He is exposed only to those risks that the occupier is exposed to.

Guest statutes also adopted distinctive rules for gratuitous transactions. Building on *Coggs*,[40] they imposed a higher standard on the driver of an automobile who chauffeurs strangers for a fee than one who drives guest passengers as a friend. The modern cases reject the old distinctions, sometimes on equal protection grounds.[41] This modern position reduces the need to make distinctions between cases, and thereby spares courts such marginal determinations as whether the passenger who splits the cost of gasoline should be regarded as a guest or as a commercial customer. But since such marginal cases seem few, it is doubtful that the "reasonable care under the circumstances" test marks any improvement.

IV. Frustration and Impossibility

Coggs also influenced *Taylor v. Caldwell*,[42] the major precedent on frustration and impossibility. *Taylor* arose out of the destruction of the Surrey Gardens Concert Hall by fire "without the fault of either party,"[43] between the time of the license agreement and the first of four scheduled performances. Addressing impossibility, Justice Blackburn cited *Coggs* for the proposition that a bailee under a contract of commodatum is excused from liability if the thing perishes because of an act of God or a third party.[44] Clearly, any excuse that works for a party held to the highest standard of care will work for bailees in the other five categories – where the standard of care is less onerous. In

38 443 P.2d 561 (Cal. 1968) (en banc).

39 *See* 443 P.2d at 569 (Burke, J., dissenting).

40 *See* Massaletti v. Fitzroy, 118 N.E. 168 (Mass. 1917), *defended in* Andrew Kull, Comment, *The Common Law Basis of Automobile Guest Statutes*, 43 U. Chi. L. Rev. 798 (1976).

41 *See, e.g.*, Brown v. Merlo, 506 P.2d 212 (Cal. 1973) (en banc). Earlier challenges at the federal level had been rebuffed in Silver v. Silver, 280 U.S. 117 (1929).

42 *See* Taylor v. Caldwell, (1863) 3 B. & S. 826, 122 Eng. Rep. 309 (Q.B.).

43 *Id.* at 312.

44 *See id.* at 314.

Blackburn's hands, this proposition lays the foundation for the general principle of impossibility, which excuses the building owner from providing his facility under its licensing arrangement with the plaintiff.

The analogy to bailments works because this license for use created divided interests in the property. But this license differs from a bailment in one key particular: there was no separation of possession and ownership when the fire occurred. The analysis thus turns to the role of "fault" in the case. Blackburn starts with the general rule that liability in contract is strict, so that "the contractor must perform it or pay damages for not doing it, although in consequence of [an] unforeseen accident, the performance of his contract has become unexpectedly burthensome or even impossible."[45] That overbroad proposition does not account for the different standards of care found in the bailment cases. Sensibly enough, Blackburn therefore subjects his initial proposition to two further qualifications. The first, based in part on *Coggs*, subjects this absolute duty to an express or implied condition about the continued existence of some particular thing that lies at the foundation of the agreement – in this case, the music hall.

Blackburn then distinguishes prior cases where a promisor promises to marry or to paint a picture, only to die before he has any chance to perform. The long-established rule excused the executor from paying damages,[46] here on the sensible ground that contractual enforcement is not needed to provide incentives to perform. No promisor kills himself to escape performing a contract. In the domain of sudden death through accident or misfortune, why go through the difficult exercise of calculating damages when it is cheaper to just call the whole arrangement off?

But what of Blackburn's qualification that this excuse in the personal service contracts is not available to a defendant who was previously at fault?[47] Nothing, really. Strikingly, none of these frustration cases takes the fault question seriously. Rather, the absence of fault is largely presumed, and rightly so. Everyone has strong incentives to take care of his own life. No one kills himself to escape a winning contract (which most contracts are). In effect, each person's life offers a huge performance bond to his trading partner, so that contractual liability is at best an afterthought. The total absence of moral hazard rightly pushes the entire "fault" question into the background. In short, it is better to let the whole matter lie where it is than to try to use damage remedies to fine-tune behavior.

[45] *Id.* at 312.

[46] *See id.* at 313 (citing Hyde v. Dean and Canons of Windsor, (1597) Cro. Eliz. 552, 78 Eng. Rep. 798 (Q.B.)).

[47] *See id.* at 314.

A key variation on *Taylor* arises when the thing destroyed is not owned by either party, as in the sequel to *Taylor*, *Krell v. Henry*.[48] *Krell* involved a license to use the windows in rooms overlooking Pall Mall to watch the coronation procession for Edward VII, which was suddenly canceled when he became ill. The lease did not mention the coronation, but its inflated price was only intelligible against this public backdrop. The Court of Appeal held that the doctrine of impossibility extended to the destruction of something external to both parties, where it is even *stronger* than in *Taylor*, given the total absence of moral hazard since neither party to the lease could have influenced the cancellation of the coronation. Letting the losses lie where they fall therefore makes sense in a rough justice sort of way, given that legal intervention is of little value in purely distributional disputes.

Yet note the uneasiness. Lord Justice Vaughan Williams desperately tried to distinguish Krell's letting of the rooms from the hiring of a cab to take a rider from London to Epsom to watch the derby, at a suitably enhanced rate of ten pounds.[49] But he never explains why the unstated derby should not be a precondition for the deal when the unstated coronation is. To be sure, the rooms let were uniquely suited to the coronation while the cab was, well, just a cab. But so what, when neither party had anything to do with the cancellation of either event? Again, why not let the losses lie where they fall? Vaughan Williams's willingness to award the cabman his fee (presumably, less expenses forgone) likely stems from class-based distributional concerns not found in a fancy lease between members of the privileged classes. Yet the one substantive difference actually cuts the other way. The coronation was never rescheduled, so the old arrangement could not be carried over to a new date. But the hypothetical Epsom Derby would, in all likelihood, have been rescheduled (like a World Series game), which meant that the cab could fetch a premium rate the next time around, if not from this customer, then from someone else. There is no reason to require what is in effect double payment.

Conclusion

One central mission of contract law is to allocate the risk for the loss or destruction of property. Seeking a single optimal rule that covers the full range of circumstances is a hopeless task, which is why the ambiguity in the term "fault" serves a useful function by hinting broadly at the diversity of circumstances. Respecting diverse circumstances does not, however, commit us

[48] [1903] 2 K.B. 740.

[49] *Id.* at 750–1.

to a hopelessly ad hoc inquiry. Rather, it invites an intelligent categorization of cases, each with its own applicable standard of care. Historically, the highly influential classification scheme for bailments set out in *Coggs v. Bernard* provides an imperfect guide as to how that is done. At no point, however, does that synthesis opt for the cost-benefit rule of the Hand formula, with its high decision costs and inconsistent results. Of course, the common law should minimize the risk of loss from certain transactions.

That said, the Hand formula cannot live up to its grand aspirations. More concrete situational standards of the Roman law do far better when tested against modern conceptions of social welfare. With professionals, the uniform standard of care reduces search costs and impose liability on those who remain in business because they know they can reach a high standard of care. With casual transactions, the nondiscrimination principle protects the volunteer while allowing his opposite number to select friends in whom he has confidence. These rules thus induce an efficient level of search for the right trading partner. How ironic that finding the efficient standard of fault is a task best left to those who do economics without really trying.

NINE

The Productive Tension Between Official and Unofficial Stories of Fault in Contract Law

Martha M. Ertman

Most people separate concepts of contract and fault. But that separation is only the official story. An equally true, quieter, and unofficial story traces the path of fault slipping in and out of contract doctrines such as willful breach. While some contract theorists argue for a simple, clear story of strict liability, others discuss the richness that the unofficial story brings to contract law by blurring boundaries between contract and tort, and between private and public realms. This chapter refuses to choose between these alternatives, arguing instead that the official and unofficial stories complement one another, reflecting a productive tension that helps contract law provide both certainty and, when necessary, equity-driven justice.

It is hard to invoke the concepts of "contract" and "fault" in the same sentence, unless you want to echo Justice Holmes's assertion that "the wicked contract-breaker should pay no more in damages than the innocent and the pure in heart."[1] But that separation of contract and fault is only the official story. An equally true, but quieter, and unofficial story complements the official one. The unofficial story traces the path of fault slipping into contract law through doctrines such as willful breach. Some contract theorists respond to the seeming tension between official and unofficial stories by seeking to impose discipline on their discipline, policing the message to convey a simple, loud, and clear story of strict liability. Others would publicize the richness that the unofficial story brings to contract law, despite, or perhaps because of, the fact that it blurs boundaries between contract and tort, and between private

Thanks to Karen Lash, Jana Singer, Michael Van Alstine, and the University of Maryland faculty workshop for helpful comments on earlier drafts of this chapter; to Gabriel Steel for able research assistance; and to the University of Maryland and Thurgood Marshall Law Library for research support. The University of Maryland Summer Research Fund provided generous financial support.

[1] Oliver Wendell Holmes, The Common Law 236 (Mark de Wolfe Howe, ed., 1963) (1881).

and public realms.[2] This chapter, like much of this volume, tends toward the latter approach. But rather than defend fault in contractual terms,[3] it argues that the official and unofficial stories operate in tension to facilitate ex ante planning and, when necessary, look backward at reasons for breach to reach a just result.[4] The official story of contract law expresses a general rule of strict liability furthering that planning, tempered by considering fault in exceptional circumstances. Thus framed, fault's occasional appearances in contract law reflect a common pattern in which legal doctrine first articulates a general rule, then enumerates one or more exceptions.

The analysis here proceeds along doctrinal and theoretical lines. First, it identifies the common pattern where contract doctrine articulates a general rule, then one or more exceptions in contract formation, enforceability, breach, and damages. Often, the general rule facilitates planning by providing certainty, while the exception allows courts to look backward at equitable considerations like fault and fairness. In each instance, the official and unofficial stories coexist, continually in tension, to prevent the exception from swallowing up the general rule. This tension allows courts to reach coherent and justified results most of the time. In other words, fault, properly constrained, facilitates rather than undermines contract law.

Second, this chapter makes a normative argument defending the coexistence of the fault and no-fault stories. Contract theory itself tolerates coexisting, disparate views. One classical liberal approach, vastly simplified, tells a story about autonomy in which parties self-regulate through words on the page, which courts passively enforce to produce certainty and efficiency.[5] This approach might narrowly construe the duty of good faith, and enforce the terms of a preprinted cruise-ship ticket.[6] A competing theory tells a realist

[2] *See, e.g.*, Second Restatement of Contracts ch. 16, introductory note (1981). *Compare* Richard A. Posner, Economic Analysis of Law 117–20 (4th ed. 1992), *with* George M. Cohen, *The Fault Lines in Contract Damages*, 80 Va. L. Rev. 1225 (1994), and Daniel S. Markovits, *Contract and Collaboration*, 113 Yale L. J. 1417 (2004). Alternatively, fault might indirectly enter contract law through the law of restitution by providing remedy for restitutionary disgorgement when a party breaches deliberately, profits from the breach, and contract damages are inadequate. Restatement (Third) of Restitution and Unjust Enrichment § 39 (Tentative Draft No. 4, 2005).

[3] *See, e.g.*, Steve Thiel & Peter Siegelman, Fault in American Contract Law; and Oren Bar-Gill & Omri Ben-Shahar, Fault in American Contract Law.

[4] Other productive tensions operate in contract law as well as other doctrinal areas, such as law/equity, rules/standards, autonomy/fairness, and freedom/equality. While this chapter focuses on the fault/no-fault tension within contracts doctrine, one could also view this tension as a subset of the larger dichotomies between law and equity or rules and standards.

[5] *See, e.g.*, Charles Fried, Contract as Promise (1981); Richard A. Epstein, *Unconscionability: A Critical Reappraisal*, 18 J.L. & Econ. 293 (1975).

[6] *See, e.g.*, Kham & Nate's Shoes No. 2, Inc. v. First Bank of Whiting, 908 F.2d 1351 (7th Cir. 1990); Carnival Cruise Lines, Inc. v. Shute, 499 U.S. 585 (1991).

story of much greater state involvement in contract law, as when courts fill gaps in contracts or refuse to enforce terms on unconscionability grounds.[7] Still other views seek to provide a general theory of contract, yet none, alone, explains the range of state and party interests in contract law.[8] One theory might apply best in large transactions between sophisticated parties, while another justifies a good result in consumer, employment, or premarital contracts. The range of options helps courts target the pendulum between certainty and fairness as appropriate. Contract theory and doctrine are strengthened, rather than weakened, by the dualism.

This chapter mirrors that plurality. If contractual purists object to fault as an incursion of a tort-based principle into contract law, the discussion here offers a dual defense of that incursion. First, it concedes the bifurcation of tort and contract, and then it defends the occasional leakage of tort into contract through fault. The diagram below illustrates the argument.

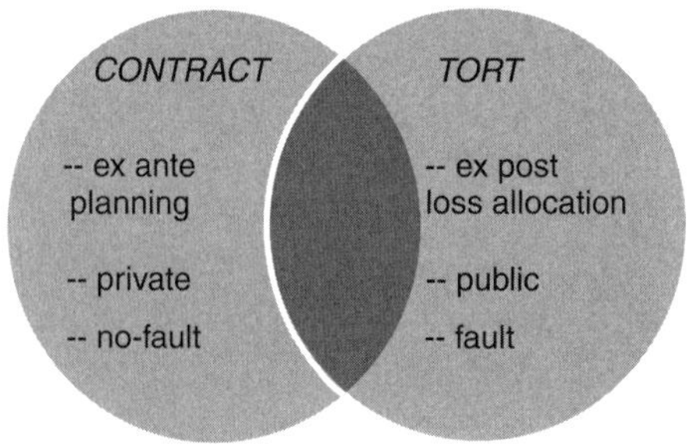

If tort and contract were two circles in a Venn diagram, we could conceive of the overlapping area as a semipermeable membrane that allows a bit of ex post evaluations fault to leak out of tort and into contract, and also some ex ante strict liability rules to leak from contract into tort. While most of each circle remains separate, this small crossover reflects the complementarity of contract and tort through their tandem operation.

This chapter develps this argument in three parts. First, it describes how contract doctrine tells both the official and unofficial story of contract law through a system of general rules complemented by exceptions. Fault, in this view, no more undermines the integrity of contract theory or doctrine than

[7] Morris R. Cohen, *The Basis of Contract*, 4 Harv. L. Rev. 553 (1933); Melvin Aron Eisenberg, *The Bargain Principle and Its Limits*, 95 Harv. L. Rev. 741 (1982); Lowden v. T-Mobile USA, Inc., 512 F.3d 1213 (9th Cir. 2008).

[8] Brian H. Bix, *Contract Rights and Remedies, and the Divergence Between Law and Morality*, 21 Ratio Juris 194 (2008).

other equitable exceptions. Second, it offers a theoretical justification for this doctrinal pattern by contending that the official and unofficial stories operate in productive tension. Third, and most provocatively, it explains its defense of both contract/tort bifurcation and overlap through a body-based metaphor. If private law can be viewed as a system that functions akin to a human body, we might view contract as analogous to the brain and tort like the heart. Each performs specialized tasks with its particular mechanisms and needs cooperation from the other. In short, contract law without fault, in proper measure, would fail as quickly as a brain deprived of blood supply.

I. Official and Unofficial Stories Appear Throughout Contract Doctrine

Before getting to the body, however, another metaphor helps explain the operation of general rules and exceptions in legal doctrine. Gore Vidal pointed out that "even a pancake has two sides."[9] Similarly, many, and perhaps most, contract doctrines consist of a general rule and one or more exceptions. Most relevant for present purposes, conventional wisdom indicates that contract law passively implements the intention of the parties,[10] yet it occasionally takes into account fault and other equitable considerations.

Buy why force the unofficial story into the shadows? We may sacrifice accuracy for simplicity out of laziness, omitting part of the story to save time and effort. Alternatively, efficiency may caution against wasting breath by mentioning a seldom-utilized doctrinal exception. Or perhaps ignoring or downplaying the unofficial story masks the operation of power, as when the official story undermines consumers' arguments that unequal bargaining power constrained their consent. Yet another explanation is functional, assigning the official story the task of channeling parties to clearly articulate contract terms. Instead of testing these explanations, this chapter contends that letting the general rule speak for the whole conveys a mostly accurate picture (especially at a distance), while the exceptions facilitate parties trusting one another. At a more abstract level, the general rule and exceptions together support the ideological underpinning for the liberal state's foundational norms of freedom, equality, and plurality.

[9] Gore Vidal, *The Meaning of Tim McVeigh*, Vanity Fair, Sept. 2001 (quoting his grandfather).

[10] *See, e.g.*, Sun Printing & Pub. Ass'n v. Remington Paper & Power Co., 139 N.E. 470, 471 (N.Y. 1923) (Cardozo, J.) (refusing recovery where damages could be calculated in different ways, asserting "we are not at liberty to revise while professing to construe.").

The doctrinal case starts with the very definition of contract. Common law defines contract as mutual assent paired with a consideration, but also recognizes limited circumstances in which detrimental reliance can create contractual liability.[11] At the formation stage, an offeree generally may accept orally or in writing, or a court might infer acceptance from conduct,[12] but not from silence. However, in exceptional circumstances, an offeree can assent by silence or inaction.[13] In *Register.com, Inc. v. Verio*,[14] for example, the Second Circuit bound a web site user to terms he never agreed to, reasoning that merely using the web site subjected the user to its terms of use.[15] Similarly, at the level of enforceability, the common law generally enforces standard form contracts, but not where the drafter had reason to know that the other party would not have agreed if she knew the terms of the writing.[16] Along the same lines, contract law generally requires parties to perform the precise terms of their contract, but relaxes this rule for innocent breach of an inessential term.[17] Finally, contract doctrine generally awards expectation damages to compensate victims of breach for the value of their planned-for gains from the transaction, explicitly rejecting punitive damages as overcompensation.[18] Nevertheless, it also, in extraordinary cases, authorizes greater damages to punish willful breach.[19] This final example most explicitly imports fault into contract doctrine.

The following section defends fault in contract law by arguing that the official and unofficial stories produce an analytic framework allowing contract

[11] Second Restatement of Contracts §§ 17, 90 (1981).

[12] *Id.* at § 4.

[13] *Id.* at § 69 (allowing silence to constitute acceptance only where the offeree took the benefit of services with reason to know they were offered for compensation, where the offeror let offeree know that silence or inaction could constitute assent and the offeree intended to accept, where prior dealings justify requiring the offeree to notify the offeror of nonacceptance, and when offeree acts inconsistent with the offeror's ownership of the property, as long as the terms are not manifestly unreasonable).

[14] 356 F.3d 393 (2nd Cir. 2004). Courts continue to struggle with the issue of Seller's silence about contract terms at the time of sale, providing them later in the box with the goods. *Compare* Hill v. Gateway 2000, Inc., 105 F.3d 1147 (7th Cir. 1997) with the approach of the Illinois Supreme Court that abrogated *Hill's* holding in Razor v. Hyundai Motor Am., 854 N.E. 2d 607 (Ill. 2006), *as recognized in* Trujillo v. Apple Computer, Inc., 578 F. Supp. 2d 979 (N.D. Ill. 2008).

[15] *Id.* at 402 (distinguishing *Ticketmaster Corp. v. Ticket.com*, 2000 U.S. Dist. LEXIS 12987 (C.D. Cal. Aug. 10, 2000)), which required users to manifest assent by, for example, clicking an "I agree" icon on the webpage to be bound to its terms).

[16] Second Restatement of Contracts § 211.

[17] Jacob & Youngs, Inc. v. Kent, 129 N.E. 889 (N.Y. 1921); Edgewater Constr. Co. v. 81 & 3 of Watertown, Inc., 769 N.Y.S.2d 343 (N.Y. App. Div. 2003).

[18] Second Restatement of Contracts § 347; UCC § 1–106 (2004).

[19] *Compare* Tongish v. Thomas, 840 P.2d 471 (Kan. 1992) (applying UCC § 2–713 damages instead of lower UCC 1–106 damages where breach is willful) *with* Allied Canners & Packers v. Victor Packing Co., 209 Cal. Rptr. 60 (Ct. App. 1984) (applying UCC § 1–106 damages instead of § 2–713 damages where breach was caused by heavy rains rather than willful breach).

law to facilitate planning by providing relative certainty, and also, as necessary, to account for ex post consideration of fault. The tension between the official and unofficial stories, in this light, produces justifiable outcomes most of the time.

II. Official and Unofficial Stories Make Theoretical Sense

Returning to pancakes, you might see contract law as a tall stack, alternating between big and little ones. The big pancakes represent a pile of general rules, with the little ones sandwiched between them as their exceptions. The very structure of default and immutable rules follows this pattern. If contract law is a set of default rules, occasionally complemented by an immutable rule, then it mostly tells a story of freedom of contract, until you come across one of those immutable exceptions. The Uniform Commercial Code (UCC) codifies this approach by establishing a default rule in favor of default rules.[20] But at the very moment of codification that supposedly set the Code apart from other contract doctrines, the UCC also built in overlap by allowing the UCC to be supplemented by principles of law and equity such as estoppel, fraud, misrepresentation, duress, coercion, and mistake.[21] Thus, parties can alter most commercial law rules, but that right is constrained by immutable rules like the duty of good faith and nonenforceability of unconscionable terms.[22]

Despite these exceptions, intent defines the parameters of contract law, just as the big pancakes determine the shape of the stack. Contract doctrine guides contracting parties as they express their intent by drafting their agreements, mandating, for example, that the contract terms must be reasonably certain.[23] Certainty is required because contracts plan for future events. Yet sometimes, things do not turn out as planned. Then, breach of contract comes into play, allocating losses in the wake of nonperformance or botched performance.

The productive tension between intent and fault echoes the larger tension between contract and tort. Fault's very association with tort generates

[20] UCC § 1–302.

[21] *Id.* at § 1–103.

[22] Other immutable rules rest on functional grounds. UCC Article 9's immutable choice of law provisions, for example, dictate the state in which a financing statement must be filed, precluding secured creditors from contracting with their debtors for perfection in some other state. If the Article 9 choice of law rule were a default rule, allowing creditors and debtors to pick their own state for filing financing statements, subsequent creditors would not know where to search to determine whether the collateral was encumbered. Thus, the Article 9's immutable exception to the default rule that rules are mostly default rules protects the integrity of public record systems, and the structural integrity of the whole Article 9 scheme of balancing creditor, debtor, and third-party interests UCC §§ 9–301, 9–307.

[23] Second Restatement of Contracts § 33 (1981).

contractual purists' objection (and surprise) at the "pockets of fault" in contract law.[24] Yet this very separation facilitates contract and tort's tandem operation.

Say you slip walking up the stairs to my house. To recover for your losses in tort, you must show a duty, breach of duty, causation, and damages.[25] At each stage, public considerations take priority over private agreement, referencing consent, for the most part, only as a defense that would preclude tort liability. My duty to maintain my steps free of "unnatural accumulations,"[26] is publicly determined, as it must be, since if I had you sign an agreement establishing standards beforehand we would be in the realm of contract. My breach is likely accidental, but if I poured water on my already icy steps in anticipation of your arrival, that action would reflect my will alone. If you were unsteady on your feet, having quaffed a pitcher of margaritas in anticipation of my company, tort law would decrease your damages to account for your contributions to the loss. Finally, your damages will be determined by a jury or judge, speaking for the public by awarding actual and perhaps even punitive damages to punish me and to deter other reprehensible hosts.

At no point is there a reciprocal exchange, at least not until settlement, which is the most likely outcome once you send me the complaint. I'll check the terms of my homeowners' insurance contract and call my insurance company, happy that my bank (contractually) required the insurance before financing the home purchase. I'll contract for a lawyer's services, and he will meet with your lawyer. They will hammer out a settlement agreement based on my insurance coverage and other assets, and we will sign it. In other words, contracts play a crucial role in resolving a tort action.

Other stories can be told about your fall on my steps. A radical realist or critical legal studies scholar might reach a different conclusion, contending that publicly driven state determinations override any pretense of private agreements' primacy.[27] In this analysis, all law is public law because even purportedly private contracts require state enforcement and the state influences contractual terms through legislation and other mechanisms. Indeed, a rich body of scholarship attacks the analytical clarity of the public/private distinction.[28]

[24] Eric A. Posner, *Fault in Contract Law, in* Fault in American Contract Law.

[25] Second Restatement of Torts § 281 (1965) ("The Elements of a Cause of Action for Negligence").

[26] *See, e.g.*, Budahl v. Gordon & David Assoc., 323 N.W.2d 853, 854, 855 (S.D. 1982)

[27] Morris R. Cohen, *The Basis of Contract*, 4 Harv. L. Rev. 553 (1933); Clare Dalton, *An Essay in the Deconstruction of Contract Doctrine*, 94 Yale L.J. 997 (1985).

[28] Symposium, *The Public/Private Penumbra: Fourteen Years Later*, 130 U. Pa. L. Rev. 1289 (1982).

In spite of such scholarly handwringing, legal doctrine, and, accordingly, the first-year curriculum, continue to distinguish between tort and contract. This bifurcation of tort and contract survived Grant Gilmore's 1974 assault,[29] though a handful of law schools briefly experimented by combining the two areas in a single course called "Contorts."[30] The remainder of this chapter uses metaphor to defend both tort and contract's general bifurcation and their occasional overlap.

III. Civil Obligation's Brain Is Contract and Its Heart Could Be Tort

Cognitive linguist George Lakoff suggests that people often think in terms of body-based metaphors.[31] Under his theory of embodied cognition, common bodily experiences inform thought and language by providing metaphors to describe that experience. Anger, for example, creates physiological effects, including increased body heat and internal pressure (through increased blood pressure and muscular tension).[32] Consequently, we think and talk about anger in ways that reflect this embodied experience. Idioms relating to anger (i.e., "he lost his cool," "you make my blood boil," and "she's just letting off steam") refer back to the physiological experience of anger.[33] Building on Lakoff's analysis, we can profitably understand the relationship of contract and tort in terms of a body-based metaphor.[34]

Imagine the first-year curriculum or civil law generally, as a human body. In this view each doctrine operates both separately and cooperatively with other doctrines, like systems of the body. The brain processes thought, imagination, and intellect. Contract law similarly specializes in rationality by accommodating parties' thought-out plans for an imagined future. Tort, in turn, can be analogized to the heart. We often contrast the brain's capacity to reason against the heart's association with emotion, especially love. The phrase "no-brainer," for example, denotes a problem requiring little thought to solve, while the adjective "heartless" describes an unfeeling person. Thus,

29 Grant Gilmore, The Death of Contract (1974).

30 Jay M. Feinman, *Change in Law Schools*, 16 N.M. L. Rev. 505 (1986).

31 George Lakoff & Mark Johnson, Metaphors We Live By (1980).

32 *Id.* at 381.

33 *Id.* at 380–1.

34 Contract might map onto the body in different ways. In an earlier piece, I examined links between hands (and handshakes) and contractual thinking. Martha M. Ertman, *As Natural as Status*, *in* Reconceiving the Family 284 (Robin Fretwell Wilson, ed., 2005). There, and here, I use the term metaphor loosely, while linguists distinguish among metaphor, analogy, and metonym. *See* Lakoff & Johnson, *supra* note 31, at 19.

contract, like the brain, prizes rationality, while tort recognizes the importance of emotion through doctrines such as the intentional infliction of emotional distress and damages for pain and suffering. Contract law, in contrast, tends to ignore emotion. These doctrinal differences mirror structural differences between brains and hearts. Each organ is composed of tissues that are specially formed to perform different tasks, and both require cooperation with the other. Brains transmit electrochemical impulses through neurons, and hearts pump blood with striated muscle fibers. Yet the brain requires some blood to operate properly, and the heart gets its operating instructions from the lower brain.

The analogy is hardly an equation. We "cross our hearts" to designate the seriousness of a promise, and use our brains to memorize song lyrics "by heart." A longer piece might explore whether tort might be more like the skin, perhaps, than the heart, since it is public and mediates sensation. This chapter's modest aim is to make a contract/brain analogy, bringing forth the tort/heart analogy largely for contrast. Even here, the analogy may not bear much more pressure. The brain is marginally more private than other body parts, in that thought alone has no third-party effect that would trigger public concerns, while hands can slap and feet can depress a gas pedal to cause a car accident. Still, hands and feet generally require direction from the brain. The contract/brain metaphor, despite its limitations, supports the idea that contract law requires a little help on occasion to do its own job.

Metaphors operate by designating a source to make sense of a target, and work best when the two share deep structural commonalities. For example, the metaphor of sound-as-wave (evident in the phrase "sound waves") works because both water waves and sound waves evidence periodicity and amplitude, even though sound is neither blue, cold, nor wet.[35] The argument here identifies some structural similarities that the target (contract law) shares with the source (the brain). Stated most succinctly, they share a central concern with rational thought.

Rational thought produces intent. Agreement is one result of intent, and contracts are enforceable manifestations of intent to enter agreements. I am hardly the first to associate contract law with the brain. Classical contract theory rested on a brain-based metaphor when it defined contracts as a "meeting of the minds." While this purely intentional and subjective understanding of contract evolved into a hybrid of subjective and objective standards, contract formation still largely rests on intent. It requires an objective manifestation of

[35] Thomas W. Joo, *Contract, Property, and the Role of Metaphor in Corporations Law*, 35 U.C. Davis L. Rev. 779, 783–5 (2002).

assent, yet also requires that this manifestation lead a reasonable person, and the receiving party, to believe in the promisor's intent.[36]

The bodily manifestation of assent mirrors this objective/subjective hybridity. Hands manifest intent by clicking "I agree" on a computer screen, but the decision to click, and the neural signals controlling the finger, emanate from the brain. Indeed, you could say that the brain operates as the nerve center for contract.[37] Just as the nerve center of a business organization directs and receives support from satellite operations, the brain requires a controlled flow of oxygenated blood from the heart.[38]

A second aspect of Lakoff's metaphorical analysis in turn mirrors the duality of a nerve center interacting with satellites. According to Lakoff, people think in terms of both basic examples and radial categories. For something to be a basic example, there have to be other, less central, instances of the same thing. For example, people across cultures asked by researchers to identify the best example of the category "furniture," tend to pick "chair," and designate "rocker" as a subordinate category.[39] Applying this analysis to legal regulation, we might see the basic-level example of "mother" as a status held by a woman who gives birth and raises a child, and thus carries all maternal rights and responsibilities. Radial extensions are quasi-contractual variations, where women agree to a subset of rights and obligations as adoptive mothers, birth mothers, foster mothers, or surrogate mothers.[40] Legal doctrine recognizes both the primacy of the basic category and the occasional relevance of radial extensions. For example, the women who fall within the basic category of "mother" carry greater rights and responsibilities than special cases like surrogate or birth mothers.

Law's simultaneous, and differential, recognition of basic-level and radial categories facilitates orderly and principled dispute resolution. One could go so far as to say that the productive tension between basic and radial categories at issue here – no fault and fault in contract law – produces the legitimacy of the liberal state. The state enjoys a monopoly on force, which it sometimes delegates

[36] Second Restatement of Contracts § 24 (1981) ("An offer is the manifestation of willingness to enter into a bargain, so made as to justify another person in understanding that his assent to that bargain is invited and will conclude it."); Lucy v. Zehmer, 84 S.E.2d 516, 522 (Va. 1954).

[37] Secured Transactions law applies the "nerve center" test to determine parties' location. *See, e.g.*, U.C.C. 9–307 (2004).

[38] Strict products liability doctrine in tort law similarly indicates that tort operates well with a measure, but only a measure, of strict liability.

[39] Lakoff & Johnson, *supra* note 31, at 46, 51.

[40] *Id.* at 91. Basic-level categories include assumptions. For example, the basic-level example of "bachelor" includes assumptions about marriageability. Thus, John Kennedy, Jr., was often described as a bachelor prior to his marriage, while Liberace and the Pope are not. *Id.* at 70.

to private parties.[41] Under the official story, contract law constitutes such a delegation, in that the contract, rather than the courts, for the most part, dictates parties' rights and responsibilities. Even so, the state remains ever-present, since it both created the doctrine and continually reshapes it. This unofficial story of continual and quiet state engagement in contract law is most obvious in doctrines that seek to ensure genuine consent and limit harm to third parties by refusing to enforce, for example, agreements to sell a kidney or a baby. A state that ordered specific performance of a baby-selling agreement would be a far cry from the individuality-honoring liberal democracy that classical contract law both presupposes and purports to support. Similarly, contract disputes would be all but inevitable if a homeowner, for example, could evade his duty to pay the contractor who built his house by finding a tiny, peripheral instance of noncompliance.[42] In short, the very legitimacy of the state's assignment of authority to parties through contract law rests on a capacious understanding that includes, and shadows, continued state oversight of contractual relations through fault-based and other equitable doctrines.

Lakoff's rubric of basic-level and radial categories show the functionality of contract law's official strict liability story working in conjunction with an unofficial fault-based story. If strict liability is the basic category of contractual thinking, fault can exist alongside it as a radial category. To insist that fault be relegated to an entirely different category is akin to insisting that because genetic mothers who raise their children are the best example of "mother," that we shouldn't recognize variations like surrogate, adoptive, or foster mothers. In short, Lakoff's rubric of basic and radial categories explains both why liability and fault can (and should) coexist in contract doctrine, and also why some contracts scholars vigorously resist any incursions of the radial fault category into contract doctrine, for fear it will taint the basic category of strict liability.

Like the human body, legal doctrine is a complex entity performing many jobs, some of which it does better than others. Most obviously, it provides an orderly system of allocating rights and duties, and assigning liability for losses. Each doctrine tailors itself to particular problems faced in one segment of human interactions. At the level of ideology, each doctrine also plays a role. The role of contract law is particularly grand, I think, undergirding Western democracy and capitalism by providing an infrastructure for planning relationships and resolving disputes, and thus encouraging parties to enter agreements because they can, more or less, trust the state to intervene

[41] *For example*, UCC Article 9 authorizes secured creditors to use self-help repossession to satisfy debts, as long as they satisfy the requirements for attachment and do not breach the peace. U.C.C. §§ 9–203, 9–601, 9–609.

[42] *See, e.g.*, Jacob & Youngs, Inc. v. Kent, 129 N.E. 889 (N.Y. 1921).

to enforce those agreements and protect parties who might not be able to protect themselves.[43] Contract law serves this function in the liberal state by implementing values of autonomy, equality, and plurality that ideally mirror democracy's social contract in which citizens participate in government processes and the state respects citizens' personal autonomy. Applying these lofty ideas to the twinned official and unofficial stories of fault in contract law, we might say that the official story buttresses the planning or certainty side of contract law, while the unofficial, fault-sensitive, story furthers ex post considerations of fault. If contract law served only certainty, refusing to temper it with occasional recognition of fault, that simplicity could both encourage opportunistic breach and defeat its own goals by creating uncertainty. Moreover, the ossification of contract law could cause damage far afield from particular contract disputes.

Conclusion

It is hardly surprising that contract law generally follows a strict liability approach but also, occasionally, accounts for fault. Legal doctrine often articulates general rules, then enumerates exceptions. This chapter dubs these two approaches the official and unofficial stories of contract law. Surprisingly, a number of contracts scholars seem to blanch at the unofficial story and either seek to excise fault out of contract law or resolve the tension by merging contract with tort. They fail to recognize that the official and unofficial stories comfortably and effectively operate in tandem at the level of both doctrine and theory. Doctrinally, fault and other equitable exceptions temper each element of the cause of action for breach of contract. Theoretically, official and unofficial stories operate in productive tension, as illustrated by metaphorical analysis of the highly abstract relationships among tort, contract, and fault. Drawing on the research of cognitive linguist George Lakoff, we can analogize the law governing civil obligations to the human body to reveal deep structural similarities between contract law and the brain, as well more attenuated similarities between tort law and the heart. Contract and tort, like the brain and heart, perform specialized work, but regularly rely on the other to get the job done. In this view, fault's occasional appearance in contract law is no more out of place than the blood circulating to the brain to facilitate neural activity. A bloodless approach to contract law that values only certainty, ignoring fault entirely, could not long survive.

[43] Jurgen Habermas, Between Facts and Norms (William Rehg, trans., 1996).

PART IV

WILLFUL BREACH

TEN

When Is a Willful Breach "Willful"? The Link Between Definitions and Damages

Richard Craswell

The existing literature on willful breach has not been able to define what should count as "willful." This chapter argues that any definition we adopt has implications for just how high damages should be raised in those cases where a breach qualifies as willful. As a result, both of these issues – the definition of "willful" and the measure of damages for willful breach – need to be considered simultaneously. Specifically, if a definition of "willful" excludes all breachers who behaved efficiently, then in theory we can raise the penalty on the remaining inefficient breachers to any arbitrarily high level ("throw the book at them"). But if, instead, a given definition of willful would catch even some efficient breachers in its net, the damages assessed against willful breachers should be more limited. In that case, damages for willful breach might still justifiably be raised, but they should be raised only to the level that is economically efficient.

Liability for breach of contract is often described as a form of strict liability, in which the measure of damages is unaffected by the culpability of the breach. However, courts sometimes do award higher damages, under various legal doctrines, if the behavior of the breacher seems especially culpable. When they do, they may describe the breacher's behavior using labels such as *willfully*, or *in bad faith*, or *fraudulently*, or *maliciously* or, as Dickens once put it, "otherwise evil-adverbiously."

Unfortunately, labels like these are not self-defining. Over fifty years ago, Corbin was scathingly critical of their use:

> The word most commonly used is "willful"; and it is seldom accompanied by any discussion of its meaning or classification of the cases that

With thanks for helpful comments from (most recently) Barry Adler, Curtis Bridgeman, Christine Jolls, Ariel Porat, Eric Posner, and Alan Schwartz, as well as participants in workshops at the Chicago, Columbia, Northwestern, NYU, Stanford, and Yale law schools.

> should fall within it. Its use indicates a childlike faith in the existence of a plain and obvious line between the good and the bad, between unfortunate virtue and unforgivable sin.[1]

In this chapter, I make three claims. First, I argue that willful breaches cannot be defined merely by reference to the breacher's mental state, and that (as a result) the existing literature on willful breach lacks an adequate definition of "willful." Second, I argue that any definition of "willful" we adopt will have important implications for just how high damages should be raised in those cases where a breach qualifies as willful, so that both of these issues – the definition of "willful" and the measure of damages for willful breach – should be considered simultaneously. Third, I argue that these issues also require consideration of the fact-finding demands that each choice would place on courts.

I. Defining a "Willful" Breach

I begin with the problem of defining "willful." One natural interpretation of that term links it to the defendant's mental state: Willful breaches are knowing or intentional breaches. The problem with this definition is that adjectives suc[illegible] "knowing" and "intentional" are most easily applied to specific [illegible]each, by contrast, is not an action but a state of affairs. If I prom-[illegible]o deliver widgets to you by next Tuesday, then I am in breach if Tuesday arrives and you have no widgets, but your being widgetless on Tuesday is not itself an action. Your widgetless state may be the *result* of an action, of course; but typically it is the result of a whole sequence of actions: of all the things that were done (or not done) in the days leading up to Tuesday. Thus, before we can apply tests such as "knowingly" or "intentionally," we need to know the individual actions in that sequence to which those terms should be applied.

To illustrate, consider two staples of the contracts curriculum: *Jacob & Youngs, Inc. v. Kent*, and *Peevyhouse v. Garland Coal & Mining Co.* In *Kent*, a builder promised to use a particular brand of pipe to build a house; in *Peevyhouse*, a mining company promised to make certain repairs to the land after they finished mining the coal. The builder in *Kent* used the wrong brand of pipe, apparently by accident; but the mining company in *Peevyhouse* decided the promised repairs would cost too much, so it simply refused to

[1] Arthur Linton Corbin, Corbin on Contracts 545 (1951). As this passage demonstrates, we do not even have any consensus on spelling: "willful" and "wilful" are both common.

make the repairs. Described in this way, *Peevyhouse* sounds deliberate or willful, while the breach in *Kent* sounds accidental.

However, *Kent* can be characterized as a willful breach if we focus on other events in the sequence. After all, as soon as the builder discovered his mistake, he could have torn the house down and started over, this time using the right brand of pipe. (Much of the pipe was in the interior walls and foundations, and so could not be replaced without demolishing the house.) The builder chose not to do this, for demolishing the house would have been extremely expensive, but there is no question that this choice, the choice not to demolish the house, was deliberate. Thus, if the intentionality of *this* part of the sequence is what matters, *Kent* must be classified with *Peevyhouse* as a deliberate or willful breach.[2] Granted, we can avoid this characterization of *Kent* if we focus instead on the builder's earlier, unintentional mistake about what brand of pipe was being installed. But why should the intentionality of *that* event control our characterization of the breach, rather than the intentionality of the subsequent decision not to tear down the house and start over?

Indeed, if we are free to pick and choose which decision to focus on, the breach in *Peevyhouse* was not necessarily willful. True, the coal company deliberately chose not to repair the land once they learned how much it would cost to do so. Under at least one reading of the facts, though, the coal company originally thought there was sufficient coal near enough to the surface that the promised repairs would have been relatively easy. As it turned out, the coal was deeper and less plentiful, and this made the repairs more expensive than they might have been.[3] Thus, if we focus on the coal company's mistake about the coal, that event in the sequence looks just as involuntary as the builder's mistake about the pipe. And if the answer is, "the coal company should have known there was a risk it might be mistaken," why not say that the builder should also have known there was a risk it might get the brand of pipe wrong?

The problem here is fundamental. In the vast majority of cases, the parties do not intend to breach at the time they enter a contract. Instead, they hope the contract will be performed as planned, but then something else happens. Costs go up, or a better offer is found elsewhere, or work is performed incorrectly, and what originally looked like a good deal becomes less appealing to one party. Sometimes that party grits her teeth and performs anyway, but the

[2] The only commentator I have found who even mentions this similarity between *Peevyhouse* and *Kent* is Carol Chomsky, *Of Spoil Pits and Swimming Pools: Reconsidering the Measure of Damages for Construction Contracts*, 75 Minn. L. Rev. 1445, 1449–50 (1991).

[3] Judith L. Maute, Peevyhouse v. Garland Coal & Mining Co. *Revisited: The Ballad of Willie and Lucille*, 89 Nw. U. L. Rev. 1341, 1368–9, 1419–24 (1995).

litigated cases are those in which she decides she will not go through with the deal. If we look at the entire sequence of the defendant's decisions, there will almost always be some that were deliberate, thus potentially allowing us to classify the breach as willful. But there will also usually be some events that were not deliberate – the increase in costs, or the work that was done incorrectly, or the better offer that came along at the last minute – so if we focus on *that* event, we will classify the breach as resulting from an unintentional decision.

Indeed, even when breaches were in some sense intended from the beginning, we can always (if we try) find nondeliberate events that played a role. Consider a sleazy aluminum siding company that lures customers in by quoting a very low price, planning all along to take their down payment and disappear. While this sounds like the quintessential example of a deliberate breach, consider that even this company might have lived up to its contract if, after the contract was signed, an eccentric millionaire had unexpectedly offered it a reward for completing the job. Thus, even this breach can be described as resulting from a sequence of two events: an earlier event that was beyond the siding company's control (the failure of any millionaire to offer a reward), followed by a later, deliberate decision about how to respond to that event (the decision not to install the siding). Focusing on the second of these events makes the breach seem deliberate, but if we focus instead on the first event, it is hard to distinguish this example in any formal way from cases like *Kent* or *Peevyhouse.*

Of course, quibbles like these do not stop most of us from condemning the siding company's breach as "willful," even if we cannot articulate a formal definition of that term. Apparently, in some cases (like my aluminum siding example) we naturally select the breacher's deliberate decisions to focus on, and we see the resulting breach as willful. In other cases (perhaps *Kent*?), we decide to focus instead on the chance event or the mistake, and see the breach as accidental. Often, these choices are made without our being consciously aware of them, though behavioral researchers are beginning to investigate these choices more systematically, as I discuss in Section I.B.

A. *Analogies in Criminal Law*

Viewed in these terms, the problem is not unique to contract law. A close analogy can be found in criminal law, in cases where it matters whether the defendant acted "voluntarily," and where the application of that label may depend on our choice to focus on earlier or later events in the sequence that led up to a crime. For example, a badly intoxicated driver may be literally unable to control her car, so if we focus entirely on her actions while she is behind the wheel, the resulting crash will seem involuntary. But if we look instead at her earlier decisions (made while she was sober) to drive to a party where she intended to drink, and to do so without making any arrangements for a designated driver, *those* decisions make the accident seem more the result of a voluntary choice.[4]

Criminal law must also deal with the problem of conditional intentions, in cases where statutes impose longer sentences for crimes committed with a particular intent. For example, if a prison inmate takes a hostage and threatens to kill her *unless he is released from prison*, does this make the inmate guilty of assault "with intent to kill?" Or is he guilty only of ordinary assault, since he did not intend unconditionally to kill the hostage, and probably hoped he would not have to kill her?[5] This problem is at least somewhat similar to trying to decide whether a breach of contract was intentional if the contractor intended to perform *unless it turned out to be too expensive*, or if the aluminum siding company intended to breach *unless a millionaire offered to reward it for performing.* And while criminal law scholars have not agreed on any general solution to this problem, they do agree that characterizing a conditional intent is not simply a matter of discovering some fact about what the defendant was actually thinking.[6]

B. *Lay Assessments of Culpability*

Rather than looking for solutions in the theories of scholars, we might instead look to laypeople's intuitive judgments about which actions qualify as "intentional." As I noted earlier, few observers would hesitate to condemn my aluminum siding company as a willful breacher, even after they understand that the company would have been perfectly willing to perform if only a millionaire had offered them a bribe. I can also report that my first-year contracts

[4] For a useful discussion of this issue in criminal law, *see* Mark Kelman, *Interpretive Construction in the Substantive Criminal Law*, 33 Stan. L. Rev. 591, 600–11 (1981). For an example of a closely analogous problem in contract law, compare Commercial Discount Co. v. Town of Plainfield, 180 A. 311, 313 (Conn. 1935) (decision by contractor to stop working when the contractor was in severe financial difficulties and was simply unable to pay its workers held not to be a "willful" breach), with Billigmeier v. Concorde Marketing, Inc., No. 04-01-324, 2001 WL 1530356, at 7 (Minn. Ct. App. Dec. 4, 2001) (breach triggered by defendant's financial difficulties held to be "willful" when the financial difficulties themselves were caused by the defendant's wrongful behavior).

[5] *Cf.* State v. Irwin, 285 S.E.2d 345, 349 (N.C. Ct. App. 1982) (reducing the verdict to simple assault without intent to kill).

[6] For a recent review of the controversy, *see* Gideon Yaffe, *Conditional Intent and Mens Rea*, 10 Legal Theory 273 (2004).

students regularly (and, in most years, nearly unanimously) consider the breach in *Peevyhouse* to be an intentional breach, but do not apply that label to the breach in *Kent.*

Behavioral researchers have recently begun to study laypeople's assessments of culpability when contracts are broken. While those studies have not focused specifically on terms like "willful," some of their findings are nevertheless of interest. For example, in one survey, lay subjects were asked to assess brief descriptions of hypothetical cases in which the breaching firm broke its contract either (a) to earn greater profits, when a better-paying opportunity arose elsewhere; or (b) to avoid suffering a loss, when the firm's costs of performance increased. Consistent with other work on heuristic distinctions between gains and losses, the subjects systematically tended to judge the first kind of breach as the more culpable.[7] Other studies, though not focusing on breach of contract in particular, found that subjects' willingness to describe any given outcome as "intentional" varied depending on whether they were judging the intentionality of normatively desirable behavior, where they might be concerned with assigning credit; or the intentionality of normatively undesirable behavior, where they might be concerned with assigning blame.[8]

While this research is promising, it is subject to several limits. For one thing, the research is still at an early stage, so the patterns (if any) in lay judgments about breach are still unclear.[9] Moreover, even if we could identify precisely which breaches most lay observers considered culpable, we would still have to decide whether those lay judgments about culpability ought to be endorsed and embodied in the law or should, instead, be considered "heuristic errors" that the law should reject or try to overcome. Obviously, the answer will depend in part on why we want to single out willful breaches for extra punishment.

In this chapter, though, I take no position on the question of *why* we might want to single out certain breaches for extra punishment. There are, of course,

[7] Tess Wilkinson-Ryan & Jonathan Baron, *Moral Judgment and Moral Heuristics in Breach of Contract*, 6 J. Empirical Legal Stud. 407 (2009).

[8] For surveys of this literature, *see* Joshua Knobe, *The Concept of Intentional Action: A Case Study in the Uses of Folk Psychology*, 130 Phil. Stud. 203 (2006); Alfred R. Mele, *Intentional Action: Controversies, Data, and Core Hypotheses*, 16 Phil. Psychol. 325 (2003).

[9] For another recent survey, also containing some intriguing results, *see* Steven Shavell, *Is Breach of Contract Immoral?*, 56 Emory L.J. 439 (2006). An earlier survey, though one less useful for present purposes, can be found in David Baumer & Patricia Marschall, *Willful Breach of Contract for the Sale of Goods: Can the Bane of Business Be an Economic Bonanza?*, 65 Temple L. Rev. 159 (1992). Baumer and Marschall's questionnaire explicitly told respondents that the hypothetical breach was "deliberate" and "willful," *id.* at 184, so their survey sheds no light on the question of when respondents themselves would use those labels.

standard economic arguments for doing so, based mostly on the need for additional deterrence if ordinary damages are too low; and there are also standard noneconomic or moral arguments for extra punishment. Rather than engage in either of those debates, I simply posit that we have already decided (for some reason) that penalties ought to be higher for at least some breaches.

C. *Two Ways of Defining "Willful"*

I present the issue in this way in order to focus on the choice between two different *methods* of raising damages, involving two different definitions of "willful." As I discuss below, these two methods correspond loosely to the difference between negligence and strict liability in tort law. The first method, corresponding to negligence, is one in which the only breaches that qualify as willful, and, hence, the only breaches that are subject to extra damages, are those where the breacher behaved inefficiently in some way. The second method, corresponding to strict liability, is one in which even breachers who behaved efficiently can be found to have committed a willful breach.

Obviously, the first method (the one corresponding to negligence) requires courts to be able to tell whether a breacher behaved inefficiently, so in that respect the first method is more demanding of courts. However, the second method (the one corresponding to strict liability) requires courts to calibrate the amount of the higher damages more precisely, making the second method more demanding in that respect. Table 10.1 summarizes these differences.

Table 10.1. *Demands placed on the courts*

Definition of "willful"	Evaluate the breacher's efficiency	Calibrate the extra damages precisely
Negligence	**Yes**	Less
Strict Liability	No	**More**

II. The Analogy to Negligence

A. *Defining a Negligence Regime*

Consider, first, a legal regime in which the label "willful" is applied and higher damages are awarded only when the breacher behaves inefficiently in some way. Under this regime, breachers who behave efficiently would still be liable for ordinary contract damages, whatever ordinary damages are taken to be. In that respect, it differs from negligence regimes in tort law, where defendants who are not negligent pay no damages at all. But the regime I describe is still *analogous* to a negligence regime in torts, in that (1) it requires courts to evaluate the defendant's behavior; and (2) defendants whose behavior was inefficient are then subjected to harsher legal consequences. In this case, the harsher consequence is that defendants who are found to have behaved inefficiently must pay the *extra* measure of damages charged against willful breachers.

More specifically, a negligence regime (as I use the term here) depends on the law as it is actually applied, not on its black-letter doctrine. For example, even if the law were to explicitly define "willful" to mean "resulting from inefficient behavior," that would not qualify as a negligence regime unless it actually succeeded, in practice, in imposing extra damages only on those breachers who behaved inefficiently. As will become clear, the economic effects of any definition depend on what courts actually *do*, not on what black-letter doctrine says they do.

I should also clarify that, when I speak of breachers behaving inefficiently, I intend to include more than just inefficient breach. In *Kent*, the builder's final decision not to rebuild the house (once the mistake with the pipe was discovered) probably was not inefficient, as the value to the buyer of replacing the pipe was surely less than the high cost of doing so. But even if *that* decision was efficient, the builder might still have made an inefficient decision at an earlier stage, for example, when it decided how many precautions to take in checking each shipment of pipe. A regime that imposed extra damages on builders who made an inefficient decision at the precaution stage would still be a negligence regime, as I use that term.

Indeed, since most breaches result from an entire sequence of events, there are usually any number of decisions that might have been inefficient. In some cases, the charge might be that the breacher had failed to efficiently investigate the potential risks before agreeing to perform the contract. In others, a breacher who had adequately investigated the risks might nevertheless be accused of failing to disclose those risks to its contracting partner, if circumstances would have made such disclosures efficient. If the risk of not being able to perform was sufficiently high (as in my aluminum siding example), and if that risk was not adequately disclosed to the other party, it might then be argued that it was inefficient for the breacher to offer the contract in the first place. Inefficiencies might also be alleged with respect to the breacher's litigation behavior, if (for example) the breacher raised frivolous legal claims whose likelihood of success was too low to justify the costs of litigating them.

In short, there are many possible ways in which any given breacher *might* have behaved inefficiently. A negligence regime, as I use that term, is one in which the only breaches that are deemed willful (in actual practice) are ones in which the breacher behaved inefficiently in one or more of these ways.

B. *"Willful" as a Test for Inefficiency?*

It might seem unlikely that any test for willfulness could ever correspond (in actual practice) to a judgment about the inefficiency of the breacher's conduct. However, as long as the law has not resolved the definitional problems discussed in Part I, it is difficult to rule out *any* of the possible ways in which a willfulness test might be applied. For example, it would not be implausible if a breach like the one in *Kent* was especially likely to strike jurors as willful if the mistake with the pipe resulted from the builder's choice to take an inefficiently low level of precautions in inspecting each pipe delivery.[10] If jurors were less inclined to find willfulness in a case where the builder took efficient precautions and merely got unlucky, that tendency would move the law in the direction of a negligence regime.

C. *The Demands that Negligence Makes of Courts*

Obviously, it will often be difficult for courts to evaluate the efficiency of a breacher's decisions. Indeed, this difficulty is closely akin to the difficulty of evaluating the efficiency of a tortfeasor's decisions in a typical negligence case, which is why I have borrowed the "negligence" label.

At the same time, though, negligence regimes may be *less* demanding of courts with respect to the exact amount of the higher damages that are assessed, in those cases where the breacher is found to have behaved inefficiently and the breach is deemed willful. To be sure, the exact size of the award is not completely irrelevant under negligence, for it is important that the damages be high enough to deter the inefficient behavior. But as long as the damages exceed that minimum, they can (in theory) be raised to any arbitrarily high level; we can "throw the book at" the inefficient breachers, as Richard Posner has suggested,[11] without producing overdeterrence or any other adverse economic effects. This is because negligence rules, if they are

[10] The dissenting judge in *Kent*, who would have awarded higher damages, seems to have held something close to this view, for he described that breach as "either intentional or due to gross neglect which, under the uncontradicted facts, amounted to the same thing…" Jacob & Youngs, Inc. v. Kent, 129 N.E. 889, 892 (N.Y. 1921) (McLaughlin, J., dissenting).

[11] Richard A. Posner, The Economic Analysis of Law 119 (7th ed. 2007).

accurately applied, offer a safe harbor for efficient breachers: As long as the breacher is confident that she has behaved efficiently in every respect, she should never have to worry about liability for extra damages. As a result, those extra damages can be set at any arbitrarily high level without inducing efficient breachers to further alter their behavior or their prices. While this feature of negligence rules has not been emphasized in the contracts literature, the same point has often been made in connection with tort law.[12]

The catch, however, is that courts have to be able to identify efficient behavior *perfectly* in order to avoid any adverse effects from arbitrarily high damage awards. Moreover, it is not enough if courts are always able to make perfect decisions with hindsight, after a case has come to trial. To avoid adverse effects, potential defendants must be able to know in advance what kind of behavior the courts will judge inefficient, and hence subjected to larger penalties. Such certainty is difficult to achieve in the real world, especially if the legal criteria for higher damages are defined in such vague terms as "willful."

III. The Analogy to Strict Liability

Accordingly, I turn now to regimes in which even breachers who behave efficiently still face some risk that their breaches will be deemed willful, and that they will be made to pay extra damages. As before, the key for my purposes is how such a regime is applied in practice, not what formal label the law adopts. Thus, I include here not just regimes that explicitly define "willful" in a way that applies to efficient breachers, but also regimes that purport to adopt a narrower standard but whose judges or juries apply that standard inaccurately in some cases, so that efficient breachers are sometimes erroneously subjected to higher damages. In this sense, my classification is meant to be all-inclusive: Any regime that does not qualify as a negligence regime (as defined in the previous section) will qualify as a strict liability regime.

Obviously, strict liability regimes reduce the demands on courts in one respect, since courts no longer need to be accurate in evaluating the efficiency of the breacher's behavior. Indeed, strict liability regimes can (in theory) dispense with the need for any evaluation whatsoever of the efficiency of the breacher's behavior.

[12] *See especially* Robert Cooter, *Prices and Sanctions*, 84 Colum. L. Rev. 1523 (1984). For discussions of the analogous point in connection with punitive damages, *see* Bruce Chapman & Michael Trebilcock, *Punitive Damages: Divergence in Search of a Rationale*, 40 Ala. L. Rev. 741, 806–08 (1989); or Keith N. Hylton, *Punitive Damages and the Economic Theory of Penalties*, 87 Geo. L.J. 421 (1998).

On the other hand, strict liability regimes increase the demands on courts with respect to the exact amount of the higher damage awards, for it now becomes important that the damage awards be neither too low *nor too high*. Damages that are too high are not a concern under negligence regimes, because efficient breachers would never have to pay those damages anyway. But strict liability regimes (by definition) take away this safe harbor for breachers who behave efficiently, with the result that any increase in the higher damage awards will affect the behavior of even efficient breachers.

To be sure, this effect on breachers might be good if the normal contract damages would otherwise be too low, and if the higher awards merely move the total damages closer to whatever level is optimal. But if the higher awards go *too* high – more precisely, if they go beyond the level of damages that is optimal, in a sense that I define below – then a strict liability regime must worry that the larger awards will cause breachers to modify their behavior excessively. This can lead to overdeterrence, higher prices, and other undesirable effects.

A. *The Cost of Excessive Awards Under Strict Liability*

This last point may require further explanation, because some writers assume that the only economic argument against large damage remedies is that they would deter efficient breaches. These writers then note (correctly) that the threat of large awards should not block an efficient breach if the parties can renegotiate, for if performance is truly inefficient then the potential breacher should always be able to buy her way out of the contract. They conclude, as a result, that there should be no economic objection to higher damage awards as long as renegotiation costs are low.

What this analysis misses, however, is that the threat of higher damages will raise the price the potential breacher must pay in any subsequent renegotiation, and this can have further efficiency effects. At a minimum, it makes such contracts less attractive to some parties; for example, builders will face the risk of having to make a larger payment if and when they make a serious mistake, and they will therefore probably have to raise the price of their houses to cover that increased liability risk. Builders may also take extra precautions to reduce the risk of making a mistake; for example, a builder may now find it worthwhile to instruct two employees rather than one to double check every shipment of pipe, if a mistake will now require they make an even larger payment, because of the threat of larger damage awards. To be sure, these may be good rather than bad effects, for there is some value (up to a point) in having builders take precautions. At some point, though, if the threatened payment becomes large enough, the builder will have an incentive to take too many precautions, so the legal rule will produce costs rather than benefits. In short, strict liability can produce good effects only if damages are increased up to the optimal level, but no further.

More precisely, in a strict liability regime it will not matter if damage awards are randomly too high or too low, so long as the average or expected value of those awards is at the optimal level. But a regime of strict liability does require that the *expected* damage award be optimal, in order to give potential breachers just the right incentives to modify their behavior.[13] Thus, when it comes to the exact measure of damages that are assessed against willful breachers, strict liability regimes make greater demands on courts than negligence regimes do.

B. *Optimal Damages Under Strict Liability*

In response, it is sometimes suggested that determining the optimal damage measure (under strict liability) must be easier than judging the efficiency of the breacher's behavior (under negligence). After all, if the optimal damage award is exactly compensatory, we can calculate it by knowing only the *costs* inflicted by the breacher's behavior, but to evaluate the actual efficiency of the breacher's behavior, we usually need to know both its costs and its *benefits*. There are many cases, however, in which the optimal damage award will *not* be exactly compensatory, so calculating the optimal award will require courts to know more than just the amount of the nonbreacher's loss.

In some cases, awards that are less than compensatory can improve efficiency. For example, if the nonbreacher has more control over some aspects of the loss, either by mitigating damages after the breach or by taking precautions of his own beforehand, it could be better to award a smaller amount in order to improve the nonbreacher's incentives to control those losses efficiently. Smaller awards might also be more efficient if the nonbreacher is less risk-averse than the breacher, or if the loss is a nonmonetary one that nonbreachers prefer not to insure against, or if the nonbreachers differ in their susceptibility to damages in ways that the breacher cannot reflect by charging them a different price. In some cases, smaller awards might also be a more efficient way of optimizing various incentives at the precontractual stage, or

[13] Specifically, optimal deterrence can be achieved as long as the damage award that defendants expect, at the time they choose their actions, is the same as the expected value of the amount of harm that their actions are likely to cause. This condition will be satisfied if both courts and defendants are accurate on average. Louis Kaplow & Steven Shavell, *Accuracy in the Assessment of Damages*, 39 J.L. & Econ. 191, 199–200 (1996).

of reducing problems caused by potentially judgment-proof defendants. And if the size of the award affects the number of lawsuits that are brought (as seems likely), the resulting effect on litigation costs could also reduce the size of the optimal award. Identifying the award that best balances all of these factors would challenge an expert economist, much less an ordinary judge or jury.

To complicate matters further, in some cases the optimal award might be *larger* than the above analysis suggests, possibly even larger than strictly compensatory damages. Among other possible justifications, if there is some chance that a breacher might escape having to pay damages at all, that could reduce the deterrent effect of any given award. A common recommendation in these cases is to multiply whatever award would otherwise be optimal by one over the probability that the award will actually be assessed. But this solution requires courts to be able to determine what that probability is, thus increasing the informational demands in one respect.

Moreover, in most cases, the optimal solution will not involve a "simple" correction like multiplying the damages by one over the probability of punishment. Though the point has not been widely recognized, that solution creates incentives for optimal decisions at the margin only under a few special conditions that rarely hold in real legal institutions.[14] Specifically, that multiplier will be optimal only if (1) the probability of punishment is the same for all breachers, regardless of the harmfulness of their breach; or (2) the multiplier is adjusted individually, case by case, to reflect the probability of punishment each individual breacher faces. The first condition almost never holds, because more harmful breaches cause greater damages and thus are more likely to trigger a lawsuit; and if there is any dispute about the underlying liability, more harmful breaches are probably more likely to be judged a breach. Moreover, the second condition requires that the harshest penalties be imposed on those breachers who committed the *least* harmful breaches (since those are the ones least likely to be held liable), which is exactly the opposite of how most punitive sanctions are used.

Instead, under more plausible assumptions about real-world enforcement, imperfect enforcement can lead to either underdeterrence or overdeterrence, implying that the optimal adjustment may require either increasing *or decreasing* the size of the damage award. As a result, it may be even harder for courts to identify the damage award that would be exactly optimal.

[14] I discuss this point at more length in Richard Craswell, *Deterrence and Damages: The Multiplier Principle and Its Alternatives*, 97 Mich. L. Rev. 2185 (1999).

Conclusion

In short, Corbin was right, and defining "willful" is harder than it might appear. In this chapter, I have tried to expand on Corbin's remarks in three ways. First, the existing literature has not yet developed *any* adequate definition of "willful," mostly because it has not addressed the question of which event in the sequence leading up to the breach should be assessed for deliberateness or intentionality.

Second, the desirability of any particular definition cannot be judged without simultaneously considering the measure of damages that will be applied to those breaches picked out by the definition, because different definitions of "willful" have different implications for the amount of extra damages that ought to be assessed. Specifically, definitions of "willful" that reach only inefficient breachers can be paired with damage awards that are quite high, and do not need to be calibrated very precisely; but definitions of "willful" that include efficient breachers will require damage awards that are more restrained. As a result, the real task is to choose a *pair* of policies, that is, a combination of a definition of "willful" and a measure of damages, rather than trying to choose a definition of "willful" in isolation.

Third, and finally, each pair of policies that we might choose makes different demands on the courts. Some policies require courts to be good at evaluating the breacher's behavior, while others require courts to be good at identifying the optimal level of damages. If the legal rules are chosen wisely, one or the other of these tasks can be deemphasized, by moving toward either strict liability (thus sparing courts from having to evaluate the breacher's behavior) or negligence (thus freeing courts from having to calibrate the measure of damages precisely). But since there is no way to free courts from both tasks simultaneously, they will have to attend to one or the other.

ELEVEN

Willful Breach: An Efficient Screen for Efficient Breach

Steve Thel
Peter Siegelman

Willful breach doctrine should be a major embarrassment to contract law. If the default remedy for breach is expectation damages designed to put the injured promisee in the position in which she would have been had the contract been performed, then the promisor's behavior – the reason for the breach – looks to be irrelevant in assessing damages. And yet the cases are full of references to "willful" breaches, which seem often to be treated more harshly than ordinary ones based on the promisor's bad/willful conduct. This chapter's explanation is that willful breaches are best understood as those that should be prevented or deterred because the parties have implicitly agreed that the promisor would not breach in those circumstances. When willfulness, so understood, is present, courts rightly award remedies that serve to deprive the promisor of any incentive to breach and to assure the promisee of getting her full expectation.

Willful breach is an embarrassment to contract law. The standard remedy for breach of contract is expectation damages, which are designed to put the injured promisee in the position in which she would have been had the contract been performed. Yet courts often award greater remedies when they find "willful breach," even though the willfulness of a breach can have little to do with the promisee's expectation interest, which is measured with reference to the harm suffered by the injured promisee, and that is the same whatever motivated the *promisor's* breach. Commentators have typically sought to explain courts' reference to willfulness by suggesting that while the promisee's expectation is not affected by the willfulness of the breach, expectation can often be measured or interpreted in many ways, and when a breach is found to be willful, the defendant's bad behavior grants license to pick the most generous definition of the plaintiff's expectation.[1]

[1] *See, e.g.*, E. Allan Farnsworth, Farnsworth on Contracts §12.17a (2d ed. 1998); Robert A. Hillman, *Contract Lore*, 27 J. Corp. L. 505, 509 (2002).

We show that, in fact, willfulness matters not because it screens for a more generous expectation measure, but because it identifies those breaches that should be prevented or deterred – that is, all breaches that could have been avoided at little or no cost to the promisor. When willfulness, so understood, is present, courts rightly award remedies that exceed the promisees' expectation but serve to deprive the promisor of any incentive to breach.

Although some commentators are quite upset by willful breaches,[2] contract law generally does not concern itself with the morality of breach in any direct way. In the context of bargains, this approach has much to recommend it. People enter into contracts in hopes that the promises made to them will be kept, and when a promise is broken, the promisee's injury is typically the same whatever the reason for the breach. A disappointed promisee ought to be satisfied with full expectation, regardless of what motivated the breach. Moreover, the ex ante price of a promise is in part a function of the remedies that will be available upon breach, and promisees who seek nothing more than the benefit of their bargains will not want to pay a premium for the right to receive more than expectation in case of any breach, willful or otherwise.

Nonetheless, courts often talk about the willfulness of breach, and a number of doctrines seem to turn on willfulness. The special treatment of willful breach can be justified without recourse to any concern for fairness or the morality of promise keeping. Indeed, the best explanation of willful breach doctrines is not promisee centered at all. Instead, the willful breach rules provide a mechanism by which promisors can bind themselves in a manner that promising parties would and do adopt ex ante. Courts appropriately give special treatment to breaches that contracting parties, at the time they enter into their contract, expect the promisor to be able to avoid at little or no cost to the parties as a whole – that is, willful breaches. The remedies courts award for willful breach effectively and appropriately bind the promisor not to commit such a breach, even if those remedies sometimes overcompensate the promisee's expectation.

Thus understood, the special treatment of willful breach is consistent with the proposition that promisees want nothing more than to have the promises made to them kept, and thus will not bargain for anything more than a right to expectation, regardless of the reason why breach has occurred.[3] The problem is that promisees (and promisors) know that courts seldom award

[2] *See, e.g.*, William S. Dodge, *The Case for Punitive Damages in Contracts*, 48 Duke L.J. 629 (1999).

[3] Alan Schwartz, *The Myth that Promisees Prefer Supracompensatory Remedies: An Analysis of Contracting for Damage Measures*, 100 Yale L.J. 369 (1990).

full expectation.[4] Thus promisors cannot credibly commit to efficient performance, because the ex post damages courts actually award will likely leave promisees undercompensated.

Promisors will get more in exchange for their promises if they can credibly commit not to breach. The level of commitment for which parties will bargain depends on the cost to the promisor of avoiding breach: The more costly it is to avoid breach, the more a promisor will charge to accept liability for such breach. When bargaining parties know that a breach will damage the promisee and can be avoided by the promisor at no net cost to the two parties taken together, they will not want to permit it.[5] Since a commitment not to breach in these circumstances will be of value to the promisee, the promisor will receive more for her promise when she makes that commitment. Moreover, the promisor will get that premium at little or no cost, since she can, by definition, avoid enhanced liability at no cost simply by not breaching willfully.

The various willful breach doctrines screen for those opportunistic breaches that produce no net benefit for the parties – this is the best definition of willful breach, and often turns out to be what concerns courts. The doctrines enable promisors to commit credibly to perform their promises when they should. Moreover, if a promisor for some reason *wants* to preserve the right to commit a cost-free breach, she is free to do so by opting out of the rules, but only at the cost of revealing that she is willing to commit such a breach and foregoing what the promisee would pay for a firm commitment to perform.

The efficiency of the willful breach rules is enhanced by the sanction for their violation – a sort of promisor expectation, or disgorgement, in which the breaching promisor is put in the position in which she would have been had she had kept her promise. At the same time, the remedy also effectively assures the *promisee* of getting her expectation as well, inasmuch as she can use the promisor's profit to accomplish performance. This remedy may award the promisee more than her expectation, but the point is not to compensate the promisee for some special harm imposed by willful breach, but instead to destroy the promisor's incentive to breach willfully. Indeed, the remedy would work just as well if it were paid to a third party, and the beauty of the doctrines is that if they work, there are no breaches.

[4] *See* Daniel A. Farber, *Reassessing the Economic Efficiency of Compensatory Damages for Breach of Contract*, 66 Va. L. Rev. 1443, 1444–45 (1980); Alan Schwartz, *The Case for Specific Performance*, 89 Yale L.J. 271, 275 (1979). Among the factors frequently leading to undercompensatory expectation awards are doctrines limiting recovery for damages not proven with certainty, consequential damages, and attorneys' fees.

[5] *See* Steven Shavell, *Damage Measures for Breach of Contract*, 11 Bell J. Econ. 466, 467–9 (1980).

The *promisor's* expectation (disgorgement) remedy adopted by willful breach doctrines also avoids untoward incentives. The promisor is not punished for a willful breach, but simply denied any benefit therefrom. The disgorgement remedy does not lead the promisor to take inefficient precautions, since it applies only to breaches that can be avoided with no precautions at all. The remedy does not distort the promisee's incentives either. Inasmuch as the remedy is not dependent on the promisee's actions, the prospect of an enhanced remedy for willful breach will not lead the promisee to rely excessively on the promise. Nor do the willful breach rules undercut the effectiveness of rules that depend on permitting undercompensation in some cases. For example, since a promisee cannot expect a willful breach at the time he enters a contract, the prospect of receiving a supercompensatory remedy in case of willful breach does not at all undermine his incentive to disclose his circumstances to avoid the rule limiting consequential damages.[6]

We use two sets of cases to show that willful breach doctrines require those who commit breaches that could be avoided without cost to the parties as a whole to surrender the profits they gain from breach. One group addresses the question of whether to award the difference between contract and market price when the buyer would have much less had the contract been performed. The other are the famous cost-of-completion/diminution-in-value cases. In all the cases, the choice is between awarding the promisee the promisor's expectation or her own, and the choice almost always turns on willfulness.

I. Applying an Expectation Cap to the Contract-Market Differential

Courts have taken varied approaches to the challenging problem that arises when market prices change dramatically after a middleman simultaneously contracts to buy goods and to resell them at a markup to an end user. If the supplier breaches, but for some reason the middleman is not liable to the ultimate buyer when he fails to deliver, the breach by the original supplier poses a difficult problem. The middleman seeks the conventional contract-market price differential provided by Section 2–713 of the Uniform Commercial Code (UCC), but the supplier insists that the buyer is entitled only to his expectation, the (smaller) markup he would have realized if the contract had been performed. Courts have split on this question, awarding contract-market differential when the breaching supplier sells the goods to someone else, but

[6] *See, e.g.*, Ian Ayres & Robert Gertner, *Filling Gaps in Incomplete Contracts: An Economic Theory of Default Rules*, 99 Yale L.J. 87, 101–04 (1989).

limiting recovery to the markup when the supplier was unable to deliver and did not sell the goods to someone else.

Commentators differ on whether this result is defensible, and we do not undertake here to defend the approach the courts have taken. We simply argue that the courts have rightly recognized that the cases are fundamentally different, and the case for the contract-market differential remedy is strongest when the breach is willful.

Consider, first, the case in which the supplier breaches and sells the goods to someone else at the enhanced market price. This breach is willful in the sense that it does not save any real resources but is instead pure transfer from the promisee (and his customer) to the promisor, with no net gain to the two parties taken together. In this situation, courts have awarded the middleman the contract-market differential, often referring to the breach as willful.[7] Yet this leaves the middleman in a better position than he would have occupied if the contract had been performed (in which case he would have realized only his markup). Importantly, however, the lost markup would not fully compensate the middleman for his expectation. Even if he does not have to pay damages to the ultimate buyer, his relationship with that buyer will be damaged, and the award of his markup will not compensate him for this loss. Put another way, if the middleman and the ultimate buyer had considered the possibility when they entered the contract, they presumably would not have agreed that the supplier should be able to breach and realize all the increase in market price, because the increased price would be lost to both the middleman and the ultimate buyer.[8]

Breach is also not efficient here. While the supplier gains more from breach than the middleman loses, once the loss to the ultimate buyer is factored in, the gains from breach exactly equal the losses – indeed, in one of the reported cases, the breaching supplier actually sold the goods to the ultimate buyer (skipping the middleman) for market price.[9] For the same reason, this breach is also one that can be avoided at no net cost to the contracting parties. To be sure, the supplier realizes an extra profit by breaching, but this profit is fully lost to the middleman and his customer. The breach is motivated not by the transfer of the goods to a higher-value user or savings to be realized by not producing the goods, but instead merely by the supplier hoping to take advantage of a quirk in the relationship between the middleman and the ultimate buyer.

[7] *See, e.g.*, TexPar Energy, Inc. v. Murphy Oil USA, Inc., 45 F.3d 1111, 1113–14 (7th Cir. 1995); KGM Harvesting Co. v. Fresh Network, 42 Cal. Rptr. 2d 286, 289–93 (Ct. App. 1995); Tongish v. Thomas, 840 P.2d 471, 475–76 (Kan. 1992).

[8] *See* Goldberg, Framing Contract Law: An Economic Perspective 225–32 (2006).

[9] *See* TexPar Energy, 45 F.3d at 1113.

While the contract-market differential remedy may overcompensate promisees, it is not punitive in any conventional sense. It does not punish the supplier beyond requiring her to disgorge her gains from breach – she is no worse off than she would have been had she performed. Because the remedy exactly matches the breaching promisor's expectation interest, it deprives the supplier of any profits from her breach, and thus of any incentive to breach and sell to a third party.[10] The remedy awarded in these middleman cases can be justified without importing moral disapproval of breach into contract law. It is simply the result the parties would have agreed upon if they had considered the situation when they entered into the contract.

At the time they entered into their contract, both parties would have recognized that if the middleman were to recover only his markup in case of breach, he would not receive his expectation. Accordingly, the supplier would have received less for her promise than she would have if she had been able to commit to performing *even if she subsequently received a better offer*. By making that commitment – and agreeing to give up any profits realized from a resale to a third party – the supplier would get more for her promise. Moreover, she would incur no costs in making this promise, beyond the loss of any future profits that would result from potential breaches she agreed to forgo. She would not have to make any investment to avoid selling to a third party, since she could hardly do so inadvertently. She would be sacrificing the ability to take advantage of a rising market, but this is exactly the purpose of the contract. The present value of expected future price changes was probably zero at the time the contract was made in any case, and if she had wanted to gamble on price changes, she would not have entered into the contract in the first place. Thus, by committing to pay the contract-market price differential in case she sold to a third party at a higher price, the supplier-promisor benefitted. Although the remedy is supercompensatory, the parties would choose it because the *promisor* preferred it.

Now consider the case in which the supplier breaches not to sell the goods to someone else at a higher price, but because she *cannot* perform, for example, because the goods are destroyed before she delivers. In this case the courts typically award the middleman only his markup, and the supplier is not required to disgorge the amount she saved by breach.[11] In other words, the middleman receives something less than expectation, and the supplier

[10] *See* Richard A. Posner, Economic Analysis of Law § 4.10, at 119 (7th ed. 2007) (suggesting that the sanction for opportunistic breach should be calculated to deter and not to punish breach).

[11] *See, e.g.*, H-W-H Cattle Co. v. Schroeder, 767 F.2d 437, 438 (8th Cir. 1985); Allied Canners & Packers, Inc. v. Victor Packing Co., 209 Cal. Rptr. 60, 61–62 (Ct. App. 1984).

is better off than she would have been had she performed by buying and delivering substitute goods or making them at substantial expense.

This is a case of nonwillful breach, since the supplier would have had to expend real resources to avoid being unable to perform. The breach is probably also efficient, even when the interests of the ultimate buyer are considered. The efficiency of the breach depends on whether the supplier could have procured or produced the goods for less than the ultimate buyer paid for them. If it would cost the supplier more to produce substitute goods than the market price of those goods at the time of breach, the breach is efficient. If the supplier would have had to procure substitute goods in the market at the price the ultimate buyer paid, the breach is a wash in terms of efficiency.

If the middleman is entitled to the contract-market differential remedy when the supplier breaches because her goods are destroyed, he has bought protection against accidental damage to the supplier's property; by contrast, the middleman who buys protection against willful breach has insured himself only against the supplier changing her mind. The middleman might want to buy protection against such destruction of property, but that protection will cost more than protection against willful breach (i.e., the supplier breaching and selling to a third party), since the supplier will have to expend real resources to avoid the inadvertent breach.[12] Even if the supplier is in the best position to protect her property, the middleman will be hesitant to pay for this protection, inasmuch as his goal in entering the contract is only to get his expectation, which the contract-market differential remedy will exceed in this circumstance.[13] Moreover, the supplier will not always be the lowest-cost provider of insurance against the destruction of her property, especially with respect to destruction not caused by her negligence, therefore, even if the middleman wants to be protected against destruction of the goods, he might not want to buy that protection from the supplier. Accordingly, while at the time of entering a contract the parties will almost always agree that the supplier will not profit from selling to a third party, they will not always agree that the supplier will perform regardless of her real costs of performance.[14] The middleman cases – which award contract-market price damages if, but only if, the supplier breaches willfully – can then be seen as an approximation

[12] The seller will, of course, have her own reasons to protect her property, but to the extent this is so, the middleman has no incentive to pay extra for the contract-market price remedy.

[13] Indeed, the effect of a perfect willful breach rule is to prevent such breaches, so that no such damages are ever actually paid. By contrast, a rule entitling the middleman to the contract-market price remedy in the event of nonwillful breach will not prevent this type of breach, and will in fact result in windfall awards.

[14] Shavell proves that the optimal complete contract will entail performance only when the cost of performance is lower than the buyer's valuation. Shavell, *supra* note 5, at 467–69.

of the remedies the contracting parties would choose rather than a reflexive reaction to immoral breach.

II. Cost of Correction Versus Diminution in Value

When a promisor fails to perform in order to save expenses, rather than to take advantage of a more profitable transaction, the computation of expectation damages presents some of the most famous issues of contract law. Allan Farnsworth offers a useful hypothetical for analyzing promisors who benefit from breach by avoiding expenses they have agreed to undertake:

> Suppose that [we] contract to build a house for you according to your plans for $150,000. [We] then find that by substituting cheaper materials [we] can do the job for $25,000 less than if [we] follow the plans. [We] make the switch, but you do not discover this until the house is built and you have paid [us] the $150,000. The price at which you can sell your house on the market is diminished by $10,000, and it would now cost $60,000 to replace the materials to conform to the plans, largely because of the cost of undoing and redoing the work.[15]

Courts typically award one of two remedies in this situation. The first is the diminution in value to the promisee – here, the $10,000 by which the house's market value has been impaired because of the breach. The second is the cost of correction – here, the $60,000 it would take to tender a conforming house. The award of the larger measure is often justified on the basis of the willfulness of the promisor's breach, with especially blameworthy breaches singled out for higher damages.[16] That is, a promisor who breaches deliberately is much more likely to be required to pay the cost of correcting his breach than one who breaches accidentally.[17] Again, our claim is that what willfulness is

15 E. Allan Farnsworth, *Your Loss or My Gain? The Dilemma of the Disgorgement Principle in Breach of Contract*, 94 Yale L.J. 1339, 1382 (1985).

16 Although the $60,000 cost of correction can be thought of as protecting the buyer's expectation interest, it often overcompensates that interest. The diminution in market value will not fully compensate a promisee who places idiosyncratic value on the completed project. However, the award of the cost of correction will overcompensate that idiosyncratic value if the promisee values performance more than the market does but not as much as the cost of correction.

17 *Compare* Kangas v. Trust, 441 N.E.2d 1271, 1275–76 (Ill. Ct. App. 1982) (emphasizing deliberateness), *and* City School Dist. v. McLane Constr. Co., 445 N.Y.S.2d 258 (App. Div. 1981) (same), *with* H.P. Droher & Sons v. Toushin, 85 N.W.2d 273 (Minn. 1957) (emphasizing good faith). *See also* George M. Cohen, *The Fault Lines in Contract Damages*, 80 Va. L. Rev. 1225 (1994); Hillman, *supra* note 1, at 509 ("[I]n construction contracts, the degree of willfulness of a contractor's breach helps courts determine whether to grant expectancy damages measured by the cost of repair or the diminution in value caused by the breach, the latter often a smaller measure."); Patricia H. Marschall, *Willfulness: A Crucial Factor in Choosing Remedies for Breach of Contract*, 24 Ariz. L. Rev. 733 (1982).

really doing here is screening for those breaches that parties would want to forbid ex ante. Willfulness itself is largely epiphenomenal, serving as a kind of indicator that a promisor's actions are contrary to what the contract expressly or implicitly called for.

A. *Three Variants on Jacob & Youngs*

1. **Inadvertent Breach** Farnsworth's hypothetical suggests a variation on the famous case of *Jacob & Youngs v. Kent*,[18] and the application of willful breach doctrine can be illuminated by considering several variants on that case. In *Jacob & Youngs*, the builder contracted to supply Reading pipe, but – apparently inadvertently – substituted identical-quality Cohoes pipe instead, without realizing any cost savings at all.[19] This appears to be a classic example of an inadvertent breach.[20] The pipe substitution could have been avoided with sufficient precautions.[21] Given that the parties might not want to invest in such precautions, however, the appropriate stance is not to prevent or deter such a breach unless the parties contract for a particular level of precautions (as they are free to do). The law takes this approach by limiting the promisee to any diminution in value, and by not classifying the breach as willful.

2. **Deliberate Breach That Transfers Wealth Between the Parties** Now, imagine a variant in which the builder deliberately substitutes Cohoes pipe, which is cheaper (but just as good), with the intent of keeping the savings. Should this be treated as a willful breach? We suggest that it should.[22]

[18] 129 N.E. 889 (N.Y. 1921).

[19] *See id.* at 890. The breach was discovered only after the pipe had been installed, which made the cost of correction vastly greater than would have been the case if the correct pipe had been used in the first place. *See id.*

[20] Richard Craswell effectively deconstructs the distinction between "deliberate" and "accidental" breaches, and we acknowledge that the distinction is much more difficult to sustain than has previously been recognized. Richard Craswell, *When Is a Willful Breach "Willful"? The Link Between Definitions and Damages*, this volume.

[21] While the following text offers an example of willful breach, one that could be avoided without cost, the analysis suggests that breaches should be treated as willful even if they are costly to prevent, so long as the cost of prevention is less than the benefit of performance to the promisee. Defining a willful breach as one that can be avoided at *no* net cost to the parties suggests a negligence limitation to willful breach doctrine.

[22] "There is no general license," Cardozo wrote in *Jacob & Youngs*, "to install whatever, in the builder's judgment, may be regarded as 'just as good.' " 129 N.E. at 891 (quoting Easthampton Lumber & Coal Co. v. Worthington, 79 N.E. 323, 325 (N.Y. 1906)); *see also id.* ("The willful transgressor must accept the penalty of his transgression. For him there is no occasion to mitigate the rigor of implied conditions. The transgressor whose default is unintentional and trivial may hope for mercy if he will offer atonement for his wrong." (citations omitted)); O.W. Grun Roofing & Constr. Co. v. Cope, 529 S.W.2d 258, 261 (Tex. Civ. App. 1975) ("The [substantial

True, the breach looks to be efficient: Assuming the owner really did not care which pipe was used (since the two brands are of identical quality),[23] both builder and owner could be made better off by substituting cheaper Cohoes for more-expensive Reading and splitting the savings. Of course, our breaching contractor did not share the savings. But he could have, and the parties might well have agreed ex ante to permit the builder to substitute identical materials at lower cost and keep any savings so realized. That would provide the appropriate party with incentives to look for cheaper materials, and consequently, a rule permitting breach here could be justified in a way that it could not in the middleman cases.

The problem, of course, is that a builder also has an incentive to substitute cheaper *inferior* materials. This is especially true in a construction contract, where substitutions are often difficult to detect. In the face of this problem, treating the breach as willful and awarding the owner the cost-of-correction measure provides the appropriate incentives for the builder to inform the owner of the opportunity for savings, and to negotiate for consent to deviate from the contract. Granted, this might sometimes lead to inefficient performance, for example, by reducing the builder's incentive to seek out cheaper sources of pipe, or by creating bargaining costs over division of the savings if cheaper pipe *is* found. But since the parties could have adopted a "cheaper substitute" rule and chose not to do so, it makes sense to read the contractual specification as a requirement and treat the conscious choice to use something else as willful.[24] When the substitution is deliberate, and *does* save money, the builder's motives are questionable and the homeowner would be poorly positioned to judge whether or not the substitution was permissible. Hence, he (and, from an ex ante perspective, the builder) might be well served by a "Reading-only" rule that obviated the risk of harm if Cohoes was not really "just as good."

performance] doctrine does not bestow on a contractor a license to install whatever is, in his judgment, 'just as good.' ").

[23] This case also shows that promisor-centric willfulness rules do not create perverse promisee incentives. Suppose that you are a member of the Reading family and so value living with Reading pipe that you will, indeed, correct the situation. Notwithstanding your real injury, however, under the consequential damage rules, you will not be able to recover your special loss if you did not inform us of your unique concern at the time we entered the contract. The fact that you might nonetheless recover the cost of correction if we breach does not undermine the information-forcing effect of the consequential damage rules, however, since you can neither predict nor cause our willful breach.

[24] In fact, this may be the best explanation for the use of the phrase "Reading pipe" in the contract – it might not have been a shorthand for a particular quality or kind of pipe. *Cf.* Richard Danzig, The Capability Problem in Contract Law: Further Readings on Well-Known Cases 111 (1978).

3. **Deliberate Breach That Is Costless to Prevent** Consider a final variant in which the builder substitutes Cohoes pipe (still identical in quality and cost), but does so just as a joke. This is a strong case for willfulness. Such a breach would not save money, and it would have been costless to prevent because all the builder needed to do was decide that the joke was not really all that funny. Put another way, there would be no real resource costs involved in performing, since this is not a case where "precautions" to prevent breach are necessary, or even meaningful. This should therefore be considered a willful breach, and awarding the cost-of-completion remedy seems appropriate.[25]

B. *Treatment by the Courts*

Now consider two of the best-known cases from the contracts classroom that are also suggested by Farnsworth's hypothetical: *Peevyhouse v. Garland Coal Mining Co.*,[26] which suggests that you are entitled to the $10,000 diminution in value, and *Groves v. John Wunder Co.*,[27] which suggests that you get the $60,000 cost of correction. Both cases involved leases to extract valuable materials from land, with an obligation to return the land in its original condition. Restoring the land turned out to cost much more than the difference in value between the degraded and restored land.

Peevyhouse and *Groves* are typically taken as presenting two answers to the question of what it takes to protect the promisee's expectation interest.[28] In choosing between these measures, which is notoriously difficult, both courts relied on willfulness to some extent. The court in *Groves* explained that "[d]efendant's breach … was wilful. There was nothing of good faith about it. Hence, that the decision below handsomely rewards bad faith and deliberate breach of contract is obvious. That is not allowable."[29] The *Peevyhouse* majority did not mention willfulness (or discuss the defendant's motives at all), but the dissent did suggest that the failure to return the land in its specified

[25] If joke breaches are rarely, if ever, litigated, it may not be because breaches can never be funny. Rather, it likely reflects the fact that since joke breaches are willful, jokesters know that they will be on the hook for cost-of-completion damages if they breach. Only a very funny joke indeed would be worth the substantial sum it would cost to rip down the walls and replace Cohoes with Reading pipe. The cost-of-completion measure does its job when it deters joke breaches.

[26] 382 P.2d 109 (Okla. 1962); *see also* Eastern S.S. Lines, Inc. v. United States, 112 F. Supp. 167 (Ct. Cl. 1953) (restoration of ship); City of Anderson v. Salling Concrete Corp., 411 N.E.2d 728 (Ind. Ct. App. 1980) (landfill not brought to level specified in lease).

[27] 286 N.W. 235 (Minn. 1939).

[28] *See* Timothy J. Muris, *Cost of Completion or Diminution in Market Value: The Relevance of Subjective Value*, 12 J. Legal Stud. 379 (1983).

[29] *Groves*, 286 N.W. at 236. Of course, the term "wilful" could just be a makeweight or place maker that a court uses to justify the remedy it prefers for other reasons.

condition was "wilful," which it took as an argument for awarding the cost of completion.[30]

Our take is that both cases were wrongly decided. However, neither breach should be seen as willful, in our understanding, since both would have been costly to avoid. Promisees who did not expressly negotiate for the cost-of-correction measure ex ante probably would not want such protection, so, in the usual case, there is no reason a failure to restore the land should be treated as willful or otherwise entitle the promisee to correct the breach. On this analysis, *Groves* presents a poor case for willfulness and the cost-of-correction measure. Although the majority characterizes the breach as willful, no justification at all is offered for this label, nor can we see one. Yet if the breach in *Groves* was not willful, it is hard to see how the breach in *Peevyhouse* was any more so. Nevertheless, the award of diminution in market value in *Peevyhouse* was incorrect, not because the breach was wilful but because, as many commentators have pointed out, there was good evidence that the Peevyhouses actually did want the land repaired.[31]

Put another way, the cost-of-correction remedy serves two separate purposes: First, it works to compensate those promisees who have high idiosyncratic value (and really do want the land cleaned up). This is an ordinary expectation theory for awarding the cost of performance, and in the case of the Peevyhouses, the history of the negotiation between the parties makes it entirely compelling, although apparently not to the Oklahoma Supreme Court.[32]

Second, the cost-of-correction remedy can also serve to *prevent* breaches that the parties would not have wanted to excuse ex ante, by forcing the breaching promisor to surrender all of the expenses saved from such breaches.[33]

[30] The dissent noted:Defendant admits that it failed to perform its obligations that it agreed and contracted to perform under the lease contract and there is nothing in the record which indicates that defendant could not perform its obligations. Therefore, in my opinion defendant's breach of the contract was wilful and not in good faith.Peevyhouse, 382 P.2d at 115 (Irwin, J., dissenting).

[31] Indeed, they negotiated for nonstandard contractual language, waiving the right to the usual payment of $3,000 for surface damage in exchange for a promise to return the land to its original condition.

[32] That said, an award of the cost of correction may overcompensate even a promisee who places idiosyncratic value on completion, if she values correction more than the market does but less than the cost of correction. Nonetheless, courts typically restrict themselves to either diminution in value or cost of correction, perhaps because determining idiosyncratic value is difficult. For an unusual case in which the court estimates the buyer's loss of subjective value and compensates that directly, rather than awarding either diminution in value or cost of correction, see Ruxley Electronics & Construction Ltd. v. Forsyth, [1996] 1 A.C. 344 (H.L.) (appeal taken from Eng.) (U.K.).

[33] Moreover, the prospect of this remedy assures the promisee that she will get her expectation if she wants it, since she is free to go ahead with correction.

Neither *Groves* nor *Peevyhouse* fits this description, however, because both promisors might very well have wanted to preserve their ability not to perform when cleanup of the land turned out to be very expensive and the effects of failing to clean up minimal. Hence, these are not the kind of breaches that the willfulness designation is calculated to prevent. Where the promisor does wish to bind himself ex ante not to breach, however, this rationale should hold, even if the promisee in fact suffered little or no idiosyncratic harm from the breach.

Conclusion

Not all intentional breaches are willful, and willful breaches are not especially injurious to promisees. Instead, they are breaches that promisors would want to commit themselves ex ante not to undertake. It follows that the remedy for such breaches is and should be the surrender of any gains they engender for the breaching promisor, even when this overcompensates the promisee. This remedy sustains promisors' credible commitments not to breach in those circumstances where such commitments are valuable. Accordingly, the availability of this remedy for willful breach furthers the interests of all contracting parties, and particularly promisors, even when it exceeds promisee expectation.

TWELVE

An Information Theory of Willful Breach

Oren Bar-Gill
Omri Ben-Shahar

This chapter argues – in contrast to conventional law and economics wisdom – that supercompensatory damages for willful breach are justified. Willful breach, it argues, reveals information about the "true nature" of the breaching party – that he is more likely than average to be a "nasty" type who readily chisels and acts in dishonest ways, and may have acted in other self-serving, counterproductive ways that went undetected and unpunished. Willful breach triggers extra resentment for what underlies it – for all the other bad things that the breaching party likely did, or, more basically, for the ex ante choice he made to engage in such a pattern of behavior. Thus, when the party is caught in the act of willful breach, he is punished not merely for this act, but for the (probabilistically) inferred mesh of bad conduct. This account provides a concrete foundation for the notion that willful breach violates the "sanctity of contract." We show that some remedial doctrines are consistent with the information-based account.

Introduction

A. *The Puzzle*

Is willful (opportunistic) breach worse than inadvertent breach? Is it more wrongful and deserving of a harsher sanction? Strikingly, two opposite views now have a long-standing tradition within contract law, and they have not been successfully reconciled. On one end, the official position of the common law, as expressed in the Second Restatement of Contracts, is that the intent to breach is largely irrelevant:

> "Willful" breaches have not been distinguished from other breaches. ... In general, therefore, a party may find it advantageous to refuse to

We are grateful to Richard Craswell, Saul Levmore, Ariel Porat, Eric Posner, and conference and workshop participants at the University of Chicago and NYU for helpful comments.

perform a contract if he will still have a net gain after he has fully compensated the injured party for the resulting loss.[1]

This view is supported by the standard law-and-economics account that the optimal remedial regime is strict liability.[2] Since the main goal of remedies is to provide incentive to breach or to perform, all that matters is to equate the remedy to the harm. Intentional breach is no different from negligent or innocent failure to take precautions – all ought to be subject to the same sanctions, and in general the expectation remedy is sufficient to provide optimal deterrence.[3] Indeed, the law-and-economics notion of efficient breach, as well the Holmesian notion of a contractual promise being no more than an option to breach and pay damages, does not consider compensated breach to be wrongful. In fact, if it is efficient, it may be commendable. A willful efficient breach need not be deterred, merely priced, and the price tag need not include a fault premium.

On the other end, there is a more popular and intuitive sentiment that regards willful breach – even if followed by full compensation – as opportunistic and wrongful, and rejects the alleged normative equivalence between deliberate and inadvertent breach. One need only recall Cardozo's famous dicta: "The willful transgressor must accept the penalty of his transgression. For him there is no occasion to mitigate the rigor of implied conditions. The transgressor whose default is unintentional and trivial may hope for mercy if he will offer atonement for his wrong."[4] Indeed, a closer look at contract law doctrine reveals numerous pockets of fault within the ostensibly strict liability regime.[5] This added hostility toward willful breach transcends jurisdictions,[6] and is shared by both commentators[7] and transactors.[8]

[1] Second Restatement of Contracts ch. 16, introductory note (1981).

[2] *E.g.*, Richard A. Posner, Economic Analysis of Law 118–26 (7th ed. 2007); Steven Shavell, *Is Breach of Contract Immoral?*, 56 Emory L.J. 439 (2006).

[3] Lucian Arye Bebchuk & I.P.L. Png, *Damage Measures for Inadvertant* [sic] *Breach of Contract*, 19 Int'l Rev. L. & Econ. 319, 329 (1999); Robert Cooter, *Unity in Tort, Contract, and Property: The Model of Precaution*, 73 Cal. L. Rev. 1, 32 (1985).

[4] *Jacob & Youngs, Inc. v. Kent*, 129 N.E. 889, 891 (N.Y. 1921) (citations omitted).

[5] *See, e.g.*, George M. Cohen, *The Fault Lines in Contract Damages*, 80 Va. L. Rev. 1225 (1994); Patricia H. Marschall, *Willfulness: A Crucial Factor in Choosing Remedies for Breach of Contract*, 24 Ariz. L. Rev. 733, 734–7 (1982).

[6] James Gordley, Foundations of Private Law: Property, Tort, Contract, Unjust Enrichment 408–11 (2006) (describing the law in France and Germany).

[7] Bruce Chapman & Michael Trebilcock, *Punitive Damages: Divergence in Search of a Rationale*, 40 Ala. L. Rev. 741, 764–2 (1989); Daniel Friedmann, *The Efficient Breach Fallacy*, 18 J. Legal Stud. 1, 13–23 (1989); Ian R. Macneil, *Efficient Breach of Contract: Circles in the Sky*, 68 Va. L. Rev. 947 (1982).

[8] *See* Lisa Bernstein, *Private Commercial Law in the Cotton Industry: Creating Cooperation Through Rules, Norms, and Institutions*, 99 Mich. L. Rev. 1724, 1733–4 (2001).

Thus, we observe two opposite views, one that deems fault to be irrelevant and another that attaches harsher consequences to different types of willful, blameworthy, breach. How can we reconcile the tension between these two polar approaches? If all that matters is the harm caused by breach, why is the intent of the breaching party relevant as a factor that increases the remedy?

B. *The Traditional Explanation*

The traditional explanation for the hostile sentiment toward willful breach invokes notions of the sanctity of contract. Willful breach is worse, so goes the argument, because it undermines more than just the expectation of the current promisee; it demonstrates indifference and disregard toward the "institutions" of contractual commitment and trustworthiness, and it conflicts with the fundamental maxim of *pacta sunt servanda*.

The problem with the "sanctity of contract" account is that it assumes the conclusion: It does not explain why the contractual "institution" is violated by willful-but-compensated breach. For most contracting parties, however, a contract is not a gospel subject to some perceived sanctity, but merely a mutually advantageous instrumental arrangement that is negotiated in order to create value. Why condemn an attempt by one party to increase the overall contractual pie through, say, a willful search for more profitable opportunities? If such opportunities benefit one party and do not harm the other, why are they regarded with distaste? Indeed, had the parties written a complete contract that anticipated potential breach opportunity, they would likely have included an express term permitting, even encouraging, deliberate, efficient breach.[9] If both parties are made better off by allowing a deliberate breach to occur, why should they be saddled with the costly burden of the sanctity of contract?

C. *An Information-Based Explanation*

We argue that willful breach triggers a stronger resentment not because of the harm it causes, but rather because of the harm it reveals. Willful breach is not any more harmful, nor does it infringe any broader societal interest. Rather, willful breach is a probabilistic indication that the breaching party is the type of transactor who readily chisels and acts in a dishonest way, and has likely exercised such bad faith on other occasions without being sanctioned. An

[9] Steven Shavell, Foundations of Economic Analysis of Law 308 (2004).

act of willful breach reveals the true nature of the contracting partner: one who would take any opportunity to divert value, if he can get away with it. This party may act in other self-serving, counterproductive ways that often go undetected and unpunished. Occasionally, when this party's opportunistic act is observed and its true nature is revealed, it triggers resentment for what underlies it – for all the other bad things that he likely did, for the choice he made to engage in this pattern of behavior. That is, when this party is caught in the act of willful breach, he is punished not merely for this act, but for being a nasty type.

To be sure, this explanation is not in conflict with notions of "sanctity of contract." Rather, it provides a grounding for this notion. The sanctity of contract is infringed not by the willful breach per se, but by the propensity to disregard the full scope of the contractual obligation and to chisel away at it. Since every contract is in various ways incomplete, the less than fully specified obligations ought to be performed in a way that preserves the reasonable expectations of the parties. The sanctity of contract, under this view, is nothing more than a reasonable supplementation of underspecified or underenforced terms. A party infringes the sanctity of contract when he acts in a way that is inconsistent with this expectation. Sometimes it is called bad faith. But since this party can often escape detection, the sanction needs to be multiplied when the bad faith is detected. If the nasty types were caught every time they misbehaved, there would be no need for supracompensatory sanctions, and no need for a willful breach multiplier.

This imperfect-detection explanation for supracompensatory damages for deliberate breach of contract builds on the economic rationale for punitive damages in torts.[10] It has also been recognized in passing by contracts commentators.[11] In an important way, though, the justification we develop for supracompensatory sanctions differs from these prior imperfect-detection explanations. In a standard imperfect-detection account, the offender commits a wrongful act that is detected only by chance. The lower this detection chance, the higher the necessary damage multiplier. This account, however, fails to explain the prevalence of punitive damages in cases of deliberate aggression (the metaphorical "punch in the face"), since those are often the easiest to detect. Indeed, in our account, willful breach is detected with certainty. Thus, even if it were subject only to regular compensatory damages, it

[10] Robert D. Cooter, *Economic Analysis of Punitive Damages*, 56 S. Cal. L. Rev. 79, 79–80 (1982); A. Mitchell Polinsky & Steven Shavell, *Punitive Damages: An Economic Analysis*, 111 Harv. L. Rev. 869 (1998).

[11] *See, e.g.*, Richard Craswell, *When Is a Willful Breach 'Willful'?: The Link Between Definitions and Damages*, this volume.

would be properly deterred. There is no need, then, for a damages booster to deter the isolated act of willful breach.

Where our account differs from the standard detection rationale is in noting that willful breach is part of an underlying pattern of behavior, most of which is undetectable. When a willful breach occurs, it indicates that other wrongful, but undetectable, behaviors are (statistically) more likely to have happened than was previously assumed. Given that they went unpunished (and undeterred), the court takes the present damage-infliction opportunity to increase the sanction. Thus, the damages booster that is attached to willful breach targets the *inferred* undetected harm. It is intended to change the underlying incentive to become the type of rent-seeking transactor that exploits opportunities to chisel and performs in subpar fashion.

This feature of the information-based theory – that is, that one breach reveals information about other, potentially very different breaches – raises the question of scope. How broad and far-reaching are the inferences that courts can draw from a breach of contract? Can a breach of contract teach us that the breaching promisor is a low-integrity type who is also more likely to cheat on taxes or misrepresent insurance claims? Should we raise damages for breach of contract to punish the promisor for this increased likelihood of tax or insurance fraud? No, we should not. Our theory of willful breach is a theory about the optimal design of default rules in contract law. This theory recommends a supracompensatory damages default when the contracting parties would have adopted such a rule themselves, absent impediments to more complete contracting. The parties would want to impose supracompensatory damages for a breach that reveals information about other, undetected breaches of their contract. They would not want their contract to subsidize the state's tax-enforcement efforts or insurance companies' fraud squad.

As should be apparent by now, our definition of willful breach has nothing to do with the mental state of the breaching promisor. Rather, we adopt a functional approach, defining as willful a breach that merits the imposition of supracompensatory damages, because it reveals information about other undetected breaches. Still, this functional approach resonates with the moral intuitions that separate more and less blameworthy breaches: A breach is more blameworthy if it is the product of an underlying trait or inadequate precaution that links this breach with other (undetected) breaches.

Section I develops the information theory of willful breach. Section II applies this theory to prominent doctrines of willful breach.

I. An Information Theory of Willful Breach

A. *The Model*

In this section, we present the basic analytical argument through a stylized example. In the next section, we discuss how the argument extends to more general settings.

1. **Framework of Analysis** Imagine a service contract for a prepaid price. The parties have a complete understanding as to the scope of the work, but cannot fully describe it in the contract, because some aspects of performance are nonverifiable (that is, cannot be proven in court). A useful example to have in mind is a food catering contract – it is hard to prove in court how the food tasted.

Specifically, we make the following assumptions: It is up to the service provider (hereinafter, the "promisor") to set the quality of performance, which can take one of three levels – Standard ("*S*"), Mediocre ("*M*"), and Terrible ("*T*"). Standard performance produces a value of $50 for the client (the "promisee"), Mediocre performance produces a value of $40, and Terrible performance produces a value of $0. Courts can tell when performance is Terrible, but they might or might not be able to distinguish between Mediocre and Standard, and we consider both cases in the following analysis.

The cost to the promisor of performance depends on three factors. First, it depends on the quality of performance – *S*, *M*, or *T* – and the better the quality, the higher the cost. Second, it depends on a general ex ante investment or effort expended by the seller. We assume that the seller can choose either High ("*H*") or Low ("*L*") investment. *L* costs $0; *H* costs $25. Intuitively, this investment can be in things like inventory, special skills, market contacts, high-end equipment – anything that is costly and renders the expected performance quality higher and/or reduces the cost of high-quality performance. Third, the cost of performance depends on some random factors that cannot be influenced by the parties (e.g., price of materials, climate effects). We assume, for simplicity, that these random factors can have one of two realizations, Good ("*G*") or Bad ("*B*"). Prior to the contract, these random factors are summarized by a probability distribution. We denote by q (a number between 0 and 1) the probability that the state of nature will be *G*; $1 - q$ is therefore the probability that the state of nature will be *B*. In state *G*, performance costs are generally lower than in state *B*.

We assume that the three factors affect the cost of performance as specified in Table 12.1 below.

Table 12.1. *Cost of performance to promisor in dollars*

Quality of performance	High investment		Low investment	
	G-state	*B*-state	*G*-state	*B*-state
Standard	0	20	25	100
Mediocre	0	20	20	75
Terrible	0	0	0	0

Notice that the cost of Terrible performance is assumed to be always $0. Otherwise, High investment makes it cheaper to produce *S* quality regardless of the state of nature. High investment also reduces the cost differential between *M* quality and *S* quality, and for expositional purposes we assume a zero-cost differential between *M* and *S*. With Low investment, *M* quality is cheaper to produce than *S* quality. Finally, notice that there is one contingency – Low investment, Bad state – for which the cost of performance is higher than the value.

The timing of the model is the following: At time 0, the promisor makes an investment (*H* or *L*) that is unobservable to the client and cannot be verified in court. At time 1, the parties enter a contract for a fixed price and the client pays the price in full. The contract requires the promisor to provide *S* quality. At time 2, the state of nature is realized, either *B* or *G*. At time 3, the promisor chooses the quality of performance, *S*, *M*, or *T*, and incurs the corresponding cost. Finally, at time 4, if the promisor delivers less than *S* quality, there might be damage consequences imposed by courts.

2. **Efficient Performance** Should the promisor take the costly High investment? Should he deliver the Standard performance, given the effort he took and the state of nature?

If the promisor takes High investment, the total expected social value, $W(H)$, is

$$W(H) = -25 + 50q + (50 - 20)(1 - q) = 5 + 20q$$

Investment costs $25; with probability q, the cost for *S* performance will be 0, hence net value of performance will be 50; and with probability $(1 - q)$, the cost of performance will be 20 for *S* and for *M*. So given that *S* creates value of 50 and *M* a value of only 40, it would be efficient to deliver *S*, hence net value of performance will be (50 – 20).

If the promisor takes Low investment, the total expected social value, $W(L)$, is

$$W(L) = (50 - 25)q + 0 \cdot (1 - q) = 25q$$

Investment costs \$0; with probability q, the cost of performance will be 25 for S and 20 for M. So, given that S creates value of 50 and M a value of only 40, it would be efficient to deliver S. Hence net value of performance will be (50 – 25); and with probability $(1 - q)$, performance will cost 100 for S or 75 for M. So it will be efficient to breach (net value of 0).

Comparing the expected value of High and Low investment, $W(H) > W(L)$ for all $q < 1$, which means that High investment is socially desirable. The reason is that High ex ante effort, while costly, more than compensates for this added cost by reducing the ex post cost of performance and increasing the net gain from delivering S quality.

3. **Expectation Damages with Perfect Information** We now turn to examine the incentives of the promisor. We begin with the benchmark case in which courts can distinguish between the different qualities of performance. Here, the client will be able to recover expectation damages of \$10 when quality is M or \$50 when quality is T.

If the promisor takes High investment, then his expected cost, $C(H)$, will be

$$C(H) = 25 + q \cdot 0 + (1 - q) \cdot 20 = 45 - 20q$$

Investment costs \$25; with probability q, the cost for S quality (to which he is obligated under the contract) will be 0; and with probability $(1 - q)$, the cost will be 20 for S and for M, and, given the liability that M entails, it would be better to deliver S.

If the promisor takes Low investment, then his expected cost, $C(L)$, will be

$$C(L) = q \cdot 25 + (1 - q) \cdot 50 = 50 - 25q$$

Investment costs \$0; with probability q, the cost of performance will be 25 for S and 20 for M, and since M leaves him with liability of \$10, he will choose S and avoid the liability; with probability $(1 - q)$, the cost of performance will be 100 for S or 75 for M, so the promisor will breach and pay \$50 damages.

Comparing the private payoff for the two investment levels, we can see that $C(H) < C(L)$ for all $q < 1$, which means that the promisor will always choose the socially optimal High investment level. The difference between the private costs of H and L is exactly equal to the difference between the social value from H and L, for the familiar reason that expectation damages provide full internalization.

4. **Expectation Damages with Imperfect Information** The key assumption we will make now is that courts cannot detect Mediocre quality and cannot assess damages for the difference between Standard and Mediocre. This is why we introduced the Mediocre level into the model: to capture the notion that performance can deviate from what is promised in ways that are clear to the parties but are too subtle for courts to see (e.g., the taste of the catered food). Thus, if the promisor delivers M, he will escape liability and will not have to pay the $10 decline in value. It will not be surprising to see that when certain breaches go undetected, the promisor is more likely to commit such breaches. We show that this will affect his ex ante choice of investment.

If the promisor takes High investment, his expected cost, $C(H)$, will now be

$$C(H) = 25 + q \cdot 0 + (1 - q) \cdot 20 = 45 - 20q$$

exactly as under the perfect-information benchmark.

If the promisor takes Low investment, then his expected cost, $C(L)$, will be

$$C(L) = q \cdot 20 + (1 - q) \cdot 50 = 50 - 30q$$

Investment costs $0; with probability q, the cost of performance will be 25 for S and 20 for M, and, since there will be no liability for M, he will choose M and bear a cost of $20; with probability $(1 - q)$, the cost of performance will be 100 for S or 75 for M. The promisor will therefore breach and pay damages of $50.

Comparing the private payoff for the two investment levels, we can now see that $C(H) < C(L)$ for all $q < ½$. Whenever $q > ½$, the promisor will inefficiently make Low investments. The reason for the distortion has to do with the undetectability of M quality. For L investments, when the state is G the promisor will deliver only M quality and escape liability, thus failing to take into account the full social benefit of High investment in terms of the increase in the (net) value of performance.

5. **Supracompensatory Damages** When M quality performance cannot be detected, there is no occasion for the court to impose damages for this conduct. The only time the court imposes any kind of damages is when the promisor delivers T quality. So far, we assumed that damages are compensatory,

restoring the promisee's expectation of \$50 value. We now show what happens when damages ("D") for T quality are increased above \$50, and demonstrate that this can correct the promisor's ex ante choice of inefficient Low investment.

If the promisor takes High investment, then his expected cost, $C(H)$, will be unchanged relative to the expectation-damages regime, since he would never choose T quality and thus would never pay any damages. His cost, $C(H)$, continues to be $45 - 20q$. If, instead, the promisor takes Low investment, then his expected cost, $C(L)$, will be higher relative to the expectation-damages regime, because in the B state he would choose T quality and pay damages of $D > 50$ (as long as $D \leq 75$):

$$C(L) = q \cdot 20 + (1 - q) \cdot D$$

The promisor will choose H, if $C(H) < C(L)$, or

$$D > \frac{45 - 40q}{1 - q}$$

Note that, for $q \leq 0.5$, $D \leq 50$, which means that no increase in damages above 50 is needed. Of course, $q \leq 0.5$ is the case in which there is no distortion in the first place, and indeed there is no need to correct the promisor's incentives. But for any $q > 0.5$, which is when (as we saw earlier) the distortion would otherwise occur, the formula above implies $D > 50$. If, say, $q = 0.75$, then $D = 60$, representing a 20 percent multiplier over expectation damages of 50. If, instead, $q = 0.8$, then $D = 65$, a 30 percent multiplier. Thus, the court can correct the distortion in investment effort by imposing supracompensatory damages.

B. *Informal Lessons from the Example*

The analysis demonstrates how a party's choice of Low investment can lead this party to breach in situations where, had he taken higher (and more efficient) investment, he would have chosen to perform. Increased liability for ex post breach can correct the ex ante incentive to invest.

In the model, a promisor who delivered Terrible quality "revealed" himself to be one who made Low investment – it is only when a promisor made such Low investment that he might end up preferring (in the Bad state of nature) to breach, deliver Terrible quality, and pay damages. The reason why a damage multiplier was needed in this situation of Terrible quality was not to achieve full compensation for some excess harm, nor to correct for some underdetection of Terrible quality. It was needed because the information that was revealed suggested that this promisor invested Low effort and thus was more likely to commit *undetected* breach of a different kind (Mediocre quality) and escape liability in some situations. The added liability was an indirect way to pay for other types of wrongdoing.

In the willful breach analogy, a promisor makes a choice – analogized to the Low/High investment decision – of what type of practices to follow. High investment is analogous to a practice of high integrity: It costs more to build, but once it is in place it guarantees a higher ability to perform in a satisfactory way. Thus, a party can invest in quality controls, excess capacity, training, information, reputation of its brand, good will, and networking – anything that makes it less likely, even if a bad contingency occurs, that this party will have an incentive to commit willful breach. When a party does commit willful breach, the inference that is drawn is that this party is of the low-integrity or low-capacity type, and that this must have put him in a position to occasionally commit various sorts of undetected breach.

The essential assumption that, we believe, makes the model applicable to the willful breach context is the idea that willful breach – or, for that matter, any conduct within a contractual relation – is not an isolated incident that just happens to take place. Rather, it is systematically related to other contractual behaviors, it is part of a pattern, and this propensity is determined by some underlying choice or disposition of the promisor (which itself can be either detectable or undetectable). We modeled this choice/disposition as an investment that costs money. In the model, once this investment was made, it had a systematic effect on two behaviors of the promisor – the frequency of detectable (Terrible quality) and nondetectable (Mediocre quality) breaches. In the real world, once a party invests in building his integrity and capacity, these have a systematic effect on many behaviors down the road, one of which is the decision to commit willful breach. The party with low integrity is more likely to commit willful breach.

In the numerical example, as in the real world, the supracompensatory increment of damages depends on the likelihood of detection and the harm from undetected breach. It is not plausible that courts would know these variables with precision. Still, our analysis provides an understanding of the factors that ought to be considered when damages are assessed.

C. *The Efficiency of Supracompensatory Damages*

This model provides a different account of efficient damages from the standard "efficient breach" paradigm. The standard paradigm requires damages to equal the lost value from breach, or else efficient breach would be deterred. In the model here, this form of ex post allocative efficiency can indeed be compromised, because the promisor might prefer to perform even at a high cost rather than breach and pay the supracompensatory damages.

This effect was absent in the numeric example studied above, since Terrible performance was never chosen when the ex ante investment was high, and the optimal supracompensatory damages were never high enough to induce inefficient performance when the ex ante investment was low. In real situations, supracompensatory damages can lead to inefficient performance both when ex ante investment is low and when ex ante investment is high.

In these situations, the two efficiency perspectives seemingly collide: Supracompensatory damages are good because they improve the ex ante investment and they are bad because they deter efficient breach. Still, it is a standard view that the latter problem (but not the former) can be easily overcome by renegotiation. That is, if a contingency arises in which it is efficient to breach but too costly because of high damages, the parties can agree to release the promisor from its obligation. This private solution cannot solve the ex ante underinvestment problem because, by virtue of its precontractual timing, it is not contractible.

D. *From Moral Hazard to Adverse Selection*

The model developed in Section A is a moral hazard model. A common, unobservable ex ante investment influences the probability of both sanctionable and nonsanctionable breaches, creating a "technological" linkage between the sanctionable and nonsanctionable breaches. Imposing supracompensatory damages on the sanctionable breaches compensates for the inability to impose damages on the nonsanctionable breaches, thus inducing efficient ex ante investment.

While our focus is on this moral hazard model and the technological linkage that it assumes, we briefly discuss the alternative, adverse selection model that provides a similar rationale for increased sanction by assuming a "character" linkage between the sanctionable and nonsanctionable breaches. In the adverse selection model, there are two types of promisors, a low-integrity type and a high-integrity type. Individuals' integrity types are unobservable. According to one interpretation, integrity can be thought of as a nonmonetary fairness cost that the promisor bears when he tenders low-quality performance. A high-integrity promisor bears a high fairness cost, and thus will provide high-quality performance even when the breach is expected to be nonsanctionable. The low-integrity promisor, on the other hand, bears a low fairness cost and thus might shade and provide low-quality performance when breach is nonsanctionable.

The imperfect detection theory explains how supracompensatory damages can be used to align the incentives of the low-integrity promisor. When detection is stochastic, the low-integrity promisor will face an expected sanction equal to the probability of detection multiplied by the damages amount. If only compensatory damages are assessed for detected breaches, the ex ante expected sanction will be too low to deter all inefficient breaches. Supracompensatory damages increase the expected sanction and improve efficiency. They compensate for those breaches that go undetected. When low integrity underlies a detected breach of contract, it is fair to assume that other, undetected breaches were committed. The detected breach reveals information about the promisor's type, and it is this information that justifies the increased damages award.[12]

II. Willful Breach Doctrine

In this section, we review several applications of the willful breach doctrine and examine whether they are consistent with the theoretical model developed in Part I.

A. *Overcompensatory Expectation Damages*

Courts sometimes award overcompensatory expectation damages. In theory, overcompensatory expectation damages are an oxymoron. In practice, contract doctrine allows much flexibility in measuring expectation damages, and courts choose higher measures when they consider the breach willful or in bad faith. These questions arise most often in construction contracts and other service contracts, when the court is required to choose between the lower, diminution-in-market-value measure of the defective service and a higher measure based on the cost of completing the performance (or repairing a noncomplying performance).

In *Jacob & Youngs, Inc. v. Kent*,[13] the builder used a different brand of pipe than what the contract specified. The installed pipes were equally good, hence no diminution in value, and it would have been prohibitively costly to fix the nonconformity and replace the pipes. Judge Cardozo, in the passage quoted in the introduction, emphasized the role of willfulness. Since the nonconformity was considered unintentional, the lower measure of damages applied.

[12] While in the moral hazard model there was one type of breach that is always detected and another type that is never detected, in the adverse selection model there is only one type of breach that is detected with some probability.

[13] *See* Jacob & Youngs, Inc. v. Kent, 129 N.E. 889, 890 (N.Y. 1921).

Had it been deliberate, the contractor would have been liable for the full cost of repair. Many courts follow this heuristic.[14]

Our information theory can rationalize this doctrine. Construction contracts usually contain detailed specifications of multiple performance dimensions. When the contractor deliberately breaches one specification, it becomes more likely (as a matter of statistical inference about past behavior) that the contractor had an underlying "propensity" or policy to chisel. This does not have to be an outright policy of active search for opportunities to "save" or chisel. It can also be the product of a general lack of attention to contractual terms or a general laxity in quality control – what we modeled as a low ex ante investment. This ex ante choice of a general inadequate adherence to quality may well have resulted in many other undetected deviations. It is this underlying choice that is being (indirectly) scrutinized by the damage measure.

While willfulness is a central factor in *Jacob & Youngs*, the meaning of willfulness is notoriously illusive (in fact, the dissent in *Jacob & Youngs* differed with Judge Cardozo on this issue).[15] The information theory developed here directs the court to identify willfulness with a high likelihood that the conduct in question is part of a hard-to-detect pattern.

B. *Tort Damages for Bad-Faith Breach*

In the United States, where contract damages are intended to be compensatory, supracompensatory damages are sometimes available through tort law. One of the most prominent examples is the tort remedy for bad faith breach of an insurance contract by the insurer. An insured can recover more than contract damages, including punitive damages, if the insurer denied benefits intentionally, knowing that there was no reasonable basis for the denial.[16]

Often, this doctrine is justified on the basis of increased harm (e.g., emotional distress to an aggrieved insured, increased secondary harm from delay, or attorney's fees). But it is striking that in justifying the infliction of punitive damages, courts often make reference to the insurer's systematic and hard-to-detect *pattern* of deviations from the spirit of its obligation, which went beyond the specific denial at issue. In the leading case, *Campbell v. State Farm Mutual Automobile Insurance Co.*, State Farm Insurance argued that its breach (the denial of benefits) was a singled-out "honest mistake," but the Utah Supreme Court found that it was part of a national scheme intended to pay claimants less than what their policies entitled them – a pattern of

[14] *See* Marschall, *supra* note 5.
[15] *See* Jacob & Youngs, 129 N.E. at 892.
[16] *See, e.g.*, Anderson v. Cont'l Ins. Co., 271 N.W.2d 368 (Wis. 1978).

"trickery and deceit."[17] Because this systematic conduct " 'would evade detection in many instances,' " it should be more heavily sanctioned " 'on those few occasions where it was discovered.' "[18] Put differently, State Farm had to pay more than compensatory damages because it chose a low-value, low-integrity *policy*.

While the U.S. Supreme Court, in reviewing the *Campbell* decision, rejected the pattern-of-systematic-bad-behavior justification,[19] the "pattern" theory pervades much of the insurance law damages doctrine and provides justification for increased damages. Moreover, there are a few other contexts in which courts invoke the "pattern" theory to justify exemplary damages.[20]

C. *Restitution*

In some circumstances, the law enables the aggrieved party to recover in restitution in lieu of expectation damages, even if this remedy is compensatory.[21] High restitution awards are traditionally rationalized as necessary to prevent unjust enrichment from an intentional breach. In some cases, they can also be justified under our information theory.

For example, after signing a detailed contract the promisor deviates from the contractual specifications in a way that reduces the cost of performance without affecting the market value of the performance to the promisee. According to the proposed Third Restatement of Restitution, the promisee is entitled to recover the reduction in performance costs.[22] This rule can be justified under the information theory if the detected deviation, which did not harm the promisee, was likely accompanied by additional undetected deviations that did harm the promisee.

Conclusion

There are two striking aspects to the law of willful breach. The first is the pervasive sense that willful breach is worse, and deserving of greater sanction, than inadvertent breach. The second is the difficulty in defining willful

[17] Campbell v. State Farm Mut. Auto. Ins. Co., 65 P.3d 1134, 1147–57 (Utah 2001), *rev'd*, 538 U.S. 408 (2003).

[18] *Id.* at 1151 (quoting Crookston v. Fire Ins. Exch., 860 P.2d 937, 941 (Utah 1993)).

[19] State Farm Mut. Auto. Ins. Co. v. Campbell, 538 U.S. 408, 422–3 (2003) (emphasis added).

[20] For exemplary damages in banking and employment cases, *see* Joseph M. Perillo, 11 Corbin on Contracts: Damages 386–7 (rev. ed. 2005).

[21] Second Restatement of Contracts § 345 (1981); Third Restatement of Restitution and Unjust Enrichment § 39 (Tentative Draft No. 4, 2005).

[22] Third Restatement of Restitution and Unjust Enrichment § 39, illus. 7, 9.

breach, given that most breaches are a result of some voluntary decision by the promisor, but not all are abusive. The thesis developed in this chapter tries to clarify both aspects. It suggests that the definition of willful breach lies not in some intrinsic characterization of the mental state of the promisor. Rather, willful breach is the tag attached to behaviors that reveal information about some underlying bad trait, distinct from the breach itself. What makes a trait bad is that it is associated with a pattern of undetected value-skimming conduct. Thus, willful breach in our theory is a device that encapsulates information. It is this information that justifies the harsher remedial consequence.

THIRTEEN

Contract Law and the Willfulness Diversion

Barry E. Adler

As a general matter, American contract law imposes strict liability for breach. The willfulness doctrine, under which the damages awarded apparently depend on the reason for the promisor's failure to perform, seems an exception to the strict liability approach. For an influential set of willfulness cases, however, the exception is merely apparent. In these cases, fault seems not to be truly part of the judges' willfulness conception and punishment seems not to be part of their goal. Rather the judges use the esoteric legal term of willfulness in a mundane process: the calculation of expectation damages.

Introduction

Expectation damages for breach of contract are generally awarded on a strict liability basis. That is, in the typical case, the reason for the promisor's breach is irrelevant. It is often stated that an exception to this general rule occurs in the event of "willful" breach, which is said to justify special damages. The supposed exception has led to a conundrum because every instance of anticipatory repudiation is in some sense willful as is every refusal to cure a deviation from promised performance, yet in only a subset of these cases is the "willful" label attached as a reason for a high damages award. Why then are some, but not all, intentional breaches singled out for condemnation?

This chapter answers this question by denying the premise, at least for an influential group of willfulness cases. In these cases, willful breaches are not disfavored, rather they are of a sort that tends to impose relatively high actual damages on the victim. That is, damages awarded in willful breach

The author thanks Oren Bar-Gill, Omri Ben-Shahar, Dick Craswell, Kevin Davis, and Ariel Porat for helpful comments.

cases – or at least those addressed here – can best be described as the ordinary benefit-of-the-bargain type, where strict liability remains the rule, and where there is no punishment for illicit motives.

The argument is spelled out in steps. Part I sets up the debate with a brief description of the connection between expectation damages and willful breach. Part II then describes three hoary cost-of-completion cases, each a staple of the first-year contracts curriculum. For each case, "willful" is described as a label a judge attaches to a breach that causes substantial injury; in each case, it is the perceived size of the victim's injury, not the nature of the breach, that best explains the remedy the judge recommends. Finally, a conclusion is offered.

I. Expectation Damages and Willful Breach

The standard remedy for breach of contract is expectation damages, which are to provide the promisee the full benefit of his bargain. In terms of the Second Restatement of Contracts, §347, expectation damages owed the injured party are measured by "the loss in the value to him of the other party's performance caused by its failure or deficiency" less any savings from the victim's not having to perform.[1] No mention is made of the reason for breach and there is no prescribed penalty, or augmentation of damages, for willful breach.

The Restatement's description of the remedy for breach is not an accident or oversight; the omission of supplemental damages for an intentional failure to perform is deliberate. As stated in the introduction to the Restatement's chapter on remedies:

> The traditional goal of the law of contract remedies has not been compulsion of the promisor to perform his promise but compensation of the promisee for the loss resulting from breach. "Willful" breaches have not been distinguished from other breaches, punitive damages have not been awarded for breach of contract, and specific performance has not been granted where compensation in damages is an adequate substitute for the injured party. In general, therefore, a party may find it advantageous to refuse to perform a contract if he will still have a net gain after he has fully compensated the injured party for the resulting loss.[2]

This sentiment was famously summarized by Grant Gilmore, who noted that according to the traditional approach, "the wicked contract-breaker

[1] Second Restatement of Contracts §347 (1981). Under this provision, expectation damages are defined to include also compensation for incidental and consequential injury.

[2] Second Restatement of Contracts ch. 16, introductory note (1981).

should pay no more in damages than the innocent and the pure in heart."[3]

Defined in this way, the expectation remedy fits the basic economic theory of breach and damages, which, roughly speaking, favors an award for breach that reflects the harm caused the promisee so that the promisor will have the right incentive to take precaution against breach and the incentive to perform if, but only if, performance is efficient.[4] A penalty for willful breach could encourage too much precaution against breach and discourage efficient termination of contracts at least in part because a promisor who wanted out of a contract would have to negotiate and pay for a release or face the penalty.[5] The result could be a failure of the parties to maximize their joint wealth. Economic analysis, moreover, has fed back into doctrinal analysis, an observation confirmed by the Restatement, which in an introductory note to its chapter on contract remedies observes the agreement between the common law's adoption of the expectation remedy and the economic theory of efficient breach.[6]

[3] Grant Gilmore, *The Death of Contract* 15 (1974). Even where fault does not play a role in the award of damages in the event of breach, it may be relevant to other contract doctrines such as those that relate to formation, interpretation, or excuse. *See, e.g.*, George M. Cohen, *The Fault that Lies Within Our Contract Law*, 107 Mich. L. Rev. 1445 (2009); Melvin A. Eisenberg, *The Role of Fault in Contract Law: Unconscionability, Unexpected Circumstances, Interpretation, Mistake, and Nonperformance*, 107 Mich. L. Rev. 1413 (2009). Analysis of these doctrines is beyond the scope of this essay.

[4] *See, e.g.*, Richard Craswell, *Contract Remedies, Renegotiation, and the Theory of Efficient Breach*, 61 S. Cal. L. Rev. 629 (1988); Steven Shavell, *Damages Measures for Breach of Contract*, 11 Bell J. Econ. 466 (1980); Charles J. Goetz & Robert E. Scott, *Liquidated Damages, Penalties and the Just Compensation Principle: Some Notes on an Enforcement Model and a Theory of Efficient Breach*, 77 Colum. L. Rev. 554 (1977); Richard A. Posner, *The Economic Analysis of Law* 56–7 (1972). Note, however, that the text is overly simplistic in its description of economic theory. In addition to the references just cited, *see, e.g.*, Albert Choi & George Triantis, *Completing Contracts in the Shadow of Costly Verification*, 37 J. Legal Stud. 503 (2008) (modeling the role of litigation costs in optimal damages); Eric L. Talley, *Contract Renegotiation, Mechanism Design, and the Liquidated Damages Rule* 46 Stan. L. Rev. 1195 (1994) (modeling renegotiation into optimal remedy); Richard Craswell, *Precontractual Investigation as an Optimal Precaution Problem*, 17 J. Legal Stud. 401 (1988) (describing, *e.g.*, the role of mitigation in optimal damages); Charles J. Goetz & Robert E. Scott, *The Mitigation Principle: Toward a General Theory of Contractual Obligation*, 69 Va. L. Rev. 967 (1983) (same); Robert D. Cooter, *Unity in Tort, Contract, and Property: The Model of Precaution*, 73 Cal. L. Rev. 1 (1985) (describing, *e.g.*, how expectation damages may induce too much precaution); A. Mitchell Polinsky, *Risk Sharing through Breach of Contract Remedies*, 12 J. Legal Stud. 427 (1983) (describing how risk aversion affects parties' preferences for remedies). An extended discussion of the economic theory of contract damages is beyond the scope of this essay.

[5] *See, e.g.*, Craswell, 61 S. Cal. L. Rev. 629, *supra* note 4. There are, at least in theory, occasions when a promisor's anticipation of paying high damages for breach will optimize investment incentives. *See, e.g.*, Lars A. Stole, *The Economics of Liquidated Damage Clauses in Contractual Environments with Private Information*, 8 J. L. Econ. & Org. 582 (1992), but a discussion of these circumstances, like the discussion of the circumstances under which compensatory damages are not optimal, see *supra* note 4, is beyond the scope of this essay.

[6] *See* Second Restatement of Contracts ch. 16, introductory note (1981).

There appears to be harmony, then, between practice and principle, almost. A growing number of commentators have observed that, despite the general pronouncements of the Restatement and the cases on which it relies, some courts use the willfulness of breach as a justification for an award of high damages.[7] Not only is a willfulness supplement to damages seemingly inconsistent with economic theory, it also creates a doctrinal conundrum because not all intentional breaches provoke judicial disapproval. Consider, for example, a routine case of anticipatory repudiation, wherein a promisor announces in advance of the time for performance that she will not keep her promise. Unsurprisingly, such repudiation gives rise to a claim for damages, but the typical damages in this case are only for the "protection of [the promisee's] expectation that the obligor will perform."[8] There is no general enhancement of the damages even though an anticipatory repudiation seems quintessentially willful.

Various theories have arisen to explain and defend courts that only sometimes saddle intentional breaches with the willfulness label. For example, George Cohen has argued that courts appropriately award high damages, even supracompensatory damages, when a promisor behaves opportunistically,[9] and the designation of willful breach, along with the associated high damages, properly corresponds with and may deter such behavior. In a more recent example, Oren Bar-Gill and Omri Ben-Shahar have proposed that "willful breach is a probabilistic indication that the breaching party is the type of transactor who readily chisels and acts in a dishonest way, and has likely exercised such bad faith in other occasions without being sanctioned."[10] A high, supracompensatory damages award for willful breach is justified under this approach because the prospect of such damages deters transgressions by promisors who know they will not be caught in every instance of breach. There is merit in these, and other, explanations or justifications of a special damages award under the willful breach doctrine.[11] But there is also, in my view, a simpler way to explain at least some of the judicial precedent.

[7] *See, e.g.*, Oren Bar-Gill & Omri Ben-Shahar, *An Information Theory of Willful Breach*, this volume; Richard Craswell, *When Is a Willful Breach 'Willful'?: The Link Between Definitions and Damages*, this volume; George M. Cohen, *The Fault Lines in Contract Damages*, 80 Va. L. Rev. 1225 (1994); Patricia H. Marschall, *Willfulness: A Crucial Factor in Choosing Remedies for Breach of Contract*, 24 Ariz. L. Rev. 733 (1982).

[8] Second Restatement of Contracts §253, comment a (1981). *See also, e.g.*, Harwood v. Avaya, Inc., 2007 WL 2407054 (S.D. Ohio); Walker v. Concrete Creations 2005 WL 2101191 (Del.Com.Pl.).

[9] *See* Cohen, *supra* note 7. For a broader view of the role fault does or should play in contract law, *see* the symposium contributions summarized in Omri Ben-Shahar & Ariel Porat, *Foreword: Fault in American Contract Law*, this volume. Some but not all of these contributions are discussed elsewhere in this chapter.

[10] Bar-Gill & Ben-Shahar, *supra* note 7 at 176.

[11] Additional approaches to willful breach are discussed in context below.

The scholars who address the topic of wilful breach are attracted to a particular set of exemplars, referred to by one as the "building, grading, and mining contractor cases."[12] These cases, described more fully below, present the same essential facts: A promisor fails to perform according to contractually specified standards and the promisee claims that its injury should be measured by the cost of completion to those specifications; in response, the promisor claims to have substantially performed and offers to pay not cost-of-completion damages but the lower difference between the market value of the performance as promised and the market value of the performance as delivered. In these cases, the majority or dissenting opinions highlight willfulness as a justification for cost-of-completion damages or lack of willfulness as a reason for the lower, market-based measure.

The contention of this chapter is that, at least in this set of cases, the courts do not use willfulness either to augment or to deny a discount from compensatory damages. Rather, I argue, the judges in these cases, whether in majority or dissent, use a determination of willfulness or its absence to indicate whether compensatory damages are high or low; that is, the judges merely seek to give the breach victims the benefits of their bargains as the judges see these bargains. The willfulness label is not used or considered in every opinion, but where it is invoked, I argue, it is employed in service to the ordinary expectation remedy.

II. Willfulness, Material Breach, and Damages

As observed above, it is not uncommon for a court to award expectation damages without mention of willfulness, even when a breach is intentional. Yet, in some cases, courts determine a damages award only after deciding whether a breach is willful. One might wonder, then, what the difference is between the sort of intentional breach that gives rise to a willfulness analysis and the sort that does not.

The distinction between a merely intentional and a willful breach can be illuminated by analogy to a comedian's distinction between nude and naked. "Nude," the joke goes, "is having on no clothes; 'naked' is having on no clothes while up to no good." A mere intentional breach, like nudity, is no reason for alarm or disapprobation. A willful breach, like nakedness, *is* reason for concern. This approach to willfulness is, in any event, the one adopted by judges in a well-known series of contract cases that required the courts to determine whether a breach victim is entitled to cost-of-completion damages or a lesser remedy of market-based damages.

12 Marschall, *supra* note 7 at 741.

The first case in the series, *Jacob & Youngs v. Kent*,[13] is best understood in connection with the Second Restatement of Contracts §241, which describes the conditions under which a breach will be deemed material. A relevant factor is whether "the behavior of the party failing to perform or to offer to perform comports with standards of good faith and fair dealing." A comment to this section observes further that a failure of good faith or fair dealing is sometimes described as a "willful" breach.[14] To illustrate, by contrast, a circumstance under which there was no failure of good faith or fair dealing, and thus no willful breach, this comment offers the case of *Jacob & Youngs*, where a contractor's breach was deemed immaterial despite its failure to install pipe of a contractually specified brand into a customer's home. A closer look at *Jacob & Youngs* illuminates the relationship among willfulness, materiality, and damages.

The contractor, Jacob & Youngs, Inc., agreed to build a house for Kent in exchange for about $80,000. The house was completed and Kent took possession, whereupon he discovered that the house had been built with Cohoes (and other) brand pipe; the contract called for Reading brand. Kent, through his architect, then asked Jacob & Youngs to replace the off-brand pipe with the specified brand; because most of the pipe was by that time enclosed in the walls, this would have required demolition of the structure. Jacob & Youngs, which installed the wrong pipe accidentally, refused the request and sued Kent for the portion of the contract price still unpaid, about $3,500. Kent defended that he was not obliged to pay this amount because the contractor's failure to supply Reading pipe was a material breach of the contract; in any case, Kent contended, he was entitled to an allowance (damages) equal to the large cost of demolition and construction that replacement would then entail. In response, Jacob & Youngs argued that because it had substantially performed on the contract, Kent was obligated to the make the final payment subject only to an allowance for the difference in value between a house with Reading pipe and a house with the off-brand pipe, a difference that the contractor said was negligible at best because the different brands of pipe were of identical quality.

Speaking through Judge Cardozo (later a Supreme Court justice), the New York Court of Appeals sided with Jacob & Youngs. After noting that "the omission of the prescribed brand of pipe was neither fraudulent nor willful" and that the only difference between the brands of pipe was "the names of the manufacturer stamped upon it," the court warned against "a purpose to visit

[13] 129 N.E. 889 (NY 1921).

[14] Second Restatement of Contracts §241, comment f (1981).

venial faults with oppressive retribution." In the court's view, Jacob & Youngs had substantially performed. This conclusion ruled out material breach and precluded Kent's excuse from performance.[15] Significantly for the subject of this chapter, the determination that there was substantial performance also established the measure of Kent's damages as "not the cost of completion, which would be great, but the difference in value, which would be either nominal or nothing."

Perhaps anticipating criticism (and a dissent), Cardozo conceded the difficulty of achieving the proper result in cases such as this and tried to explain the reason for the court's holding despite that difficulty:

> Where the line is to be drawn between the important and the trivial cannot be settled by formula.... We must weigh the purpose to be served, the desire to be gratified, the excuse for deviation from the letter, the cruelty of enforced adherence.... This is not to say that the parties are not free by apt and certain words to effectuate a purpose that performance of every term shall be a condition of recovery [and justify an allowance for the cost of completion]. This is merely to say that the law will be slow to impute the purpose, in the silence of the parties, where the significance of the default is grievously out of proportion to the oppression of the forfeiture. The willful transgressor must accept the penalty of his transgression ... [but the] transgressor whose default is unintentional and trivial may hope for mercy if he will offer atonement for his wrong.

As already noted, the court thought the contractor's breach trivial and "atonement" for the wrong was here measured by the difference in value – implicitly the market value – between Reading and off-brand pipe rather than by the higher cost of completion, but one might ask why. That is, inasmuch as the court concedes that parties may expressly contract for whatever outcome they choose, how does the court know the significance of the default, and why, in the absence of express provision, should the willfulness of the breach affect whether damages are high or low?

The answer I propose is that, as the court used the term here, a willful breach would not necessarily be one that justified high damages but rather could be one that *reflected* high damages. What likely drove the court to conclude that Jacob & Youngs' breach was not willful was its determination that Kent suffered no injury. In the court's view, despite his initial (perhaps

[15] Where a promisor has materially breached, she has not substantially performed, while where she has not materially breached, she has substantially performed. As Allan Farnsworth put it, "the doctrine of material breach is simply the converse of the doctrine of substantial performance." *See* Allan Farnsworth, *Farnsworth on Contracts* 518 (3d ed., 2004).

feigned) request for demolition of the house, ultimately what Kent wanted was not performance but money, deserved or otherwise, at least as an offset to the amount he owed the contractor. That is, in the court's opinion, despite the contractual provision for Reading brand pipe, Kent had no preference for that brand over other pipe of the same quality and merely sought to exploit Jacob & Youngs' harmless error, something the court would not allow.[16] Indeed, this is the interpretation given the case by the Second Restatement of Contracts, which in an explanatory comment to section 348 (on the measure of damages), explains that Kent lost because of his failure to provide "proof of any special value that Reading pipe would have to him."[17]

Imagine an alternative version of the case. Assume that Kent contracted for Reading pipe in his home even though he was aware that Reading was more expensive than Cohoes pipe and even though he was aware that, for the purposes of home construction (as opposed to industrial construction), the market assessed the quality of the pipe brands as identical; assume that Jacob & Youngs was also aware of these facts.[18] Assume too that in this hypothetical version of the case all of the pipe was to be exposed in a basement, rather than enclosed in the walls, so that the cost of performance would not change following the initial installation of off-brand pipe. If, under these hypothetical circumstances, Jacob & Youngs installed the less expensive pipe, then refused to replace it, the court likely would not have permitted it later to claim that the breach was trivial. Even though the market would treat the substitution as inconsequential, this breach likely would render the contractor liable for cost-of-completion damages (subject to offset for any resale value of the installed Cohoes pipe). In the actual case, Judge Cardozo hints at this result with the suggestion that Kent might have prevailed had he asked only for the replacement of exposed pipe.[19]

Under the ordinary expectation remedy, cost-of-completion damages would be appropriate in this hypothetical version of the case because there is every reason to believe that Kent idiosyncratically values Reading pipe more

[16] An alternative defense of the holding is that the specification of pipe brand was meant only to indicate quality and did not, in fact, require installation of any particular brand. In that case, *Jacob & Youngs* would not even be in breach of the contract. But the court did not rely on such an interpretation of the contract.

[17] Second Restatement of Contracts §348 comment c, illustration 4 (1981).

[18] That, in this hypothetical version of the case, Kent was aware of the cost difference between the pipe brands as well as the market's judgment as to the brands' qualities would logically exclude the possibility that Kent meant the designation of Reading pipe merely as an indication of quality.

[19] In the actual case, the court observed that "[s]ome of the exposed sections [of pipe] might perhaps have been replaced at moderate expense," but that the "defendant did not limit his demand to them, [and instead] treated the plumbing as a unit to be corrected from cellar to roof."

than Cohoes pipe by at least as much as the added cost[20]; after all, in this version of the case, the higher cost of the Reading pipe, of which Kent was aware at the time of agreement, was presumably incorporated in the contract price for the home's construction.[21] If Jacob & Youngs intentionally installed the wrong pipe, the court would label the breach willful, but intentional or accidental, the contractor likely would not be able simply to pocket the savings from having installed off-brand pipe.

It is instructive to place the actual and hypothetical versions of *Jacob & Youngs* side by side. In the actual case, the court concluded that the accidental installation of the wrong pipe followed by the pipe's enclosure in the structure raised the cost-of-completion damages above the promisee's actual injury from breach. The court unhelpfully folds this conclusion into a determination that the contractor's breach was not "wilful," but the circumstance of the cost increase, not of the promisor's ultimate failure to perform, is the basis for the court's determination. In the hypothetical version of the case, where there is no mistake as to cost or value or accident to raise the cost of performance, there is a strong case to be made that the promisee's injury would be properly recompensed with cost-of-completion damages rather than the lower, market-based remedy. In this case, a court would deem the breach willful if the promisor knowingly installed the off-brand pipe, but in any event the court likely would award the higher damages; such damages would not constitute a penalty. Again, "willfulness" of the breach is not a particularly helpful rationale, but close analysis reveals an underlying logic.

Willfulness as a reflection of injury also explains another case in the pantheon of willful breach doctrine, *Groves v. John Wunder Co.*[22] In that case, a landowner, Groves, leased his property to Wunder. The lease contemplated that Wunder would strip from the land sand and gravel, which it could retain for its own purposes. Under the lease, Wunder was obligated to restore the property to "a uniform grade." Wunder made the required lease payments but returned the stripped property in a "broken, rugged, and uneven" condition. This was an undisputed breach of the agreement. The question was one of damages. The difference between the market value of the property if

[20] The observation that cost-of-completion damages may be used to compensate for idiosyncratic value is also made in Steve Thel & Peter Siegelman, *Willfulness Versus Expectation: A Promisor-Based Defense of Willful Breach Doctrine*, this volume. *See also* Timothy J. Muris, *Cost of Completion or Diminution in Market Value: The Relevance of Subjective Value*, 12 J. Legal Stud. 379 (1983).

[21] The observation that cost-of-completion damages may be incorporated into the contract price is also made in Robert E. Scott, *In (Partial) Defense of Strict Liability in Contract*, this volume. *See also* Muris, *supra* note 20.

[22] 286 N.W. 235 (Minn. 1939).2

returned as promised and the market value of the property as returned in fact was no more than about $15,000, while the cost of returning the property to uniform grade was more than $60,000. Wunder was willing to pay the former amount; Groves demanded the latter. The Supreme Court of Minnesota sided with Groves, holding that because Wunder's breach was "willful" and in "bad faith" cost-of-completion damages was the appropriate remedy.

To support its holding, the *Groves* court appealed to Cardozo's dictum from *Jacob & Youngs* that "the willful transgressor must accept the penalty of his transgression." As for the different outcome in the two cases, the *Groves* court concluded that the facts of *Jacob & Youngs* were "distinctly the opposite." One might ask why the cases are opposites. Put another way, one might ask why the contractor in *Jacob & Youngs* was innocent while the lessee in *Groves* was a ne'er-do-well. The mere intent to breach does not provide a satisfactory answer because, like the reprobate lessee in *Groves*, the hapless contractor in *Jacob & Youngs* ultimately intentionally refused to perform according to the contractual terms. Some other distinction is required.

Grappling with this problem, the *Groves* court fixed on the concept of waste. In *Jacob & Youngs*, the *Groves* court observed, full performance would have resulted in "wrecking a physical structure, completed, or nearly so." Absent such "waste," the court reasoned, relying in part on the Restatement of Contracts, an award based on the cost of completion was the appropriate remedy.[23] But this distinction is analytically unhelpful because "wrecking a physical structure" is wasteful only if the remedy the wreckage allows is worth less than the cost of the destruction and repair; it is not always wasteful to tear down and rebuild. Along the same lines, returning land to a uniform grade, the performance at issue in *Groves*, may be wasteful even if nothing is wrecked in the process. If the benefit of uniform grade is less than the cost, then even restoration can be wasteful. So the court got sidetracked when it equated waste with the destruction of a structure. But the question of whether the cost of completion would be justified by the benefit created is the right one when the objective is to award a promisee the benefit of his bargain.

Ultimately, the *Groves* court arrived at a sensible analysis. The court noted that it is not wasteful for a person with idiosyncratic preferences to customize his property in a way that does not maximize its market value: "The owner's right to improve his property is not trammeled by its small value. It is his

[23] The court relied on the First Restatement of Contracts §346 comment b (1932) (observing that the law does not require damages based on wasteful performance); *see also* Second Restatement of Contracts §348 (1981) (providing that cost of completion damages will not be presumptively awarded where the cost is disproportionate to the probable value).

right to erect thereon structures which will reduce its value." With a focus on this language, *Groves* stands for the proposition that cost-of-completion damages are appropriate where the value of performance to the promisee is at least equal to the cost. In *Groves*, just as in the hypothetical version of *Jacob & Youngs* discussed above, absent mistake or changed circumstances, it seems reasonable to conclude that the original contract price incorporated the ultimate cost of completion, which, in turn, must have been no more than the value of performance to the promisee.[24] The same cannot be said of the actual *Jacob & Youngs* case, which is thus reconcilable with *Groves*, each awarding merely compensatory damages, with the amount of those damages simply different. In this light, the question of willfulness in these cases is seen as a mere diversion.

Peevyhouse v. Garland,[25] with facts remarkably similar to those in *Groves*, completes the triumvirate of building, grading, and mining contractor cases. In *Peevyhouse*, property owners, the Peevyhouses, leased their land to Garland Coal Mining Co., which was permitted to mine the land for its own purposes but required to restore the land before returning it to the owners. Garland made the lease payments but refused to perform the required restoration. The market value of the remedial work was trivial, while the cost of completion was substantial, and the Peevyhouses sued for the cost of completion, relying on the reasoning of *Groves*. Garland offered to pay only market-based damages, relying on the reasoning of *Jacob & Youngs*.

In *Peevyhouse*, the Oklahoma Supreme Court considered *Groves* and *Jacob & Youngs* as well as the Restatement and other authorities. In the process, the court identified "waste" as the "prime consideration." The court went on to describe waste in functional, economic terms, rather than by reference to whether anything was "wrecked." What matters, said the court, is the "relative economic benefits." In other words, the question is whether the benefit of completion to the promisee justifies cost-of-completion damages.

[24] This said, the court may well have misread the facts of the case. A dissent in the case observed that there was "no showing made, nor any finding suggested, that this property was unique, specially desirable for a particular or personal use, or of special value as to location or future use different from that of other property surrounding it. Under the circumstances here appearing, it seems clear that what the parties contracted for was to put the property in shape for general sale." If it is true that Groves was going to sell the land on the open market, then any idiosyncratic taste he had for restoration would have been irrelevant and the proper damages would be market based. In that case, one might presume that there was a mistake or changed circumstances since the time of contract; perhaps the parties erred as to the true cost of restoration or perhaps Groves only later decided to sell.

[25] 382 P.2d 109 (Okl. 1962).

The court recognized that it is sometimes difficult to determine the benefit of performance to a promisee, and so for mining cases such as this one, at least, the court concluded that:

> [The measure of damages] is ordinarily the reasonable cost of performance of the work; however, where the contract provision breached was merely incidental to the main purpose in view, and where the economic benefit which would result to lessor by full performance of the work is grossly disproportionate to the cost of performance, the damages which lessor may recover are limited to the diminution in [market] value resulting to the premises because of the non-performance.

Put another way, if promised performance is likely of special significance to the promisee or if the market-based value of performance is roughly the same as the cost of performance, then it is reasonable to conclude that the true value of performance at least equals its cost, justifying cost-of-completion damages. Otherwise, market-based damages are likely to be fully compensatory.

Applying its rule to the facts, the court found no evidence that the obligation to restore the land was anything but an incidental term and concluded that the cost of performance was grossly disproportionate to the market-based value of performance.[26] The court, therefore, held in favor of Garland and awarded the Peevyhouses only market-based damages.

Nowhere in the opinion does the *Peevyhouse* court make reference to willfulness or good or bad faith. This is not surprising, because the court turned directly to a comparison between the cost and the value of performance, what it described as "relative economic benefits." The court had no need for lack of "willfulness" or "good faith" as a proxy for its decision. There was, however a dissent, which fell back on this terminology. According to the dissent, Garland's breach was both willful and in bad faith and thus should have required the company to pay cost-of-completion damages. Of particular interest is the reasoning the dissent offers in support of its conclusion: "The cost of performing the contract in question could have been reasonably approximated when the contract was negotiated and executed and there are no conditions now existing which could not have been reasonably anticipated by the parties." That is, according to the dissent, there was no mistake, no accident, and thus no reason to doubt that the promisees valued performance by at least its cost.

[26] The dissent calls into question the court's conclusion that the restoration term was unimportant, but that does not affect the validity of the court's reasoning conditional on the facts it found.

Terminology aside, then, it seems that the disagreement between the *Peevyhouse* majority and dissent went not to the nature of the appropriate damages, but merely to the amount of those damages. Each sought to award damages that compensated the promisees for their injury. The majority suspected that the promisees did not place an idiosyncratically high value on the promised performance while the dissent thought otherwise. The majority used lack of centrality of the contract term as a basis for its decision while the dissent used the lack of mistake or changed circumstances for its determination. The majority did not mention willfulness, while the dissent did, but the dissent's use of the term – like that of *Jacob & Youngs* and *Groves* – was a label applied to a conclusion, not an instrument of analysis.

The story told here, even if correct, is incomplete. It does not, for example, address the question of why a court ever awards cost-of-completion damages without also requiring the promisee to complete the project. The prospect that a court would require completion could induce a strategic promisee – one who does not idiosyncratically value performance – to accept a settlement amount close to her actual, market-based injury.[27] This result would reduce promisee overcompensation as compared to an unconditional award of cost-of-completion damages based on a court's erroneous conclusion that the promisee specially suffered from breach. But in the cases described here, the courts may not have considered an order of completion a remedy available to them, and so the claim that the judges attempted to award merely compensatory damages, given the available choices, seems reasonable.

The analysis above also neglects the situation where cost-of-completion damages would be overcompensatory while market-based damages would be undercompensatory. Consider again the hypothetical version of *Jacob & Youngs* discussed above, but now assume that in the hypothetical version of the case, just as in the actual case, the pipe was enclosed in the walls before Kent discovered the substitution, so that the cost of performance changed between the time of contract and the time of the contractor's ultimate refusal to perform. Here, just as in the actual case, the cost of demolition, replacement, and reconstruction could well exceed the value of performance to Kent, but just as in the earlier hypothetical version of the case, because Kent was aware of the price difference between and relative quality of Reading and Cohoes pipe, there is every reason to believe that he idiosyncratically values Reading pipe more than Cohoes pipe, a preference likely incorporated into the contract price. In this case, neither cost-of-completion damages nor

[27] *Compare* Ian Ayres & Kristen Madison, *Threatening Inefficient Performance of Injunction and Contracts*, 148 U. Pa. L. Rev. 45 (1999).

market-based damages is likely to be the true expectation measure, and a court would find it difficult to calculate the true expectation award because the idiosyncratic value to Kent of Reading brand pipe has no ready referent. (The added cost, prior to enclosure, of the Reading pipe would seem a minimum award but would not necessarily fully compensate Kent for his idiosyncratic value because, after the walls are closed, this added cost is insufficient to pay for the installation of the preferred pipe.)

In a case such as this, if a damages award of some amount is the only available remedy, cost-of-completion damages are attractive even though they would be overcompensatory, particularly if the promisor intentionally tendered defective performance. As observed by Steve Thel and Peter Siegelman in work that builds on Cohen's earlier contribution, anticipation of a cost-of-completion award under these circumstances could prevent promisor breach that would be inefficiently encouraged were the lower, market-based measure employed.[28] Bob Scott and Alan Schwartz have observed that courts often decline to award the higher remedy despite promisor fault.[29] But even if a court would apply a willfulness label to this case and award cost-of-completion damages, the reason need not be a desire to award supracompensatory damages or to deny any sort of good-behavior discount. For better or for worse, were they calculable,[30] a court might still prefer merely compensatory expectation damages.

Conclusion

The iconic cases discussed here – *Jacob & Youngs*, *Groves*, and *Peevyhouse* – display the work of judges who use "willfulness" of breach as a way to signal their determination that a promisee has suffered substantial harm from a promisor's failure to perform. Fault seems not to be truly part of the judges' willfulness conception and punishment seems not to be part of their goal. Rather these judges use the esoteric legal term of willfulness in a mundane process: the calculation of expectation damages. In a sense, the courts are following the path prescribed by Dick Craswell, who warns that when a court

[28] *See* Thel & Siegelman, *supra* note 20; Cohen, *supra* note 7. *See also* Muris, *supra* note 20.

[29] *See* Robert E. Scott, *In (Partial) Defense of Strict Liability in Contract*, this volume; Robert E. Scott & Alan Schwartz, *Market Damages, Efficient Contracting, and the Economic Waste Fallacy*, 108 Colum. L. Rev. 1610 (2008).

[30] An ambitious court might seek to determine the true value the promisee places on performance through a structured settlement process imposed on the parties. *See* Ayres & Madison *supra* note 27. Or a court might find reason to replace a determination of such value with an award based on the bargaining power of the parties. *See* Omri Ben-Shahar, *A Bargaining Power Theory of Default Rules*, 109 Colum. L. Rev. 396 (2009). But these interesting ideas are beyond the scope of this essay.

applies strict liability to a determination of willfulness – that is, when willfulness is not fault based – the court should carefully measure the damages award yielded by such a determination, lest the rule create inefficient incentives.[31] In these cases, the courts are, to the best of their abilities, carefully measuring damages, as part of the standard expectation remedy.

This is not to say that other willful breach theories are mistaken. In some cases, for example, it may well be sensible to adjust damages or to apply a penalty, as deterrence, for instance – ideas proposed by Cohen, Thel and Siegleman, and Bar-Gill and Ben-Shahar.[32] Or one might believe that certain breaches should be met with a particular imposition of damages based on the promisor's immorality.[33] And the case law may well offer examples of courts that adopt these approaches. But the best-known building, grading, and mining contractor cases, the standard set of exemplars for the supposed willful breach penalty, have another explanation.

[31] *See* Craswell, *supra* note 7.

[32] *See supra* notes 9, 10, and 28 and accompanying text. These approaches contemplate selective application of the willfulness doctrine. In contrast, Bob Scott and Alan Schwartz have proposed that to induce precaution and provide restitution, cost-of-completion damages should be awarded routinely, without regard to possible overcompensation. *See* Scott & Schwartz, *supra* note 29. George Cohen also addresses the role of restitution in these cases; *see* Cohen, *supra* note 7, a topic beyond the scope of this chapter.

[33] For a recent debate on questions of fault and morality in contract law, *compare* Seana Shiffrin, *Could Breach of Contract Be Immoral?*, 107 Mich. L. Rev. 1551 (2009), and Steven Shavell, *Why Breach of Contract May Not Be Immoral Given the Incompleteness of Contracts*, this volume. The morality of breach is a separate question from that presented by fraudulent promises. Regarding the latter, *see*, Ian Ayres & Gregory Klass, *Insincere Promises: The Law of Misrepresented Intent* (2005). An analysis of either question is beyond the scope of this chapter.

PART V

COMPARATIVE FAULT

FOURTEEN

A Comparative Fault Defense in Contract Law

Ariel Porat

This chapter calls for the recognition of a comparative fault defense in contract law. Part I sets the framework for this defense and suggests the situations in which it should apply. These situations are sorted under two headings: cases of noncooperation and cases of overreliance. Part II unfolds the main argument for recognizing the defense and recommends applying the defense only in cases where cooperation or avoidance of overreliance is low cost.

Introduction

In the 1970s, the comparative fault defense (CFD) in tort law began to spread across the United States,[1] about thirty years after it became prevalent in the United Kingdom.[2] Both legislatures and courts throughout the United States adopted this defense, with the latter applying it in tort cases on a daily basis. Today, few will call for the restoration of the doctrine that preceded it: the contributory negligence defense. That defense enabled courts to either impose full liability on the injurer (when there was no contributory negligence) or leave the burden of harm completely on the victim's shoulders (when there was contributory negligence). The CFD rejects this binary approach to fault, instead allowing apportionment of damages between the injurer and the contributorily negligent victim.

Over the years, the CFD has spread into the contract law of many countries (e.g., Canada, the United Kingdom, and Israel), albeit primarily in cases where a party breached a contractual duty of reasonable care or in cases of

[1] Dan B. Dobbs, The Law of Torts §201 (2001). Dobbs also notes that several states had adopted it earlier.

[2] W.V.H. Rogers, Winfield & Jolowicz on Torts §§6.38–6.41 (16th ed. 2002).

concurrent tort and contract liability.[3] Yet the same shift has been slow to occur in American contract law.[4]

This chapter calls for a reversal of this state of affairs and the recognition of a CFD in American contract law. Part I begins by presenting the nature and scope of the advocated CFD. It also illustrates the categories of cases to which it should apply: cases where (1) efficiency requires that the promisee take steps during performance to reduce the probability of a breach (to cooperate) or to reduce his potential losses (to avoid overreliance); and (2) the cooperation or avoidance of overreliance is low cost. Part II unfolds the main argument for applying the defense in American contract law. It argues that the CFD is warranted because it would provide the promisee with incentives to cooperate and rely efficiently, while at the same time maintaining incentives for the promisor to perform the contract even if the promisee failed to fulfill his part. The CFD would also encourage the promisor to efficiently reduce the need for the promisee's cooperation and avoid overreliance, thereby decreasing the losses from failure to cooperate or avoid overreliance.

I. The Nature and Scope of the Comparative Fault Defense

The CFD should be available to a breaching party ("promisor") against an aggrieved party ("promisee") when the latter's fault has contributed to his own losses. The promisee should be considered "at fault," and should shoulder part of the loss, when he fails to meet a legal burden to reduce his potential losses by cooperating with the promisor or avoiding overreliance. Below, I present eight categories of cases in which the promisee should be considered at fault and a CFD applied. These are sorted under two headings: cases of noncooperation and cases of overreliance. In all eight categories, efficiency requires the promisee to take steps either to reduce the probability of breach or otherwise to reduce his potential losses, and prevailing contract law mostly fails to provide him with adequate incentives to do so.

A. *Noncooperation*

In the cases that can be classified as instances of noncooperation, the promisee fails to take steps to prevent or reduce the likelihood of breach during performance. Example 1 presents the case where a promisee fails to assist in performance by act or omission. Example 2 presents the case where a promisee

[3] *See, e.g.*, Law Comm'n, Contributory Negligence as a Defence in Contract para. 1.4 (1993).

[4] For refusal to apply the CFD to contracts, *see* Fortier v. Dona Anna Plaza Partners, 747 F.2d 1324 (10th Cir. 1984). For willingness to apply the defense to contracts, *see* American Mortgage

could have reasonably prevented the breach by clarifying the promisor's legal rights and duties under the contract for her. In Example 3, the promisee fails to provide the promisor with information necessary for performance, while in Example 4 he fails to inform the promisor of the high potential losses he would incur in the event of breach. In both cases, the failure to provide information contributes to the breach of the contract. In the fifth and final example, the promisee is responsible for creating apprehensions that he will not perform, thereby inducing the promisor to breach.

Example 1. Failing to assist in performance. A undertakes to construct a building for *B*. During the last stage of performance, *B* gives *A*'s employees confusing instructions on the construction work required. In the end, there is a delay in the completion of performance; moreover, some of the construction work is found to be defective. Had *B* refrained from instructing *A*'s employees, the contract would have been adequately performed.[5]

Prevailing contract law would take a binary approach to such situations: either *A* or *B* would shoulder any losses due to nonperformance in their entirety. The choice between the two alternatives would hinge on the interpretation of the contract.[6] Courts rarely opt for an intermediate solution that apportions damages between the parties.[7]

Example 2. Failure to clarify misunderstandings. A is a subcontractor and *B* is a primary contractor. They enter a contract for *A* to perform construction work and for *B* to pay installments at different stages of the work. At a certain point in time, *A* argues that she has reached one of these payment stages and is therefore entitled to an installment. In fact, *A* is not entitled to any payment, because she failed to meet an additional condition stipulated by the contract. *A* is not aware of this additional condition because of an oversight on her part. *B* refuses to pay, stating that he is not obliged to do so under the contract, but *B* provides no other explanation. *A* then stops her work, causing loss to *B*. Only after a month, during which *B* stubbornly refuses to meet with *A*, does *B* explain to *A* why she was not entitled to payment.

Traditional contract law would impose liability on *A* since she breached the contract. The fact that *B* could have easily clarified the misunderstanding

Inv. Co. v. Hardin-Stockton Corp., 671 S.W.2d 283 (Mo. Ct. App. 1984). There is an increasing willingness to apply the CFD to implied-warranty cases. *See* 1 James J. White & Robert S. Summers, Uniform Commercial Code §11–8, at 758–60 (5th ed. 2006).

[5] This example is an adaptation of Lesmeister v. Dilly, 330 N.W.2d 95 (Minn. 1983), in which the court apportioned damages between the parties.

[6] *E.g.*, AMPAT/Midwest, Inc. v. Ill. Tool Works Inc., 896 F.2d 1035, 1041 (7th Cir. 1990); Second Restatement of Contracts §205 cmt. d (1981) (asserting that noncooperation could be considered a breach of the duty of good faith).

[7] Lesmeister, 330 N.W.2d at 102.

and prevented the breach is seen as irrelevant: After all, *B* is not *A*'s legal advisor, and it is *A*'s responsibility to fulfill her obligations under the contract. Under a different approach, which finds some support in the case law, when one party is aware of the other party's ignorance of his legal rights and duties and can easily clarify them, he is under obligation to do so. *B* would not be allowed to take deliberate advantage of *A*'s oversight, and he could not recover for *A*'s breach.[8] The CFD is a third option: In this type of case, it would make both *A* and *B* responsible for the losses.

Example 3. Failure to provide information necessary for performance. *A*, a contractor, and *B*, the owner of a certain piece of land, enter a contract for the performance of construction work. Due to geological difficulties, there is a delay in performance that causes *B* substantial losses. It becomes evident, however, that *B* knew about these obstacles at an early stage (although not prior to entering into the contract with *A*). Had he revealed this to *A* in due time, the delay could have been prevented.

Contract law imposes a limited duty of disclosure at the contract formation stage.[9] In shaping this duty, courts balance the interest the party possessing information has in using it for his own benefit against the interest the other party has in not being misled.

Traditional American contract law does not impose *any* duty to disclose information at the performance stage. However, one might expect an even broader disclosure duty at this stage: Disclosing the information necessary for performance, especially when it is costless (or nearly so), increases the surplus of the contract without distributional effects. As I argue in Part II, under certain conditions, applying the CFD is a better solution than imposing a duty of disclosure.

Example 4. Failure to warn of a high potential loss. *A*, a carrier, undertakes to ship a crank shaft from *B*'s mill for repair and to bring it back in one week's time. *A* instead brings the shaft back after two weeks, which results in high consequential losses to *B*, who could not find a substitute shaft. At the time of contracting, the parties were aware of a small risk that a substitute shaft would not be available. A week later, it had become clear to *B*, but not to *A*, that this risk had materialized. Had *B* conveyed this information to *A* on time, *A* would have taken costly precautions to ensure that he would return the shaft on time, thus preventing the breach.[10]

Under the *Hadley v. Baxendale* principle, *A* would be liable for *B*'s losses, since the unavailability of a substitute shaft was foreseeable at the time of contracting.

8 Mkt. St. Assocs. Ltd. P'ship v. Frey, 941 F.2d 588, 596–8 (7th Cir. 1991).

9 *See* Melvin A. Eisenberg, *Disclosure in Contract Law*, 91 Cal. L. Rev. 1645 (2003).

10 The inspiration for this example is, of course, Hadley v. Baxendale, (1854) 156 Eng. Rep. 145.

Yet, had *B* informed *A* of his potentially high losses when he realized that a substitute shaft was not available, the inefficient breach would have been avoided.[11] One way to provide promisees with incentives to convey such information would be to deprive *B* of his entitlement to damages.[12] A less extreme approach would be to make the CFD available to *A* and reduce his liability accordingly.[13]

Example 5. Creating apprehensions. B constructs a building for *A*. At a certain point in time, *B* brings heavy equipment to the construction site and places it on a concrete floor that was poured only a few days earlier. At *A*'s request, the equipment is removed to avoid damaging the floor. *A* suspects that it is already damaged, however, and demands its replacement. *B* refuses. *A* forbids *B* from continuing the construction work, and both suffer losses. It later becomes evident that the concrete floor was not damaged and that *B*'s placement of the heavy equipment on the floor was no more than a minor breach that did not warrant *A*'s repudiation. It also becomes evident that *B* could have assured *A* that the floor was not damaged or, alternatively, that it would be repaired if necessary. Had *B* provided such assurances, *A* would not have repudiated.[14]

Under traditional contract law, *A* should be found liable for breach of contract – her suspicions of damage are her own problem and do not affect *B*'s rights and duties under the contract. In contrast, the modern approach, as reflected by the Restatement, allows a party who has reasonable grounds to suspect that the other party will not perform his or her contractual obligations to demand adequate assurance of due performance. If the party fails to provide assurances, the requesting party can treat the contract as having been repudiated.[15] The Restatement does not explicitly discuss cases in which the

[11] The following illustrates numerically the principles behind Example 4: Assume that, at the time of contracting, the probability of losing $1,000 was 0.1, yielding an expected loss of $100, but that a week after contracting, the probability of loss increased to 1, yielding an expected loss of $1,000. Assume now that by investing $500 in precautions, *A* could prevent the breach. So long as *A* assumes the expected loss to be $100, he won't make this investment, whereas if he is aware that it has risen to $1,000, he will. Since efficiency requires making the investment, efficiency also dictates that *B* should convey the information regarding his high potential loss to *A*.

[12] Others have supported the use of this solution in analogous cases. *See* Melvin A. Eisenberg, *The Duty to Rescue in Contract Law*, 71 Fordham L. Rev. 647, 670–2 (2002); Charles J. Goetz & Robert E. Scott, *The Mitigation Principle: Toward a General Theory of Contractual Obligation*, 69 Va. L. Rev. 967, 1012–14 (1983).

[13] Another situation in which the *Hadley v. Baxendale* principle would allow recovery, and where applying the CFD could be valuable, is one in which the high potential losses are foreseeable (objectively) but unforeseen (subjectively) by the promisor at both the time of contracting and later on. Here, too, if the promisee realizes during performance that the promisor is unaware of the high potential loss entailed by a breach, efficiency requires conveying the information to the promisor. The CFD would provide incentives to achieve this result.

[14] This example is an adaptation of Carfield & Sons, Inc. v. Cowling, 616 P.2d 1008 (Colo. Ct. App. 1980).

[15] Second Restatement of Contracts §251 (1981).

apprehensive party responds by breaching the contract (as in our example). However, there is an implicit assumption that that party would be considered in breach and liable for the ensuing consequences. As Part II explains, a better solution for Example 5 would be apportionment of damages under the CFD.

B. Overreliance

Three categories of cases can be classified as instances of overreliance – where efficiency would have required the promisee to restrain his reliance, but he failed to do so. In the sixth example, the promisee engages in reliance despite knowing the promisor will likely breach. In the next example, the promisee has no concrete reason to suspect an imminent breach, but his reliance prior to the breach is nonetheless unreasonable. In the last example, the promisee unreasonably assumes that the contract was performed and thus fails to minimize his expected losses.

Example 6. Failure to restrain reliance in the face of a concrete risk of breach. A agrees to sell his house to *B*. As the time of delivery of possession approaches, there are signs of a substantial risk that *A* will not make timely delivery because *A*'s lessee is refusing to vacate the premises. Even though *B* is well aware of this risk, he enters into a contract with a contractor to refurnish the house starting on the day set for delivery. He also incurs expenses advertising the house for rent. In the end, *A* breaches due to late delivery, and *B* suffers losses due to forfeiting the contractor's deposit and his advertising expenses. These losses would have been prevented had *B* waited to see whether the contract would be adequately performed.

Assuming the expected losses of reliance exceeded the expected gains of reliance, *B*'s reliance on the contract was unreasonable. But since contract law does not sanction for overreliance, *B* could externalize his costs and internalize his gains. Consequently, the risk that he would overrely was a substantial one. Note that Example 6 is not a case of anticipatory breach, where the mitigation of damages defense would apply,[16] and thus provide efficient incentives for *B* to restrain his reliance. In situations represented by Example 6, then, the application of the CFD would unambiguously improve *B*'s incentives relative to those currently provided by contract law. The CFD would also be *superior* to the mitigation of damages defense, as will be explained in Part II.

Example 7. Failure to restrain reliance when there is no concrete risk of breach. A undertakes to guard *B*'s house, where valuable goods are stored. However, *B* fails to activate the alarm system. *A* breaches the contract by neglecting to guard the house. As a result, thieves steal *B*'s goods and inflict

[16] *Id.* §350 cmt. f.

bodily injury on *B*. Had *B* activated the alarm system, all losses would have been prevented. *B* also could have taken other precautionary measures to reduce the risk of theft.[17]

Even if *B* had no concrete reason to suspect that *A* would breach the contract, it could still have been unreasonable for *B* to rely only on *A* for protection. To determine whether his reliance was unreasonable, it is necessary to consider the value of the assets, the risk of theft and bodily injury, the capabilities of *A* as a guard, the cost of additional precautionary measures and their effectiveness, and so on. Applying the CFD if *B*'s reliance was unreasonable would provide incentives to similarly situated promisees to make reasonable efforts to protect their property. Conditioning *A*'s liability on *B*'s activating the alarm system or taking other precautionary measures would be an inefficient solution, as will be clarified in Part II.

Example 8. Relying on the mistaken belief that the contract has been adequately performed. *A* constructs a heating system for *B*'s business. The heater malfunctions due to *A*'s failure to fulfill her contractual obligations, and *B* suffers property losses. As a result of these losses, *B* is unable to perform third-party contracts and suffers additional losses. A few hours prior to the malfunction, there were signs of something going wrong. A reasonable person could have inferred the impending malfunction and taken steps to avoid losses.[18]

Here, as in the sixth and seventh examples, the mitigation of damages defense does not apply because *B* was not aware of the breach at the relevant points in time.[19] The CFD provides a compromise between the two extreme solutions of either *A* or *B* bearing *all* the losses. And, indeed, some courts have allowed the defense in similar situations – as when the promisor breached an implied warranty and consequential losses ensued.[20]

II. The Argument for Adopting the Comparative Fault Defense

A. *Setting the Stage*

The most significant argument against recognizing the CFD in American contract law is that it would impair the promisee's reliance and planning abilities. Were the CFD applicable, the argument runs, the promisee could no

[17] *Cf.* Astley v. Austrust Ltd. (1999) 197 C.L.R. 1, 14.

[18] This example is an adaptation of Signal Oil & Gas Co. v. Universal Oil Prods., 572 S.W.2d 320 (Tex. 1978).

[19] Second Restatement of Contracts §350 cmt. f.

[20] *See, e.g.*, Karl v. Bryant Air Conditioning Co., 331 N.W.2d 456 (Mich. 1982); Signal Oil & Gas Co., 572 S.W.2d. 320.

longer be certain of full compensation for an unfulfilled contractual promise. He could no longer "sit and wait" until the promisor fulfilled her contractual obligation, but would have to assist, supervise, and take precautionary measures with regard to either the other party's performance or his own potential losses.

In the analysis below, I posit that, under certain conditions, most contractual parties would benefit ex ante from the availability of a CFD, making it an efficient default rule for contract law. If my argument holds, the reliance and planning argument unravels: Even if the promisee's ex post reliance and planning abilities are impaired, this does not justify rejecting the CFD since it is consistent with both parties' ex ante interests.

My analysis assumes the following sequence of events: First, the promisee observes the behavior of the promisor or some part of it; second, the promisee responds by taking or not taking steps to cooperate or avoid overreliance; third, the promisor observes the response of the promisee; and fourth, the promisor responds by performing or not. The analysis also assumes that the relevant behaviors are verifiable – in other words, that they can be proven in court. Finally, it is assumed that renegotiation is costly and the parties would prefer their rights and duties to be regulated from the outset.

B. *Noncooperation*

1. **When Should Cooperation Be the Default Rule?** Below, I argue that cooperation should be the default rule where cooperation is low cost. But before explaining why, let me clarify what I mean by "costs of cooperation" and by "high-cost" and "low-cost" cooperation. Costs of cooperation do not refer only to the costs of executing the cooperation; they also include the costs associated with monitoring the promisor's performance to anticipate a need to cooperate, as well as the costs necessary to infer from the circumstances that a need to cooperate arose. The two latter costs are often far more substantial than the former type, as most of the examples discussed in Section I.A illustrate. Thus, in Example 2 (clarifying misunderstandings), the promisee's costs of clarifying for the promisor that she was about to breach the contract were close to zero; however, in order to know that such a clarification was needed, the promisee would have had to monitor the promisor's behavior and infer such a need when it arose. These costs of monitoring performance and inferring a need to cooperate, even if not high, are not nil.

There is no bright-line rule for distinguishing between high-cost and low-cost cooperation. While it is relatively easy to conceive of the two poles, it is difficult to draw the line between them. The costliness of cooperation is certainly a function of the surplus created by the contract: Cooperative efforts that are high cost in the context of a contract for renting an apartment could be low cost in the context of a contract for performing a huge construction project. For the purposes of this chapter, I define "low-cost cooperation" as any cooperation that a reasonable person would not consider to materially affect the division of the contract surplus. I define all other forms of cooperation as "high cost."

a. *High-Probability, High-Cost Cooperation* When the parties to a contract anticipate a high probability that the promisor will need the promisee's cooperation during performance and the costs of cooperation are high, they tend to address this need in their contract. The parties can set either a burden or a duty of cooperation for the promisee, so that noncooperation will result in deprivation of the promisee's entitlement to damages (a burden) or the promisee's liability for the promisor's losses (a duty). In contrast, silence on this matter can indicate that the parties did not intend to impose a high-cost burden or duty of cooperation on the promisee, at least when the parties anticipate that the need for the promisee's cooperation is highly probable.

But the question arises whether, in order to save transaction costs, there should be a default rule imposing a burden or duty of cooperation when the need for cooperation is highly probable and cooperation is *high* cost and *efficient*. I believe that the answer is no.

First, it is often hard to know whether the parties would have preferred high-cost cooperation and, if so, to what extent. Occasionally, different modes of cooperation are available, and there is no clearly preferable choice among them. Moreover, the need to cooperate and the efficiency of doing so could be debatable and could fluctuate from case to case.[21]

Second, when cooperation is high probability and high cost, it becomes part of the substance of the exchange. From both positive and normative points of view, default rules do not and should not regulate the substance of the exchange but only its ancillary terms; the substance of the exchange should be left for the parties to regulate.

Third, on many occasions the promisee could refuse to undertake a burden or duty of high-cost cooperation – or the parties could deem it inefficient – because of the parties' asymmetric information and control regarding the

[21] The parties will sometimes prefer to leave the question of cooperation open for future negotiation. However, that can be done only when the costs of renegotiation are not prohibitively high.

conditions relevant to cooperation. Typically, the promisor knows more than the promisee about the promisor's ability to perform and about her expected need for the promisee's cooperation. The promisor will try to underestimate the likelihood of this need arising while negotiating the contract, and the promisee, well aware of this fact, will be reluctant to bear a burden or duty of high-probability and high-cost cooperation. But more important, in addition to possessing better information, the promisor often has better control over the conditions giving rise to a need for cooperation. Knowing that the promisee bears a burden or duty to cooperate, the promisor may try to manipulate the promisee or to maneuver events so that greater cooperation is required than efficiency would dictate.[22] Often, such inefficient behavior is unverifiable and therefore cannot be deterred.

All three of these reasons are compelling grounds for a default rule under which there is *no* burden or duty of high-cost cooperation where the need for it is highly probable, instead leaving the parties to regulate cooperation as they see fit.

b. *Low-Probability, Low-Cost Cooperation* However, a different situation arises when one or more low-probability contingencies that require low-cost cooperation are expected to transpire. Regulating any low-probability contingency by contract yields high, even prohibitive, transaction costs for the parties, thereby encouraging them to leave many contingencies unregulated. When the potential cooperation is low cost, the argument that default rules should not regulate the substance of the exchange also collapses: It is precisely in such cases that default rules are most needed. And the above-discussed issue of asymmetric information and control over the circumstances giving rise to the need of cooperation is decidedly less acute. Therefore, given that specific low-cost cooperative behavior on the part of the promisee is typical in many contractual settings, it is desirable to shape a clear default rule regulating such behavior. The five categories of cases represented by the five examples discussed in Section I.A could set the framework for five sets of default rules regulating repeat low-cost and *efficient* cooperative modes of promisee behavior.

Example 1 (assistance) can be used to illustrate this. In that example, the owner failed to cooperate by issuing confusing instructions. While not

[22] Sometimes the parties may overcome this hurdle by imposing a duty (or burden) of cooperation on the promisee and a duty for the promisor to compensate the promisee for his costs. But since this solution could work only for some cases (e.g., it would not work when transaction costs involved in measuring the costs of cooperation and in transferring payments for cooperation are high), it cannot serve as a default rule.

necessarily costless, cooperation would not have been high cost. But many parties would not regulate such contingencies when the default rule is noncooperation. Even when cooperation is efficient, regulating these kinds of contingencies would involve high transaction costs that the parties would not willingly shoulder. A default rule encouraging cooperation would be desirable in such cases. And the same conclusion holds with respect to the other examples presented in Section I.A. In most of those examples, a substantial part of the cooperation costs were related not to executing the cooperation, but rather to monitoring the promisor's performance and inferring from the circumstances that cooperation was needed. The latter types of costs are typically "fixed." The promisor's manipulations and maneuvers cannot significantly affect the magnitude of fixed costs, so the promisee will be more willing to bear them in the first place. Therefore, in Examples 1 through 5, and especially when most of the cooperation costs are fixed, efficiency mandates that the promisee assume a burden or a duty of cooperation.

c. *High-Probability, Low-Cost Cooperation* The crucial need for a default rule favoring low-cost cooperation when it is *unlikely* to be needed does not preclude a default rule requiring low-cost cooperation when it is *likely* to be needed. Indeed, even for high-probability contingencies, a default rule could operate efficiently by reducing the parties' transaction costs. Suppose that in Example 5 (apprehensions), the parties anticipate a high probability that the owner will be uncertain, at different stages of the work, as to whether performance is adequately executed, but that assurance of performance will not be high cost. With a default rule of noncooperation, the parties will probably regulate cooperation in their contract for such a contingency. However, a cooperation default rule would save them the transaction costs of negotiating and drafting a contract provision.

d. *Low-Probability, High-Cost Cooperation* The case of *low-probability, high-cost* cooperation is different, mainly because of the above-mentioned problem of asymmetric information and control. A burden or duty of cooperation could spur the promisor to take advantage of the promisee by creating conditions in which cooperation is required too often and *inefficiently*. The fact that cooperation is high cost could provide good grounds for rejecting a rule of cooperation from the outset.[23]

[23] But if most of the costs are fixed and their magnitudes are not dependent on the promisor's behavior, a different conclusion could be warranted. *See supra* Section II.B.1.b.

2. **The Remedy** One way to encourage low-cost cooperation in the cases depicted by Examples 1 to 5 is to impose a duty of cooperation on the promisee – or a full burden of cooperation, which has a similar effect when he is the only party expected to incur losses – so that if he fails to fulfill his duty, he will shoulder all losses from a breach. When the promisee expects to internalize the entirety of the costs stemming from his inefficient noncooperation, he will tend to cooperate. But there is still a flaw in this solution: It provides no incentive for the promisor to perform efficiently if the promisee fails to cooperate. In an ideal world, if the promisee expected to internalize all the costs of his inefficient noncooperation, he would always cooperate efficiently; but in our nonideal world, he will often fail to do so. The parties may therefore be willing to give the promisor incentives to perform in the event that the promisee fails to cooperate. But placing full liability (or full burden) on the promisee will not achieve this goal.

Just as full promisor liability creates a moral hazard for the promisee, full promisee liability creates a moral hazard for the promisor. Example 3 (providing information necessary for performance) can illustrate such an outcome. In that example, the owner failed to convey geological information to the contractor. It could still have been efficient to perform on time without knowledge of this information. But if the contractor knew that the owner would bear all the losses because he had failed to inform her, she might inefficiently refrain from performing on time.

The CFD could solve this problem. Since the defense apportions damages between the parties, it leaves substantial incentives for the promisor to perform even when the promisee has failed to cooperate. Thus, in Example 3, the contractor would have incentives to perform on time even if she did not receive the information at an early stage and even if she knew of the promisee's omission. These incentives are admittedly imperfect since the CFD forces the promisor to bear less than the amount of the full losses generated by the breach. But, given the importance of the promisee's cooperation, this is a price worth paying.

There is yet another cost of using the CFD over a duty (or full burden) of cooperation: the loss of perfectly efficient incentives for the promisee to cooperate (which exist when he fully internalizes *all* the costs of the breach). However, this cost is trivial in the context of low-cost cooperation, where much less than the threat of full liability is necessary to induce the promisee to cooperate. In such cases, it is typically sufficient to threaten the promisee with an expected burden (or liability) that is higher than his costs of cooperation *even if it is much lower than the costs of noncooperation*. Using Example 3 to demonstrate this, much less than the threat of full liability is necessary to induce the owner to convey the geological information to the contractor. Granted, there is still the potential for strategic behavior on the part of the promisee: Aware that the promisor has sufficient incentives to perform even if cooperation is not rendered, the promisee may choose from the outset not to cooperate. But this is not a major concern. As illustrated by Examples 1 to 5, the promisee typically knows there is significant risk that the promisor will not perform in the absence of cooperation. In light of this knowledge and given the low-cost burden of cooperation, the promisee will cooperate because he expects to bear part of his losses. To illustrate with Example 3, the risk that the owner will not convey the geological information to the contractor to save cooperation costs is very low. He must realize that the failure to convey this information would not only make performance more costly, but could also lead to a breach with him facing part of the consequences.

In addition to providing efficient incentives for the promisee to cooperate and for the promisor to perform when the promisee fails to cooperate, the CFD offers at least one other important advantage over a duty or full-burden rule. It provides the promisor with more efficient incentives to reduce the expected losses from breach before the need for cooperation arises, which is crucial because of the promisor's superior information and control over the circumstances giving rise to the need for cooperation. If the promisee bears all the costs of noncooperation (as a duty rule would mandate), then the promisor will covertly, inefficiently, and too often create situations in which the promisee is required to cooperate. Given that cooperation is low cost, it would seem this is an insignificant risk. But since the outcome is sometimes a *high-cost failure* to cooperate, reducing the probability of the *need* to cooperate – even if cooperation is not high cost – could be cost justified. The CFD, as opposed to its alternatives, provides incentives for the promisor not only to perform when cooperation has been withheld, but also to reduce the need for cooperation in the first place.

The following numerical example illustrates the incentivizing effects of the CFD in such situations. Assume that, without cooperation, the probability of breach is 0.5, and the loss the promisee is expected to incur due to the breach is $80, yielding an expected loss of $40. Also assume that, with the promisee's cooperation, which costs him $2, the probability of breach is expected to be reduced to 0.25, with losses remaining at $80, thereby yielding expected losses of $20. Under such circumstances, cooperation is efficient. If the CFD is applied and the promisee failed to cooperate and a breach occurred, it would be sufficient that he be made to bear only $5 of the total $80 loss. This would create an ex ante threat of $2.50 for the promisee (0.5 x $5) and would induce him to cooperate from the outset. At the same time, it would leave most of the costs of the breach to be borne by the promisor. This would typically provide her with sufficient incentives to efficiently perform if the promisee failed to cooperate and to reduce the need to cooperate in the first place.

To conclude, in cases of low-cost cooperation, noncooperation should lead to reduced damages under the CFD. Ideally, from an efficiency perspective, this reduction should be no more than the minimum amount necessary to provide the promisee with incentives to cooperate.

C. Overreliance

1. **When Should Avoiding Overreliance be the Default Rule?**

a. *High-Probability, High-Cost Avoidance of Overreliance* When overreliance is anticipated at a high level of probability and its avoidance is high cost,[24] the parties are expected to regulate the extent of reliance in the contract if they want it controlled at all. They can regulate it directly when overreliance is verifiable or indirectly when it is not. Indirect regulation can take the form of a liquidated-damages clause that sets the damages the promisee is entitled to in the event of breach. In such a case, the promisee would internalize both the costs and the benefits of his reliance and would rely efficiently.[25] A default rule regulating reliance is not suitable where overreliance is highly probable and avoiding that overreliance is high cost, for the same reasons that a default rule is not suited for regulating high-probability, high-cost cooperation cases.[26]

b. *Low-Probability, Low-Cost Avoidance of Overreliance* In cases of low-probability, low-cost avoidance of overreliance, however, a default rule that encourages efficient reliance could be justified.[27] Let us return to Example 6 (concrete risk of breach). There could be many contingencies in which a risk of breach on the part of the seller of the house could emerge. Regulating each and every such contingency would entail high transaction costs, and most parties would not even attempt to do so. Thus, developing default rules adapted to various types of overreliance could be the best solution. Examples 6 to 8 could serve as paradigmatic cases from which more detailed and nuanced default rules could evolve.

[24] The distinction between high-cost and low-cost overreliance is analogous to that applied to high-cost and low-cost cooperation. *See supra* Section II.B.1.

[25] *See* Robert Cooter, *Unity in Tort, Contract, and Property: The Model of Precaution*, 73 Cal. L. Rev. 1, 14–15 (1985). Note that this solution does not work for noncooperation cases. On handling overreliance, *see* Richard Craswell, *Performance, Reliance, and One-sided Information*, 18 J. Legal Stud. 365, 367–8 (1989). For various doctrines in prevailing contract law that reduce overreliance, *see* George M. Cohen, *The Fault Lines in Contract Damages*, 80 Va. L. Rev. 1225 (1994).

[26] *See supra* Section II.B.1.a.

[27] For the argument that overreliance is not a severe or prevalent problem in contract law, *see* Melvin A. Eisenberg & Brett H. McDonnell, *Expectation Damages and the Theory of Overreliance*, 54 Hastings L.J. 1335 (2003).

c. *Other Situations in the Avoidance of Overreliance* To avoid unnecessary repetitiveness, I will not discuss at any length the desirability or undesirability of setting a default rule for cases of *high-probability, low-cost* avoidance of overreliance and for cases of *low-probability, high-cost* avoidance. The arguments regarding the desirability of default rules in the corresponding contexts of cooperation apply here as well. It suffices to say that a default rule for *high-probability, low-cost* avoidance of overreliance would be efficiency justified since it would save transaction costs; in contrast, a default rule for *low-probability, high-cost* avoidance of overreliance would be unwarranted because of the promisor's superior information and control.[28]

2. **The Remedy** One way to encourage low-cost avoidance of overreliance would be to deprive the promisee of damages for the reliance losses he inefficiently increased or failed to reduce. The buyer in Example 6 (concrete risk of breach), for example, would not be compensated for his deposit or his advertising costs because they resulted from unreasonable reliance. This solution is tantamount to applying the mitigation of damages defense at the stage before a known breach transpires. It is flawed, however, in that it would reduce the promisor's incentives to perform efficiently: She would know that she would not have to shoulder any of the promisee's overreliance losses. In Example 6, given the buyer's overreliance, efficiency requires that the seller take extra steps to deliver on time. But if the seller knows she is exempt from any liability for the buyer's overreliance losses, she will make less-than-efficient efforts to perform.

By contrast, applying the CFD would result in a reduction of the promisee's damages for losses resulting from his overreliance. This would provide the promisee with efficient incentives to undertake low-cost avoidance of overreliance. No less important, it would create greater incentives for the promisor to perform efficiently when there is a known risk of or tangible promisee overreliance. Relative to situations in which the promisor shoulders all of the losses, as is the case under prevailing contract law, the CFD would create somewhat weaker incentives for the promisor to perform efficiently. But this is a price worth paying to improve the promisee's incentives to avoid overreliance, a point well illustrated by Example 6. Under the CFD, the buyer would be expected to bear some of the advertising costs and the cost of the forfeited deposit. This would provide him with incentives to delay reliance until he saw whether the contract was performed on time. But if the buyer were to inadvertently overrely, the seller would have incentives to take extra precautions, ensure timely performance, and prevent overreliance losses.

[28] *See supra* Section II.B.1.d.

As was the case with noncooperation, the asymmetry in information and control over the conditions generating a need to avoid overreliance also provides reasons to prefer the CFD over a rule that leaves all overreliance costs on the promisee's shoulders. Unlike that latter rule, the CFD induces the promisor to reduce the need to avoid overreliance. The advantage to this is that it ameliorates the risk of high-cost overreliance, which can result when the promisee fails to avoid overreliance.

In sum, in cases of low-cost avoidance of overreliance, as in cases of low-cost cooperation, the CFD is preferable to a binary approach that leaves one party with the entire burden of loss. Here as well, from an efficiency perspective, the burden borne by the promisee should amount to no more than the minimum necessary to provide him with incentives for efficient reliance.

Conclusion

This chapter calls for recognition of a comparative fault defense in American contract law. It presents the categories of cases to which this defense should apply and argues that a precondition for its application is low-cost promisee cooperation or low-cost promisee avoidance of overreliance. Other relevant factors affecting the desirability of the CFD include (1) the benefit to be derived from the expected cooperation or avoidance of overreliance, (2) the extent of asymmetry in the information and control the parties wield over the conditions giving rise to the need to cooperate or avoid overreliance, and (3) the probability of that need arising. The higher the benefit from cooperation or avoidance of overreliance, the less asymmetry in information and control, and the lower the probability of the need to cooperate or avoid overreliance materializing, the stronger the case for the CFD.

While the chapter does not present an in-depth consideration of the criteria for apportioning damages under the CFD, the discussion does imply that courts should assign the promisee no more than the minimum burden necessary to efficiently induce him to cooperate or avoid overreliance. This would often result in imposing a greater share of losses on the promisor.[29]

Only forty years ago, American tort law was governed by a binary approach to liability and a comparative fault defense had yet to be recognized. Courts and legislatures rightly changed that. The same should be done in contract law.

[29] This is the outcome when cooperation or avoiding overreliance is low cost and the probability of a breach without cooperation or avoidance of overreliance is high. *See supra* Section II.B.2 (providing a numerical example).

FIFTEEN

Stipulated Damages, Superstrict Liability, and Mitigation in Contract Law

Saul Levmore

The remedy of expectancy damages in contract law is conventionally described as strict liability for breach. Parties sometimes stipulate damages in advance, and may agree that the damages they stipulate shall be the exclusive remedy for breach. This chapter advances two claims. First, that the familiar expectation remedy is correctly understood to involve elements of fault. There is litigation over the question of fault with respect to the mitigation of damages. Stipulation, on the other hand, makes contract liability stricter because it takes the mitigation question away from courts. Second, while law is generally described as being suspicious of, or even hostile to, stipulation, in fact, law encourages stipulation. It does this by sometimes declining to award expectancy damages, often in the very situations where stipulation seems sensible, and also by providing expectancy damages where the award of stipulated damages is regarded as a penalty. These two claims illuminate cases on such diverse matters as residential leases, construction contracts, product warranties, service contracts with liability waivers, and no-show customers and their service providers.

Introduction

The remedy of expectancy damages plays a central role in the conventional statement of American contract law. Specific performance is a smaller but well-recognized feature, and it is prominent in some subsets of contract law, such as those concerned with unique goods and land transfers. Both rules are usefully described as providing strict liability, though occasional academic campaigns draw attention to the ways in which fault permeates contract law. Fault is, of course, the foundational rule of American, if not all, tort law, and there it is strict liability that plays the supporting role.

The conventional statement also has something to say about stipulated damages, a term I use to include liquidation to an amount of money, as well as limitations on damages, scheduled damages, and other means of specifying the remedy for breach in advance and by bargain. It is when these damages are "too high," measured either by actual damages expected at the time of contract formation or damages suffered by breach, that courts will often disregard them as "penalty damages," perhaps because gambling is in the air. The disappointed party is then normally free to revert to collecting expectancy damages. There is also a small literature on "underliquidated damages," and while these might also be toxic to courts that hue to the expectancy damage line of authority, they are more often acceptable. Indeed, many waivers of liability can be understood as successfully stipulated low, if not rock bottom, damages.

This chapter proceeds as follows. Section I locates the remedy of stipulated damages in the firmament of fault, and shows that stipulated damages outflank expectancy damages on the strict liability spectrum. Contract law has been understood as deploying strict liability, but it is strict liability only to a point – because once the "duty to mitigate" is at issue, fault comes into play as courts consider the reasonableness of the post- and even the prebreach mitigation efforts. Through a variety of means, courts can modulate damages according to the parties' relative shortfalls in these efforts. In contrast, when the parties stipulate damages, they leave courts with less room in which to operate. With stipulation, the parties agree not only to take expectancy damage determinations away from the court, but also to remove questions about mitigation. Expectancy damages thus constitute a mixed system; there is, famously, strict liability with respect to breach, but then there is fault – and really a kind of comparative fault – with regard to mitigation. A stipulated damage remedy can therefore be characterized as superstrict liability because it does not normally vary according to the fault of the parties, even when we take postbreach behavior into account. I explore this conception of contract remedies, and the idea of stipulated damages as superstrict liability and as a means of removing mitigation from the purview of the courts. In doing so, I illuminate classes of cases where courts are more or less inclined to accept stipulated damages.

Section II proceeds to a second, independent point as it reexamines the conventional wisdom that law is leery of, or in effect discourages, stipulated damages – if only by dismissing those deemed to be "penalty damage" clauses. I suggest that the opposite is true. In fact, the law may actually push contracting parties toward stipulation. For example, the expectancy damage remedy is sometimes eviscerated by courts and, knowing this, parties will sometimes choose to stipulate damages in advance. Alternatively, they may simply prefer more strict liability. The real rule of contract remedies is probably that contracting parties *should* stipulate damages, at least when a postbreach assessment of damages would require something more than a comparison of market and contract prices. If this is right, then it follows that contract law, at least in this realm, seems to prefer superstrict liability. This reconception of contract remedies focuses attention on the strengths and weaknesses of stipulated damages, especially as it pertains to mitigation.

I. Stipulation, Fault, and Mitigation

A. *The Effect of Stipulated Damages on the Nonbreaching Party*

Consider a case where the parties stipulate damages and custom, law, or perhaps even the contract itself leads to the conclusion that the stipulation is, or approaches the status of, an agreed-upon exclusive remedy. Common residential leases fit this description. *A*, an apartment building owner, might agree in July to rent premises to *B* for a one-year period, beginning September 1, at a rent of $2,000 per month. Imagine that the lease agreement provides for a $1,500 deposit in the event of damages beyond normal wear and tear, and also for a $2,000 deposit to guarantee that the apartment will be held for the September occupancy. The latter money can be applied toward the last month's rent in August. In reality, the damage deposit is unlikely to be understood as stipulated damages, and to do so would create a series of problems. For example, were *B* to destroy the apartment, we would expect *A* to be able to collect more than $1,500 from *B*, and if damage done by *B* were modest, we would expect B to get some of the deposit returned. But consider the situation in which the tenant, *B*, fails to materialize on September 1, or announces just before that date that he will break the lease. My interest here is in expectancy damages versus implicit stipulation, and in the parties' mitigation efforts. Imagine that *A* is immediately able to find another tenant, *C*, who agrees to pay the rent *B* had promised. As a result, *A*'s damages are close to zero, and yet in most cases we expect *A* to retain the $2,000 deposit, perhaps because it is hard for *B* to learn of the agreement with *C*, because *A* is seen as a kind of lost-volume seller, or because the deposit compensates *A* (in a manner courts might subtly recognize without articulating) for those other occasions when it is very difficult to locate a new tenant. This is the situation where *A* does not find a new tenant for some time, say ten months. In theory, *A* might then collect $20,000 from *B*, but these expectancy damages are rarely awarded. Parties to a residential lease have come to believe that if this part of the deposit is forfeited, it is the landlord's exclusive remedy. This belief or implied provision that this "deposit" amounts to stipulated damages, is like that we attach to a storekeeper's sign declaring that there will be a $25 charge for a bounced check. The amount is understood to be the exclusive remedy available to the storekeeper, though it could turn out to be higher or lower than the actual damages, despite the fact that Section 2–719(1)(b) of the Uniform Commercial Code (UCC) insists that a contract be clear about an exclusive remedy. In the case of both the breaching tenant and the bouncing check, the stipulated amount is apt to be regarded as a reasonably good (ex ante) estimate of expectancy damages. In the case of the check, actual damages might include another bank's fee assessed against the storekeeper's account, as well as the loss that occurs when the storekeeper writes checks based on an incorrect assessment of her own bank balance – all of which could be reasonably thought to add up to, or to average, $25. Similarly, in the residential lease case, we might imagine that *A*, or even the typical landlord, averages one month to find a replacement tenant.

This apparent treatment of the deposit as stipulated damages seems efficient in this context. *A* is in the superior position to find a replacement tenant. The fixed damage amount gives *A* the right incentive to find *C*, and at the best possible price. If instead, the rule were that *B* retrieved the deposit in the event that *A* quickly found a replacement, *A* would have diminished incentive to expend resources on the search. An expectancy damage rule runs a yet more serious risk that *A* will underinvest in the mitigation process. It is tempting to observe that custom has produced the more efficient rule. It is, after all, custom that has glorified the deposit to a point where it has become the automatic and exclusive remedy for breach, at least in most residential settings, despite the ostensible rule that expectancy damages constitute the default and preferred remedy for breach in American law.

If the law were to abide by expectancy damages, *A* would have an obligation to mitigate, and the court would have to confront obvious fact-finding questions as to whether *A* advertised, searched, and priced the place in a reasonable fashion as well as whether *A* was a lost-volume seller. It is not that the parties know in advance much more than the court will know following breach, but rather that they may agree not to expend resources arguing about this matter. All in all, the stipulated damage norm is nicely efficient in getting *A* to undertake the mitigation, as *A* internalizes the costs and benefits associated with the task of going forward once *B* breaches. And it does this without imposing the fact-finding costs associated with comparative fault, which is a way of describing the usual treatment of the parties' mitigation efforts.

B. *The Effect of Stipulated Damages on the Breaching Party*

The contrast with comparative fault draws attention to *B*'s as yet unexplored behavior. Even if we assume that *B* has no capacity to find a subletting tenant or other substitute, *B* is in control of the information regarding his own likelihood of breach. He can inform *A* of his plans early or late in the game, and often decrease or increase *A*'s (and the social) losses in this way. In principle, expectancy damages take this into account; the reasonableness of *A*'s mitigation efforts will be a function of *B*'s, for mitigation is a joint venture. Thus, at first blush, superstrict liability is likely to be inferior when efficient mitigation requires precautions by both parties. Expectancy damages left room for an element of comparative fault with respect to mitigation. Stipulated damages appear to give one party, but one party only (*A*, the landlord, in our example) a strong incentive to mitigate.

Stipulated damages can, however, have some effect on *B* through additional stipulation, or what amounts to more careful contracting by the parties. This form of more detailed stipulation is common in certain settings. For example, newly admitted law students are accustomed to terms under which they forfeit an increasingly large fraction of the first tuition payment as the date of their withdrawal, or change of heart, falls later in the calendar. Similarly, in the preceding example, *A* and *B* might have provided for *B* to forfeit a larger fraction of the deposit as the date of breach approached September 1. Without such refinement, stipulated damages may be superstrict in the sense that there is no fault determination, but also less than strict because the damages are capped. (In our example, the $2,000 deposit is owed without any inquiry into mitigation, but it is less than strict liability in the sense that it offers only $2,000, rather than the $24,000 that an expectancy damage remedy might generate.) As detail is added, stipulation can encourage mitigation on the part of both parties.

The preceding example illustrates that while expectancy damages may not normally depend on the reason for, or morality of, a failure to keep a promise, these damages are supposed to be sensitive to the parties' mitigation efforts, and in this regard reasonableness of behavior is very much at issue. We can imagine a fault-based system that inquires into the reasonableness of the breach itself, and we can understand stipulated damages as a system that comes close to eliminating fault as a factor in both pre- and postbreach activity. The expectancy damage remedy normally falls in between these two, representing a kind of mixed (fault-strict liability) system, because once a breach is contemplated, losses that could have been avoided through mitigation are assigned according to a comparative fault inquiry. In most cases, a strict liability remedy, such as the homemade one of stipulated damages, can give (at least) one party an incentive to mitigate.

The novel element in this picture of stipulation is that the parties may reason that a commitment not to spend resources trying to show that the other party was at fault will be cost effective. This is the key to the argument in Part II, where I suggest that in many situations courts may share or simply accommodate this sense regarding the folly of calculating not only expectancy damages, but also the costs and benefits of various mitigation strategies. In these settings, the parties can see that they might need to forgo expectancy damages – and they can choose to stipulate damages instead, or adjust to a high likelihood of (undeterred) breach.

The argument advanced thus far, that stipulated damages should be seen as a kind of superstrict liability, is meant to supplement the familiar notion that stipulation is simply a means of self-assessment, where the parties have more information about losses from breach ex ante than courts will have ex post. Under this view, when losses are easy to calculate ex post, as they are when a defendant breaches the promise to deliver a good with an easily determined market price, there is no reason to encourage stipulation, and the parties themselves should have no reason to stipulate damages in advance. The connection between the relative ability of the parties and courts to assess damages, on the one hand, and the cost of encouraging and monitoring mitigation efforts on the other, will become clearer when we add to the picture the inclination of courts to encourage stipulation.

II. Encouraging Stipulation

A. *How Courts Encourage Parties to Stipulate*

Courts often decline to award contract damages because they are "too speculative." In one representative case, a manufacturer delivered defective carpet to a dealer, yet the dealer's lost prospective profits were regarded as too speculative and conjectural to warrant recovery.[1] And in the famous case of *Chicago Coliseum Club v. Dempsey*, the club collected most of its provable expenses following the boxer's breach of an agreement to appear in an exhibition fight, but not its lost profits, because they were "dependent upon so many different circumstances that they are not susceptible of definite legal determination."[2] When new ventures are derailed by contractual breaches, it continues to be likely that courts will decline to impose expectancy damages, because the disappointed party's expectation is seen as difficult to measure,

1 Aldon Indus. v. Don Myers & Assoc's, 517 F.2d 188 (5th Cir. 1975). The court declined to go along with a "general rule" that the anticipated profits of a commercial business ought always be regarded as too speculative, but it did say that, where anticipated profits are concerned, a plaintiff has a difficult burden of proof.

2 265 Ill. App. 542 (1932).

inasmuch as there is no track record of past profits from which to extrapolate damages.[3] Courts will, however, respect the stipulated damage provisions in these sorts of contracts.[4] It remains difficult to predict when courts will decline to award damages because of their speculative nature. Even if we set new ventures aside, there will often be wild and genuine disagreement over the damages caused by the breach of a commercial contract. Dempsey's escape from serious liability is easy to ridicule with the observation that, although most losses are speculative, courts can marshal predictive evidence much as entrepreneurs do their best to assess the profitability of various investments. Yet, it is not uncommon for expectancy damages to be denied because of the speculative character of these predictions.

When courts deny expectancy damages, they effectively encourage stipulation in future transactions, especially because parties have nothing to lose by stipulating; even if courts disregard the stipulation, the option of expectancy damages remains. Conventional wisdom, however, suggests that contracting parties should be cautious about stipulation primarily because, if the specified amount looks high ex post, there is the danger that a court will say it was also unreasonably high ex ante, when the parties ought to have been assessing expected damages. If so, the provision will be labeled a penalty and disregarded. But a better, and certainly contrarian, view is that, on balance, the law actually encourages stipulation. If the parties do not stipulate, the danger exists that damages will be regarded as speculative. Stipulation allows the parties to avoid that result. And if stipulation is disregarded because of the penalty clause doctrine, the injured party can still ask for and receive expectancy damages. The cost of stipulation is, therefore, the cost of assessment and negotiation (at least insofar as there will be no breach later on, so that these are wasted expenditures) and also the cost associated with the danger of underliquidation. This last cost, however, can normally be avoided by the parties specifying that the stipulated damage term is a floor and not an exclusive remedy. If, however, the stipulated damages are described as the exclusive remedy, then we can surmise that either the parties prefer their own ex ante assessments (and bargain) over a court's ex post determination or that they wish to commit to avoid litigation costs. Note that courts are not simply saving themselves work in one place – damage assessment – only to take it back

[3] *See* Drews Co. v. Ledwith-Wolfe Assoc's., 371 S.E.2d 532 (S.C. 1988) (finding insufficient certainty to award lost profits but deciding to join the majority of jurisdictions in applying the "new business rule" as a rule of evidentiary sufficiency and not as an automatic preclusion to recovery of lost profits by a new enterprise).

[4] *See, e.g.*, XCO Int'l v. Pac. Sci. Co, 369 F.3d 998 (7th Cir. 2004) (upholding $100,000 per year in liquidated damages where assignee allowed assignor's patent to expire, and noting that it was sensible for parties to stipulate damages where damages are difficult to determine).

on when evaluating claims that stipulated amounts should be excluded as "penalties." The latter inquiry is more relaxed, as courts need not be precise r to rule whether or not penalties have been provided.

B. *Two Advantages of Stipulation: Knowledge and Mitigation*

I have already suggested that stipulation allows parties to opt for strict liability with respect to the question of mitigation. And we know that stipulated damages are also a means of estimating damages where the parties think that their knowledge and bargain are likely to be superior to the courts' determination of expectancy damages. The courts have the advantage of viewing the actual damages, while the parties cannot wait until after breach to assess damages because, by then, their interests are opposed. On the other hand, the parties have local knowledge and can vary the price of their contract. We might label this familiar, first-order reason for stipulation as "knowledge." "Mitigation" could refer to the possibility of profitably, avoiding the costs associated with litigating the consequences of various mitigation strategies, even at the expense of reducing the incentive to mitigate. Stipulated damages might thus offer *knowledge* and *mitigation* advantages. And one way to think about the cases is to ask whether they present one or both of these features.

Of course, one risk of stipulation is that the parties sacrifice the comparative fault inquiry that is buried within expectancy damages, as it pertains to mitigation; the parties may not want superstrict liability. Fortunately, when parties are encouraged to stipulate they are usually able to count on one party's mitigation efforts, precisely because the stipulated damage clause gives that party a strong incentive to mitigate – as *A* was encouraged to do in the residential lease example above. The other party can then be induced into contributory mitigation with more refined stipulation.

A natural question to ask at this point is whether it is good that knowledge and mitigation are "bundled" in the single tool of stipulated damages. The parties might agree to avoid litigating over mitigation, but they may think that a court's ex post damage assessment is superior to their own ex ante guess. Conversely, they may prefer their own ex ante assessments, but be willing to risk the costs of later litigation over mitigation because of the incentive effects on mitigation. In principle, these problems can be solved and the solutions unbundled. Parties could stipulate damages in order to gain the knowledge advantage, but could provide that the stipulated damages they specify "should be increased or decreased if either or both parties fail to take steps to mitigate the losses caused by breach." I have not seen such a contract. Lawyers may sense that courts will misinterpret or fail to enforce such a mixed message about their own competence, or they may simply not have thought about unbundling. Parties could also try to waive solely the duty to mitigate. An agreement could provide that "the tenant shall take possession on September 1, and shall owe no damages whatsoever for failing to provide any notice regarding anticipated breach to the landlord before that date." And, in between, contracts could try to specify what should or should not be taken into account in determining damages. In practice, parties inclined to stipulate damages in order to avoid litigation over mitigation will surely want to avoid litigation about expectancy damages, where they also enjoy a knowledge advantage. The reverse is less obvious. Parties may wish to exploit their own knowledge and take the determination of expectancy damages away from the court, but they may still fear losses from the failure to mitigate enough to tolerate litigation over those losses. Careful stipulation will help. For example, the carpet manufacturer (that may know its product is defective in time for dealers to stock other inventory), Dempsey, and surely the tenant, *B*, can all be encouraged to reveal coming breaches early in the game, just as the withdrawing law student has an incentive to do so, with clauses that increase their damages as the revelation date is delayed.

In some settings, parties turn to insurance, but this does not mar the point about bundling mitigation and knowledge. Thus, when a construction company is employed to build a bridge or renovate a place of business, the customer fears delay or abandonment. It might obtain or require a performance bond, and include that premium in the price of the contract. The surety's price is one check on the feasibility of the project, and on the schedule of payments due from the customer, because it must stand ready to hire another firm to complete the project. Concurrently, the construction company may buy or require a payment bond, so that each side's performance under the contract may be guaranteed. If the construction company abandons the project, the customer (and the insurer with a right of subrogation) may make a claim for this breach. Under these circumstances, stipulation may be less attractive. The parties might respond to the unavailability of expectancy damages by demanding these sureties, and thus we can think of the premium paid to an insurer as a kind of stipulated damages, but paid ex ante. This is surely a form of superstrict liability, where payment follows the activity rather than the breach.

Dempsey is a case where unbundling the knowledge and mitigation attributes of stipulated damages might have been useful. The club could have stated its expected damages ex ante, and Dempsey could then have priced the contract accordingly. It seems unlikely, though, that the parties would have chosen to stipulate in order to avoid the comparative fault inquiry we associate with the duty to mitigate. The club might have mitigated, and received some return on its preparatory expenditures, by looking for a substitute – though heavyweight champions are hard to find. Dempsey could have tried to do the same. The main claim here is that the very possibility of a court's declaring expectancy damages to be "too speculative" encourages future parties to stipulate. If they prefer a court to police mitigation, then the benefits of stipulation come at a substantial cost, although the parties can minimize this cost by agreeing on a schedule of stipulated damages.

Fretwell v. Protection Alarm Co.[5] provides a contrasting case, in which the court upheld a contract between a homeowner and burglar alarm company.[6] The contract stipulated $50 as the "limit of liability," but negligence by the company's employee, who failed to notify the police, arguably caused the homeowner's $90,000 loss. In contrast to *Dempsey*, not only did the parties stipulate here, but their concern would also surely have been about litigating over mitigation rather than assessing damages. Parties to such a contract can anticipate that damages will be easy to assess, because the homeowner will provide proof of stolen property. There is, however, the risk that questions surrounding mitigation will consume resources. For instance, the alarm company can argue that even though it is strictly liable for nonperformance, the property owner has the obligation to mitigate, or at least not to be contributorily negligent; in the extreme, the homeowner cannot possibly collect if he or she gave information to the thief and enabled the crime. It is easy to imagine litigation over less dramatic contributions to the loss – and the parties might sensibly choose to stipulate in order to avoid such litigation.

These unbundled cases, where stipulation is responsive either to the parties' superior ability to assess damages or to the difficulty of evaluating mitigation efforts in court, are relatively rare. When expectancy damages are hard to assess, both will often be difficult to evaluate, if only because knowledge and mitigation are intertwined. A common example is that of a product sold with a repair-or-replace warranty, or stipulation. Imagine that a photographer, *P*, purchases a camera made by *N*, offered with just such a warranty, and that *P* suffers losses when the unit malfunctions. Stipulation makes sense because damages can be quite difficult to assess even ex post, and since they

[5] 764 P.2d 149 (1988).

[6] A well-known outlier is Samson Sales, Inc. v. Honeywell, Inc. 465 N.E.2d 392 (1984), where a similar liquidated damages clause was thrown out as a penalty, both because it was not a reasonable estimate of damages and because damages would normally be easy to ascertain. The parties' language was perhaps unfortunate, and the court might have treated the clause differently had it been fashioned as a limitation on liability. Fretwell also raises the issue of a clause fashioned as liquidated damages, but treated by the court as involving a limitation on liability, and therefore not subject to the claim that it was an inapt estimate of damages.

take the form of a limitation on damages, they do encourage some mitigation on *P*'s part. For instance, *P* might travel with a backup camera. There may be no incentive for *N* to mitigate, but in most cases there is little *N* can do by way of mitigation. If some disclosure by *N* would be useful, as when *N* learns of a problem from other users, it is possible that the contract or legislation will step in to encourage disclosure, or mitigation. Moreover, where damages include personal injury, as is the case where automobile and pharmaceutical manufacturers could provide notice of dangers, stipulation is likely to fail in the first place. In any event, *P*'s mitigation will not completely eliminate the damages *P* suffers, but these damages are difficult to assess.

I do not mean to say that stipulation is always encouraged by courts or desirable for parties. First, there are cases where ex post determination is easy, as when there is the failure to deliver or to purchase a widely sold commodity, and where ex ante stipulation is more difficult or would simply be deflected to an insurance contract. It happens that in these cases the task of mitigation is easily allocated by contract or by default, so stipulation would sacrifice little on that front, but stipulation is simply not needed in the first place, because expectancy damages are easily assessed. Second, there are cases where the ability of courts to modulate damages in the manner of comparative fault with respect to mitigation (or breach itself) is palpably valuable because both parties may contribute to the delay or other breach. The parties may choose to stipulate in these settings, and to sacrifice this benefit, but then they need to make their intentions clear. If their underliquidation or overliquidation is too serious, we know that courts may think they erred too much. A straightforward way to think about this is not to emphasize what courts "think" or encourage, but rather to understand parties as sometimes choosing superstrict liability for themselves.

C. *Stipulation Through the Lens of Mitigation*

The arguments advanced here are largely positive, for I do not make a claim as to when courts ought to encourage stipulation. A normative argument would require some confidence in our ability to estimate the costs of determining fault and the costs suffered by encouraging a remedy, stipulated damages, that is more difficult to modulate according to the relative fault of the parties. The positive-normative line would be blurred somewhat if there were more obvious patterns with respect to courts' disregarding stipulated damages or with regard to their encouraging stipulation by denying expectancy damages. But when one studies the cases, it becomes apparent that the denials do not seem linked to the breacher's wrongdoing, willfulness, or opportunistic behavior; they do not seem tied to the identity of the claimant; and they do not come more readily when the stipulation is customized or boilerplate. The argument advanced here is thus cast as a positive one, explaining repair-or-replace clauses and a variety of other cases, as we have seen.

Consider, finally, everyday cases where the conventional rules of contract remedies appear to be ignored. *R* orders a taxi from *T* in order to travel to an airport. If *T* fails to materialize as agreed upon, and *R* loses the value of a non-refundable ticket (as could have been well anticipated by *T*), we do not expect *R* to recover these expected damages from *T*. Symmetrically, if *T* appears at *R*'s door and *R* had accepted a ride with a friend, *T* may have lost other business, but does not expect to collect from *R*, unless damages were stipulated. In some sense, the case is mysterious; it is almost as if all we read in contract treatises has no application in the real world. After all, the damages here are not particularly difficult to determine ex post, so that stipulation does not seem superior to expectancy damages on the usual grounds. We might imagine highlighting the nonspeculative costs associated with taking a later flight, and *T*'s pointing to the time wasted because of *R*'s breach, in hopes of recovering at an hourly rate. But the case can be described neither as one of strict liability for failure to perform nor as one reflecting the imposition of fault or comparative fault. Even if *R* could easily have called *T* to cancel the trip, or *T* could have contacted *R* two hours in advance to encourage *R* to find another means of transport to the airport, we know that, in the absence of stipulation, no damages will be paid for the failure to take these steps. While at first glance this might seem like the wrong result, the picture is easier to rationalize once we bring mitigation into play. It would be hard to know how easy it really would have been for *R* to rush to the airport by another means, or for *T* to find other business. We might think of customary law as offering a default stipulation of zero damages, so that the parties need not litigate the facts of mitigation.

There is the lingering question of why parties to this kind of contract so rarely agree on stipulated damages. We do see some expensive restaurants asking for credit card information when taking reservations, and then imposing a stipulated fee for the patron's failure to materialize. Even if the taxi company stipulates $*x* for *R*'s failure to wait, *R* may breach either because the alternative ride is free or because *R* fears missing a flight. And if $*y* is stipulated for *T*'s failure to pick up *R* as promised, *T* will still breach if another customer, *S*, pays a sufficiently higher price – though we have no reason to think that *S* values the ride more than *R*, whose fare was likely determined by a fixed schedule. But bargaining can encourage earlier transmittal of information. It might pay for *R* to stipulate that "I will pay you $50 if I am a no-show, but only $30 if I give more than one-hour notice." Similarly, we do find restaurants excusing the penalty with enough notice. But it is also possible that we do not often find more detailed stipulation because such stipulation might be thought to encourage breach, as it offers a price for breach and thus psychologically encourages the other party to "buy a breach." Still, at the right price, breach ought to be welcome. Some restaurants and airlines do seem comfortable with no-shows, once fees have been included.

Conclusion

As a normative matter, there is something to be said for complete freedom of contract. From this position, it is easy to rail against cases that do not enforce the parties' stipulations, and then to complain about cases that do not provide expectancy damages, or another remedy, where the parties appear to have planned on the supply of the given remedy. On the other hand, over- and underliquidation can cause inefficiencies that parties may not have anticipated, and these may be avoided if courts judiciously intervene to prevent palpable waste. To this calculus we must now add the idea that just as parties might sometimes wish to avoid a court's assessment of expectancy damages, so too they might sometimes choose to avoid a court's assessment of their mitigation efforts. Stipulation in various currencies thus produces superstrict liability in contract law. It does so by adding strict liability regarding mitigation to the usual strict liability as to the fact of breach. Where mitigation is important, contract law is a comparative fault regime, and its strict liability component fades in the background. In an important subset of these cases, the parties will prefer strict liability and they will stipulate damages – sometimes partial and sometimes a good estimate of full expectancy damages – in order to achieve this result. In another subset, they will count on courts to police their efforts in comparative fault fashion. And in a surprisingly significant third group of cases, they will not stipulate, even knowing that courts will decline to impose liability.

The other reconception suggested here, that contract law effectively encourages the stipulation of damages, is a weaker though more startling claim. The doctrinal knowledge of most lawyers is, after all, limited in this regard to the fact that one must be careful not to overliquidate and enter the realm of penalty damages. But as we look at the variety of cases, it is apparent that expectancy damages are disrespected by courts at least as much as stipulated damages. And inasmuch as expectancy damages are still available when penalty damages are disregarded, there will be many circumstances in which parties will do well to stipulate damages. Certainly such stipulation does sometimes introduce the problem of an insufficient incentive to mitigate, especially when mitigation requires joint effort, but this problem can be reduced with yet more detailed stipulation. Courts may want to take these points into account when striking or enforcing stipulated damage clauses and when adjudicating mitigation disputes. As is often the case, a positive theory of the behavior of parties and courts is likely to bear on the normative questions associated with legal rules and private practices.

SIXTEEN

Creditor's Fault: In Search of a Comparative Frame

Fabrizio Cafaggi

This chapter compares the role of the promisee's conduct in contractual relationships in U.S. and European legal systems. Different approaches to comparative negligence and mitigation are considered first, and then a more general analysis of doctrines dealing with the promisee's position in the contractual relationship and the role of cooperation is carried out. In this area, legal systems display significant divergences. Continental European systems recognize a strong role for comparative negligence and the duty to cooperate, while common law jurisdictions limit the scope of comparative negligence and the duty to cooperate while attributing a wider role to the duty to mitigate.

This chapter offers an "institutional" explanation to these divergences. The lack of comparative negligence in the United States, when considered along with the deployment of other forms of risk-sharing and apportionment of losses stemming from breach of contract, conforms to the idea that contract law is mainly directed at risk allocation. In European continental systems, the recognition of a general rule of comparative negligence and mitigation delineates a general principle based on the law of obligations, applicable to both contract and tort. Contractual relationships are generally characterized in these systems by a legal framework fostering a higher level of cooperation, including reallocation of risks between time of contract and time of performance.

Introduction

In this chapter, I compare the role of the creditor's (promisee's) conduct in contractual relationships in US and European legal systems. I first consider

Many thanks to the participants to the Chicago conference organized by O. Ben Shahar and A. Porat for comments and suggestions and to C. Gillette and A. Porat for comments on a later draft of this chapter. Thanks to D. Fortune, L. Gorywoda, and A. Janczuk for their excellent research assistance.

different approaches to comparative negligence and mitigation, and then carry out a more general analysis of doctrines dealing with the creditor's position in the contractual relationship and the role of cooperation.

In this area, legal systems display significant divergences – partly rooted in their historical antecedents, and partly related to different concepts of contracts and contractual relationships. Continental European systems (with significant differences between Germany and France) recognize a strong role for comparative negligence and the duty to cooperate, while common law jurisdictions (with important differences between England and the United States) limit the scope of comparative negligence and the duty to cooperate while attributing a wider role to the duty to mitigate.[1]

The divergence between the Continental European and common law regimes can largely be explained by their different forms of regulatory capitalism, as market structures and contractual interdependencies, especially in the context of business transactions, may influence the emergence and operation of a system's comparative negligence rule.[2] In particular, the different role of the judiciary in relation to private autonomy and contractual freedom can at least partly be explained by the different relationships between states and markets.[3] The resulting comparative negligence and mitigation rules not only influence parties' ex ante risk allocation, but also have an impact on adjustments made in light of unanticipated events – including the choice between remaining in the contractual relationship versus deploying market alternatives. Where markets are thin and likely to fail, the relevance of the creditor's conduct will be heightened. As is common in many contractual relationships, new circumstances may require contract or market adaptations. Market prices of the traded commodity may increase or decrease to unexpected levels, new technologies may make the goods unsuitable for the buyer, or the seller may face an unexpected rise of production costs. But where markets are thin or substitute performance is difficult to obtain, due to high specific investments and/or interdependencies, the need for cooperation within the transaction will be amplified.

The duty to cooperate gains further importance in the case of collaborative contracts,[4] wherein the exchange of performances is aimed at achieving

[1] For a comparative analysis, *see* A. Porat, *Contributory Negligence in Contract Law: Toward a Principled Approach*, 28 U. Brit. Colum. L. Rev. 141 (1994). In general comparative fault in contract law has been denied in the United States: *see, e.g.*, Haysville U.S.D. No. 261 v. GAF Corp., 666 P.2d 192, 199 (Kan. 1983). I should clarify that, in relation to the United States, I will examine only the Second Restatement of Contract, leaving out the UCC.

[2] On the role of regulatory capitalism and its different models, J. Braithwaite, Regulatory Capitalism: How It Works, Ideas for Making It Work Better (Edward Elgar, 2008).

[3] *See* C. Milhaupt & K. Pistor, Law and Capitalism (University of Chicago Press, 2008).

[4] *See* Fabrizio Cafaggi, *Contractual Networks and the Small Business Act: Towards European Principles?*, 4 Eur. Rev. of Contract Law 493 (2008).

a common objective unlike conventional sales contracts.[5] In the context of "business-to-business" transactions, where parties agree to codesign a product or jointly develop a research project, the role of the creditor in ensuring conforming performance by the debtor gains significance. The creditor's failure to cooperate may affect both the likelihood of breach and the consequences flowing therefrom. In some contractual relationships, such as joint ventures, the distinction between creditor and debtor may be difficult to maintain, and a failure to achieve the agreed-upon outcome will often be the result of a lack of mutual cooperation.

As we shall see, the rules of comparative negligence and mitigation incentivize different types of behavior among contracting parties. While the comparative negligence rule is primarily aimed at fostering contractual cooperation, mitigation encourages parties to seek alternative performance in the market.[6]

Often, within the contractual relationship, performance is the outcome of a sequential game wherein the debtor and the creditor interact strategically. The creditor's conduct may precede or succeed the debtor's (promisor's) performance, and the interaction may generate reliance on the promise and its execution by the debtor, which in turn may affect the decision-making process of the debtor concerning performance or breach. Reliance may occur before the contract is signed or after the promise becomes binding. In light of the fluid nature of the contractual relationship, the creditor's conduct should be analyzed with regard to this sequential frame. Although the optimal level of a creditor's reliance and his related levels of investment in precautions and performance are not directly controlled by the doctrines of comparative negligence and mitigation, these doctrines play a significant role in shaping rules concerning the creditor's conduct.

I. Comparative Negligence and Mitigation in Contract Law Compared

The core investigation concerns the relationship between comparative negligence and mitigation as regulatory principles of the creditor's conduct and its effect on debtor's decision-making process. The first issue is whether these divergent rules concerning the creditor's conduct can still be traced back to a unitary principle of cooperation among contracting parties, or if they

[5] *See* R. J. Gilson, C.F. Sabel, & R.E. Scott, *Contracting for Innovation: Vertical Disintegration and Interfirm Collaboration*, 109 Colum. L.R. 431 (2009).

[6] *See* C. J. Goetz & R. E. Scott, *The Mitigation Principle: Toward A General Theory of Contractual Obligation*, 69 Va. L. Rev. 967 (1983) (hereinafter Goetz & Scott, *The Mitigation Principle*).

instead perform different functions, varying in accordance with the nature of the contractual relationships and market structures. Legal systems currently provide three answers: (1) to combine comparative negligence and the duty to mitigate into a unitary principle; (2) to group them under a common principle of mitigation, but subdivide operational rules between the duty to mitigate and comparative negligence; and (3) to radically distinguish them by referring to different functions (i.e., deterrence and compensation).

In Continental Europe, legal systems such as those of Germany, Austria, and Italy adopt a unitary principle, differentiating between pre- and post-breach; while in other systems, comparative negligence and mitigation are distinguished. In France, comparative negligence (*faute de la victime* or *du creancier*) has been adopted by the Cour de Cassation, but the duty to mitigate has been rejected.[7] In England, the duty to mitigate is widely recognized while contributory negligence with apportionment, which was introduced in tort with the 1945 act, is limited in contract common law.[8] In the United States, mitigation is well recognized while comparative negligence is not.[9] It should be underlined that even those jurisdictions that reject or limit comparative negligence in the context of a two-party contract often allow apportionment, based on fault, in multiparty contracts.[10]

Comparative negligence and the duty to mitigate share the common feature of being defenses pleaded by the debtor. They are not affirmative claims, unlike the duty to cooperate, whose breach by the creditor can give rise to an obligation of the debtor to pay damages. The two differ concerning the applicable standard: care in comparative negligence and reasonableness in mitigation. These differences may lead to different considerations concerning an individual party's ability to act in order to prevent the breach or minimize its consequences. Reasonableness, in the context of mitigation, often allows subjective elements to be factored in, including, to a limited extent, impecuniosity. These elements are less frequently considered in comparative negligence. However, the key difference between comparative negligence and mitigation relates to creditor's expectations. In the case of comparative negligence, precautions by the creditor are based on the expectation of performance, not

[7] C. André, *Le fait du créancier contractuel* (LGDJ, Bibliothèque de droit privé, 2002), S. Reifergeste, *Pour une obligation de minimiser le dommage* (PUAM, 2002).

[8] *See* E. Peel, Treitel, The Law of Contract (12th ed., Thomson Sweet & Maxwell, London, 2007), 1064–6.

[9] *See* Second Restatement of Contracts § 350. For general rule that there is no apportionment of contractual damages based on comparative fault of parties, *see* III Farnsworth on Contracts (3d ed. 2004) §12.8, pp. 195–6.

[10] D. J. Bussel, *Liability for Concurrent Breach of Contract* 73 Wash. Univ. Law Q. 97, 124, 126 (1995).

on that of breach. The opposite is true for mitigation, where the creditor is required to act on the knowledge of breach or on the expectation, after repudiation, that the debtor will breach. One additional difference between comparative negligence and mitigation, present in all legal systems to varying degrees, is that expenses the creditor incurs in taking precautions may not be recovered under comparative negligence but will be recoverable under mitigation if deemed reasonable.

We find comparative negligence in systems that have opted for strict liability for the debtor as well as in fault-based regimes. Thus, comparative negligence, when adopted, does not require a particular rule of debtor's liability, being compatible with both strict liability and fault. However, modes of apportioning damages may change depending on what debtor's liability regime is in place. In a strict liability regime with comparative negligence, the debtor will bear all losses but for those "attributable" to the creditor's negligence. In a negligence-based regime, the creditor will bear all the losses from the breach but for those "caused" by the debtor's fault.

II. Comparative Negligence

Comparative negligence in contract is expressly recognized by legislation in Germany and Italy, Austria, the Netherlands, and Switzerland.[11] Similar principles apply in Poland and Slovenia.[12] In France, recognition has occurred through judicial interpretation.

The rule applied both to contractual and extracontractual liability is often framed within the broader context of causation and is explicitly associated with the limitation of damages.[13] The creditor who has contributed to the breach (or whose conduct has increased the losses flowing therefrom) cannot be fully compensated.[14]

Creditor's conduct may concern a duty to take precautions affecting probability of breach – for example, a duty to provide information about the effects of debtor's future performance on creditor's economic activity, a duty to warn about risks associated with debtor's performance, or a duty to inspect the good or services and verify lack of conformity once performance

[11] In Germany, a general principle of contributory negligence, applying to both tort and contract, is provided for by §254 BGB. In Italy it is regulated by art. 1227 CC. In Austria by §1304 ABGB, in the Netherlands by art. 6. 101 BW, and in Switzerland by art. 44 CO.

[12] In Poland art. 362 CC and in Slovenia arts. 243–44 CC.

[13] *See* G.H. Treitel, *Remedies for Breach of Contract (Courses of Action Open to a Party Aggrieved)*, Chapter 16, International Encyclopedia of Comparative Law 75–6 (J.C.B. Mohr (Paul Siebeck), Tübingen and Mouton, The Hague 1976).

[14] Paradigmatic is §254 BGB.

is rendered.[15] There is, then, a wide array of creditor's conducts that do not directly affect the probability of breach, but instead impact its consequences (e.g., the amount of losses[16]).

The creditor's cooperation may often be necessary to the debtor's performance. A failure to cooperate, making performance more difficult or impossible, may lead to the reduction of damages and/or to discharge of damages entirely. Even when the creditor's cooperation is not required, negligent or intentional conduct by the creditor, which makes the debtor's performance more difficult, may limit the creditor's recovery. The boundaries between comparative negligence associated with breach and impossibility, due to creditor's negligent behavior, are not always clear-cut.[17] When creditor's cooperation is "necessary," a non-negligent failure by the creditor to cooperate may still place the entire burden on the debtor, while a negligent or intentional violation of the duty to cooperate may affect (a) the choice of remedies available (e.g., making specific performance unavailable); (b) the level of recoverable damages; or (c) the possibility of creditor's discharge. In the latter case, the creditor may have contributed to making performance either more burdensome or partially or wholly impossible. This may occur due to the creditor's fault or even due to his faultless conduct. Legal systems attribute different roles to creditors' negligence that causes impossibility.[18]

In Germany, §254 finds its origins in the principle of good faith.[19] In France, where no codified rules relating to comparative negligence exist, the negligent conduct of the creditor can diminish recoverable damages on the basis of causation even while no mitigation of damages is recognized on the basis of full compensation principle.[20]

In England, contributory negligence (equivalent to comparative negligence) as a means to apportion losses was introduced by statute in the area of tort law in 1945.[21] Its application to contract law has been limited, however, in order to

[15] For a detailed examination concerning different groups of cases, *see* A. Porat, *A Comparative Fault Defense in Contract Law*, this volume (hereinafter Porat, *Comparative Fault Defense*).

[16] For this distinction *see* R. Cooter, *Unity in Tort, Contract and Property: The Model of Precaution*, 73 Cal. L. Rev. 1 (1985), and Porat, *Comparative Fault Defense*.

[17] F. Cafaggi, *Comparing Comparative Negligence in Contract Law: In Search for a Framework*, unpublished, on file with the author.

[18] *Id.*

[19] *See* R. Zimmerman & S. Whittaker, Good Faith in European Contract Law 173–4 (Cambridge University Press, Cambridge 2000).

[20] *See* M. Fabre Magnan, Droit des obligations, 1 Contrat et engagement unilateral, Themis de droit 661–2 (PUF, 2008); Y. M. Laithier, Etude Comparative sur l'inexecution du contrat (LGDJ, 2004); S. Le Pautremat, *Mitigation of Damages: A French Perspective*, 55 ICLQ. 205 ff. (2006).

[21] The Law Commission, Contributory Negligence as a Defence in Contract, w.p. 219, London, 1993, para 1.4.

avoid shifting the task of risk allocation from parties to courts. The application of contributory negligence to contract is well accepted when a breach of contract coincides with a tort.[22] Contributory negligence has also been applied to those cases, as in service provision, where the standard of liability is care rather than strict liability. It does not apply when liability for breach of contract is strict and not associated with carelessness, and its applicability is disputed when the defendant is liable for a contractual duty of care but carelessness does not make him liable in tort.[23] In some circumstances, English courts have apportioned damages under causation, thereby allowing for a similar result to what would have been achieved under comparative negligence.[24]

In the United States, the application of comparative negligence to contractual liability has generally been rejected.[25] Although a small handful of Courts have begun to explicitly recognize its applicability in certain circumstances, the majority of courts and the Second Restatement of Contracts continue to hold the opposite view.[26]

Among those legal systems that expressly recognize the principle of comparative negligence, many identify the degree of negligence as a criterion relevant to the apportionment of liability.[27] Thus, while the presence of debtor's fault affects the "if" question of liability (e.g., whether the debtor can be held liable) regardless of the degree of fault, the level of creditor's fault is important to the question "how much" liability will be attributed to the creditor. In some legal systems, creditor's negligence becomes relevant only when it is preponderant, that is, beyond 50 percent. In other systems whichever percentage is relevant will be deducted.

Two concluding remarks should be made. First, those systems that have introduced a specific rule to apportion liability for breach of contract distinguish this case from that of causation. Comparative negligence is typically depicted as conduct that concurs to the breach, without breaking the causal link. Second, there are no strong reasons to exclude apportionment based on causation, even in a pure strict liability regime where both parties have "contributed" to the breach with no fault. For example, it is possible to allocate losses between parties by alternatively looking at comparative foreseeability.[28]

22 Forsikringsaktieselkapet Vesta v Butcher [1989] AC 852 ('Vesta v Butcher').

23 *See* G.H. Treitel, An Outline of the Law of Contract 397 (Butterworths, London 1995).

24 *See* Tennant Radiant Heat Ltd v Warrington Development Corp [1988] 1 E.G.L.R. 41.

25 *See* R. Scott, *In (Partial) Defense of Strict Liability on Contract*, this volume; and Porat, *Comparative Fault Defense*.

26 *See, e.g.*, Gateway Western Railway Co. v. Morrison Metalweld Process Corp., 46 F.3d 860 (8th Cir. 1995).

27 *See* the Italian Civil Code under art. 1227 para. 1

28 *See* Richard Danzig, Hadley v. Baxendale: A Study in the Industrialization of the Law 4 J. Leg. Stud. 249 (1975).

III. Mitigation

The principle of mitigation has been widely adopted, but its scope and domain vary across legal systems.[29] Mitigation is well recognized in common law jurisdictions, such as those of the United States and England. Mitigation has been recognized within a general principle in Continental European countries such as Germany, Italy, Austria, the Netherlands, Poland, Slovenia, and others. In France, mitigation has been rejected, although similar results may be attained through the principle of *faute de la victime*.[30] This alternative route, however, allows substitute performance by a third party at the expense of the debtor, when judicially ordered.[31] Outside of the European Union, the rule of mitigation is recognized in the new Russian Civil Code.[32]

The scope of the mitigation rule, however, varies even within Continental European countries. In Germany, it includes at least two situations: First, a creditor cannot recover if she could have avoided the losses flowing from the debtor's breach at a reasonable cost; and second, damages are reduced to account for any gains accrued to the creditor as a result of the breach.

Other legal systems distinguish between cases in which the injured party has acted after the breach, increasing the amount of losses, and cases in which she has failed to reduce losses causally linked to the breach by the debtor. In the former hypothesis, courts often refer to causation and consider the creditor's conduct to be an intervening cause, interrupting the causal link and thus preventing full recovery. In the second hypothesis, they frame the conduct as mitigation and exclude recovery of the losses that the injured party could have avoided with a reasonable effort.[33] In case of violations by the creditor, the difference concerns the liability standard; in case of compliance the difference relates to the costs of precautionary measures: borne by the creditor in comparative negligence, by the debtor in mitigation.

[29] *See* Goetz & Scott, The Mitigation Principle, 967–8.

[30] In two judgments of June 19, 2003, the French Supreme Court explicitly rejected the introduction of a general principle of mitigation in the French law of tort, thereby departing from the solutions reached in England and other legal systems: Cass 2ème civ (June 19, 2003) No 930 FS-PBRI, Xhauflaire c/Decrept and No 931 FS-PRBI, Dibaoui c/ Flamand, Bull Civ II No 203, D 2003 Jur 2396; Petites Affiches 2003, No 208, 16.

[31] While the duty to mitigate imposes a legal obligation on the injured party without any need for judicial intervention, in France the creditor can seek an alternative performance at the expense of the debtor only if authorized by the judge. *See* S. Whittaker, *Contributory Fault and Mitigation; Rights and Reasonableness: Comparisons between English and French Law* in L. Tichý (ed.), Causation in Law (Univerzita Karlova v Praze 2007) [hereinafter Whittaker, *Contributory Fault and Mitigation*] (p. 17 of the file with author).

[32] *See* Art. 404 of the Russian Civil Code.

[33] In England, often even the duty to mitigate is framed under causation principle. *See* Whittaker, *Contributory Fault and Mitigation* (p. 2 of the file with author).

Mitigation is generally required after breach has occurred, and forces the creditor to seek alternative performance in the market or, when alternative performance is unavailable, to act reasonably to minimize losses flowing from the breach.[34]

Mitigation can occur in two cases: (a) where the contract has been terminated by the injured party after a material breach; or (b) where the obligations under the contract are still in force, and the injured party has not been discharged from performing its own obligation.

The duty to mitigate is generally referred to in the latter case, but in some legal systems it may also operate in the former. In the latter, the creditor will have to counterperform and seek alternative performance in the market. In the former, the content of the duty may be affected by the decision to terminate. The creditor faces some uncertainty stemming from the risk that termination was wrongful. If that proves to be the case, then seeking alternative performance may be deemed unreasonable mitigation and the creditor may have to bear the costs associated with its decision to seek such alternative performance.[35]

Does mitigation impose a duty to deal with the breaching promisor? Rarely, a duty to mitigate will translate into a duty to renegotiate the contract after breach. More frequently, mitigation is framed as part of the duty of good faith or, in the international contract law context, the duty of cooperation.[36] The implications are related to criteria concerning the distribution of gains and losses following renegotiation.

When is mitigation reasonable? What is the standard for the mitigator? Generally speaking, the injured party is required only to take reasonable steps to mitigate. This reasonableness is frequently measured both subjectively and objectively. At least two dimensions of reasonableness are considered: one relating to the performance of the specific contract and the costs of mitigation (e.g., repair or cure by the injured party), and the other relating to the market structure. The two dimensions are related when the court has to define what constitutes substitute performance and how far the injured party must go in accepting substitute performance. This issue concerns both the

[34] In the United States, mitigation duties arise after repudiation. *See* Edward M. Crough, Inc. v. Department of General Services, 572 A.2d 457, 467 (D.C. 1990); Second Restatement §350, comment B.

[35] In relation to England, *see* Whittaker, *Contributory Fault and Mitigation* (p. 11 of the file with author). For a more detailed analysis, *see* Cafaggi, *Comparing Comparative Negligence in Contract Law*.

[36] *See* Unidroit Principles of International Commercial Contracts 2004, Article 5.1.3: ("Each party shall cooperate with the other party when such co-operation may reasonably be expected for the performance of that party's obligations.").

offer of a substitute performance by the debtor and the search for an alternative performance in the market.[37]

Mitigation through cover is more likely to be reasonable when the market is competitive and alternative performances are easily available. The less competitive the market, the more difficult it becomes to find alternative performances and the more "unreasonable" mitigation through cover becomes, forcing parties to find alternative solutions within the relationship. Thus, the market form is an independent variable that, via reasonableness, affects the existence and the breadth of the duty to mitigate.[38]

The doctrine of mitigation, particularly as it has been applied in Continental Europe, has important drawbacks insofar as it fails to account for market form. Rarely European continental Courts look at market structure when defining the existence and scope of the duty to mitigate. If the market is competitive, it is generally accessible to both the debtor and the creditor. A duty should arise for the creditor only if it is cheaper for him to seek alternative performance than it is for the debtor. If the market is not competitive, it will be difficult for either party to seek alternative performance. In this case, cover is unavailable and mitigation will consist of reducing the losses stemming from the breach by negotiating contractual modifications (e.g., reduced quantity, providing alternative goods). The current mitigation doctrine available in Continental Europe, unlike in the United States, does not provide a sufficiently clear menu of choices for cover between debtors and creditors interacting in competitive markets, and does not give clear indication of what the promisee should do when alternatives in the markets are unavailable.

IV. Reasonable Reliance

While the role of creditor's reliance in contract law is widely recognized via several doctrines in the United States, it is less relevant in Continental European systems, except during the precontractual stage. Beneficial reliance is protected by making promises enforceable or by ensuring damages if there is unreasonable refusal to conclude a contract. Detrimental reliance is discouraged through a number of doctrines, among which causation and foreseeability bear a primary role. To induce reasonable reliance implies discouraging overinvestment by both parties: by the creditor seeking to maximize the gains from performance and by the debtor in precautions taken to avoid breach and in facing unanticipated circumstances. To a certain extent,

[37] *See* Whittaker, *Contributory Fault and Mitigation*.

[38] This is one of the most important insight of Goetz & Scott, *The Mitigation Principle* 1024.

protection of only "reasonable" reliance may lead to similar results to those achieved by comparative negligence in Continental European systems.

The different doctrines that promote reasonable reliance operate as functional equivalents to comparative negligence only to a limited extent. They share with comparative negligence the fact that reasonableness of reliance becomes legally relevant only if the debtor breaches, and it reduces compensation only for those losses incurred by making reasonable commitments to take advantage of the expected performance. Unreasonable reliance of creditor, outside of breach, cannot constitute an affirmative claim for the debtor. It differs from comparative negligence because it deals predominantly with decisions influencing the consequences of excuses and breach and not the breach itself. In fact, conducts relevant under reasonable reliance concern more the consequences of the breach (L) than its probability (P). Though the issue is hotly debated and Courts have not reached uniform results, reasonableness related to reliance should not be associated with the probability of breach but with that of impossibility or impracticability of performance. Creditors should rely on performance by debtors and reasonableness should limit the level of investments in relation to impossibility due to *force majeure* and hardship or frustration. As in comparative negligence, when reasonable reliance applies, the creditor should expect performance unlike in mitigation, when she reacts to a breach that has already materialized.

When reliance damages are granted instead of expectation damages, two goals are pursued: protection of the creditor's interest and provision of incentives to rely reasonably on the promised performance. Absent comparative negligence, reliance damages may provide the creditor with better incentives than expectation damages to invest reasonably.

The fault standard, deployed to reduce recoverable damages in comparative negligence when the creditor is negligent, may bring about different results from the reasonableness standard used in reliance when the promisee has overrelied.

V. Causation

Comparative negligence, associated with causation as a means to apportion liability between contracting parties, plays an important role in Germany, countries that follow the German system, as well as Italy and France. In England, causation operates more as an alternative to comparative negligence.[39] In general, causation does not lead to apportionment, since it operates through

[39] In regard to England, *see* The Law Commission (Law Com. No. 219), Contributory Negligence as a Defence in Contract (1993), cit. §3.9 and 3.10.

either-or mechanisms.[40] Only in rare cases have courts been willing to apportion losses under "comparative" causation.[41]

Causation as a means to allocate liability from breach has two dimensions: (a) the domain of the risk associated with performance; and (b) the risk's distribution between the debtor and the creditor. When a loss is deemed to be too remote, courts conclude that the risk is not part of the contractual allocation and thus place the burden entirely on the creditor.[42] But remoteness can also be used to distribute the risk among parties. If the risk was contemplated by both parties, the creditor's conduct may operate as an intervening cause, breaking the causal link.[43] More often, however, a lack of contemplation is framed within foreseeability. In this context, the relevant question concerns whether the risk, associated with the creditor's conduct, was contemplated by the parties and, if so, how that risk was allocated.[44]

Causation can thus have two consequences on creditor's conduct: (1) If the creditor's conduct breaks the causal link, the debtor is not liable and the creditor bears all the losses; or (2) if she only contributes to the breach, liability is "shared" and apportionment of damages follows. In the first scenario, what is really considered is the but-for-causality of the creditor's conduct and negligence is not relevant. In the second scenario, the existence of fault and the degree of negligence are relevant to the apportionment of the consequences of the breach. However, in this case, direct references to comparative negligence are more frequent, given the "resistance" to applying comparative causation, deploying an apportionment criterion regardless of the relative fault of the parties. The second scenario is very rare, since risk distribution in causation generally operates as an either-or rule.

VI. Foreseeability

Foreseeability as a means to allocate risks and liabilities between contracting parties plays an important role in France and Italy but not in Germany.[45] It has great relevance in Anglo-American law under the cases following the doctrine announced in *Hadley v. Baxendale*.[46] In particular, it has been used

[40] *See* A.S. Burrows, *Contributory Negligence in Contract: Ammunition for the Law Commission*, 109 L. Q. Rev. 175 (1993).

[41] *See* Tennant Radiant Heat, [1988] 1 E.G.L.R. 41.

[42] In regard to the United States, *see, e.g.*, Suitt Constr. Co. v. Ripley's Aquarium, LLC, 108 Fed. Appx. 309, 314 (6th Cir. 2004).

[43] In regard to the United States, *see* Suitt Constr. Co., 108 Fed. Appx. 309, for premise that only damages proximately caused by the debtor's breach are recoverable to the creditor.

[44] For the United States, *see* Second Restatement of Contracts §351, comment A.

[45] *But see* creditor's duty to warn under §254 II BGB.

[46] Hadley v. Baxendale, 9 Exch. 341, 156 Eng. Rep. 145 (1854).

in the United States, as an alternative to comparative negligence and a means to control reasonable reliance.[47] The rule does not directly affect the role of the creditor, but it can influence the allocation of risks and losses. However, there are several dimensions in which the doctrine of foreseeability may indirectly affect the creditor's conduct in relation to debtor's breach.

On the one hand, foreseeability incorporates into the contract the debtor's expectations concerning the creditors' conditions. These expectations may concern the creditor's needs, but might also relate to his economic or physical conditions relevant for debtor's performance.

On the other hand, foreseeability reduces the creditor's incentive to opportunistically increase the losses related to a potential breach between the time of formation and the time of breach. For instance, additional investments aimed at "exploiting" opportunities from the use of the good to be delivered by the debtor may not be recoverable because they are unforeseeable and thus not contemplated by the parties at the time of contract.[48]

The foreseeability rule is aimed at promoting communication among parties for risks known to the creditor or that ought to be known at time of contracting.[49] On the basis of the foreseeability rule, a risk and the occurrence of a loss can be transferred from the creditor to the debtor only if the former informs the latter, making him aware of the risk.[50] If the creditor fails to inform the debtor about the specific contingencies, damages are not recoverable because unforeseeable. In this case, only those losses associated with ordinary market ones can be recovered.[51] Whether the failure to inform depends on negligent conduct is, in principle, irrelevant when foreseeability is applied, unlike in the case of comparative negligence.

VII. Explaining the Differences Between Anglo-American and Continental Europe Approaches

The degree of convergence or divergence between the United States and Continental Europe depends on the level of analysis: If we consider only comparative negligence in contract, divergences are relatively high, but when mitigation is included, divergences decrease. Furthermore, if – when the debtor's

[47] For the United States, *see* B. Hermalin, A. Katz, & R. Craswell, *The Law and Economics of Contracts*, in Handbook on Foundations of Law and Economics 104 (M. Polinsky & S. Shavell, eds., Elsevier 2007).

[48] *See* Illustration 2 to Second Restatement §351.

[49] I Ayres & R. Gertner, *Filling Gaps in Incomplete Contracts: An Economic Theory of Default Rules*, 99 Yale L. J. 87 (1989).

[50] *See* Goetz & Scott, The Mitigation Principle.

[51] *See* Transfield Shipping Inc v. Mercator Shipping Inc. the Achilleas [2009] 1 A.C.

performance is rendered impossible due to the creditor's own conduct – the creditor's duty to cooperate is integrated into the analysis, divergences over the existence of a general principle further decrease. The brief and extremely synthetic examination of different doctrines across jurisdictions has shown that some of them combine allocation of liability and apportionment of damages while others allocate liability on the basis on an either-or criterion without apportioning damages.

In the former category, we should include comparative negligence, mitigation, reasonable reliance and, to a limited extent, foreseeability. Only indirectly, the reciprocal duties of cooperation and good faith constitute a means to apportion damages. In the latter category stand causation and impossibility that deploy primarily either-or mechanisms, although for the latter, fault and some type of apportionment are sometimes considered.[52]

The Continental European approach, with important differences among its legal systems, adopts a cooperation principle, highlighting the relevance of creditor's pre- and postbreach conduct based on risk sharing and leading toward loss apportionment.

The United States seems to distinguish sharply between a creditor's pre- and postbreach conduct, limiting the mitigation principle to the postbreach phase, despite proposals to introduce comparative negligence principles in contract law.[53] However, on deeper scrutiny, the principle (not the rules!) of apportionment related to comparative fault emerges in several contract doctrines where part of the loss is allocated to the creditor primarily because the risk was initially borne by her or because the risks' allocation has shifted over time, due to unanticipated circumstances. In particular, reasonable reliance, and to some extent foreseeability when apportionment is allowed, seem to play functions similar to comparative negligence in allocating both liabilities and damages in the case of breach: providing incentives to adopt precautionary measures to tackle risks of nonperformance and to avoid overinvestments.[54]

How can the differences between the United States and England, on the one hand, and part of Continental Europe and international regimes, on the

[52] For broader and more detailed analysis, *see* Cafaggi, *Comparing Comparative Negligence in Contract Law.*

[53] For proposals concerning the introduction of comparative negligence, *see* A. Porat, *The Contributory Negligence Defence and the Ability to Rely on the Contract* 111 L.Q. R. 228 (1995).

[54] For premise that the use of foreseeability functions in a similar fashion to comparative negligence on the part of creditor, *see* Afram Export Corp. v. Metallurgiki Halyps, SA, 772 F.2d 1358, 1368 (1985) (stating that debtor could not foresee "imprudent" conduct by creditor and thus damages attributable to creditor's imprudent conduct not recoverable) and Rexnord Corp. v. DeWolff Boberg & Associates, Inc., 286 F.3d 1001, 1003–05 (7th Cir. 2002) (noting that the result in *Hadley* "may have depended on the mill's failure to have protected itself against the

other, be explained? There are three categories of complementary explanations: historical, philosophical, and functional.

Historically, the departure from contributory negligence as a total bar from recovery in both contract and tort predates codifications in Continental Europe. The approach taken by European codifications relates to the law of obligations, including both contractual and extracontractual relationships. The reference point in the law of obligations is the creditor as both a promisee and a potential victim of the breach. The regime referred to the law of obligations has been designed to be applicable to contractual and extracontractual settings.

The departure from contributory negligence and binary risk allocation is much more recent in the United States, in the context of tort law. In contract law, the application of comparative negligence has been generally rejected while other doctrines, primarily those promoting reasonable reliance, foreseeability, and causation, have operated as functional equivalents to affect the creditor's conduct and the allocation of risks that reduced the need for comparative negligence.

Though they may operate as functional equivalents, divergences are still relevant, going to the core of the different approaches to contractual relationships and contract law in Anglo-American and Continental European systems, with all the internal distinctions pointed out earlier. Differences between the United States and England – the two common law systems – seem to be more a matter of degree than a divergence between the foundations on which they are grounded. Overall, considering the deployment of other doctrines, England seems to preserve the more traditional view of Anglo-American contract law as a risk-allocation device, despite the introduction of comparative negligence, whereas the growing importance of reliance in US contract law partially counteracts strong opposition in the United States to comparative negligence.

The philosophical explanation for this divergence builds on the distinction between the greater emphasis on corrective justice in Continental Europe and the more realist and consequentialist approach in the United States. which is grounded on risk allocation. This distinction may contribute to explaining the use of different doctrines to achieve similar results. Comparative negligence, more so than mitigation, can be grounded in corrective justice,[55] reducing recoverable losses "caused" by the negligent conduct of the creditor,

consequences of a delay by the carrier by having a spare part on hand" and there "was a sense in which the mill was the author of its own loss").

[55] On corrective justice as a foundation of continental contract law, *see, e.g.*, R. Zimmermann, Roman Law, Contemporary Law, European Law: The Civilian Tradition Today (Oxford

whereas the use of foreseeability and mitigation can be better justified on consequentialist grounds. Comparative negligence, whose introduction can also be justified on efficiency grounds, recalls the concept of reciprocity and the obligation to "protect" the other party's interest. Failure to do so would impose an additional and unfair burden on the debtor.

Beyond the historical and philosophical explanations, there is perhaps a functional distinction that may shed further light on the different places of comparative negligence in contract and tort law in the United States and the (theoretically) uniform regime, based on the law of obligations, of some Continental European systems.

Contract law in the United States and England is still predominantly seen as a risk-allocation device.[56] While it is recognized that contract law can also perform other functions such as fostering cooperation and preventing opportunistic behavior, these other functions are seen as ancillary.[57] This could explain reluctance to adopt a comparative negligence regime that aims at fostering cooperation and is at odds with risk allocation. The duty to mitigate, distinguished from the rule of comparative negligence, reflects the idea that parties should use market alternatives, when available, to minimize losses or maximize gains stemming from new opportunities, arising outside the contractual relationship. Thus, the duty to mitigate is perceived as compatible with risk allocation or fostering optimal risk allocation across different states of the world.

European systems focus more attention on the cooperative nature of the venture created when parties enter into contractual relationships and the opportunity to share the risks of nonperformance.[58] The relevance of the market structure and the availability of alternative options when one party is in breach bear a more limited role than that of cooperation. When the emphasis is on the cooperative venture and risk sharing, comparative negligence becomes more appropriate.

To what extent does the increased focus on risk allocation over cooperation in the United States explain the resistance to the introduction of comparative

University Press, Oxford 2001); and J. Gordley, Foundations of Private Law: Property, Tort, Contract, Unjust Enrichment (Oxford University Press, Oxford 2006). In general, *see* A. T. von Mehren, *A General View of Contract*, ch.1, in International Encyclopedia of Comparative Law 64–5 (J.C.B. Mohr (Paul Siebeck), Tübingen and Mouton, The Hague 1982).

56 *See, e.g.*, O. W. Holmes, The Common Law 299–301 (Dover Publications, Inc., New York 1991); A. Schwartz & R. E. Scott, *Contract Theory and the Limits of Contract Law*, 113 Yale L. J. 541, 556 (2003); R. A. Posner, *Let Us Never Blame a Contract Breaker*, this volume.

57 *See* Market Street Associates v. Frey, 941 F.2d 588 (7th Cir. 1991); *see also* R. A. Posner, Economic Analysis of Law 94–95 (7th ed. 2007).

58 On the role of different institutional environments in shaping contracting practices, *see* S. Deakin, Ch. Lane, & F. Wilkinson, Contract Law, Trust Relations, and Incentives for

negligence in US contract law? In theory, risk can be allocated by using either an either-or system (e.g., strict liability or negligence without defense) or a "sharing" system allowing defenses that include apportionment. In practice, however, US courts continue to be reluctant to address risk allocation through an apportionment-based, risk-"sharing" system.

Conclusion

In this chapter, I have shown that the great divergence concerning the rule of comparative negligence in contract law between England and the United States, on the one hand, and Continental European systems with the exception of France, on the other, needs to be rethought. A wider range of doctrines beyond mitigation should be considered on the grounds that they act, at least partially, as functional equivalents of comparative negligence.

The divergence diminishes if we move away from specific doctrines to the general principle of creditor's cooperation. This cooperation is relevant in many doctrines of contract law in the United States and, to a lesser extent, England, although its scope differs in these two legal systems. In England, where comparative negligence has limited application, the doctrines of causation and foreseeability provide some recognition of creditor's conduct and apportionment of losses. The narrow and very limited recognition of the rule of comparative negligence in the United States is "compensated" for by reference to other apportionment techniques in different doctrines such as those fostering reasonable reliance, mitigation, and foreseeability.

In Continental Europe, the doctrine of comparative negligence is widely recognized, and its influence has spread into international commercial laws such as CISG and Unidroit principles, where both comparative negligence and mitigation are explicitly recognized. The principle of creditor's cooperation is well grounded in Continental European legal systems and has also found its way into the new proposal from PECL to DCFR.

The potential explanation for this divergence may vary if we consider the rule of comparative negligence or the principle of creditor's cooperation and its apportionment of losses regime as encompassing different doctrines. The recognition of the principle, under different doctrines but with different weight, does not eliminate the divergence; rather forces us to rethink its reasons. The lack of comparative negligence in the United States, when considered along

Co-operation: A Comparative Study, in Contracts, Co-operation, and Competition 105–39 (S. Deakin & J. Michie, eds., Oxford University Press, Oxford 1997); and G. Teubner, *Legal Irritants: Good Faith in British Law or How Unifying Law Ends Up in New Divergences* 61 Modern Law Rev. 11 (1998).

with the deployment of other forms of risk sharing and apportionment of losses stemming from breach of contract, conforms to the idea that contract law is mainly directed at risk allocation. In Continental European systems, the recognition of a general rule of comparative negligence and mitigation delineates a general principle based on the law of obligations, applicable to both contract and tort. Contractual relationships are generally characterized by a higher level of cooperation. These divergences have been explained with reference to different business practices and community norms that legal systems have internalized. This "institutional" perspective can shed some light on these divergences, but needs to be complemented by a deeper understanding of the core function of contract law and business rules.

PART VI

THE MORALITY OF BREACH

SEVENTEEN

Why Breach of Contract May Not Be Immoral Given the Incompleteness of Contracts

Steven Shavell

There is a widely held view that breach of contract is immoral. In this chapter I suggest that breach may often be seen as moral, once one appreciates that contracts are incompletely detailed agreements and that breach may be committed in problematic contingencies that were not explicitly addressed by the governing contracts. In other words, it is a mistake generally to treat a breach as a violation of a promise that was intended to cover the particular contingency that eventuated.

There is a widely held view that breach of contract is immoral.[1] Yet it is manifest that legal systems ordinarily do allow breach – the law usually permits breach if the offending party pays damages[2] – and it is a commonplace that breach occurs. Thus, a tension exists between the felt sense that wrong has been done when contracts are broken and the actual operation of the law. This opposition has long been remarked by commentators.[3]

Recently I wrote on the question of when breach of contract should be considered immoral.[4] My primary point was that breach may often be seen

I thank Louis Kaplow for comments and the John M. Olin Center for Law, Economics, and Business for research support.

[1] *See, e.g.*, Second Restatement of Contracts ch. 16, introductory note at 100 (1981); Tess Wilkinson-Ryan & Jonathan Baron, *Moral Judgment and Moral Heuristics in Breach of Contract*, 6 J. Empirical Legal Stud. 405–23 (2009).

[2] Second Restatement of Contracts ch. 16, introductory note at 100 (1981); *see also* John D. Calamari & Joseph M. Perillo, The Law of Contracts § 16.1 (4th ed. 1998).

[3] *E.g.*, O.W. Holmes, *The Path of the Law*, 10 Harv. L. Rev. 457, 462 (1897) ("The duty to keep a contract … means … that you must pay damages if you do not keep it.… But such a mode of looking at the matter stinks in the nostrils of those who think it advantageous to get as much ethics into the law as they can.")

[4] Steven Shavell, *Is Breach of Contract Immoral?*, 56 Emory L.J. 439 (2006) [hereinafter Shavell, *Is Breach of Contract Immoral?*]. Many of the points of that article are first made in Steven Shavell, *Damage Measures for Breach of Contract*, 11 Bell J. Econ. 466, 466–9 (1980) [hereinafter Shavell, *Damage Measures*], and are amplified in Louis Kaplow & Steven Shavell, Fairness

as moral once one appreciates that contracts are incompletely detailed agreements and that breach may be committed in problematic contingencies that were not explicitly addressed by the governing contracts. In other words, because of contractual incompleteness, it is a mistake generally to treat a breach as a violation of a promise that was intended to cover the particular contingency that eventuated.

Seana Shiffrin has critically examined my analysis of the immorality of breach in her symposium contribution.[5] Here, I want to respond to her – mainly to disagree, but partly to agree. I first review my prior argument and then comment on Shiffrin's argument.

I. Summary of the Argument that Breach May Not Be Immoral Given the Incompleteness of Contracts[6]

A. *Definition of Moral Behavior in a Contingency*

To discuss the immorality of breach, one must, of course, state what constitutes moral behavior in the contractual context. I make two simple definitional assumptions. First, I presume that if a contract provides explicitly for a contingency, then the moral duty to perform in that contingency is governed by the contract. Second, I suppose that if a contract is incomplete in the sense that it does not provide explicitly for a contingency, then the moral duty to perform in the contingency is governed by what a completely detailed contract addressing the contingency would have stipulated, assuming that the parties know what this hypothetical contract would have stated.[7]

Consider, for example, a contract concerning the clearing of snow from a person's driveway and the contingency that the seller's snow clearing equipment is stolen. Suppose that the contract specifies that if such a theft occurs, the seller still has an obligation to clear snow (perhaps because he can readily rent snow clearing equipment). Then the seller is assumed to have a moral duty to clear snow even if his equipment is stolen. However, if the contract

Versus Welfare 155–223 (2002). *See also* Steven Shavell, Foundations of Economic Analysis of Law 304–12, 338–55, 638–40 (2004).

[5] Seana Shiffrin, *Could Breach of Contract Be Immoral?*, 107 Mich. L. Rev. 1551 (2009) [hereinafter Shiffrin, *Breach of Contract*]; *see also* Seana Valentine Shiffrin, *The Divergence of Contract and Promise*, 120 Harv. L. Rev. 708 (2007).

[6] I here sketch the argument of Shavell, *Is Breach of Contract Immoral?*, *supra* note 4. This section is reprinted with permission of the *Emory Law Journal*, and appeared in part in Shavell, *Is Breach of Contract Immoral?*, *supra* note 4.

[7] In reality, what a contract would have said about a particular contingency might not be known with confidence by the parties, implying that they might not know their moral duties with confidence.

mentions the possibility of theft and says that in that event the seller does not have to clear snow (perhaps because it would be very difficult to rent substitute equipment on the spot), then the seller would not have a moral duty to perform should his equipment be stolen. And, if the contract does not mention the contingency of theft explicitly, the seller's obligation to clear snow in that circumstance would be determined by what a hypothetical complete contract would have said, assuming that the parties know its nature.

The appeal of the foregoing definition of moral obligation derives from the observation that a contract that provides explicitly for a contingency is similar to a promise that provides explicitly for a contingency, and that there are well-known grounds for finding that individuals have moral obligations to keep such promises.[8] I will return to the subject of the appeal of my definition of moral obligation in the contractual domain in Part II. For the remainder of this part, I put that matter to the side and develop the implications of my definition.

B. *The Observed Incompleteness of Contracts*

That the definition of moral obligation applies when contracts do not explicitly mention the contingency that arose is important because this may well be the state of affairs. We see that in reality contracts are far from completely detailed. Although a contract for removing snow from a person's driveway might mention a number of conditions, for instance, whether clearing is to be done on Christmas day, it will typically omit a practically endless number of events that could matter to the seller – theft of his snow clearing equipment, illness of his crew, snow so deep that it makes roads impassable – or to the buyer – unexpected travel out of town over the winter, sale of her home, inheritance of snow clearing equipment.

It is true that contracts will often provide implicitly for many, and perhaps all, contingencies. Suppose that a contract states that "snow is to be cleared from the buyer's driveway if the snow is over five inches deep," and that the contract mentions no other conditions. This contract implicitly covers the contingency of theft because in a formal sense the contract covers all contingencies: it divides them into two general categories, those in which the snow is up to five inches deep (whatever else happens), and those in which the snow is over five inches deep (whatever else happens). But because the contract does

8 *See, e.g.*, David Hume, A Treatise of Human Nature §3.2.5 (David Fate Norton & Mary J. Norton eds., Oxford University Press 2007) (1739); Immanuel Kant, Groundwork of the Metaphysics of Morals 15, 32, 38 (Mary Gregor ed. & trans., Cambridge University Press 1997) (1785); John Rawls, *Two Concepts of Rules*, 64 Phil. Rev. 3 (1955).

not mention theft explicitly, I consider the contract to be incomplete as to that contingency.

Why are contracts substantially incomplete in that they omit explicit mention of numerous contingencies? Most obviously, it is because time is needed to discuss and to include contingent provisions in contracts. If a contingency like theft of snow clearing equipment is sufficiently unlikely, the probability-discounted benefit of providing for it in the contract will be low and will be outweighed by the cost of the time that would be spent to do so. Other significant reasons for contractual incompleteness are that a contingency (such as whether a person had a stomachache) might be hard for a court to verify, which would make a clause depending on its occurrence unworkable; that parties might be able to renegotiate if a problematic circumstance arises; and that parties might be able to commit breach and pay damages if a difficulty arises. In all, then, the existence of significant contractual incompleteness is not surprising.

C. *The Morality of Breach When Contracts Are Incomplete*

Given the importance of incompleteness of contracts, we know that questions about the morality of breach will often concern situations in which the contingency that occurred was not specifically mentioned in the contract. If a snow clearing company breaches its contract to clear my driveway when its equipment was stolen but the contract did not explicitly address that contingency, we cannot assess the morality of the breach by pretending that the contract did address the contingency (in which case the breach would be immoral by hypothesis). We must engage in further inquiry. To ascertain whether the breach was moral under my definition, we have to determine whether performance would have been called for had the contingency been expressly addressed in the contract, that is, we need to understand the character of hypothetical complete contracts.

D. *The Nature of Obligations to Perform in Hypothetical Completely Detailed Contracts*

We can deduce a very important characteristic about the nature of a hypothetical complete contract agreed upon by rational parties. Namely, *performance will be required in a contingency if and only if the cost of performance to the seller would be less than the value of performance to the buyer.*

The logic leading to this conclusion is that if the contract were otherwise, it could always be altered in a way that both parties would prefer – hence they would never settle on a contract unless it were of the claimed type. To illustrate, suppose in our snow clearing example that the buyer and the seller consider a contract that calls for performance in a contingency in which the cost of performance to the seller would be $300 and would exceed the value to the buyer of $100. Thus, the contemplated contract is different from the claimed type. Let the contemplated contract be changed only in the term covering this contingency: under the adjusted contract, the snow does not have to be cleared, and the seller must make a payment to the buyer of $110 (in addition to whatever other payment might have been stipulated in the contemplated contract). Clearly, the buyer would be better off in the contingency at issue under the new contract, for she would receive, in the $110 payment, more than the $100 value she would lose from not having snow removed. Likewise, the seller would be better off in the contingency because his payment of $110 would be less than his cost savings of $300 from not having to perform. Because both parties would be better off in the contingency in question and would be just as well off in all other contingencies (because the new contract does not change in those contingencies), both parties would prefer the new contract to the contemplated one. Hence, they would never agree to the contemplated contract calling for performance when the cost would exceed the value of performance. Similar logic shows that the parties would never agree to a contract in which there is a contingency not calling for performance even though its cost would be less than its value.[9]

The conclusion just discussed validates what should be appealing to the intuition in a qualitative sense. One would expect that if the parties were bargaining over each contingency individually, they would agree on performance when it would not be very expensive for the seller relative to its value to the buyer but agree that it is not worthwhile to specify performance when its cost for the seller would be high.

E. *The Immorality or Morality of Breach When Contracts Are Incomplete Can Be Inferred from the Willingness of the Party in Breach to Pay Damages*

If there is a breach in a contingency that was not provided for, such as theft of snow clearing equipment, how can we ascertain whether, had they discussed

[9] Although this paragraph demonstrates that the conditions under which performance is specified must be as claimed, it does not show what the contract price or possible payments made in the event of nonperformance would be. These elements of the contract would depend on characteristics of the parties and cannot be predicted on a priori grounds.

that contingency explicitly, the parties would have agreed that there would or would not be an obligation to perform?

We know from the previous section that the answer inheres in whether the cost of performance was less than its value. If it was, then the parties would have specified performance and the breach would thus be immoral; if it was not, and the cost would have exceeded the value of performance, the breach would not be immoral. Must we make a direct inquiry about the cost and the value of performance to know whether the breach was immoral? The answer is no.

We can draw an inference about the cost of performance if the breaching party paid damages for breach. We know that the party in breach must have considered the cost of performance to be greater than the damage amount. In particular, suppose that the measure of damages is the expectation, that is, the value of performance to the buyer. A seller will then commit breach if and only if his cost of performance would exceed the value of performance. In the snow clearing contract, suppose that the value of performance to the buyer is $200. Then, if the seller breaches after his equipment is stolen and pays expectation damages, we infer that his cost of performance exceeded $200.[10] Because the cost exceeds the value, this implies that had the parties discussed the theft contingency, they would have agreed there would be no duty to perform in that event. Thus, the seller's breach and failure to clear snow when his equipment is stolen is not immoral; his behavior is precisely in accord with what would have been the terms of a completely detailed contract that spoke to the circumstance – the theft of snow clearing equipment – that actually occurred.

This example illustrates the general point that when the measure of damages equals the expectation, a seller will be led to breach if and only if the cost of performance exceeds the value of performance to the buyer. Because that is exactly when a seller would not have to perform in a completely detailed contract, the seller will fail to perform in the same contingencies as the seller would be permitted not to perform in a hypothetical complete contract. Accordingly, *breach should not be characterized as immoral when expectation damages are paid for breach.*

[10] To amplify, suppose that the contract price is paid in advance. Then expectation damages would equal $200, for that amount must be received by the buyer to make her whole. Consequently, the seller would not commit breach unless the cost exceeded $200. Alternatively, suppose that the contract price, say $125, is to be paid upon performance. Then expectation damages would equal $75, for now it is this amount that must be received to make the buyer whole. Hence, if the seller commits breach, he forgoes collecting the $125 and pays $75, and so suffers a total cost of $200; again, therefore, he would not commit breach unless the cost exceeded $200.

Now assume that damages for breach are less than the expectation. Because breach will tend to occur whenever the cost of performance exceeds the level of damages, breach will occur more often than nonperformance would have been permitted in a completely specified contract – thus, breach might be immoral. In our example, if the measure of damages were, say, $50 instead of the expectation of $200, breach would occur whenever the cost of performance would exceed $50. Consequently, if breach occurred when the cost would be between $50 and $200, the complete contract would have insisted on performance. Such breach would be immoral.

F. *When Is Breach Immoral and When Is It Moral in Practice?*

Given the conclusions just reached, we can say that if damages equal the buyer's expectation, breach can be inferred to be moral because it will occur only when the parties would have allowed nonperformance in a complete contract. However, when damages are less than the expectation, we cannot make this inference and would have to inquire directly about the cost of performance relative to its value in order to make a judgment about its morality.

Are damages fully compensatory? They are intended to be. The expectation measure is, of course, the general damage remedy employed for breach of contract, where the expectation measure is defined as the amount that would restore the victim of a breach to the position this party would have enjoyed had performance occurred.[11] The expectation measure as it is actually applied, however, tends to be less than fully compensatory and may leave the victim of a breach substantially worse off than he or she would have been had there been performance. The reasons given for believing that the expectation measure is often undercompensatory include the following. First, courts are reluctant to credit hard-to-measure components of loss as damages. Hence, lost profits and idiosyncratic losses due to breach are likely to be inadequately compensated or neglected. Second, courts are inclined to limit damages to those that could have been reasonably foreseen at the time the contract was made. Third, damages tend not to reflect the considerable delays that victims of breach may suffer. Fourth, legal costs are not compensated.

Not only do expectation damages appear to be undercompensatory in a general sense, but damages for breach may be effectively nonexistent if the breach victim's losses are less than the costs of bringing suit, which is to say, below a threshold of several thousand dollars. If the losses are not this high, the breach victim will not have a credible threat to litigate.

[11] Second Restatement of Contracts §346–47 (1981); Calamari & Perillo, *supra* note 2, §14.4.

In view of these remarks about the adequacy of damages, the practical reality is that breach will often be of suspect moral quality, and the likelihood that breach is immoral will be higher the lower the damages are in relation to the true expectation.

II. Criticism and Discussion of the Foregoing Argument

Seana Shiffrin makes three criticisms of the argument that I have summarized. First, she disputes my conclusion that the hypothetical complete contract would be as I asserted – calling for performance when and only when its cost is less than its value. Second, she does not find that the hypothetical complete contract provides an appealing moral standard for the obligation to perform. Third, she believes that performance per se should possess a positive moral valence, whereas performance does not have this character in my framework. After discussing these criticisms, I consider the issue of how to choose among different definitions of moral behavior in the contractual context.

A. *The Nature of the Hypothetical Complete Contract*

Shiffrin appears to have misunderstood an assumption that I made concerning the hypothetical complete contract. I presumed that each contingent provision in a hypothetical complete contract calling for performance would definitely be enforced – so that such a contract means exactly what it says. For simplicity, I also presumed that if a contingent provision does not call for performance, no payment would be made by the seller if that contingency arose.[12] In contrast, Shiffrin seems to have thought that under the hypothetical complete contract, breach was permitted if a person paid damages.[13]

In any event, and more important, Shiffrin questions the central claim that the agreed terms of the hypothetical contract would specify performance in

[12] I considered hypothetical completely detailed contracts in Shavell, *Is Breach of Contract Immoral?*, *supra* note 4, at 444–6. The discussion there presumes that performance occurs when a contract states that it is to occur. Breach and payment of damages play no role in the hypothetical complete contract.

[13] Shiffrin, *Breach of Contract*, *supra* note 5, speculates on what the hypothetical complete contract means. She conjectures that the parties would have elected terms that "provided the promisor with a disjunctive option to perform or pay expectation damages." As I just stated in the text and in the preceding note, that was not my assumption. Also, I observe that had I made a different definition of the hypothetical contract, under which nonperformance would be accompanied by the payment of money by the seller, my conclusion about the agreed-upon conditions of performance would be the same. Indeed, the argument given in Section I.D demonstrates this.

a contingency if and only if its cost to the seller is less than its value to the buyer. In fact, the claim is correct – it is an objective claim that follows from straightforward logic and is a standard point in the economic literature on contracts.[14] The example I provided of the argument for the claim in Section I.D is essentially a general proof. It shows that if any term in a proposed contract does not have the asserted character, an altered contract with that term changed in the claimed way can be devised such that both the buyer and the seller prefer the new contract. Indeed, this argument explains why a surmise of Shiffrin is incorrect. She suggests that the claim might not hold if one were to take into account bargaining over all the terms of the contract.[15] But the argument does not depend on the other terms in the contract. The argument shows that by adjusting *only* the term applying in a single contingency, both parties will be made better off regardless of what the other terms might have been.

B. *Does the Hypothetical Complete Contract Provide an Appealing Moral Standard?*

Shiffrin questions the appeal of my definition of the moral obligation to perform. She asks, "[i]s he right to assert that there is a moral duty to perform only if the parties would have explicitly agreed to perform had they squarely faced the contingency that is the occasion for the breach?"[16]

However, she does not address head on the attraction of my definition of moral obligation. That is, if the parties to the contract know what they would have provided for in an express provision for the contingency that actually occurred – and they did not make the express provision only for some practical reason – one would think their moral duty would be governed by the agreement they would have made but for this practical reason. Suppose that the buyer and the snow clearer signed a contract reading simply that "snow clearer shall clear buyer's snow from her driveway"; that they both understand that had their contract mentioned theft of equipment, the clearer would not have to remove snow; and that they did not include a provision mentioning theft because they did not feel it was worth the trouble given the unlikelihood of theft. Realizing all of this, why would the buyer feel that the clearer has a

[14] *See, e.g.*, Benjamin E. Hermalin et al., *Contract Law, in* 1 Handbook of Law and Economics 3, 24–5 (A. Mitchell Polinsky & Steven Shavell eds., 2007); Shavell, *Damage Measures*, *supra* note 4, at 475–6.

[15] Shiffrin, *Breach of Contract*, *supra* note 5 ("Shavell fails to contemplate the entire contract and its contents. He focuses on how the contingency would have been settled in isolation.").

[16] *Id.*

moral obligation to remove snow if his equipment had been stolen, and why would the clearer feel such an obligation? It is not apparent to me that either the buyer or the seller would feel that the seller had an obligation to perform. An obligation could be felt, I think, only if the parties mistakenly conflate the incomplete contract reading "snow clearer shall clear buyer's snow from her driveway" with an explicit agreement intended to cover theft of snow clearing equipment.

Instead, among other things, Shiffrin emphasizes an issue that I did not discuss and imputes to me a view about it that I do not hold. She considers the possibility that one party to a contract might have superior information to the other. If this is so, she intimates that the party with superior knowledge could enjoy an unfair advantage if his moral obligation is determined by the hypothetical complete contract. For instance, if the snow clearer knows his equipment is likely to be stolen and the buyer does not, the buyer might be led to pay too much for the contract. I did not address such issues of asymmetry of information because they are collateral to the main point of interest for us. Had I considered asymmetry of information, I would have analyzed the moral obligation to disclose information at the time of contracting, as well as to perform, and my conclusions about the moral obligation to perform in the absence of disclosure would be different.

Shiffrin also suggests that one of the main implications of my view – that committing breach and paying expectation damages is morally permissible – violates her moral intuition. She finds it counterintuitive, offensive to her sense of right and wrong, that a party can breach and pay such damages. "So long as *A* would rather just pay expectation damages than perform, does that mean *A* does no moral wrong if she decides not to perform?"[17] My reaction to this view is twofold. First, as I explained in Section I.E, that breach induced by payment of expectation damages is moral is a logical conclusion following from my definition of morality of performance. But second, my definition of morality of performance may certainly be questioned. Although I commented above on why it might have appeal, other definitions of morality need to be considered. Let me now turn to the concept of morality in contractual behavior endorsed by Shiffrin.

C. *The Idea that Performance Per Se Has Moral Importance*

Shiffrin finds attractive notions of morality under which there is a special obligation to perform an act stated in the contract, even though she does not

[17] Shiffrin, *Breach of Contract*, *supra* note 5.

offer a precise definition or account of this opinion about moral behavior. She says, "[t]he idea that performance matters is a difficult point to support directly. It is the sort of position toward which one tends to be drawn by instinct rather than led by explicit direction."[18]

In her ensuing discussion, one point she stresses is that the purpose of a contract is to obtain performance, so that allowing breach and payment of expectation damages would "invert" the true warrant for a contract. Another point she advances is that the victim of breach loses his freedom – becoming an involuntary employee of the party in breach – because the victim has to find a replacement manner of obtaining performance.

I am sympathetic to Shiffrin's views in the sense that I believe most readers share her intuition that it is wrong to breach a contract, as I discuss in the following section.

D. *The Choice Among Definitions of Moral Behavior in the Contractual Context*

The debate between Shiffrin and me about the morality of breach of contract can be ascribed primarily to our different definitions of moral behavior. This leads to the question, how might a person choose among competing definitions of such behavior? Let me comment on three criteria by which a definition might be chosen.

First, a definition might be endorsed because it reflects the moral beliefs that individuals actually hold about the moral propriety of breach. My experience, and I suspect the reader's, has been that most individuals react to breach in the way Shiffrin supposes they do, as having an ethically incorrect aspect. Indeed, I conducted a limited survey confirming this hypothesis,[19] and a recent study by psychologists validates it as well.[20]

Why would individuals tend to hold the view that breach is wrong? The core of the explanation, I believe, is that contractual agreements are seen by individuals as close to, or as even indistinguishable from, promises made in everyday life. Such promises are statements that most people think they have a moral obligation to honor. We are taught from childhood that our promises ought to be kept, and this view is reinforced throughout our lives. Thus, it is

[18] *Id.*

[19] Shavell, *Is Breach of Contract Immoral?*, *supra* note 4, at 452–5. In particular, I found that "the individuals participating in the survey found the simple, unqualified fact of breach to be unethical on average." *Id.* at 455. However, when individuals were prompted by being asked to consider the terms of hypothetical complete contracts, they changed their opinions somewhat. *Id.*

[20] Wilkinson-Ryan & Baron, *supra* note 1.

natural for us to identify contracts with the promises that we have learned to treat as having moral valence. We do not pause to consider that contracts are, in fact, different from promises made in social intercourse, and that breaking contracts, unlike breaking promises, results in the payment of damages.

Second, a definition of the morality of breach might be selected because it has been developed from certain underlying principles with which one agrees. The definition that I have advanced is partly of this nature, as it is premised on the theory that contracts should be viewed through the lens of hypothetical complete contracts, to which there would be a moral obligation to adhere. I am not sure how to categorize Shiffrin's views, although my conjecture is that they are based on some combination of the first, empirical criterion and the second, underlying principles criterion.

Third, a definition of the morality of breach might be chosen because it promotes the welfare of contracting parties.[21] According to this criterion, my definition of the moral desirability of breach is attractive, for if the definition governs performance – if performance occurs when and only when its cost is less than its value – parties will tend to be better off than under any other standard for performance. As the reader knows, if under a proposed contract parties do not perform exactly when cost is less than value, it is always possible to find an alternative contract that both parties would prefer.

Relatedly, a regime of breach and payment of expectation damages promotes the welfare of the contracting parties relative to a regime of required performance. One way of demonstrating this point is to observe that if there is a breach and payment of expectation damages, the buyer is not harmed – by hypothesis, expectation damages are the equivalent of receiving performance – and the seller is benefited; the seller, after all, chose to commit breach so must have been made better off thereby. In other words, from an ex post perspective, the ability of sellers to commit breach and pay expectation damages benefits them but does not harm buyers. And from an ex ante perspective, the ability of sellers to commit breach and pay damages tends to help buyers affirmatively (rather than merely not harm them), for sellers can afford to give buyers a price reduction because of the anticipated benefit derived from their ability to commit breach.

In contrast, Shiffrin seems to believe that a regime permitting breach and payment of expectation damages lowers the welfare of buyers and discourages the making of contracts. She avers that if expectation damages were

[21] By the welfare of a party, I refer to the party's expected utility. In strict logic, the utility of a party could depend not only on conventional components of well-being (material goods and services, friendship, and the like) but also on satisfaction of moral notions, but I overlook this latter point for present purposes.

always paid, "[n]o promisee would ever get what she sought. As a further consequence, if this were the universalized response, the agreements would then never be made. The same is not true if performance were the universalized response to a promise to perform."[22] This is a perplexing view. As I stated in the preceding paragraph, the buyer is made whole if she receives expectation damages, so she should not be discouraged from contracting under a regime with breach and payment of these damages. Moreover, the seller becomes better off if he can breach and pay damages, so he should be positively encouraged to contract and could share his benefit with the buyer by lowering the contract price. This well-known point from the theory of contracts helps to explain why contracts flourish under our contract law that permits breach and payment of damages, and also why contracting would be unduly hindered were performance insisted upon as a matter of course.

Conclusion

I have explained in this chapter why I think that Seana Shiffrin's criticisms of the pure logic of my article are misplaced. Contracts are, I observed, substantially incomplete, so that a breach of a contract is ordinarily not a violation of an agreement that explicitly mentioned the contingency that occurred. And if one accepts my definition of moral behavior as that which would have been agreed upon in a hypothetical complete contract, it follows that breach and payment of expectation damages is not immoral, because such breaches occur only when performance would not have been specified in a complete contract.

I also asked about the appeal to the moral intuition of my definition of moral contractual behavior. Although I believe that my definition possesses attractiveness, because it reflects the notion that intended promises should be kept but not unintended ones, I also believe that its virtues can be appreciated only upon reflection. Most individuals seem instinctively to hold a different view, of which Shiffrin's is an exemplar, namely, that breach per se has an immoral dimension. I suggested that the primary explanation for why individuals hold this moral belief is that they regard contracts as simple promises and ignore the incompleteness of contracts – individuals tend to confuse the violation of a contract with the breaking of an explicit promise.

Last, I observed that different criteria may be employed for choosing among definitions of morality: consistency with the moral beliefs found in the population; derivation from favored underlying principles; and the advancement

[22] Shiffrin, *Breach of Contract*, *supra* note 5.

of the welfare of contracting parties. I stressed that according to the welfare criterion, my definition of when breach ought to occur is desirable and that breach and payment of expectation damages increases the well-being of both sellers and buyers. Conversely, a moral view under which positive weight is accorded to performance per se works against the interests of both sellers and buyers.

EIGHTEEN

Fault and Harm in Breach of Contract

Dori Kimel

This chapter offers a defense of the common law's approach to considerations relating to moral culpability in breach of contract – an approach by which such considerations tend to play a fairly limited role in devising the appropriate response to a breach. Calls for assigning fault a more central role in the law of contract are often inspired by the thought that it ought to reflect more systematically and more directly the morality of promise. The chapter seeks to expose this theoretical stance as misguided, instead locating the common law's approach to fault in broader ideas underpinning the legal and the political culture of which the common law is a product, and in particular the harm principle. The chapter concludes with an outline of what makes a law of contract moral, taking issue with the view that a moral law of contract is one that sets out to enforce morality.

Introduction

The key to the interest in the philosophical foundations of contract – inconstant as it has been in recent decades – lies, I believe, in the relationship between contract and promise. That contract is the legal equivalent of an institution with a full and independent existence outside the law, though perhaps not a source of direct interest in its doctrinal dimensions, means that this branch of the law furnishes its students with a unique opportunity to investigate a certain dimension of the relationship between law and morality.

Why is this opportunity unique? Opportunities to gain an insight into the relationship between law and morality (or law and other dimensions of our society and culture) are probably present in the study of any branch of the law. When it comes to contract, however, we find not an assortment of moral ideas and their legal manifestations, but what looks, at least, like the legal counterpart of one, whole, discrete, normative institution. The norms of promise, that is – the norms that govern the making, discharging, termination, frustration, or response to the breach (etc.) of promises – form a complete and, in many ways, discrete normative institution or practice. Thus, this legal domain furnishes us with a uniquely suitable lens through which to investigate a particular dimension of the relationship between legal and extralegal norms or normative systems.

If the relationship between contract and promise is the key to the philosophical interest in contract and contract law, it is also the key to the main puzzles encountered by those who have shown such interest. For as soon as closer attention is paid to the relationship between contract and promise, not just the foundational similarities but also some startling discrepancies between these two normative institutions come to light – the more startling the more one expects the law of contract simply to reflect promissory logic and (where applicable) enforce promissory norms. I will not attempt to catalogue all such discrepancies in the present context, but at the highest level of abstraction I think they can be grouped around two main themes: voluntariness and fault.[1]

On the voluntariness side, apparent tensions between contract and promise are bound up with the idea that if contract, like promise, were based on the recognition of the value of voluntarily assumed, self-imposed obligations, then contract law would look different: It would impose far fewer limitations and far fewer conditions on parties' ability to have their expressed wishes – and nothing other than their expressed wishes – enforced by law. Contract law doctrines such as consideration and implied terms, the relative rarity of actual enforcement (as opposed to the award of monetary compensation for breach), and much besides to do with the numerous ways in which the freedom of contract is encroached upon in contemporary jurisdictions, have been adduced as evidence in this context.

When it comes to fault, the apparent tension naturally concerns the fairly negligible role that fault plays in contract law: if the law of contract is based on

[1] There is, in fact, a third theme, to do with the fact that a promise is a unilateral undertaking whereas a contract is (typically) a bilateral one. Objections to the contract-promise analogy based on this observation have been met by suggestions along the lines that the correct analogy is between contract and an *exchange* of promises, or an exchange of *conditional* promises, etc. (For an excellent recent contribution to this debate *see* H. Sheinman, *Agreement as Joint Promise*, in H. Sheinman (ed.) Promises and Agreements: Philosophical Essays (New York: Oxford UP (forthcoming)). Such objections may or may not amount to more than a quibble, but either way, they are avoided altogether if the correct analogy is taken to be that between (legal) contracts and (nonlegal) agreements, be the relationship between "agreement" and "promise" as it may. This distinction is of little or no significance for the purposes of this chapter, so I'll continue to use, for the most part, the familiar "contract and promise" language; I think, however, that none of my arguments would be affected if "promise" is replaced with "agreement."

the morality of promise, so the thought goes, moral culpability – in breach, for instance – ought to play as much of a role here as it does there. And one of the most obvious features of contract law, as we know it, is that it does not.[2]

Saying as much, it should be noted, does not implicate a particularly far-reaching or controversial view of the role of fault in the promissory domain. It is compatible with the notion, for instance, that once a valid promise is made, keeping it is a matter of strict liability, so that *breaking* it may be excusable, or justified, or plain wrong – but always *a wrong*. For even if this is so, the normative aftermath of the breach would be significantly informed by its moral quality: An explanation might always be called for (on this view it is, after all, always a wrong), but what kind of explanation is called for, whether an apology should also be made, what efforts to make reparations are required, how the promisee, in turn, should respond (and so on) are all matters the evaluation of which would undoubtedly be bound up with the circumstances of the breach and the degree of fault (if any) attributable to the promise breaker. In contract, by contrast, not only the liability but also the remedies available to the innocent party are largely insensitive to questions concerning fault on the part of the party in breach.

I. Promise De-moralized, Contract Moralized

Other than the rather rare, outright denial that there is any instructive analogy to be drawn between the law of contract and the morality of promise,[3] such apparent discrepancies between them have been met with responses that I will describe as oriented in three directions. The first two types of response aim at explaining away or actually eroding the apparent discrepancy – either by exposing it as (for the most part) illusory, or by arguing for a reform of contract law aimed at minimizing it. The third, by contrast, takes (much of) the discrepancy to be far less troublesome; rather, is sees it as an inevitable manifestation of the fact that contract is, indeed, the *legal* equivalent – that is, the legal *equivalent* – of promise.

I refer to the first type of approach as "promise de-moralized" and the second as "contract moralized." The former consists of arguments aimed at exposing at least some of the seeming discrepancies between contract and

[2] Here and elsewhere, I do not mean to suggest that fault does not play any role in the law of contract. George M. Cohen has been foremost in giving the lie to exaggerated views on this matter; see his The Fault Lines in Contract Damages 80 *Virginia LR* 1225 (1994), as well as his contribution to the present volume.

[3] The most notable example – at least for the proposition that the morality of promise is of no use for the task of developing "default rules" in contract law – is Richard Craswell's Contract Law,

promise as illusory, in the sense that they reflect an erroneous understanding of the morality of promise. Here, we find a broad range of claims meant to falsify certain central dimensions of a certain orthodoxy in the philosophy of promise, in particular the notion (or any or all of the constituent parts of the notion) that promissory obligations are moral obligations that significantly and centrally owe their existence to intentional acts by promisors, the purpose of which is the very assumption of moral (promissory) obligations.[4] As such, it is an approach that has proved useful for quibbling with apparent discrepancies grouped around the theme of voluntariness, but which could also be brought to bear on issues concerning fault.

On the contract moralized side of things – contract *over*moralized is what I really have in mind – we find the contrasting approach: The general orientation here is to argue that, inasmuch as discrepancies between contract law and the morality of promise are *not* illusory, they represent a flaw in contract law, and one that (other things being equal) ought to be rectified. Contract law, in other words, ought to be such that it reflects as closely as possible and enforces as consistently as possible the moral norms governing promise or agreement. Although contrasting, these approaches are not entirely contradictory or mutually exclusive; one's overall view of the relationship between contract and promise may include elements of both. Having said that, it can be seen that the contract moralized approach would be the more conspicuous, and produce more scope for a critique of actual contract law regimes, the more it is rooted in an analysis of promise along the lines of what I have described, albeit loosely, as the philosophical orthodoxy in this matter – that is, the less tainted it is by the de-moralization of promise.

To stand out, and to inform a meaningful critique of contract law, however, the contract moralized approach need not be rooted in a crude version of the philosophical orthodoxy on promise. And inasmuch as such an approach is informed by a sufficiently sophisticated understanding of the morality of promise – one that eschews, for instance, radically individualistic notions of voluntariness and its implications, or eschews the simplistic notion that if promissory obligations are rooted in personal autonomy, then promisors

Default Rules, and the Philosophy of Promising 88 Michigan LR 489 (1989). For my response, *see* Remedial Rights and Substantive Rights in Contract Law 8 *Legal Theory* 313 (2002).

[4] The canonical example of the philosophical *counter*orthodoxy would, of course, be Hume. F.S. McNeily's influential *Promises De-Moralized* (81 Phil. Rev. 63(1972)) is a notable modern attack on the type of orthodoxy I have in mind. Also notable is Neil MacCormick's argument for seeing promissory obligations as located in reliance. (*See Voluntary Obligations and Normative Powers* 46 Proc. Aristotelian Soc. 59 (1972).) For a more recent contributions, *see e.g.*, H. Sheinman's *Promise as Practice Reason* (forthcoming *in* Acta Analytica), and Heidi M. Hurd, Promises Schomises (unpublished manuscript, on file with the University of Illinois Law

must have complete control over the content and the normative implications of their promises – it need not have particularly radical implications in terms of all issues concerning the meaning and the appropriate scope of voluntariness or the implications of respect for personal autonomy in contract law. It need not, for example, lead to calls for a radical expansion of the freedom of contract, or for less regulation of contract terms, and so on. On the contrary, the moralizing approach can manifest itself in the view that contract law must be such that it can be used only for moral aims, be infused by requirements of good faith or hostility to sharp practice, and so on (ideas that can and, I would argue, ought to be defended on different grounds). But it does have a direct bearing on fault, leading naturally to calls for assigning it a far more central role in contract law than it currently occupies. Such a role may have implications, among other things, in terms of eroding the traditional claimant-centric approach to remedies for breach, and with it, possibly, the principle that, quite regardless of the defendant's culpability or its absence, remedies are aimed at placing the claimant in as good a position as that in which she would have been absent the breach *and no more*; making specific performance (or injunction against breach) more readily available even where that principle does not strictly require it; rethinking the traditional aversion to punitive damages, and so on.

I said earlier that interest in the philosophical foundations of contract has been inconstant. Of late, it has certainly been on the ascent: After two decades or so during which the theory of contract, particularly in the United States, seems to have been dominated by economic analysis, recent years have seen a true revival in this particular branch of legal philosophy, and with it some instances of fresh enthusiasm for both the promise de-moralized and the contract moralized modes of analysis, with the latter, in particular, receiving a new lease of life, a phenomenon perhaps best understood as a backlash against the grand enterprise of *de*-moralizing contract (among other branches of the law) that is economic analysis.

I consider both approaches to be misguided. A substantive critique of any argument of the promise de-moralized variety can only be offered by way of a defense of a version of the philosophical orthodoxy against which it is aimed – something of no interest in this chapter.[5] I will not engage directly with contract moralized *as such*, either – tempting as it might be, it is not clearly possible (or helpful anyway) to offer a critique of a general theoretical

Review). The most notable example of the "promise de-moralized" approach in contract theory is Patrick Atiyah's in Promises, Morals, and Law (Oxford, 1981).

[5] For my own view, *see* From Promise to Contract: Towards a Liberal Theory of Promise ch.1 (Oxford, 2003). *See also* Joseph Raz's critique of MacCormick's view (*Voluntary Obligations* 46

orientation, as opposed to concrete arguments. Instead, I will use the debate over the appropriate role of fault in contract law, particularly when it comes to responses to a breach, as an opportunity to demonstrate the scope and merit of an approach that eschews both the de-moralization of promise and the (over)moralization of contract. I argue that, although contractual obligations are, in significant ways, promissory, the fairly marginal role fault has been assigned in the law of contract is, by and large, the correct one, notwithstanding the more central role it unquestionably plays in the promissory domain. As far as implications in terms of legal reform are concerned, this is therefore a conservative essay. In a different sense, however, it is meant to sound a cautionary note regarding what I see as a breed of theoretical conservatism in the analysis of the relationship between contract and promise, as well as, by implication, law and morality more broadly.

II. Contract and Promise: More on the Relationship

Establishing the proposition that contractual obligations are, in significant ways, promissory, or that contract should be thought of as the legal equivalent of promise, is not something that can be done within the confines of this chapter.[6] I should nevertheless explain what I mean by this, and, for present purposes, two interrelated points are of significance:

First, the core contractual obligation is the obligation to perform, and the core contractual right is the right to performance, whereas "performance" means carrying out the actions specified in those terms of the contract in which performance is defined. So if a contract is for "the construction of a garden shed or adequate compensation for a failure to construct a garden shed," either constructing the shed or adequately compensating for the failure to do so amounts to performance. But if a contract is for the construction of a garden shed, constructing the shed is performance, compensation for the failure to construct it is compensation for a failure *to perform* – it is not performance.[7]

Second, a central part of the justification for facilitating and enforcing contracts is the recognition of the value of voluntarily undertaken obligations.[8]

Such claims can have – and, for those who make them, usually do have – both a descriptive and an evaluative or critical dimension. They are, if you

Proc. Aristotelian Soc. 79 (1972)) and of Atiyah's (*Book Review: Promises in Morality and Law* 95 Harv. L.R. 916 (1982)).

[6] My take on this issue was offered in detail in *id*.

[7] The emphasis is meant to clarify that my view is not vulnerable to a critique such as Richard Craswell's in Expectation Damages and Contract Theory Revisited (Stanford Public Law Working Paper No. 925980, 2006).

[8] For an explanation of why the second point entails the first, *see supra* note 5, ch. 4.

like, interpretive claims about the law of contract. For those who offer them in this way, at least, the first claim entails that the core contractual obligation is performance, *and aptly so* – it does not deny that a law of contract (or something like it) that does not take the core contractual obligation to be performance is conceivable, but it implies that it would be an institution inferior to the one with which we are familiar; whereas the second claim implies that the justification for facilitating and enforcing contracts that draws centrally on the value of voluntarily undertaken obligations is the best one, or the one that would justify a law of contract superior to a law that cannot be justified thus.

This does not mean, however, that those who make such claims (and who subscribe to both their descriptive and critical dimensions) are bound to think it possible or wise to systematically *make* contract more promise-like, or as promise-like as possible. Take, for instance, the second claim: It accounts for an important similarity between contract and promise, but leaves open the possibility of equally important differences. The justification for both institutions may draw centrally on the recognition of the value of voluntary obligations, but beyond that – that is, in terms of *how* the particular value is recognized or the particular reasons for recognizing it in each case – there may be crucial differences or even contrasts between them,[9] differences that, in turn, can have a bearing on the selection of the rules that best contribute to the promotion of the overall value in question. Or, when it comes to the first claim, for closely related reasons – reasons pertaining to the nature of the law in general and its impact on the institution of agreement in particular – not every implication of the fact that the core obligation is performance that we find in the promissory domain can be gainfully incorporated into contract law. Simply *enacting* promissory norms or their closest approximation can be a self-defeating business, sometimes endangering rather than making more likely the realization of the very values by which they are informed, sometimes endangering the realization of other values to which the law ought to remain sensitive.

That is also part of the reason why the conceptual relationship between contract and promise cannot be settled by *fiat*, either official or private. Lawmakers may set out to make contract law *the law of legally enforceable promises*, no more or less, and may define "contract," statutorily, in just such terms – that is, as *legally enforceable promises* – yet the success or failure of such an enterprise would not be entirely within their control: Legal

[9] On my own account, for instance, the value in the case of promise is the combination of cooperation and fostering personal relationships, whereas in contract it's the combination of cooperation and protecting personal detachment – *see supra* note 5.

enforceability on its own inevitably alters certain characteristics of promissory relations, and other features of the legal framework may similarly have a transformational (and not just protective, supportive, etc.) effect on that which it sets out to encompass. Similarly, inasmuch as contractual undertakings *are*, in certain ways, promises, a party cannot enter a contract while meaningfully declaring herself to be "making no promises" (or if she does, she says something oxymoronic).[10]

This abstract and regrettably sketchy preamble finally brings me to the issue of fault. Continuing to focus on the very limited role that considerations of moral culpability play when it comes to devising the appropriate responses to a breach, my thesis is simple. It is that, like much else when it comes to responses to a breach of contract, the role assigned to fault has a great deal to do with the harm principle – a principle that does not derive from promissory or contractual norms, but forms part of a general doctrine of political freedom and its implications in terms of the appropriate limits on the use of state power. Thus, neither confirming nor falsifying the analogy between contract and promise in terms of their intrinsic norms, the relative inattention to fault in contract owes to something that is unique to contract *as a legal institution*, as such embedded in a particular political culture and aptly governed – unlike promise – by the principles of political morality of which that culture is composed.

III. The Harm Principle and Contract Law

For obvious reasons, I will say very little here about the harm principle and its moral foundations. I will say the bare minimum required to demonstrate how a credible version of that principle can – and, in given legal-political cultures, does – have the kind of bearing on the law of contract that I am attributing to it here.

Thankfully, it is fairly straightforward. Informed by concern for personal freedom, the harm principle sets a certain threshold for the legitimate use of state power. As such, it has to be grounded in a comprehensive theory of personal and political freedom, one that lends it both a foundation and concrete content – content, that is, in terms of giving a sufficiently precise meaning to "harm." Properly so grounded, it offers up harmfulness (in the relevant sense) as a necessary condition for the use of state coercion, thus delegitimizing (among other things) the suppression or the punishment of conduct for the sole reason that it involves the commission of what amounts to a moral wrong.

[10] Compare M. Pratt, Contract: Not Promise (2008) 35 *Fla. St. U. LR* 801, 807–11.

Given the political as well as philosophical popularity and influence of the harm principle (at least since John Stuart Mill's defense of a version of it in the mid-nineteenth century), and given how prominently it features in discussions of the moral limits of the law in general, I have always found it somewhat surprising that it features so rarely in discussions of the appropriate limits on the enforcement of contracts. I can think of two explanations, both of which ultimately fail to justify this neglect. The first has to do with the fact that, as a principle of freedom, the harm principle sets a limit not on state action in general, but on action that interferes directly and significantly with freedom – that is, the imposition of legal *obligations*, or the use of state *coercion*. Thus, it is naturally associated with debates concerning criminalization and state punishment, and much less so with a branch of the law generally thought to be concerned with the extension or exercise of freedom, not its curtailment; with rules that confer powers, not impose obligations. Another explanation might be that the predominant issue, when it comes to remedies for breach of contract, is not one of identifying a harmful wrong in the first place; rather, the presence and identity of a relevant harmful wrong in this domain tends to be taken for granted – it is the wrong of breach, and the resultant harm in terms of denying the innocent party the benefit performance would have brought – whereas the real debate surrounds the question of how exactly to respond to it; *which* remedy, that is, would be appropriate. And the harm principle is sometimes thought to be oblivious to the choice of response to a wrong once the threshold it sets has been cleared; it is sometimes thought to bear exclusively on the question of when the use of power is legitimate, not on how much power or what type of power to use.

The first explanation, I think, is not only misguided, but contains a degree of irony: The harm principle is, in fact, more straightforward to establish and has a more direct and less controversial bearing when it comes to contract law than when it comes to the much more open-ended domain of criminalization. This is not a proposition I can fully defend here, but the clue is in that very open-endedness. The criminal law may respond, potentially, to any type of wrong, and for a whole variety of reasons. Criminalization, that is, has not one, but a fairly wide range of coexistent functions – protective, preventive, rehabilitative, retributive, communicative, and more – each bringing with it its own distinct justificatory apparatus.[11] This at least indicates how difficult it would be to establish that under no circumstances, and by reference to any proper function of

[11] For a nice rebuttal of the notion that different functions and justifications of the criminal law are necessarily rivals among which one must make a choice, *see* J. Gardner, *Crime: In Proportion and in Perspective*, reprinted in Offences and Defences: Selected Essays in the Philosophy of Criminal Law 213, 214–15 (Oxford, 2007).

criminalization, would it be legitimate to criminalize any instance of wrongful yet harmless conduct.[12] Of course, even inasmuch as it is agreed that something more than a bare moral wrong needs to be targeted for criminalization to be legitimate, various potential alternatives to harm present themselves (of which offense is probably the most familiar). All such complications are largely absent when it comes to contract. The remit of the law of contract is, of course, far more limited, both in terms of its functions and possible justifications and, clearly, in terms of the range of wrongs it responds to as well as the type of harms with which those wrongs are normally associated. Indeed, when it comes to breach of contract, the wrong is just that – breach of contract. I will say more shortly about the related harms, but what is clear is that, unless the function of contract law is viewed as that of enforcing the morality of promise keeping *for its own sake* – something that would not only be illiberal and ill-advised on its own, but would also significantly undermine the propensity of contract law to fulfil the functions more commonly attributed to it – the threshold for legitimate remedial responses to a breach can only plausibly be harm. The imposition of remedial duties, on this view, would not be justified unless explicable as a means of preventing or redressing the harm associated with a breach.

The second possible explanation for the rarity of allusions to the harm principle in this context reflects a simple misconception, perhaps owing to well-documented flaws with *the* classic defense of a harm principle, namely, Mill's.[13] Grounded, as it must be, in a comprehensive theory of political freedom, the harm principle need by no means be rendered silent as to the means by which harm is redressed once it has been identified. On the contrary, the same considerations establishing the imprudence of suppressing or punishing harmless conduct in the first place would normally continue to exert an inhibitive influence here. If the harm principle is grounded in the value of personal autonomy, for instance, those same considerations underlying it would not only reveal what should count as harm for its purposes, but also that the use of coercion aimed at redressing it must, other things being equal, involve the minimal cost to the personal autonomy of those against whom coercion is used.

IV. Harm, Fault, and Remedies for Breach

We are now in a position to appreciate the bearing that the harm principle has on the selection of remedies for breach of contract in general; once this is

[12] For a related critique of the harm principle in the context of criminalization, *see* J. Stanton-Ife, *The Limits of Law in* Stanford Encyclopedia of Philosophy (2006).

[13] *See, e.g.*, John Gray's comment on Mill in J. S. Mill, On Liberty and Other Essays xix (Oxford World's Classics edition, 1998).

demonstrated, we can turn our attention to its implications regarding fault in breach in particular.

Joseph Raz has argued that the harm principle lends support to reliance damages as the standard remedy for breach.[14] This view seems to implicate a particular understanding of what the relevant harm in breach is, namely, the notion that, in this context at least, denying a party what it has not yet had – that is, the benefits of the bargain – is not harming, and hence not something the redress of which the harm principle would (other things being equal[15]) sanction. For my part, having taken my cue from him in terms of investigating the implications of support for the harm principle in this domain, I quibbled with Raz's identification of the relevant harm. Thus, informed by the thought that denying a party something of value *to which it is entitled* is harming (and paradigmatically so), coupled with the notion that (again paradigmatically) parties to contract are entitled to each others' performance, my own analysis has established specific performance as the standard (logically speaking, not statistically) remedy for breach, albeit a standard from which it is rather frequently necessary to depart. Such departures are called for in two types of scenario: either where a less intrusive remedy would be *just as good* as a means of preventing or redressing the same harm, or, far less routinely, in cases where notwithstanding the fact that full redress could be achieved only through specific performance, the case for awarding it is outweighed, in the circumstances, by sufficiently potent considerations against such an award. The first type of scenario is one in which the threshold set by the harm principle for actual enforcement of a contract has not been cleared[16]; the second type is one where it has been cleared, yet independent, non-harm-principle–derived considerations counsel against it (e.g., unusual hardship befalling the defendant, the specter of large-scale economic waste, the obvious impracticality of enforcement, etc.).[17] It should be noted that the second type of scenario

[14] *Book Review: Promises in Morality and Law* 95 Harv. L.R. 916, 934 (1982).

[15] But *see* his account of how things may not be equal, *id* 937–8; and *see* my comments, *supra* note 5, 106–7.

[16] What the harm principle *does* mandate in such cases, of course, depends on the circumstances: Since the harm principle mandates only the least intrusive remedy with which to fully redress the harm, it would mandate no more than expectation damages where these would place the claimant in just as good a position, mandate no more than reliance damages where these suffice for the same purpose, and indeed rule out remedial intervention altogether where the breach causes no harm. Technically speaking, the latter type of case (e.g., in a contract for sale where another buyer is ready to step in and there are no additional losses relating to transaction costs, volume of transactions, etc.) should be described as a third type of scenario – that is, one where there is no harm to redress.

[17] Elements of the two scenarios can sometimes overlap: There may be cases, for instance, where the harm principle only mandates expectation damages (since their award would place the claimant in exactly as good a position as specific performance), yet some independent consideration

is by no means an embarrassment for a harm-principle–based analysis; rather, it is a reminder of the fact that the harm principle sets but a *threshold* of legitimacy for the use of state power. It sets a necessary condition, not one that is necessary and sufficient.

How does fault come into this? Well, it barely does – and that is exactly my point. Unlike certain harms with which species of tort and criminal liabilities are concerned, the harm against which parties ought to be protected in the context of an institution whose main function is to facilitate arm's length transactions – namely, the denial of valuable contractual entitlements – tends to be entirely insensitive to fault; its occurrence as well as magnitude does not usually correspond to the moral quality of the conduct that has brought it about. Whether nonperformance, possibly subject to the payment of appropriate damages, would cause that harm – that is, would leave the innocent party in an inferior position to that in which performance would have left it, denying it some or all of the benefits of the bargain – is a question the answer to which depends entirely on matters other than the moral culpability, if any, attending the breach – matters such as what is bought or sold, the purpose for which the parties have entered the contract, the availability and adequacy of alternatives, relevant changes in market conditions, and so on. Thus, a breach that is harmful in terms of the benefits of the bargain remains so even when committed absent fault, whereas a breach that is harmless in terms of the benefits of the bargain – say, where both parties enter the contract for profit, and damages reflecting the innocent party's expectation interest would leave it in an identical position to that in which performance would have left it – remains harmless whether intentional or even spiteful. And if the harm principle delegitimizes remedial measures beyond that which is necessary to prevent or redress harm, and the potential harmfulness of breach of contract is insensitive to fault, then fault has no central role to play in devising the appropriate legal response to a breach – not in terms of identifying the harms against which parties ought to be protected in the first place, nor in terms of selecting the means by which to do so.

To be sure, the picture does not change when the focus shifts from ex post redress to ex ante deterrence: The coercive deterrence of harmless wrongs violates the harm principle in much the same way as the excessive redress of harmful wrongs. The availability (in principle) of specific performance in cases where nothing less would do for the purposes of securing for the innocent party the benefits of the bargain, coupled with the availability (in

militates against their award and in favor of the award of a "lesser" remedy, such as reliance damages.

principle) of no more than the measure required (if any) for the same purposes in all other cases, represents all that there is for the law to do in terms of harm-prevention, both deterrence-wise and redress-wise: It redresses the relevant harm to the full but no more, and it fully deters harmful conduct but not conduct that is not harmful. By contrast, the availability *in addition* of remedies reflecting a particular judgment as to the moral culpability attending the breach – say, punitive damages for an intentional breach, or specific performance in such cases even when a less intrusive remedy would otherwise do – would usually serve no purpose other than that of, in effect, the suppression of immorality for its own sake.

Thus, it is a principle of political morality, rather than the notion that a breach is not or cannot be immoral, that explains the relative inattention to moral culpability in breach of contract, as well as the traditional aversion to punitive damages and much besides, and that, indeed, largely obviates the very question as to the (possible) immorality of a breach for the purposes of defending or criticizing remedial regimes.

I said *largely* obviates, and I said no *central* role, rather than no role whatsoever or obviates altogether. There is a reason for that – two minor twists I have thus far ignored, and which show that fault has *some* role to play after all, albeit a residual one.

The first has been implied already, in connection with the harm principle's status as setting a necessary condition only, so that considerations arising in the circumstances of particular cases can militate against the award of a particular remedy even where the failure to award it would mean a failure to fully redress the harm caused by the breach. At common law, such considerations tend to receive direct attention in court particularly when it comes to the question of whether to order specific performance, since the award of that remedy is always discretionary. And in considering whether to exercise this discretion in favor of the claimant, courts sometimes advert to the question of fault, and rightly so, not only in light of the formal rule (a historical accident, really) by which specific performance can be granted only to a claimant who comes to court with "clean hands,"[18] but also since it can sometimes shed light on the precise weight to be ascribed to specific considerations that potentially militate against enforcement. Take, for example, cases involving the judgment that the award of specific performance would be excessively harsh on the defendant in the circumstances: Such a judgment, like most other judgments to the effect that the position of the defendant merits special sympathy

[18] This rule, as well as the discretionary status of specific performance, reflects this remedy's origins in Equity.

even to the detriment of the (otherwise deserving) claimant, is one that is almost invariably sensitive to the question of the culpability of the defendant; a measure that may seem harsh when taken against a blameless defendant may not seem so in the case of a culpable one.

I would describe this particular role of fault as residual or noncentral, since it is limited, by its very logic, to exceptional cases – cases the particular circumstances of which (possibly) justify a departure from what is taken to be the general rule. The same is true of the other twist I have in mind. To introduce it, I need to say a bit more about the harm in question.

V. Fault and Institutional Harm

The discussion thus far has focused on the harm a breach causes to the innocent party. My characterization of this harm as involving the denial of the benefits of the bargain – no less but also no more – was, of course, informed by a certain understanding of the functions of contracting (and hence also of the legitimate expectations to which a contract may rise, so that their frustration through breach constitutes the wrong the harm of which ought to be redressed), one that takes the main purpose of the institution to be the facilitation of transactional cooperation outside the context of already-existing personal relationships while allowing parties who so wish to preserve their mutual detachment in the process.[19] Be that as it may, the harm principle encompasses not only harms to individuals, but also harms to valuable institutions; accordingly, legal obligations can, sometimes, legitimately be imposed with the aim of preventing harm of the latter kind, even inasmuch as no harm to individuals is at issue. Now, when it comes to conduct that engenders harm to the institution of contract, the two types of harm tend to overlap, as do the means by which to redress them: The straightforward way to protect the institution from, say, disrepute, is to protect those who legitimately deploy it from all relevant harms. And so long as this is done – when it comes to remedies, with a remedial regime aimed at placing claimants well and truly in as good a position as that in which they would have been absent the breach, or anyway doing so in all but exceptional cases the exceptional nature of which is readily understandable – the related threat to the institution's standing (relative to a correct perception of its functions) is removed. In this context, it may be worth noting again that the same conclusions emerge from the ex ante and the ex post perspectives just the same: Given its particular functions, the institution of contract would not benefit from the deterrence of

[19] I have defended this view at length elsewhere; *see supra* note 5.

harmless breach any more than it would from its punishment, and would not benefit from the disproportionate deterrence of a harmful breach any more that it would from its excessive punishment. On the contrary, the institution's capacity to fulfil its true functions would only diminish if it did so, as parties would be more reluctant to deploy it if by doing so they were subjecting themselves to an otherwise unnecessary, potentially coercive scrutiny of their moral rectitude.

Yet exceptional cases may exist wherein the two types of harm do not entirely overlap – cases where the potential harm to the institution of contract a breach may engender is independent of, or markedly exceeds, the harm caused to the innocent party. And I suspect that fault can sometimes be intrinsic to this sort of harm in a way it usually is not when it comes to harm to contracting parties.

The type of case I have in mind here is a particular subcategory of cases where the breach is a constitutive part of a profitable enterprise, not just by removing an obstacle to undertaking it (as in the case of the standard, so-called efficient breach) or making it more profitable than it would have otherwise been (as in another type of efficient breach),[20] but by facilitating it in the first place. It is this type of case that has presented perhaps the greatest temptation to depart from the claimant-centric norm, to award disgorgement damages or punitive damages, and at any rate, to fashion a response that directly reflects a judgment as to the defendant's moral culpability. But whereas such a response may fall foul of the harm principle inasmuch as the harm suffered by the defendant is concerned, it may be justified, on occasion, by reference to the need to protect the institution of contract. The circumstances of the famous *Blake* litigation[21] – where the defendant made a profit from the proceeds of a memoir published in breach of a confidentiality clause (which, being a spy, he never intended to keep) in his contract of employment with the claimant, and disgorgement damages were sought – provide a good example for the possible combination of all such elements. In a case such as this, a remedial response limited to redressing the harm suffered by the claimant, and thus, potentially, leaving the defendant with a significant profit, can indeed fall short of redressing the likely *institutional* harm at stake, and the latter would indeed be a function of fault on the part of the defendant: It is precisely the fact that the defendant is allowed to keep an ill-gotten gain – ill-gotten, that is, in the sense of having been accrued

[20] Namely, where the expectation interest of the first buyer forms a platform for price negotiation with the second.

[21] Attorney General v. Blake [2001] 1 AC 268 (HL). For a detailed account, *see* J. Edelman, Gain-Based Damages ch. 5 (Oxford, 2002).

directly through calculating, fraudulent, and in any event clearly blameworthy conduct – that can have adverse ramifications in terms of the public perception of contract or the legitimate purposes for which the institution may be deployed.

I would not want to argue conclusively that the temptation to depart from the claimant-centric norm, or indeed to pay closer attention to fault on the part of the defendant, must always be resisted in such cases; perhaps it should not. But whereas I cannot here undertake the detailed analysis such cases merit, it should be noted just how exceptional they really are and, regardless, that inasmuch as they open the door to giving more of a role to fault in breach *still in line with the harm principle*, they open it very slightly. First, the obvious remedy in cases such as the *Blake* litigation is actual enforcement of the contract (i.e., in the circumstances, an injunction against breach): While best suited for protecting the legitimate interests of the claimant, it is also the remedy that would completely preempt the institutional harm in question, and *its* award need not require giving fault in breach more than its usual (non)role. Therefore, cases where this sort of institutional harm is at stake are exceptional not just in terms of the type of breach in question, but also in terms of their arising in circumstances where the obvious and standard remedial response is not available.[22] Second, such cases often involve the commission of a criminal offence or incurring liability in tort (or both), and these noncontractual liabilities often provide the best opportunity to redress both the individual and the institutional harms associated with the breach. Third, inasmuch as the implications of focusing on the defendant's fault in the context of an action for breach of contract is thought to counsel in favor of awarding damages exceeding the harm suffered by the claimant, such as the disgorgement damages sought in the *Blake* litigation, the claimant is placed (or places itself) in a tenuous moral position: It asks to benefit from the proceeds of culpable conduct that, according the claimant's own position, should not have accrued *to anyone*. That the defendant ought to be stripped of such benefits, in other words, falls short of fully explaining why they should go to the claimant; that, in turn, lends further support to the previous point, namely, that an action for breach of contract, with or without attention to fault, is rarely the ideal medium through which to redress the institutional harm that particularly culpable breaches of this sort sometimes involve.

[22] In the *Blake* case, the book was published more than 30 years after George Blake escaped from prison, where he served a sentence for spying; at the time he lived in Moscow, and the prosecuting authorities became aware of the publication too late to obtain an injunction.

Conclusion: Toward a Moral Law of Contract

My defense of a doctrinal tradition by which fault in breach of contract receives very little attention may be thought to implicate a broader view, which takes contract law as a whole to be divorced or isolated from (all but very few) moral considerations – perhaps particularly so in light of the fact that it was presented as part of a case against the theoretical trend toward overmoralizing contract law. I have hinted earlier that such an impression would be profoundly misguided, and in concluding this chapter I wish to make this point more explicit by sketching out my view as to what it means to make the law of contract moral.

I started out by describing contract as the legal equivalent of agreement. Agreement is a moral institution, the limits of which – if you like, the limits on the *freedom* of which – are delineated by the entirety of moral considerations that have a bearing on the question of what agreements it is desirable, or at least permissible, for people to make, as well as under what conditions. Thus, agreements for the furtherance of immoral aims, or agreements that are decidedly exploitative or otherwise fall outside of the relevant scope of moral permissibility, may be, and usually are (morally speaking) void.

Things are not different when it comes to contract. The facilitative nature of this legal domain – the fact that, here, the law furnishes prospective parties with the power to make legally binding transactions, thus also availing them, in the context of such transactions, of the adjudicating as well as enforcing agencies of the state – means that the law is implicated in the moral quality of the agreements it recognizes and enforces in a particularly direct and active way. When the law fails to criminalize a particular type of, say, exploitation or advantage-taking or undue influence or manipulation, or when it refrains from criminalizing otherwise reprehensible pursuits, it merely fails to do what (arguably) it ought to do. When it recognizes and enforces agreements that are similarly morally tainted, however, it actively partakes in enabling them and securing their ends.

For that reason, when it comes to the appropriate scope of the freedom of contract, the pressing question is not how far it would be legitimate or desirable for the law to go *in terms of imposing restrictions* (as the customary terms of engagements in debates over the freedom of contract would have us believe), but quite the opposite: The question is how far the freedom of contract must extend in the first place; what kind of transactions the law of contract ought to facilitate, and why. In her masterful study of the narrower debate surrounding market alienability, Margaret Radin has demonstrated, if nothing else, the inevitability of a case-by-case approach to the question of what people should be allowed to buy and sell through contracting, as well as the potential intricacy of the moral analysis that determines the result in each case.[23] All this applies with equal force to all other dimensions of the freedom of contract. And whereas that does not mean that the law of contract ought to limit itself to enforcing perfect bargains and nothing else – that would doubtless be self-defeating – it does mean that the comprehensive moral foot-work involved in establishing the case for or against extending the freedom of contract over any type of transaction (or any type of circumstances under which transactions are made, etc.) is an integral part of the ongoing endeavor of making the law of contract such that it contributes to, or at least does not undermine, all those forms of human flourishing (to use Radin's language) on which it can have an effect.

Thus, a moral law of contract is not a punitive law of contract, nor a law of contract that sets out to simply enforce moral norms, promissory or otherwise. A law of contract law that allows contracts for, say, the sale of human beings, or fails to protect vulnerable parties from the worst repercussions of inequality of bargaining power and enforces exploitative terms against them, can be said to be immoral, and in quite a paradigmatic way: It facilitates immoral conduct and avails those who engage in it with powerful means with which to secure the rewards. By contrast, a law of contract that does not enforce the moral norms of promise keeping beyond that which the harm principle permits does not facilitate immoral conduct; it merely holds back from enforcing morality for its own sake. The mistake of conflating these two propositions, if adopted as a starting point for legal reform, would result in a law of contract not more, but significantly less moral. It may not lend itself as much as the law as it is apparently does to being misinterpreted as setting out to actively *encourage* the commission of harmless wrongs (justified wrongs, excusable, or otherwise),[24] but it would become divorced from one of the foundational tenets of a political morality that gives freedom, correctly interpreted and aptly integrated into the overall scheme of good government, the place it deserves in informing the appropriate limits on the use of state power. Morally speaking, that can only be a step in the wrong direction.

[23] Market-Inalienability 100 Harv. L.R. 1849 (1987).

[24] An anxiety expressed by Seanna Shiffrin in The Divergence of Contract and Promise 120 Harv L.R. 708 (2007).

NINETEEN

Fault in Contracts: A Psychological Approach

Tess Wilkinson-Ryan

Although the role of fault in contract law has traditionally received little theoretical or doctrinal attention, it is central to commonsense moral theories of contract. Most people believe that breaking a promise is wrong, and that breach of contract is a form of promise breaking. Parties' moral intuitions may affect their willingness to breach when it is otherwise efficient to do so, their ability to reach settlement once a contract has been breached, their predictions about legal rules of contract, and their post hoc assessments of appropriate damages. This chapter reviews experimental research on the effects of moral norms on contracting. Behavioral studies show that many people believe that breach of contract is a moral harm irrespective of actual losses suffered by the promisee. It is argued in the chapter that moral norms often act as default rules in legal decision making about contracts when a contingency is unspecified in the contract.

Although the role of fault in contract law has traditionally received little theoretical or doctrinal attention, it is central to commonsense moral theories of contract. Most people believe that breaking a promise is wrong, and that breach of contract is a form of promise breaking. In fact, evolutionary psychologists have identified the rule of honoring contracts as one of only three universal moral norms.[1]

Behavioral research has begun to address the role of moral intuition in legal decision making. This chapter reviews experimental research on the

This chapter borrows in part from Tess Wilkinson-Ryan & Jonathan Baron, *Moral Judgment and Moral Heuristics in Breach of Contract*, 6 J. Empirical Legal Stud. 405 (2009); and Tess Wilkinson-Ryan, *Do Liquidated Damages Encourage Efficient Breach: A Psychological Experiment*, 108 Mich. Law Rev. (2010).

[1] Paul Robinson, Robert Kurzban, & Owen Jones. *The Origins of Shared Intuitions of Justice*. 16 Vand. Law Rev.1631–89 (2007).

effects of moral norms on contracting. First, I offer evidence from psychology that many people believe breach of contract is a moral harm irrespective of actual losses suffered by the promisee. Second, I review empirical studies on the notion of the "reference profit," which suggest that people are more sympathetic when a party to a contract breaches in an attempt to preserve the expected profit than when the breach is motivated by an opportunity to exploit the market for an increased profit. Finally, I argue that moral norms often act as default rules in legal decision making about contracts when a contingency is unspecified in the contract.

This review includes studies that directly examine legal decision-making processes as well as others that seem to have a natural application to the legal context. This research offers some evidence that parties may not behave in line with economic expectations. Parties' moral intuitions may affect their willingness to breach when it is otherwise efficient to do so, their ability to reach settlement once a contract has been breached, their predictions about legal rules of contract, and their post hoc assessment of appropriate damages.

I. Breach as Moral Harm

Research on attitudes toward promise and contract indicates that there is a special psychological harm in breaching a contract, a harm that is conceptually separate from the financial or actual losses of the promisee. When people perceive a moral wrong, they are apt to focus on the punishment that the breacher "deserves" rather than the rules that would create the most efficient incentives. The rule of expectation damages sets optimal economic incentives for the making and breaking of contracts. However, we know that people are often insensitive to these kinds of incentives, especially when the incentive structure fails to punish adequately for moral harms. Jonathan Baron and Ilana Ritov have studied intuitions about penalties and compensation in tort law.[2] Though subjects were highly sensitive to moral distinctions, they ignored the information about deterrence altogether, uniformly imposing punishments based on the moral rule that the punishment should be proportionate to the outrageousness of the act, whether the punishment would be useful, pointless, or even harmful. In the criminal context, John Darley and Paul Robinson[3] have repeatedly shown that subjects are more sensitive to morally salient information than they are to factors associated with deterrence

[2] Jonathan Baron & Ilana Ritov. *Intuitions about Penalties and Compensation in the Context of Tort Law.* 7 J. Risk Uncertainty 17–33 (1993).

[3] Paul Robinson & John Darley. *The Utility of Desert.* 91 Northwestern Univ. Law Rev. 453–99 (1997).

rationales, and that people punish in line with retributive theories of justice. However, when parties interact under an assumption of mutual trust, they may be particularly disappointed by a breach, insofar as the breach feels like a betrayal.

Recently, Cass Sunstein has described a phenomenon he calls the "betrayal heuristic."[4] People seem to respond more negatively, and more punitively, to harms caused by a trusted agent than identical harms not caused by a trusted agent. In an empirical study on betrayal, Koehler and Gershoff asked two groups of subjects to assign punishments for five different crimes; in both cases, subjects were shown information about the professions of the respective perpetrators.[5] In one condition, the perpetrators were randomly assigned to the crimes; in the other, each crime was committed by someone who would normally be entrusted to prevent just such an occurrence (e.g., a bank robbery committed by a security guard). Subjects were more punitive when the perpetrator was an otherwise trusted agent. There might be good reasons for this. As Sunstein points out, a betrayal causes not only the harm of the crime itself, but also a disruption to the victim's propensity to be trusting in the future. However, Koehler and Gershoff also demonstrated betrayal aversion in cases in which it was arguably non-normative. In their studies, subjects preferred inferior products – products that were actually less safe – to superior products that had a small risk of betrayal (e.g., a car with no airbag and a higher risk of death in a collision vs. a car with a lower overall risk of death but with an air bag that causes death or injury in a small number of cases).

This evidence suggests that people might also be more averse to losses coming from someone who has promised to confer a benefit (e.g., a promisor) than from someone with a neutral status (say, a negligent tortfeasor). Jonathan Baron and I tested the intuitive difference between identical harms resulting from breach of contract versus negligence.[6] Using web-based questionnaires, we showed subjects a set of vignettes describing either a breach of contract or a negligent tort, and asked them to indicate the appropriate damages award.

In the contract version of each case, subjects read about an efficient breach, in which the promisor breaks the contract in order to accept a more lucrative contract elsewhere. In the control condition, the same contract is rendered impossible to complete when a third party negligently causes a harm that in

[4] Cass Sunstein. *Moral Heuristics*. 28 Behav. Brain Sci. 531–73 (2005).

[5] Jonathan Koehler & Andrew Gershoff. *Betrayal Aversion: When Agents of Protection Become Agents of Harm*. 90 Org. Behav. & Hum. Dec. Processes 244–61 (2002).

[6] Tess Wilkinson-Ryan & Jonathan Baron. *Moral Judgment and Moral Heuristics in Breach of Contract*. 6 J. Empir. Legal Stud. 405–23 (2009).

turn prevents performance. In this case, we were asking subjects not about the damages that would be paid by the promisor, who is presumably excused from the contract, but rather the liability damages paid by the third party. In each condition, the financial harm is identical, and the harm is confined to the harm of not being able to realize the benefit of the contract. An example of a scenario is as follows:

> The Millers are getting ready to sell their condo. Their real estate agent tells them that their condo will be worth $10,000 more if they get the floors refinished (and you should assume that the agent is correct). They meet with Todd, from Todd's Hardwood Floors, agree on a price of $6,000 to refinish the floors, and they all sign the contract. Todd is going to refinish the floors right before the condo goes on the market in early October.

Three of these scenarios were presented in one of two conditions, the promise condition and the no-promise condition.

> *Promise Condition* About three days before he is slated to work on the Millers' floors, Todd gets an offer to refinish all of the floors in another apartment building. If he accepts this offer, he will make much more money, but he will not be able to refinish the Millers' floors. Todd decides to take the new job and break his contract with the Millers.
>
> *No-Promise Condition* About three days before Todd is slated to start working on the Millers' floors, the owners of the next apartment down, the Bakers, are trying to move a gas line in their own condo, even though it is quite dangerous. They do not take proper precautions and the line breaks, gas leaks, and the Millers' apartment is too toxic for Todd to do his work. The Millers have already moved into their new home, so they are not personally affected by the fumes. However, the fumes are quite toxic in the Millers' condo for more than a week, so Todd is unable to refinish the floors before the condominium goes on the market. (Note that Todd does not need to be compensated, because he gets a similar, highly paying job for the same week once he is released from his contract with the Millers.)

In order to assess subjects' judgments about harm in contract and tort, I took the mean of the difference of each subject's promise and no-promise damages responses. Subjects imposed much higher damages overall in the promise cases than in the no-promise cases.

Our between-subjects tests of guilt and morality indicate that subjects thought a person who caused harm by breaking a contractual promise was more immoral and should feel more guilt than a person who caused harm

Table 19.1. *Ratio of subjects' chosen damages to expectation damages*

Mean ratios	Case 1: refinish floors	Case 2: landscape yard	Case 3: cater party
Promise condition	1.12	3.12	2.33
No-Promise condition	0.82	0.79	1.58

through negligence. On a 7-point scale where 7 is extremely immoral and 1 is not immoral at all, the average rating for a negligent wrongdoer was 3.3, and the average rating for a breacher who caused an identical loss was 5.1, a statistically significant difference. Similarly, on a 7-point scale, subjects on average felt that a negligent wrongdoer's guilt should rate a 3.3, and a breacher's guilt should rate a 5.

Subjects were also inclined to report that the promisors should honor the contract rather than pay damages and breach (even though it was clear in every case that the promisor would be better off by breaching). Responses were fairly consistent across cases, with an average of 75.8 percent of subjects responding that the promisor should honor the contract in a given case. Subjects also indicated that they thought the law should force the promisor, in many cases, to honor the contract and perform. Subjects answered a series of questions about appropriate damages (and the mean damages awards were usually above expectation value), and were then asked whether the law should require performance. The average percentage across scenarios of respondents who thought the law should require specific performance was 66.7 percent.

One reasonable objection to this interpretation of these results is that the promise/no-promise manipulation is confounded with the level of intentionality on the part of the agents: The promisor knowingly breaches, but the tortfeasor just takes an imprudent risk. In order to rule out this explanation, I conducted a follow-up study in which I kept the parties' intentions constant across conditions.[7] In the Promise condition, subjects read either that the promisor was going to take another job and had to break his deal, or that the promisor was taking another out-of-town job that would entail a 10-percent risk that he would not get back in time for the target contract. In the No-Promise condition, subjects read either that the tortfeasor knew for certain that the given action was certain to harm the neighbors or meant a

[7] Tess Wilkinson-Ryan. *What Is a Promise Worth? Reputation and Moral Intuition in Efficient Breach* (2009, on file with author).

10-percent risk of harming the neighbors (again, the harm was the neighbors' inability to get the contracted-for work done on their house). Comparing the risky breach situation to the risky tort situation, I found that subjects thought that the risky breach should be punished more severely than the risky tort. The same pattern emerged in the comparison between the certain breach and the certain tort.

The most important implication of this study for law is that intuition treats a contract like an obligation in tort. When subjects read that a promisor breached his contract in order to make more money, subjects wanted to treat him like an intentional tortfeasor, including levying punitive damages.

II. Breach and the Reference Profit

Breach of contract is efficient when performance is more costly than breach – whether the cost is in terms of an actual loss to the promisor or opportunity costs. However, most people treat losses much more seriously, and sympathetically, than forgone gains. This is one of the central predictions of loss aversion, that losses loom larger than gains. The role of loss aversion in contractual exchanges has been refined even further in research by Daniel Kahneman, Jack Knetsch, and Richard Thaler.[8] They argue that an important determinant of perceptions of fairness in contract-like transactions is the "reference transaction." Most people believe that a firm is entitled to the reference profit – the profit that the firm expected in the original or baseline situation. When a firm's reference profit is threatened, it can change the terms of the exchange at the expense of the transactor. However, a firm may not *increase* its profits by decreasing the transactor's reference profit. Two classic examples of this effect are demonstrated by comparing responses to a pair of questions. In the first example, experimenters asked some subjects whether it is fair for a landlord to raise the rent to cover cost increases, knowing that the increased rent would force the tenant to move; 75 percent of survey respondents said that was acceptable. A second question asked if it is acceptable for a landlord to raise the rent when he learns that his tenant has taken a nearby job and is therefore unlikely to move; in this case, 91 percent of respondents thought that raise was unfair. Another example was about an employment relationship. One condition asked subjects whether it is acceptable for a company that

[8] Daniel Kahneman, Jack L. Knetsch, & Richard Thaler. *Fairness as a Constraint on Profit Seeking: Entitlements in the Market*. 76 Amer Econ. Rev. 728–41 (1986).

is making a good profit in an area in which there is unemployment whether it is acceptable to reduce workers' wages by 5 percent, given that the company could easily replace its current employees with good workers at a lower wage. The other condition asked whether it is acceptable for a company that has been losing money to reduce its workers' wages by 5 percent. In the former case, 23 percent of subjects thought the wage cut was acceptable; in the latter, 68 percent. Subjects are sympathetic when a firm tries to protect its expected profit at a cost to the transactor – that is, when it is not possible to preserve the expected profit of both the firm and the transactor, it is permissible for the firm to impose a loss on the transactor. But as long as the company is able to maintain its profit, subjects disapprove of any action that eats into the transactor's expected benefit.

Although the authors did not couch their findings in terms of contracts, their examples are drawn almost exclusively from contractual relationships – landlord/tenant, employer/employee, consumer/manufacturer. Thus, it does not seem like a stretch to characterize a contract as a reference transaction, and to suggest that, given the results of the reference profit studies, we would expect to see that people think it is generally fair to breach a contract when the promisor faces a loss (say, due to the rising cost of materials) but not acceptable to breach in order to exploit increased market power (say, a better offer due to a more favorable market).

Jonathan Baron and I tested this intuition directly in an experiment.[9] We predicted that subjects would be more sympathetic to a breacher who breaks a contract in order to avoid a loss than to an otherwise identical breacher who breaks a contract in order to accept a more lucrative deal elsewhere. This is essentially a framing effect: In both cases, the breacher will make more money by breaking the contract than by honoring it. However, because people are more sensitive to the prospect of a loss than a forgone gain, we hypothesized that they would find the notion of breaching in order to gain to be more offensive than breaching to avoid a loss. We assume that subjects take the status quo to be the expected benefit of the original contract, such that a lower profit for the promisor is seen as a loss. We predicted that subjects would impose higher penalties in a breach to gain case than in a breach to avoid loss case, and that they would find the former more morally objectionable than the latter.

[9] Tess Wilkinson-Ryan & Jonathan Baron. *Moral Judgment and Moral Heuristics in Breach of Contract.* 6 J. Empir. Legal Stud.405–23 (2009).

Half of the subjects read about a breach to avoid loss, and the other half read about a breach to gain. The scenario described a contract for a kitchen renovation. In the Avoid-Loss condition, subjects read that "the contractor learns that the price of cabinets and countertop has skyrocketed, and the contract price will barely cover the cost of materials. He decides to break his contract in order to take other, more profitable work."

In the Gain condition, subjects read that "the contractor learns that there is a shortage of skilled renovators in a nearby area, and he could charge much more there for a similar project. He decides to break his contract in order to take other, more profitable work."

Subjects were asked to choose an appropriate amount of damages. Subjects who saw the Avoid-Loss condition chose, on average, an amount statistically indistinguishable from expectation level. Subjects in the Gain condition, however, chose to award damages above expectation level. They seemed to want to compensate the promisee for his loss *and* add an extra penalty to convey their moral condemnation of an opportunistic breach. Overall, subjects thought that the breacher in the Gain condition should feel significantly more guilty about his breach than the breacher trying to avoid a loss.

Given that so many subjects believed that breach of contract was a special moral harm, and that profit-seeking motives were especially problematic, the economic theory of efficient breach seemed unlikely as a behavioral prediction. Even when economic incentives weigh in favor of breach, many people will perceive contravening moral incentives in favor of performance. If moral qualms deter efficient breach, we would expect to see that more people are willing to breach when facing a loss than when offered more profit.

Evidence from a recent experiment supports this prediction.[10] In a short study about breach of contract, over half of subjects indicated that they would breach a contract if they faced a loss from performance, but only about a third said that they would breach to exploit a better deal. In a follow-up experiment, subjects indicated the lowest offer that they would accept to breach when a better offer was on the table. For each scenario, the average lowest acceptable offer was still over twice the original contract price, and one that would yield over three times the original expected benefit. In practical terms, this means that many reasonable, welfare-maximizing, Pareto-optimal offers would be rejected. A number of subjects indicated that they thought the better choice for the business would be to breach the contract, but they indicated they would not breach even so.

[10] Wilkinson-Ryan. *supra note* 7.

III. Moral Norms as Default Rules

One way to think about the behavioral role of fault in contracts is that fault matters because contracts are incomplete. No contract can specify, for example, every possible contingency for breach. This means that some eventualities are not spelled out in the text of the agreement. When rights or obligations are not specified within the contract, behavioral research suggests that parties look to social and moral norms to fill in the blanks. Where a contract is incomplete, the economic assumption is that parties will either rely on the default rule or behave strategically and negotiate for optimal terms. There is another possibility, one that a number of behavioral researchers have begun to address: When parties omit terms from the contract, they may assume that the relevant framework for their obligations is trust.[11] That is, the parties trust that they are both bound by the same set of social norms, including promise keeping and reciprocity. In the final section of this chapter, I argue that the best way to think about the role of moral intuitions regarding fault in contract law is that the moral intuitions act as default rules when contracts are incomplete.

At least three pathways exist for moral norms to affect legal decision making. First, when a strong moral norm is in conflict with a legal rule, people may mistakenly assume that the legal rule mirrors the moral rule. Second, people may fear that violating a shared moral or social norm will lead to social sanctions, no matter what the legal rule provides. Third, moral beliefs may directly affect behavior: if I think a certain behavior is immoral, I may decide not to do it even when it is financially advantageous and perfectly legal. Behavioral research supports the existence of each of these phenomena, though it is sometimes difficult to distinguish the explanatory mechanisms in the context of a given decision.

There is evidence that moral norms affect parties' understanding of contractual obligations – both moral and legal obligations – irrespective of the background rule. In particular, researchers have found that people believe contracts are enforceable as written, even when some of the clauses are unenforceable. Dennis Stolle and Andrew Slain studied the effects of exculpatory clauses in contracts on consumer behavior.[12] They found that exculpatory language in a standard form contract had a deterrent effect on subjects' likelihood to seek compensation, even when the clause would be unenforceable. Perhaps more

[11] Deepak Malhotra & J. Keith Murnighan. *The Effects of Contracts on Interpersonal Trust*. 47 Adminis. Sci. Quar. 534–59 (2002).

[12] Dennis Stolle & Andrew J. Slain. *Standard Form Contracts and Contract Schemas: A Preliminary Investigation of the Effects of Exculpatory Clauses on Consumers' Propensity to Sue*. 15 Behav. Sci. & Law 83–94 (1997).

important, the researchers found that subjects did not think that a contract with an exculpatory clause was less fair than a contract without an exculpatory clause – even though such provisions are usually unenforceable as a matter of public policy. Even more telling is that subjects did not make a moral distinction between two contracts, one of which limited the rights of the consumer much more sharply than the other. As long as the term was specified in the contract such that both parties were aware of it, they believed that all was fair.

As a follow-up question to the willingness-to-breach study reported above, I asked participants to answer questions about their understanding of the legal ramifications of breach of contract. They were asked to predict how a judge would deal with a series of breach of contract cases. Subjects could choose between damages and specific performance, and if they chose damages, they wrote in the amount the judge would impose. Over half the subjects thought that in at least one of the six presented cases, the judge would require specific performance. Legally, there is no reason to think that any of the straightforward cases presented would require specific performance, since money damages were adequate and easy to assess. This means that half the subjects were mistaken about the state of the law, and their mistakes about the law tended to reflect their moral intuitions.

This evidence does not necessarily indicate, of course, that parties' behavior would not change if they were fully informed about their legal rights and obligations – these studies suggest that there are cases in which parties may make assumptions about the law that depend on perceived moral norms. In the contracts context, erroneous assumptions about the law may never be corrected. A party's decision *not* to pursue damages for breach, or *not* to breach, is not one that courts or lawyers will have a chance to review. And, in the case that parties think their course of action is supported by their moral beliefs, they will presumably be less likely to seek better information about the legal rule.

The behavioral implications of a moral norm are more complicated in the case of informal agreements. In this context, parties may adhere to informal norms either because they fear informal sanctions or because they have internalized the norm and believe that breaking a deal is intrinsically wrong. One of the most important empirical findings about contractual relationships is the vitality of contractual norms in the absence of formal contracts. In 1963, Stewart Macaulay documented the informal means by which businesses could reach agreement on an exchange, and the ways that they would seek to enforce their deal.[13] Interviewees in Macaulay's study reported that,

[13] Stewart Macaulay. *Non-Contractual Relations in Business: A Preliminary Study*. 28 Amer. Soc. Rev. 55–67 (1963).

even in cases in which a formal contract existed, the important contractual obligations were defined by the parties' informal mutual understanding. Furthermore, breach of that understanding was remediated with renegotiation at best, and blacklisting or termination of the relationship at worst. Legal remedies were more or less ignored. Other studies have found, similarly, that when contracts are incomplete, the penalty for breach is termination of the contract.[14] In other words, when contracts are incomplete, the parties do not turn to the court to enforce money damages or renegotiate the terms; they end the business relationship.

Sandra Robinson and Denise Rousseau have also addressed the nature of commonsense understandings of contract in their work on the "psychological contract."[15] The psychological contract is defined by a person's belief about the terms and conditions of her participation in a reciprocal exchange. Studies have shown that violations of the psychological contract are distinct from unmet expectations – that is, though people respond negatively to disappointment when the reality does not meet their expectations, the emotional and attitudinal response to breach of contract is more intense. The core of this difference is in "the individual's belief that an agreement is mutual, that is, a common understanding exists that binds the parties involved."[16] This is particularly apt in the employment context, their primary focus, because even when a written employment contract exists, it is unlikely to iterate the various contributions, obligations, and inducements that characterize an employer/employee relationship over time. The psychological schema, or mental model, of the contract includes professional norms, information gathered during recruitment, societal beliefs, and formal mechanisms for the exchange of promises within the employment contract. Robinson and Rousseau found that perceived violations of the psychological contract have real effects for employers, including higher turnover and lower employee satisfaction.

Behavioral economists have recently redescribed this phenomenon in terms of trust: When the parties trust that they can rely on a certain level of reciprocal cooperation and good faith, informal agreements may actually provide a greater social surplus than a completely specified contract.[17] The norm, and utility, of reciprocity in incomplete contracts have been demonstrated

[14] Martin Brown, Armin Falk, & Ernst Fehr. *Relational Contracts and the Nature of Market Interactions*. 72 Econometrica 747–80 (2002).

[15] Sandra Robinson & Denise M. Rousseau. *Violating the Psychological Contract: Not the Exception but the Norm*. 15 J. Org. Behav. 245–59 (1994).

[16] Denise Rousseau. *Schema, Promise and Mutuality: The Building Blocks of the Psychological Contract*. 74 J. Occup. & Org. Psychol. 511–41 (2001).

[17] Yongmin Chen. *Promises, Trust, and Contracts*. 16 J. Law, Econ., & Org. 209–32 (2000).

experimentally. In one example, researchers used a game in which players interacted with each other under conditions of incomplete contract in a context modeled on an employer/employee relationship.[18] One player was the employer and the other was the worker. The employer offered some amount to the worker, ranging from a minimum wage to a generous wage, and the worker then offered some amount of effort in return. Effort was costly to the worker but profitable to the employer. In the main treatment, players did not meet one another, so all choices were anonymous. The economic prediction was that the worker would return the minimum amount (minimal effort) to the employer. The employer, expecting this selfishness, would offer the minimum wage in the first case. In fact, the experimenters found that the dominant pattern was reciprocal behavior, and that the reciprocity was intrinsic rather than driven by any particular experimental manipulation (including social approval incentives or more iterations of the game). This means that employers offered an amount significantly above the minimum wage and workers returned an effort significantly greater than the lowest possible effort. Although the contract was incomplete – that is, it did not specify how much the employer had to pay or how much effort the employee had to contribute – the parties behaved as though the social norm of reciprocity were built into their contract, and high wages led to high effort.

The role of the norm of reciprocity has been documented in part by showing how explicit sanctions can actually serve to "crowd out" the relevant social or moral norms. In other words, people may be less likely to conform to the dictates of moral norms when the contingency and penalty for breach are specified. Experimental economics games have repeatedly found that players in a game that requires cooperation or reciprocity for the best overall results are more cooperative when there is no penalty for defection and less cooperative when there is a small penalty for defection.[19] In fact, some research suggests that, when a game is fully described in terms of rewards and penalties, parties attribute one another's behavior to self-interest rather than cooperation. The theory proposes that, when a transaction is described in terms of monetary rewards and penalties, the parties to the transaction stop depending on social or moral norms to make their decisions or judgments.[20] The explicit rules crowd out the implicit norms – much as explicit terms in a contract replace default rules.

[18] Armin Falk, Simon Gachter, & Judit Kovacs. *Intrinsic Motivation and Extrinsic Incentives in a Repeated Game with Incomplete Contracts.* 20 J. Econ. Psychol. 251–84 (1999).

[19] Daniel Houser, Erte Xiao, Kevin McCabe, & Vernon Smith. *When Punishment Fails: Research on Sanctions, Intentions and Non-Cooperation.* 62 Games & Econ. Behav. 509–32 (2008).

[20] Uri Gneezy & Aldo Rustichini. *A Fine is a Price.* 29 J. Legal Stud. 1–17 (2000).

In a particularly relevant example, experimenters used a game modeled on contractual relationships to show that moderate sanctions can crowd out the norm of reciprocity.[21] In this game, the first player could offer a small sum to the second player. If the second player chose to perform, both players would get a reward. If the second player breached, one of two possible outcomes occurred. One outcome, which the authors describe as an unenforced contract, was that the second player would receive a large reward and the first player a nominal amount. The other possible outcome was that the players would receive the same payouts that they would have received had the second player performed. In this game, the enforceability of the contract varied. This means that subjects understood that in the event of breach, there was a 10, 50, or 90 percent chance that the experimenters would enforce the contract. The authors found that individuals performed when the enforcement was strong or when it was very weak, but not when it was moderate – that is, strong enough to be a salient element of the game but weak enough that defection was still the dominant strategy. The authors concluded that when the enforceability was so low as to be almost negligible, players understood that the rules of the game would conform to the moral norm of reciprocity. When the enforcement was so high as to be almost absolute, there was no point in breaching. But when the enforcement was in the middle, it crowded out the moral norm without introducing a penalty heavy enough to deter selfish behavior.

I have suggested that one mechanism for moral norms to act on legal decision making is that people may simply believe breach of contract is morally wrong, and therefore choose to punish breach even when punishment is costly or to avoid breach even when breach would be lucrative. The worker effort experiment makes an important point about the norm of reciprocity. Players did not just behave according to the norm in order to further their own self-interest. They behaved as though bound by the norm even when the game was limited to a single round, and whether or not they were playing anonymously or face-to-face. Experiments have repeatedly shown that many people engage in positive reciprocity that cannot be entirely explained by self-interest.[22] Friendly waitresses get more tips, even from customers who do not plan to return.[23] Various one-shot experimental games have also

[21] Iris Bohnet, Bruno Frey, & Steffen Huck. *More Order with Less Law: On Contract Enforcement, Trust, and Crowding.* 95 Amer. Pol. Sci. Rev. 131–44 (2001).

[22] Ernst Fehr & Simon Gachter. *Fairness and Retaliation: The Economics of Reciprocity.* 14 J. Econ. Perspectives 159–81 (2000).

[23] Kathi Tidd & Joan Lochard. *Monetary Significance of the Affiliative Smile: A Case for Reciprocal Altruism.* 11 Bull. Psycho. Soc. 344–6 (1978).

demonstrated positive reciprocity. In the traditional trust game, a Proposer is endowed with a sum of money, and permitted to transfer some or all of that money to a Responder.[24] The experimenter triples the transfer amount, so the Responder receives three times as much as the Proposer gave up. The Responder is then permitted to send some money back to the Proposer. The amount that Responders return is positively correlated with the amount transferred by the Proposer, which is to say, many Responders return something, even though they are not required to do so, will not play with the Proposer again, and, because the players do not meet in person, will never suffer any social embarrassment or sanctions.

Moral norms affect peoples' beliefs about their legal system, their beliefs about the normative expectations of their fellow citizens, and their intrinsic preferences for their own moral and legal choices. These studies suggest that the norms of reciprocity and promise keeping are powerful enough in some experimental settings to guide behavior even when they are in some tension with the background rule or self-interest.

Conclusion

Behavioral research on moral judgment in contracts has potential implications for how parties draft agreements, how they understand their contractual obligations, and whether they breach or perform. People's moral intuitions may inhibit the parties' ability to settle out of court if there is a breach, especially if they have differing notions of what constitutes fair compensation. When parties disagree about appropriate damages in light of a breach of contract, they may be less likely to settle and more likely to undertake litigation.

More sophisticated parties may also be deterred from efficient breach because they do not want to offend their customers or get a bad reputation. Empirical research has demonstrated the real effects of psychological breach. The loss of consumer trust may have financial effects that override the potential profits from the breach, no matter that the consumer's judgment seems irrational. Parties to a contract will have different interactions with one another and with the legal system depending on their beliefs about contracts. These beliefs, in turn, may be partially informed by intuitions imported from the moral domain.

"The line between legal and moral guidelines is a very blurry one in my mind," commented one subject in an experiment. The results reviewed here

[24] Joyce Berg, John Dickhaut, & Kevin McCabe. *Trust, Reciprocity and Social History.* 10 Games Econ. Behav. 122–42 (1995).

suggest that the connection between law and morality is not a philosophical abstraction; for most people, it is an entrenched component of their intuitions about legal decision making. Moral responses to breach of contract affect legal judgments. Empirical results like those reviewed here have bearing on practical legal matters, including bargaining during contract drafting as well as negotiations over the breach of a contract.

CASE INDEX

SUBJECT INDEX